Neo-Latin and the Vernaculars

Medieval and Renaissance Authors and Texts

Editor-in-Chief

Francis G. Gentry (*Emeritus Professor of German, Penn State University*)

Editorial Board

Teodolinda Barolini (*Lorenzo Da Ponte Professor of Italian, Columbia University*)
Cynthia Brown (*Professor of French, University of California, Santa Barbara*)
Marina Brownlee (*Robert Schirmer Professor of Spanish* and *Professor of Comparative Literature, Princeton University*)
Keith Busby (*Douglas Kelly Professor of Medieval French, University of Wisconsin-Madison*)
Craig Kallendorf (*Professor of English and Classics, Texas A&M University*)
Alastair Minnis (*Professor of English, Yale University*)
Brian Murdoch (*Professor of German, Stirling University*)
Jan Ziolkowski (*Arthur Kingsley Porter Professor of Medieval Latin, Harvard University* and *Director, Dumbarton Oaks Research Library and Collection*)

VOLUME 20

The titles published in this series are listed at *brill.com/mrat*

Neo-Latin and the Vernaculars

Bilingual Interactions in the Early Modern Period

Edited by

Alexander Winkler
Florian Schaffenrath

BRILL

LEIDEN | BOSTON

The Library of Congress Cataloging-in-Publication Data is available online at http://catalog.loc.gov

Typeface for the Latin, Greek, and Cyrillic scripts: "Brill". See and download: brill.com/brill-typeface.

ISSN 0925-7683
ISBN 978-90-04-38486-6 (hardback)
ISBN 978-90-04-38640-2 (e-book)

Copyright 2019 by Koninklijke Brill NV, Leiden, The Netherlands.
Koninklijke Brill NV incorporates the imprints Brill, Brill Hes & De Graaf, Brill Nijhoff, Brill Rodopi, Brill Sense, Hotei Publishing, mentis Verlag, Verlag Ferdinand Schöningh and Wilhelm Fink Verlag.
All rights reserved. No part of this publication may be reproduced, translated, stored in a retrieval system, or transmitted in any form or by any means, electronic, mechanical, photocopying, recording or otherwise, without prior written permission from the publisher.
Authorization to photocopy items for internal or personal use is granted by Koninklijke Brill NV provided that the appropriate fees are paid directly to The Copyright Clearance Center, 222 Rosewood Drive, Suite 910, Danvers, MA 01923, USA. Fees are subject to change.

This book is printed on acid-free paper and produced in a sustainable manner.

Contents

    Contributors VII

1   Introduction 1
    Alexander Winkler and Florian Schaffenrath

2   Latin and the Vernacular in Biondo Flavio's Thought and Works: a Study with a New Critical Edition of the Correspondence with the Duke of Milan, Francesco Sforza 11
    Giuseppe Marcellino

3   Latin and Vernacular Interplay: Lazzaro Bonamico as Author and Character of Sperone Speroni's *Dialogo delle lingue* 36
    Teodoro Katinis

4   *Diserte Germanice loqui*: the Cultural-Historical Status of the German Language in Franciscus Irenicus's *Germaniae Exegesis* (1518) 53
    Ronny Kaiser

5   Ludvig Holberg's *Niels Klim* (1741) and the Irony of Reading and Writing in Latin 72
    Thomas Velle

6   Neo-Latin and Vernacular Translation Theory in the 15th and 16th Centuries: the 'Tasks of the Translator' According to Leonardo Bruni and Étienne Dolet 96
    Marianne Pade

7   Ariosto *Latine Redditus*: Early Modern Neo-Latin Rewritings of the *Orlando Furioso* 113
    Francesco Lucioli

8   Rewriting Vernacular Prose in Neo-Latin Hexameters: Francisco de Pedrosa's *Austriaca sive Naumachia* (1580) 130
    Maxim Rigaux

9   Neo-Latin Epic Poetry on Telemach after Fénelon 147
    Florian Schaffenrath

10 Coexistence and Contamination of Vernacular and Latin in Alessandro Braccesi's Bilingual Tribute to Camilla Saracini: the Literatures of Siena and Florence between Illustrious Women and Neoplatonism 166
   Federica Signoriello

11 The Reception of Petrarch and Petrarchists' Poetry in Marcantonio Flaminio's *Carmina* 188
   Giacomo Comiati

12 Pietro Angeli da Barga's *Syrias* (1582–91) and Contemporary Debates over Epic Poetry 212
   Alexander Winkler

13 Didactic Poetry as Elitist Poetry: Christopher Stay's *De poesi didascalica dialogus* in the Context of Classical and Neo-Latin Didactic Discourse 232
   Claudia Schindler

   Index 251

Contributors

Giacomo Comiati

is postdoctoral research fellow at the University of Oxford and member of the AHRC-funded project 'Petrarch Commentary and Exegesis in Renaissance Italy (c. 1350–c. 1650)'. He completed his PhD at the University of Warwick (UK) in 2016, after having studied at the University of Padua (Italy) and the Scuola Galileiana di Studi Superiori. He was junior research fellow at the Dahlem Humanities Center of the Freie Universität in Berlin (Germany). His research interests and publication mainly concern the Early-Modern reception of Latin antiquity and Renaissance Italian and Latin poetry.

Ronny Kaiser

is teacher of Latin and History at a Gymnasium in Berlin, Germany. From 2009 to 2016 he worked as research assistant at the Collaborative Research Center 644 "Transformations of Antiquity" (Humboldt University of Berlin) and obtained a fellowship at the Ludwig Boltzmann Institute, Innsbruck. Besides his teaching activity, he works on the historiographical and political discourse in Neo-Latin Literature. He has published the volume "Portraying the Prince in the Renaissance. The Humanist Depiction of Rulers in Historiographical and Biographical Texts, Berlin/Boston 2016" (together with Patrick Baker, Maike Priesterjahn, and Johannes Helmrath). His most recent publication is "Caesar's Rhine Bridge and Its Practical Feasibility in Giovanni Giocondo's *Expositio Pontis* (1513), in: Knowledge, Text and Practice in Ancient Technical Writing, ed. by Marco Formisano/Philip van der Eijk, Cambridge 2017, pp. 68–92."

Teodoro Katinis

is Research Professor of Italian Literature in the Department of Literary Studies of Ghent University. In 2015–2016 he was Marie Skłodowska-Curie Fellow at Ca' Foscari University of Venice. His first monograph is on philosophy and medicine in Marsilio Ficino (Edizioni di storia e letteratura, 2007), while his second monograph is on Sperone Speroni and the rebirth of sophistry in the Italian Renaissance (Brill, 2017). Katinis has also published on other subjects, including Renaissance political literature, Torquato Tasso's poems and poetics and the early-modern dialogue. At Ghent University, his research will focus on vernacular medical texts published in Renaissance Venice and translated in Europe for a broader public.

Francesco Lucioli
is Assistant Professor in Italian and European Studies at the University College Dublin. His main areas of interest are: Early-modern Italian literature, language and culture, in both Neo-Latin and the vernacular; the relationship between literature and visual arts; the relationship between literature and religion; Renaissance and Baroque Rome; chivalric and epic poetry; ethics and conduct literature. He has published the following monographs: *Amore punito e disarmato. Parola e immagine da Petrarca all'Arcadia* (2013), and *Jacopo Sadoleto umanista e poeta* (2014). He has also edited Giuliano Dati's *Aedificatio Romae* (2012), and Cardinal Agostino Valier's conduct treatises for women (2015).

Giuseppe Marcellino
is research fellow at the Alexander von Humboldt Foundation. He received a PhD in Classical Philology, Linguistics and History from the Scuola Normale Superiore in Pisa. He has worked on topics related to both classical philology as well as Neo-Latin studies. He published the critical edition, with introduction and commentary, of Favonius Eulogius' *Disputatio de Somnio Scipionis*, (Napoli: D'Auria, 2012) and Biondo Flavio's *De verbis Romanae locutionis* (Pisa: Edizione della Normale, 2015). He is currently working on the fifteenth-century Latin production in Italy.

Marianne Pade
is director of the Danish Academy at Rome and professor of Classical Philology at the University of Aarhus. She has published widely on Renaissance Humanism, the reception of Greek historiography in the Renaissance, and Neo-Latin Studies. Among her publications are the article on Thucydides for the *Catalogus Translationum et Commentariorum* (vol. 8, 2003), *The Reception of Plutarch's* Lives *in Fifteenth-Century Italy* I–II, Renæssancestudier 14 (Copenhagen, 2007), and critical editions of Niccolò Perotti's *Cornu copiae* (8 vols., with Jean-Louis Charlet *et all.*, Sassoferrato 1989–2001) and Guarino Veronese's Latin translation of Plutarch's *Vita Dionis* (Firenze, 2013). She is currently working on Neo-Latin translation of Greek political vocabulary and its influence on western political lexicon.

Maxim Rigaux
received a master degree in Historical Literature and Linguistics at Ghent University (2013) and an advanced master in Medieval and Renaissance Studies at the University of Leuven (2014). As a predoctoral fellow of the FWO (Research Foundation Flanders) he worked at Ghent University on the project *Fictions of Lepanto: Visuality and Epic Poetry in Renaissance Iberia (1571–1587)*.

During this time, he was also co-founder of RELICS and editor of JOLCEL. Since October 2018, he is affiliated to the University of Chicago, working as a Visiting Scholar on his new research project *Before the Royal Tomb: Juan Latino's Lyric Poetry*. For this project, he was awarded two postdoctoral fellowships, by the Belgian American Educational Foundation (BAEF) and Fulbright.

Florian Schaffenrath
is Associate Professor of Classical Philology at the University Innsbruck and director of the Ludwig Boltzmann Institute for Neo-Latin Studies. His main areas of interest are: Neo-Latin epic poetry, Neo-Latin drama, and Cicero. He has published a critical edition with German translation of Ubertino Carrara's poem *Columbus* (2006), and was one of the editors of *Tyrolis Latina—Geschichte der lateinischen Literatur in Tirol* (2012). He is the principal investigator in several third party funded projects, e.g. on Jesuit theatre or Basinio da Parma.

Claudia Schindler
is Full Professor in Classical Philology at the University of Hamburg. Her main areas of interest are: Greek and Roman didactic poetry and its reception in Neo-Latin literature, epic poetry, Neo-Latin poetics, and reception studies. She has published the following monographs: *Untersuchungen zu den Gleichnissen im römischen Lehrgedicht* (2000), and *Per carmina laudes. Untersuchungen zur spätantiken Verspanegyrik von Claudian bis Coripp* (2009).

Federica Signoriello
is a librarian at the European University Institute in Florence, Italy. In recent years she has worked at the Warburg Institute, Cambridge University Library and the British Library. She completed her PhD in Italian Studies at University College London with a thesis on Satire of Philosophy and Philosophers in Fifteenth-Century Florence, dealing with comic poetry in relation to philosophy and the history of scholarship. She is currently working on the monographic version of her thesis and is editor of the unpublished comic poems of the humanist Alessandro Braccesi, which are currently being issued on hypotheses.org.

Thomas Velle
studied Classics and Modern Comparative Literature at Ghent University and successfully completed his PhD in Literary Studies at the same institution in 2018. His dissertation on Ludvig Holberg's imaginary travelogue *Nicolai Klimii iter subterraneum* (1741–1745) is currently reworked into a monograph. He is

a founding member of the international research group RELICS, and editor of the peer reviewed online journal JOLCEL. Since October 2018, he is working as a postdoctoral fellow at Ghent University on the project "The Republic of Epigrams. The Latin Epigram and the Multilingual Self in 17th- and 18th-century Europe," funded by the FWO (Research Foundation Flanders).

Alexander Winkler

is research assistant in Medieval and Neo-Latin philology at the University of Bonn. He published a German translation of the *Satire against the abuse of tobacco* by the 17th-century Jesuit Jacob Balde and is currently preparing a monograph on Pietro Angeli da Barga's (1517–1596) epic poem *Syrias*.

CHAPTER 1

Introduction

Alexander Winkler and Florian Schaffenrath

The culture of early modern Europe is fundamentally bi- or multilingual in the sense that (Neo-)Latin[1] was highly important over almost all of Europe alongside the vernacular language(s) until the 18th century, in some geographical contexts even later.[2] Latin was a European *lingua franca* that was widely used as a means of international communication in the arts and sciences, as well as in the realms of commerce and diplomacy. It was (and officially still is) the language of the Catholic Church and was important on a national level for administrative purposes, in politics, in literature, and in general, for communication in the public sphere. At the dawn of the Middle Ages, Latin was the obvious choice for any scholarly text (Dante famously chose Latin for his *De vulgari eloquentia*, the first treatise on the Italian *volgare*), it was the 'father tongue'[3] for most humanists (Petrarch, albeit nowadays too often remembered mainly for his vernacular *Canzoniere*, wrote almost exclusively in Latin), and Latin was used at the university as the most important language of academic exchange well into the 19th century.

The role, function, and standing of Latin could vary according to social context. Since Latin was considered the language of the learned and often of the social elite, it functioned as a 'prestigious' language that could serve to distinguish social classes within a speech community. At numerous early modern courts, however, the distinguished role of Latin was contested by a vernacular language. This linguistic divide between the learned and the social elites could have an impact on the prestige of the Latin language.

One's acquaintance with the language and capacity to express oneself could vary considerably for each individual, as well as in the broader geographical, cultural, and social contexts. Late Italian humanists of the 16th century, for example, occasionally acknowledged their somewhat poor command of Latin,[4]

---

1 For a discussion of the term Neo-Latin (with further reading) see Ramminger 2014. In what follows, Neo-Latin is understood primarily as a chronological term designating the Latin language used in the early modern period without regard to stylistic features.
2 A quick and useful overview of the spread of Neo-Latin in space and time is provided by the respective chapters in recent handbooks on Neo-Latin, i.e., Knight/Tilg 2015 and Moul 2017.
3 On this concept with regard to medieval Latin, see Ziolkowski 1996, pp. 506–07.
4 See the contribution by Alexander Winkler in this volume.

© KONINKLIJKE BRILL NV, LEIDEN, 2019 | DOI:10.1163/9789004386402_002

which they considered a foreign language: Neo-Latin was a "language without native speakers."[5] During the first half of the 19th century, when Latin was still *the* language of the European universities, increasing problems with students' language skills led to a loosening of the rules regarding disputations.[6] Although Latin could function as a means of communication among those who had undergone Latin schooling, it must be borne in mind that Latin was not equally accessible to everybody.

In addition to these obvious restraints, it is also important to take into account the linguistic diversity of Neo-Latin which often tends to be conceived of as a rather homogeneous, or even monolithic language modelled on the best authors of classical antiquity. This view, however, does not represent the linguistic reality of Neo-Latin, which knew a great number of stylistic ideals over the centuries. The very few common terms coined for stylistic trends in Neo-Latin, such as Ciceronianism, Tacitism, or Lipsianism, by no means cover the stylistic variety of Neo-Latin literature.

Taking into account its chronological and geographical extension, as well as its vast stylistic variety, it is evident that there is, strictly speaking, no 'Neo-Latin' *tout court*. Consequently, every single speech community in which Latin played a role (i.e., virtually everywhere in early modern Europe), possibly even every act of (Neo-Latin) communication, must be analysed in its own right, depending on the linguistic status of Neo-Latin in a particular context, which means taking into account the pertinent customs, habits, and levels of erudition and social prestige of those involved in its use.

These are genuinely sociolinguistic questions and can be best approached within a sociolinguistic framework. Peter Burke, an early advocate of sociolinguistic methodology in historical linguistics, has also made a strong case for the use of sociolinguistic methods and terminology in order to describe the role of Latin in the early modern period.[7] However, much more research remains to be done on Neo-Latin communication and its contexts.

Bi- or multilingualism is a key element of any sociolinguistic discussion of Neo-Latin in the early modern age. As stated above, European culture was largely Latin, but there was generally at least one other major language in use alongside Latin. It is again Peter Burke who, in his *Languages and Communities in Early Modern Europe* (2004), provides a magisterial overview of early modern bilingualism. In accordance with his comprehensive and 'pan-European'

---

5 Burke 2004, p. 43.
6 See Tütken 2005, pp. 277–87 for a case study at the University of Göttingen.
7 See Burke's programmatic essay in Burke 1993.

INTRODUCTION 3

approach, he pays some attention to the role of Latin.[8] When it comes to the rise of the vernaculars, however, Burke shifts his focus towards the languages that gained in importance alongside and sometimes to the detriment of Latin. This is also usually the case in books on the history of the vernaculars. Understandably, these are usually only marginally concerned with Latin when they discuss bilingualism. It is problematic, though, that they endorse a narrative of a development in which the decaying Neo-Latin hands over responsibility to an ascendant vernacular. This, of course, stems from the fact that histories of the vernaculars, for better or worse, have to focus on the language under discussion. Such a narrative, however, is partial, and disregards the importance Neo-Latin continued to have throughout early modernity. Moreover, it also discourages further inquiry into the sociolinguistic history of Neo-Latin. One hopes that the increasing interest in Neo-Latin in general and in the interactions between Neo-Latin and the vernacular(s) in particular, will eventually lead to a more detailed understanding of the history of Neo-Latin as a European language. Partly owing to the complexity of the phenomenon, however, there is regrettably still a dearth of knowledge on the social history of the Neo-Latin language. Apart from necessarily brief discussions of the matter by Wilfried Stroh (2007) and Jürgen Leonhardt (2009), Françoise Waquet's *Le latin ou l'empire d'un signe* (1998) is apparently the only attempt made so far at a comprehensive discussion of Neo-Latin in early modern culture. Waquet's book is enormously successful in charting the field but it necessarily remains eclectic in what it discusses.

Several recent publications on early modern bilingualism have provided a number of interesting case studies that pave the way for a better understanding of what it meant to use (or not to use) Latin in the early modern period. *Bilingual Europe: Latin and Vernacular Cultures—Examples of Bilingualism*, edited by Jan Bloemendal (2015), is an important collection of case studies that calls attention to the continuing importance of Neo-Latin in periods where the influence of the vernaculars was growing. *Dynamics of Neo-Latin and the Vernacular. Language and Poetics, Translation and Transfer*, edited by Tom Deneire (2014), is important because it offers precious theoretical considerations on the issue of early modern bilingualism. Deneire rightly points out that in a multilingual context, where Latin inevitably competes, interferes, or interacts with the respective vernacular(s), we have to deal with a very dynamic, heterogeneous, and thus complex form of bi- or multilingualism, that is not satisfactorily described by the influential concept of *diglossia*, a term introduced by Charles Ferguson in 1959 and defined as follows:

---

8 See especially Burke 2004, pp. 43–60.

> Diglossia is a relatively stable language situation in which, in addition to the primary dialects of the language (which may include a standard or regional standards), there is a very divergent, highly codified (often grammatically more complex) superposed variety, the vehicle of a large and respected body of written literature, either of an earlier period or in another speech community, which is learned largely by formal education and is used for most written and formal spoken purposes but is not used by any sector of the community for ordinary conversation.[9]

Ferguson proposed calling the highly codified variant, 'high variety' (H), the dialects 'low variety' (L). It is clear that the limitation to 'variants' and 'dialects' makes the strict definition of *diglossia* inappropriate to the context of Neo-Latin. It has therefore been suggested that the term 'extended diglossia' should be adopted to describe the Neo-Latin situation. Extended diglossia is meant to "encompass even a situation where H and L are not varieties of the same language."[10] Still, *diglossia* is a judgemental term that presupposes the existence of a language (variety) that is considered more prestigious than the other(s). As is evident, for instance, from a study of 16th-century Italy, this difference is by no means unproblematic. Latin was arguably as prestigious as the vernacular; it was simply the case that there were certain rules or customs that determined which language was to be used by whom in specific situations. Language choice thus depended on the speech community and the language domains: "In medieval and early modern times," Burke writes, "it was considered appropriate to use that language [*sc.* Latin] in some situations and domains."[11] The ever-shifting "division of labour between Latin and vernacular"[12] characterizes a process that spans the entire early modern period. This process is, as Deneire rightly points out, "dynamic," and therefore highly idiosyncratic and different for every single historical, geographical, cultural, and social context. The concept of *dynamics* with regard to (extended) *diglossia* or bilingualism can be seen as a very promising way to overcome the limitations associated with the idea of bilingualism (which rather suggests a distinct coexistence of two languages in a certain region or society), in order to think in terms of fluid, multidirectional, and dynamic exchange between Neo-Latin and the vernacular. The professed intention is to interpret "the interplay

---

9   Ferguson 1959, p. 336.
10 Svensson 2014, p. 91.
11 Burke 2004, p. 43.
12 Burke 1993a, p. 56.

between Latin and the vernacular as a radically dynamic, ever-shifting process of 'making cultural meaning' in a bilingual context."[13]

It is also important to bear in mind that language choice in itself can have connotation and consequently convey a message. Sometimes the code is at least *a* message. A famous and admittedly extreme example is that of Christian Thomasius (1655–1728) who was allegedly the first professor to deliver a university lecture in German. By choosing German over Latin, which would have been the most obvious language in this particular domain, he made an unequivocal statement in favour of the German vernacular. Conversely, the choice of Latin in the case of Dante's *De vulgari eloquentia* or Opitz's *Aristarchus*, two works that plead for the vernaculars, signalled that they were to be viewed in the context of the general scholarly discourse, which naturally used the Latin language. In linguistic interactions, language is never just neutral: "[T]he medium, code, variety or register employed is a crucial part of the message."[14]

Philip Ford's last monograph, *The Contest between Neo-Latin and Vernacular Poetry in Renaissance France* (2013), presents a very interesting study on language choice in the polyglossic context of early modern France. Ford points out that "for most potential writers living in France, language choice was far from obvious," as the "emerging standard French [*sc.* the *langue du roi*] was a long way from being codified in formal grammars and dictionaries, and was not part of school education, since the only language being taught formally was Latin."[15] Ford stresses the complexity of the linguistic situation reducible to "the existence of two prestige languages, Latin and French, alongside a range of commonly used and highly diverse dialects."[16] He analyses the language used by 486 French writers of the 16th century and finds that those whose mother tongue was not the prestige variant of French were more likely to use Latin than those from the region where the *langue du roi* was spoken. Ford thus confirms what has been said above: language choice appears to be influenced not least by language proficiency. But he also notes a correlation between literary genre and language choice. Languages usually "come with a certain amount of cultural and political baggage."[17] In other words, they are linked by their respective traditions to different literary forms, themes, etc. When an author uses Latin instead of the vernacular, s/he necessarily gives preference to certain reference frames or systems. These 'soft boundaries' set by tradition and

---

13   Deneire 2014, p. 5.
14   Burke 1987, p. 9.
15   Ford 2013, p. 3.
16   Ford 2013, p. 7.
17   Ford 2013, p. 7.

custom can be deliberately challenged; for instance, attempts can be made to open up genres for other language systems as well. Prominent cases are classicist movements in vernacular literatures, where themes and forms of classic literature are adapted to the requirements of the vernacular.

Language choice and "the conscious and unconscious rules for switching codes,"[18] however, are but one facet of bilingualism. Where there is a developed vernacular culture and literature alongside Latin, there are bound to be more general interactions between Neo-Latin and the vernacular culture. These interactions have received major attention in recent years. As noted above, the decision for or against one language or another determines to a varying degree what can be expressed in which forms. The decision, for instance, to write lyric poetry in Latin more often than not meant following the model of Horace, Catullus, or perhaps late antique Christian poets such as Prudentius. The vernacular, however, had a different set of options to offer. Languages come with a complex system of rules and possibilities of expression, which both limit and enable forms of understanding. Such systems can be regarded as constituting language-specific discourses with idiosyncratic features. When two or more distinct discourses come into contact, they are likely to interact. This interaction can, of course, result in further differentiation, but it is also very likely that the discourses intermingle, thus enriching one another. It is one of the purposes of this volume to illustrate the ways such interaction can take place.

While this volume avowedly owes much to the recently published works on Neo-Latin bilingualism or vernacular interactions that have been mentioned so far, its aim is to add some new perspectives to this discussion in the field of Neo-Latin studies. It is necessary to think more extensively about Neo-Latin multilingualism since multilingualism is a crucial characteristic of the early modern period in western Europe and deserves an appropriate share of scholarly attention. As historians of vernacular languages justifiably focus on the vernacular, it is up to scholars who are active in the field of Neo-Latin studies to turn their attention also to the sociolinguistic aspects of Neo-Latin. There lies considerable potential in this broadened scholarly focus as it further contributes to rendering the significance of the Latin language in the early modern period more visible.

The essays collected in this volume proceed from papers read at the seventh *Texts & Contexts* conference held at Innsbruck in April 2016.[19] The original

---

18 Burke 1993a, p. 56.
19 The editors would like to express their gratitude to Rhoda Schnur and the Pegasus Foundation for their generous financial support of the conference.

focus had been—as the title of the conference indicates—on "Vernacular Influences on Neo-Latin Literature." The breadth and variety of the papers that were delivered, however, as well as the fruitful discussions among the participants, occasioned a slightly different take on the issue. The intriguing case studies presented at the conference made it necessary to consider not only the specific monodirectional influences from the vernacular to Neo-Latin, but also to broaden the perspective in order to do justice to the interplay between Neo-Latin and vernacular discourses in all its complexity. Our aim is to provide a number of case studies that address different aspects of the interactions between Neo-Latin and the vernacular.

The essays collected in this volume are taken from a wide array of historical, geographical, and cultural contexts and therefore do not offer a systematic discussion of Neo-Latin bilingualism as such. They rather aim to deepen our understanding of what it could 'mean' to write in Latin in the early modern period. Katinis and Kaiser, for example, explore the function and 'cultural weight' of Latin in different contexts; Velle and Lucioli shed light on the impact the linguistic code has on the reception of a text, and Pade and the authors of the third section of this volume discuss the dynamics that come into being when Latin and vernacular discourses interact.

The volume is divided into three parts: The case studies in the essays in the first part (Language Choice and Its Implications) show that in a multilingual situation where both Neo-Latin and the vernacular are an option, the choice of one or the other is not a neutral decision. It rather appears that the languages have their own specific sociolinguistic domains. Giuseppe Marcellino explores the dynamics of bilingualism and language choice in the linguistically highly sensitive context of quattrocento humanism and shows that in certain circumstances even a fierce advocate of Latin resorted to the vernacular.

The diptych on quattrocento humanism is paradoxically completed by an essay on the Italian cinquecento by Teodoro Katinis who rereads Sperone Speroni's *Dialogo delle lingue* and tries to reinterpret Bonamico Lazzaro's opinion on Latin and the vernacular, confronting the stance Bonamico takes in the dialogue with ideas voiced in his own works. Ronny Kaiser discusses Franciscus Irenicus's defence against the accusation of barbarism that some Italians had levelled against the Germans. Not only do Irenicus's apologetic and polemic remarks show the cultural value commonly attached to languages, but they also exemplify the somewhat paradoxical consequences of the rules of language choice in the early modern period: namely, in order for the defence of German culture to be widely read, it had to be written in Latin. With his essay on Niels Klim, Thomas Velle ventures into an entirely different chronological, geographical, and cultural context. He explores the elusive dynamics of multilingualism inscribed into this modern and profoundly European novel that force the reader to reflect upon the role of Latin at the beginning of the modern age.

The second part addresses probably the most evident form of influence: translation and, more broadly, the rewriting of genuinely vernacular models. Marianne Pade's contribution inaugurates this section and picks up the thread of the previous part by discussing translation theories in Italian and French humanism, which appear to differ in the way they consider the vernacular. The practice of Neo-Latin translation is explored by Francesco Lucioli who looks at a hitherto disregarded partial translation of Ariosto's Italian vernacular classic *Orlando Furioso*. As Neo-Latin often speaks to a different public and caters to needs other than those of the vernacular, translations often do not limit themselves to merely rendering a text from the vernacular into Latin; rather, they often select, reconfigure, and anthologize literature in order to efficiently address the intended readership. A different approach is chosen by Maxim Rigaux who focuses on a way of rewriting in Neo-Latin that is, in certain respects, contrary to the anthologizing translation of the *Orlando Furioso*. In his discussion of Francisco de Pedrosa's *Austriaca sive Naumachia*, a six-book epic poem on the battle of Lepanto (7 October 1571), based on the vernacular historical account of the events by Fernando de Herrera's *Relación* (1572), Rigaux sheds light on the implications of translating not only into another language, but also into another entirely different genre. His comparison between the Neo-Latin epic poem and other vernacular re-elaborations of the same historical source shows some of the fundamental differences underlying Neo-Latin and vernacular poetics. The choice between Neo-Latin and the vernacular thus had a profound impact on what could be said and written. In the last essay of this section, Florian Schaffenrath explores the influence of Fénelon's *Télémaque* on Neo-Latin literature through an analysis of various Latin verse translations.

Especially in polyglossic contexts, in which the vernaculars became increasingly important, prestigious, and culturally productive, Neo-Latin literature began to orientate itself towards the increasingly successful vernacular culture. It borrowed ideas and motifs, and imitated forms and genres. This is, of course, indicative of the strength the vernaculars had gained. From a specifically Neo-Latin point of view, however, it is also a sign that Latin literature was willing to participate in contemporary literary (and non-Latin) discourses, and was capable of interacting with the rising vernacular cultures. This preponderant influence of vernacular culture on Neo-Latin literature is addressed in the third and last part of the volume. Under the heading "Neo-Latin Literature and

Vernacular Traditions," four different case studies explore different types of influence vernacular discourses have exerted on Neo-Latin literature. Federica Signoriello considers Alessandro Braccesi's bilingual lyric poetry in terms of the "coexistence and contamination of vernacular and Latin" and shows the tight links that ran between the two languages and discourses. One of the most momentous innovations that the Italian vernacular literature of the Renaissance brought forth was without doubt Petrarchism. Giacomo Comiati sheds light on the understudied reception of Petrarch's lyric poetry in Neo-Latin with reference to the example of Marcantonio Flaminio's *Carmina*. Alexander Winkler devotes his essay to epic poetry, yet another field in which the vernacular influence was vital. He explores vernacular influences on the theoretical discussions as well as on poetic practice in a case study on Pietro Angeli da Barga's *Syrias*, a 16th-century epic poem on the First Crusade. One of the last important writers of Neo-Latin didactic poetry was Benedetto Stay, whose brother Christopher wrote his dialogue *De poesi didascalica* in 1792. This dialogue is one of the very rare theoretical documents written on didactic poetry. Claudia Schindler studies it in her contribution and has a special focus on the relationship between Neo-Latin and vernacular didactic poetry.

Bibliography

Burke, Peter. "The Social History of Language." In *The Art of Conversation*, edited by Peter Burke. Cambridge, Eng.: Polity Press, 1993, pp. 1–33.

Burke, Peter. "'Heu domine, adsunt Turcae': A Sketch for a History of Post-Medieval Latin." In *The Art of Conversation*, edited by Peter Burke. Cambridge, Eng.: Polity Press, 1993a, pp. 34–65.

Burke, Peter. *Languages and Communities in Early Modern Europe*. Cambridge, Eng.: Cambridge University Press, 2004.

Bloemendal, Jan, ed. *Bilingual Europe: Latin and Vernacular Cultures—Examples of Bilingualism and Multiculturalism c. 1300–1800*. Leiden: Brill, 2015.

Deneire, Tom, ed. *Dynamics of Neo-Latin and the Vernacular. Language and Poetics, Translation and Transfer.* Leiden: Brill, 2014.

Deneire, Tom. "Introduction: Dynamics of Neo-Latin and the Vernacular: History and Introduction." In Deneire 2014, pp. 1–17.

Ferguson, Charles A. "Diglossia." *Word* 15.2 (1959), pp. 325–40.

Ford, Philip. *The Judgment of Palaemon*. Leiden: Brill, 2013.

Knight, Sarah and Stefan Tilg, eds. *The Oxford Handbook of Neo-Latin*. Oxford, Eng.: Oxford University Press, 2015.

Leonhardt, Jürgen. *Latein. Geschichte einer Weltsprache.* Munich: Beck, 2009.

Moul, Victoria, ed. *A Guide to Neo-Latin Literature.* Cambridge, Eng.: Cambridge University Press, 2017.

Ramminger, Johann. "Neo-Latin: Character and Development." In *Brill's Encyclopaedia of the Neo-Latin World,* edited by Philip Ford, Jan Bloemendal, and Charles Fantazzi. Leiden: Brill, 2014, pp. 21–36.

Stroh, Wilfried. *Latein ist tot, es lebe Latein! Kleine Geschichte einer großen Sprache.* Berlin: List, 2007.

Svensson, Johanna. "Exploring the Borderlands. On the Division of Labour between Latin and the Vernacular(s) in the Church in Scania under Danish and Swedish Rule in the Seventeenth Century." In Deneire 2014, pp. 86–107.

Thurn, Nikolaus. *Neulatein und Volkssprachen: Beispiele für die Rezeption neusprachlicher Literatur durch die lateinische Dichtung Europas im 15.–16. Jh.* Munich: Fink, 2012.

Tütken, Johannes. *Privatdozenten im Schatten der Georgia Augusta. Zur älteren Privatdozentur (1734 bis 1831).* Göttingen: Universitätsverlag Göttingen, 2005.

Waquet, Françoise. *Le Latin ou l'empire d'un signe: XVIe–XXe siècle.* Paris: Albin Michel, 1998.

Ziolkowski, Jan M. "Towards a History of Medieval Latin Literature." In *Medieval Latin. An Introduction and Bibliographical Guide,* edited by Frank A. C. Mantello and Arthur G. Rigg. Washington, DC: The Catholic University of America Press, 1996, pp. 505–36.

CHAPTER 2

Latin and the Vernacular in Biondo Flavio's Thought and Works: a Study with a New Critical Edition of the Correspondence with the Duke of Milan, Francesco Sforza

Giuseppe Marcellino

A survey on bilingualism in Italy during the 15th century cannot omit a preliminary examination of the question of what Latin and vernacular languages represented for humanists. The choice made by 15th-century scholars of whether to use Latin or the vernacular was accompanied, in most cases, by their reflections on the dignity and nature of these languages. For this reason, research on this issue should pay attention, from time to time, not only to the literary genre, recipients, and purpose of the works examined, but also to the complex and not always linear relationship between compositional practice and theoretical reflection. Biondo Flavio's case study seems to be very promising, since he was both the first theoretician of the idea that the Romance languages descended from Latin and unwittingly a crucial figure for that innovative process of valorising the vernacular, which was subsequently launched by Leon Battista Alberti starting in the 1530s.[1] As a brilliant scholar of the Roman world and an outstanding historian of the Middle Ages, Biondo lived and worked in that 'secolo senza poesia' of Italian literature—to use Benedetto Croce's popular definition—during which the study of classical antiquity and the formal restoration of Latin were the focus of most efforts of learned men. Biondo's rich literary production includes Latin works concerning linguistics, historiography, geography, and antiquarian studies, while the only evidence of the vernacular must be sought in his private correspondence. Only two letters in the vernacular idiom by Biondo are currently known to be preserved and both of them, which are held at the State Archives of Milan, were sent to Francesco Sforza, the Duke of Milan, one in 1459 and the other in 1463. In the second

---

1 For Biondo's biography and production, Nogara 1927 is still essential. See also Campana 1927, pp. 487–97; Fubini 1968, pp. 536–59; Campana 1970, pp. 634–35; Fubini 1986, pp. 339–44; Defilippis 2006, pp. 87–105; Campana 2016, pp. 21–44; Mazzocco 2016, pp. 9–34; Muecke/Campanelli 2017.

part of this essay I will examine these two documents, which are also the last known letters written by Biondo, and I will try to explain why he composed them in the vernacular. In the first part, I will go through his Latin literary production, paying attention in particular to the theoretical reflection that underlies his choice to compose in this language. At the end of this essay I provide a new critical edition of all of Biondo's correspondence with Francesco Sforza, in Latin and the vernacular.

Since some Quattrocento humanists, such as Leonardo Bruni,[2] Leon Battista Alberti[3] and Matteo Palmieri,[4] did not despise the use of the vernacular for the drafting of their works, it is worth investigating the reasons that led Biondo to almost exclusively use Latin. To at least partially answer this question, it is necessary to focus on those factors, theoretical and practical, that seem to be the basis of his linguistic choices. In 1435, he wrote his first literary work in Florence, *De verbis Romanae locutionis*, in which he challenged the recently expressed ideas of Leonardo Bruni, who had attributed to ancient times the *diglossia* of the present and believed that even in antiquity Latin was a prerogative of only learned men. Instead of now examining the content of the famous humanistic debate over the language of the ancient Romans,[5] it is my intention to focus on Biondo's choice to treat this subject in Latin. From this point of view, in fact, it is interesting to remember that Leon Battista Alberti, in order to take a position in this debate, wrote in the vernacular both the *Grammatichetta*, whose drafting is now dated by Lucia Bertolini to the period immediately following the debate of 1435,[6] and the *Preface* to the third book of *De familia*, composed before 1440–41.[7] First, it is worth noticing that through his work, Biondo, albeit unconsciously, offered a solid argument for

---

2   Leonardo Bruni composed in the vernacular idiom: *Canzone morale, De felicitate* (ca. 1424); *Canzone a laude di Venere* (ca. 1424); *Difesa del popolo di Firenze nella impresa di Lucca* (1431); *Lettera al popolo di Volterra* (1431); *Oratione detta a Nicolò da Tolentino* (1433); *Epistola mandata a Papa Eugenio IV* (1435); *Vite di Dante e del Petrarca* (1436); *Novella di Antioco, re di Siria* (1437); *Lettera allo illustrissimo conte Francesco Sforza* (1439); *Oratione fatta pe' chapitani della parte guelfa visitando i signori*; *Oratione fatta pe' chapitani della parte guelfa visitando il papa*; *Risposta agli ambasciatori del re di Raona* (1443); *Sonetto 'Spento veggio merze sopra la terra'*. For Bruni's vernacular production see Hankins 2006, pp. 11–29; Rizzi 2013, pp. 243–56.
3   Alberti wrote the following vernacular works: *Grammatichetta, Libri de familia, Protesta, Della pittura, Della tranquillità dell'anima*. For general introductions to Alberti's bilingual productions see Maraschio 1972; Maraschio 1972a; Maraschio 2007; Furlan 2013, pp. 39–46.
4   Matteo Palmieri wrote in the vernacular both the poem *La città di vita* as well as the treatise *Vita civile* (around 1434). See Carpetto 1984 and Finzi 1984.
5   For which see Marcellino 2015; Raffarin 2015; Marcellino 2016.
6   Bertolini 2004, p. 254; Bertolini 2011, pp. 56–57. Roberto Cardini dates the *Grammatichetta* after 1437, Cardini 2008, pp. XLII–XLVIII.
7   For the dating of the *Proemio*, see Furlan 1994, pp. 441–42.

those people who supported the use of the vernacular. Having proved in *De verbis* that the ancient Romans wrote in the language commonly spoken by the entire population (Latin), Alberti went on to champion in *Grammatichetta* and the *Preface* to *De familia* the idea of composing in the language used by everyone in the 15th century (the vernacular).[8] *De verbis* is a summary of an oral debate that took place in Florence, in the Convent of Santa Maria Novella, between Leonardo Bruni, then Chancellor of the Florentine Republic, and some apostolic secretaries of Pope Eugene IV, among whom were Andrea Fiocchi, Cencio Rustici, Poggio Bracciolini, Antonio Loschi, and Biondo himself. With the exception of Leonardo Bruni, who also composed several works in the vernacular, the remaining participants in this debate were all monolingual writers and supporters of the use of Latin. Moreover, it is significant that in 1441, the same secretaries Poggio Bracciolini, Biondo Flavio, and Antonio Loschi, now serving as judges, decreed that the popular vernacular poetry competition organized in Florence by Leon Battista Alberti and known as *Certame coronario* had been a failure. The choice to compose *De verbis* in Latin was undoubtedly determined by the sense of belonging to that elite of *litterati* who, at least at first, tried to limit the innovative power of the proposal by Alberti, whose name would be significantly omitted in all works concerning the debate on the language spoken in ancient Rome. In addition, *De verbis* is the first literary work of a no longer young humanist who was about to argue with the most famous humanist of the Quattrocento, Leonardo Bruni, whose writings were widely regarded as the highest example of Ciceronean "splendor of style, rhythm and embellishments."[9] For this reason, even from a formal point of view, the sophisticated and elegant style of this work represents Biondo's concrete attempt to carry on with the ancient eloquence-restoration program undertaken by Petrarch and continued by Giovanni da Ravenna,[10] Manuel Chrysoloras, and finally by Leonardo Bruni. Indeed, all of these figures, according to Biondo's vision, as we read in the famous excursus of the *Romandiola* region in the *Italia illustrata*, would have played a decisive role in the cultural renewal process of the Italian peninsula. Lastly, there are good reasons to believe that Biondo's predilection for Latin had also been influenced by the fact that, since the years of the composition of *De verbis*, he considered this language inherently superior to the Italian vernacular. It should certainly not be forgotten that Biondo

---

8   For the concept of 'vernaculus,' see Ramminger 2010.
9   "orationis nitor numerositasque et ornatus." (Blondus Flavius, *De verbis Romanae locutionis*, § 2).
10   For the different positions about the identity of Giovanni da Ravenna, see the bibliography provided by Backer 2015, p. 56 n. 71.

was the first who argued that the birth of the vernacular dates to the period of the great barbarian invasions, and considered it to be a hybrid product between *Latinitas* and the spoken language of barbarian invaders and destroyers of the Roman Empire. Beginning with his first work, he was able to meditate on the Italian vernacular, sometimes expressing words of appreciation for the literary production of Dante and Boccaccio,[11] even though during his life he abstained from composing literary works in that idiom.

In September 1443, once again back in Rome, two years after the defeat of the *Certame coronario*, Biondo undertook the drafting of the *Roma instaurata*, the first real topographical description of the city of Rome, which enjoyed immediate good fortune, even outside the Italian peninsula. The script, which was completed in 1446 and dedicated to Pope Eugene IV, is the first modern attempt at a systematic study of ancient and medieval monuments of the eternal city.[12] Both the sight of the ruins in the Campus Martius and the Vatican, as well as Biondo's need to correct misspelled topographical judgements repeated by common people about the function of many monuments, as Bartolomeo Nogara poignantly wrote,[13] significantly influenced the drafting of the *Roma instaurata*. It is not such a surprise that a work aiming at the reconstruction (through inscriptions and classical sources) of the topography and monuments of ancient Rome is written in Latin, especially if one considers that Leon Battista Alberti, who wrote several works in the vernacular, used Latin and not his own mother tongue for the short *Descriptio urbis Romae* (1450).[14] Moreover, the literary and epigraphic sources used by Biondo for this cultural operation were exclusively in Latin, a linguistic choice which seems to have been determined also by the desire to offer the work to a cultured and European-wide public that was able to access the documentation on the Roman world in the original. For example, even before completing *Roma instaurata*, Biondo was able to present a portion of the work concerning old coinage during a banquet organized in Rome by Cardinal Prospero Colonna, who was a relevant figure among the Roman humanists in the 15th century.[15] It is also worth remembering that *Roma instaurata* constitutes an attempt to match, on a literary level, the *instauratio* of Roman buildings, and in particular of the basilicas of St. Peter, St. John Lateran and the Vatican Palace, all of which were promoted

---

11   Blondus Flavius, *De verbis Romanae locutionis*, § 20.
12   For *Roma instaurata*, see the modern edition by Raffarin (Flavio Biondo 2005 and 2012). See also Della Schiava/Laureys 2013, pp. 643–65; Della Schiava 2015, pp. 41–84; Della Schiava 2016, pp. 105–31.
13   Nogara 1927, p. XCVI.
14   See the modern edition by Boriaud and Furlan (Alberti, *Descriptio*).
15   Nogara 1927, p. XCVIII.

and strongly supported by Eugene IV.[16] The *Roma instaurata* is itself a literary monument dedicated to the praise of the *Urbs*, which is significantly referred to in the preface as "mother of intellects, nurse of virtues, example of fame, column of praise and glory, and nursery of all the good things that are in the whole world."[17] It is thus not surprising that Biondo used Latin, the language of the ancient Romans, rather than the vernacular for such a literary monument of ancient Rome. For the purpose of our discussion, it is helpful to remember that in *Roma instaurata* Biondo stressed the role of Christianity as a guide for all European people by replying to those learned men who had despised the condition of contemporary Rome and believed that the downward trend of glorious Roman history had begun with the decline of imperial institutions.[18] The topographical reconstruction of pagan and Christian Rome that emerges from the pages of *Roma instaurata* is the product, indeed, of a humanist who was actively engaged in the *res publica Christiana* and worked daily by using Latin, at first as protonotary and abbreviator and then as apostolic secretary.[19] From this point of view, one can observe that the revival of classical Latin is functional not only to the study of ancient and medieval ruins, but also to the cultural restoration of the Roman Church.

The study of ancient Rome and the reconstruction of the medieval historical events forced the humanist to use Latin sources for the composition of his major works: *Italia illustrata, Historiae*, and *Roma triumphans*. Biondo's linguistic choice was certainly influenced by the desire to have his works circulate beyond the Alps. For example, in the vernacular letter addressed to Francesco Sforza, which will be taken into consideration in the second part of this essay, Biondo praised the universal power of his *Histories*, which for some time had circulated beyond the Italian borders, and wrote that the work, unlike the laudatory writings dedicated by others to the Duke of Milan and concerning local history, had been read by the King of France and other European monarchs and writers, because its object covered a wide spatial and temporal extension.[20]

---

16 Flavio Biondo, *Rome Restaurée*, vol. 1, p. 13. Eugenius IV welcomed and supported in his Curia distinguished scholars, such as Maffeo Vegio, Aurispa, Alberti, Leonardo Dati, Carlo Marsuppini, Poggio Bracciolini, Antonio Loschi, Andrea Fiocchi, and Cencio Rustici.

17 "ingeniorum parens, virtutum alumna, celebritatis specimen, laudis et gloriae columen, ac omnium quae universus orbis ubique habet bonarum rerum seminarium." Flavio Biondo, *Rome Restaurée*, vol. 1, p. 11.

18 Flavio Biondo, *Rome Restaurée*, vol. 2, p. 211. See also Raffarin 2003, pp. 643–54; Mazzocco 2012, pp. 73–88.

19 The office of protonotary and abbreviator consisted of drafting pontifical documents and correspondence, while that of apostolic secretary concerned the drafting of papal bulls.

20 Biondo began this work in 1439, starting with drafting those parts concerning the most recent events, and then devoted himself to the more remote period. The *Histories*, in

Theoretically, for the drafting of a historical work in the Quattrocento it would have been possible to make use of the vernacular. In fact, Dino Compagni and Giovanni Villani had just composed the *Cronica delle cose occorrenti ai tempi suoi* and the *Nova Cronica* respectively. Yet Biondo's choice of using Latin seems to be linked to content and practices, since he usually brought into his writings, often without any formal change, a very high number of passages coming from ancient sources. In this regard it is worth citing the famous opinion expressed by Pius II on this *operandi modus*: "Biondo was far from ancient eloquence, nor did he examine carefully enough what he wrote: he paid more attention to quantity than to historical reliability."[21] Certainly, while collecting documentary material, he made use of notebooks to record significant passages encountered during his continuous readings. The material for the construction of his literary buildings was therefore already in Latin. To this observation it should also be added that the dedicatees of the first redaction of *Italia illustrata* and of *Roma triumphans* were Nicholas V and Pius II respectively, two popes who were at the forefront of the humanist movement. The *Italia illustrata*, which was written between 1447 and 1453, represented, according to Biondo, an extension of the historical-chorographic project of *Roma instaurata*.[22] Although Italy from a political point of view was divided among the major powers at that time, Biondo indicated in the *studia humanitatis* the glue that could hold the peninsula together.[23] He believed that Cicero's eloquence had returned to life thanks largely to the work of Petrarch, Giovanni da Ravenna, and Leonardo Bruni. The latter in particular had learned and perfected the practice of translating Greek into Latin at the school of Manuel Chrysoloras, a skill that would allow ancient eloquence to be reborn and be spread among the learned men of

---

32 books, cover the ages ranging from the Visigoths' invasion under Alaric (410) until the peace of Cavriana (1441). On 13 June 1443 he sent to the King of Naples, Alfonso of Aragon, the first eight books. Nogara 1927, pp. XCII and 148; Hay 1959, pp. 102–05; Delle Donne 2016, pp. 55–74.

21   "Procul Blondus ab eloquentia prisca fuit, neque satis diligenter quae scripsit examinavit: non quam vera sed quam multa scriberet curam habuit." Pii II *Commentarii*, vol. 2, p. 711. For Piccolomini's opinion and in general for his relationship with Biondo, see Defilippis 2009.

22   The first impulse for the composition of *Italia illustrata* was given by Alfonso of Aragon in 1447. Blondus Flavius, *Italia illustrata*, pp. 40–43. A new complete edition with an English translation by Jeffrey A. White is now available: Biondo Flavio, *Italy Illuminated*, vols. 1 and 2.

23   Baker 2015, pp. 63–64: "Geography is only one aspect of Italy's coherence, others being its Roman past, the rediscovery of its archaeological and linguistic heritage, and the hope for its political and military independence from the rest of Europe. The most important, however, is the cultural and political Renaissance of the time."

the present. Among the *viri illustres* of *Italia illustrata*, the *litterati* constituted the majority, but it is worth noting here that the attention of the humanist is completely directed to the Latin production, while the vernacular literature, according to him, does not play a role in the process of cultural renewal in the peninsula.[24]

The Latin language was not only an essential tool to reach geographically distant readers who spoke many different languages other than the vernacular in use in 15th-century Italy, it also represented a fundamental element for Western Christian culture as a whole. Biondo's work, in which this pan-European linguistic vision emerges more clearly, was composed not by chance in the years immediately following the fall of Constantinople.[25] In the elegant *Prooemium* of *Roma triumphans* (1453–59), the choice of using Latin is explicitly linked to the particular subject matter and, in particular, to the grandeur and splendour of Rome: Nearly all those men of passion, vigour and outstanding intellect who have been seized by a desire to write in Latin about history and the other aspects of human life have turned to the City and people of Rome.[26] While investigating the reasons that made possible the cultural homogeneity of the Empire, the humanist not only highlights the importance of the fact that subdued populations were incorporated into the Roman political and administrative system, but also assigns a central role to the Latin language in the acculturation process:

> After the Romans had brought the largest part of the world under their sway, they made it so peaceful and so civilized it with good customs and conduct that races divided by sea and mountain and kept apart by rivers and peoples who had different languages and ways of writing were made one and the same state, through sharing the Latin language and all having the Roman magistrates in common.[27]

---

24 I do agree with Baker 2015, p. 251 n. 44, but see Albanese 2005, p. 36: "Die Liste der hier [sc. Biondo, *Italy Illustrated* I, Reg. 6, § 31, pp. 306–08] als Repräsentanten eines dreisprachigen Humanismus genannten Autoren zeigt deutlich, dass Biondo in sprachlicher und kultureller Hinsicht die gesamte Halbinsel in den Blick nimmt."

25 Mazzocco 1979, pp. 1–26; Tomassini 1985, pp. 9–80; Pincelli 2007, pp. 19–28.

26 "Ardenti virtute praestantique ingenio ferme omnes quos de gestis rebus deque ceteris mortalium vitae partibus Latine scribendi libido coepit, ut ad urbem sese verterint gentemque Romanam factum videmus." Biondo Flavio, *Rome in Triumph*, p. 6, trans. Muecke.

27 "Romani enim maximam orbis partem suae subactam ditioni ita pacaverunt cultamque bonis moribus et artibus reddiderunt, ut disunctae mari montibusque et fluminibus separatae gentes ac linguis litteraturaque differentes populi per Latinae linguae communionem perque communes omnibus Romanos magistratus una eademque civitas sint effecti, quod quidem maximum humani generis beneficium Dei potius quam hominum opus

Biondo's idea is certainly very close to that expressed by Lorenzo Valla in the *Preface* to Book I of the *Elegantiae*, where we read that the Latin language had instructed all nations and peoples in the liberal arts and opened for them the way that leads to full knowledge, thus ensuring that the barbarians could no longer be defined as such.[28] In light of the the narrow connection set by Biondo between territorial domination and civilization, however, I will limit myself here to observe that the thought expressed in the *Roma triumphans* shares more affinity with the *Oratio in principio studii* by Valla (1455), in which the spread of the Latin language is presented in a historical perspective as the positive result of Roman imperialism. The adoption of Latin by the defeated peoples is for the two humanists a crucial moment for the global acculturation process that had been activated by territorial conquest.[29] Here it is interesting to note that Biondo clearly links his linguistic choice to the fact that learned transalpine readers, who are able to read in Latin, are very keen on the history and the institutions of ancient Rome:

> Accordingly, no less than Italians, foreign people literate in Latin both eagerly read and listen with the greatest of attention to the glorious merits of the City and people of Rome, the Roman institutions and models for living, no differently from the deeds of their own parents and forefathers. Thus they seem to invite and stimulate to write those with the capacity to do so.[30]

To explain why Biondo composed this work in Latin, we should also draw attention to an aspect that has long been neglected by scholars. Besides serving as a very wide thematic encyclopaedia of the ancient world, *Roma triumphans* is a work of anti-Turkish propaganda, begun after the fall of Constantinople and completed in 1459 at the Congress of Mantua, which had been established by Pius II in order to organize Christian rulers for a crusade against the

---

fuisse videtur." Biondo Flavio, *Rome in Triumph*, p. 6, trans. Muecke). This idea is then taken up and amplified in the excursus on Latin literature in the fourth book of this work. Blondus Flavius, *De Roma triumphante libri decem*, p. 98; Marcellino 2017.

28 Regoliosi 1993, p. 121.

29 Valla, *Orazione*, p. 196, §§ 18–19. For a detailed discussion of this topic, see Marcellino 2017.

30 "Romanae igitur gentis et urbis laudes, Romanorum instituta et vitae exempla non Italae magis quam externae gentes litteris utentes Latinis haud secus quam parentum et progenitorum gesta et legunt avide et attentissima exaudiunt diligentia, ut idoneos ad scribendum invitare ac impellere videantur." Biondo Flavio, *Rome in Triumph*, p. 10, trans. Muecke.

Ottomans.[31] The propaganda sections and the heartfelt invitation to the powers of Europe were undoubtedly written to reach a pan-European audience, to which the humanist not only offered a statement of Roman grandeur and splendour, but also invoked the duty to obey Pope Pius II in order to save the *res publica Christiana*, at that moment threatened by infidels.[32] That Cicero's language was then the most suitable instrument for such a political goal is proven by Piccolomini's contemporary anti-Turkish production and orations in Latin.[33]

By retracing, albeit briefly, Biondo's literary production, I have tried to highlight the intrinsic and profound reasons that were the basis for his choice to use Latin. Now, before concluding, I would like to examine the two letters in the vernacular mentioned at the beginning of this contribution (the original copies of which are held at the Sforzesco Archive in Milan). First, it should be noted that, unlike other humanists, Biondo did not personally arrange for collecting his letters, which are now preserved in a very small number of manuscripts. It is enough to remember here that most of his letters have survived thanks to Biondo Flavio's son, Girolamo, who used manuscripts inherited from his father in order to prepare the transcription of ms. F 66 of the Saxon State and University Library Dresden, which also contains *De verbis Romanae locutionis, Roma instaurata* and *Italia illustrata*. For this reason it is necessary to use extreme caution in making a quantitative comparison between the 24 Latin letters and the two epistles written in the vernacular.[34] Second, it is possible that in his private correspondence, the humanist, especially in dealing with practical matters, usually made a more frequent use of the vernacular than the documentation in our possession allows us to believe. In this regard I wish to observe that the small number of vernacular letters by Biondo now finds a significant equivalent in the correspondence of his mentor and close friend, Francesco Barbaro,[35] of whom only a single official letter written in the

---

31 Mazzocco 2010, pp. 133–41; Marcellino 2014, pp. 163–86.
32 Not by chance Biondo wrote his four works concerning the crusade in Latin: *Oratio coram serenissimo imperatore Frederico et Alphonso Aragonum rege inclito* (1452); *Ad Petrum de Campo Fregoso illustrem Genuae ducem; De expeditione in Turchos* (1453); *De origine et gestis Venetorum* (1454). For the first two texts new critical editions are now available: Blondus Flavius, *Oratio coram serenissimo imperatore* and Blondus Flavius, *Ad Petrum de Campo Fregoso*. For Biondo's propaganda works see Defilippis 2009a; Rossi 2009, pp. 669–77; Pittaluga 2009, pp. 557–668.
33 For Piccolomini's anti-Turkish production see Helmrath 2000, pp. 79–137.
34 Biondo's vernacular letters are absent in the Dresden manuscript.
35 Biondo was also secretary to Barbaro in Vicenza in 1425 and then in Bergamo in 1430.

vernacular has been preserved beyond his huge *epistolario* in Latin.[36] Even in the case of Barbaro, as well as in that of Biondo, it is questionable whether the low amount of available documentation is not just due to the nature and linguistic circulation of these missives. Indeed, a vernacular epistle was intended to circulate less than the Latin ones, which instead were often sought as a model for epistolary composition.

On 16 January 1459 Biondo wrote from Rome to the Duke of Milan, Francesco Sforza, begging him to give to his son Girolamo the post then vacant at the Diocese of Parma (Text A).[37] From this letter we learn that even in the last years of his life he had to provide for the material needs of his "grave famiglia," which was made up of ten children. We also know that in 1459 Girolamo was already a doctor of both laws ("doctore utriusque iuris") and seemed to be endowed with very good skills. We do not know whether Girolamo succeeded in obtaining that post, and although we know that he played a key role in the spread of his father's writings, we unfortunately do not have other evidence of him. The choice of using the vernacular with the Duke of Milan might at first sight seem to be determined by the content itself of the letter, which consists of a practical request. This hypothesis would seem at first glance also to be confirmed by the other letter addressed to the Duke of Milan on 28 January 1463 (Text B), to which I referred at the beginning of this essay.[38] Writing again from Rome, Biondo on this occasion addresses Sforza in order to focus on the general theme of writing historical works and to request his financial support for the drafting of the fourth *Decas* of his *Histories*. In the *exordium* the humanist opens by declaring that the glory of "ciascun grande et virtuoso homo" is linked to the fact that there have always been writers who recounted the historical events by writing "bone et sollide historie." Biondo thus reminds readers that, except for Julius Caesar's *Commentaries*, the history "de niuno principe o altro homo antiquo romano o d'altra natione" has been preserved. The digression seems not to be made for its own sake, but in order to serve Biondo's aim, as evidenced by his claim that in the third *Decas*:

> è qualche partesella de gesti del magnanimo Sforza vostro padre e de voi e tutto ciò che vi occurse mai fare da la morte del S. Braccio fin a la

---

36 The vernacular letter has been published by Griggio 2013, pp. 191–96. For the sake of completeness it is necessary to remember that Francesco Barbaro also drafted in the vernacular Zaccaria Trevisan's testament, of which the copy transcribed by the notary has survived.

37 Nogara p. CXIX. The text has also been edited by Gabotto 1891, p. 8; Nogara 1927, p. 210.

38 The text has also been edited by Gabotto 1891, pp. 9–11; Nogara 1927, pp. 211–12. For a detailed analysis of this letter, see Ianziti 1988, pp. 77–80.

predicta pace de Martinengo, et sono li vostri gesti con veritate, ordine e bono inchiostro narrati, cioè senza frappe vane, de le quali vi vogliono vestire alcunj.[39]

The mention of "frappe vane," probably a reference to Filelfo's *Sphortias*,[40] whose redaction of eight books was completed in the early 1460s, leads us to assume that Biondo tries to distance himself from a certain laudatory production.[41] It is also to be added, in fact, that the opening words of the *Sphortias*, which explicitly criticize historical works aiming at reconstructing past events, can itself be read as an attempt by Filelfo to distance himself from that universal history project to which Biondo had dedicated great effort.[42] Moreover, before explicitly advancing his request, the humanist emphasizes the fact that thanks to his work the glorious name of the Duke of Milan resounds throughout Europe ("et vedese per certa experentia che in le mie historie disseminate per Anglia, Spagna, Franza, quanto per Italia, da tutti li notabili principi et homini litterati se lege la gloria vostra"). Indeed, among the readers of Biondo's *Histories* there is also "el Serenissimo Re de Franza," who bought a book in Rome "dal Reverendissimo mio S. Arcivescovo de Milano," Stefano Nardini, and implored Biondo to complete the work until the narration of the last years. In a simple and direct way, he implies that he can offer the Duke a service that others could not procure for him, because, while particular histories and biographies are meant to have a limited scope, the universal history ("historia universale") is the only one that can encompass a large scale perspective, because it concerns different countries and rulers. Finally, the humanist gets to the heart of the matter, by openly asking for the Duke's help in completing his literary enterprise:

> Dico tante cose per indure la S. vostra ad fare si ch'io possa scrivere la quarta deca, in la quale seria tutta la gloria vostra de Martinengo in qua. La quale deca nè altro più non posso scrivere senza alturio de chi po' et ad chi tocha.

---

39 Braccio da Montone (1368–1424) was a famous leader and politician. The "pace di Martinengo" (1441), also called "pace di Cavriana," put an end to the clash between the Duchy of Milan and the Venetian Republic.
40 Fubini 1968, p. 554, but see Ianziti 1988, pp. 78–79.
41 The first four books of the *Sphortias* were completed in 1456, while the drafting of the eight-book redaction dates to 1460. Filelfo's original plan was to compose a poem in 24 books, following the Homeric model. For the history of the composition of the work, see De Keyser 2015, pp. XI–XVIII.
42 De Keyser 2015, p. 3 vv. 1,1–2.

The "alturio" Biondo refers to is surely of an economical nature, as it is proved by the last sentence of the letter:

> Altramente, se io debbo scrivere gratis, io farò como ho facto dapoi compita la terza, che ho scripto *Roma instaurata, Italia illustrata* et *Roma triumphante* et molte altre operette.

We thus see that while on the one hand Biondo addressed Francesco Sforza in the vernacular in order to get financial support, he on the other hand sought to make him immortal by placing in the *Histories* the description of his glorious actions in Latin. First, we may wonder whether the choice of using the vernacular is related in any way to the content of the two letters, in which our humanist seems to be led primarily by the desire to deal with some practical questions in order to obtain benefits for himself and his son Girolamo. Second, one should remember that Biondo on other occasions made use of Latin always for concrete demands, as happened, for example, on 13 June 1443, when the humanist wrote a long letter to Alfonso of Aragon to send him the first eight books of the first decade of his *Histories*. Even in this case, although insistently asking the King to provide documentary material about the history of Spain, Biondo did not avoid pointing out the difficult enterprise he had undertaken.[43] However, it should be noted that together with the letter addressed to Alfonso (much more elegant and extensive than that sent to the Duke of Milan), Biondo transmitted to the Aragonese king the first eight books of the first decade. In this letter, the humanist not only sought Alfonso's aid, as in the case of Sforza, but also dwelled on the tasks that should belong to a good ruler.[44] These two writings, although they are to be included formally in the same kind of letter production, differ greatly in content and purpose.

Since Biondo was able to write with brevity and conciseness in Latin, as he did in a very short letter to Messer Nicodemus Tranchedini about some private business,[45] we should try to give a fairer explanation as to why Biondo used the vernacular while addressing the Duke of Milan. Thus, we can wonder at this point whether the linguistic choice was not perhaps to some extent related to the tastes or use of the recipient, as is the case, for example, with Francesco Filelfo's letters to Giovanni Toscanella and Antonio Metello in 1443.[46] If we consider the literary production dedicated to the Duke or written

---

43   Nogara 1927, p. 149.
44   Nogara 1927, p. 152.
45   Nogara 1927, p. 169.
46   Marcelli 2015, p. 62.

in the cultural circle gravitating around him, we might observe that there was a great number of works written in both Latin and vernacular. In the very same years, as noted above, Francesco Filelfo composed the famous epic Latin poem *Sphortias*.[47] He was the most important figure at the court of the Duke, but also other humanists, trying to guarantee his benevolence, dedicated works to him in Latin. Among them is to be numbered Pier Candido Decembrio, who in the years 1461–62 wrote the *Vita Francisci Sfortiae*, also known as *Adnotatio rerum gestarum in vita illustrissimi domini Francisci Sfortiae*. Yet one should also note that towards the end of 1462, Decembrio began to make a vernacular version of this biography, probably hoping to attract the attention of the Duke with this vernacular redaction. Moreover, in 1485 Antonio Minuti composed his *Compendio di gesti del magnanimo e gloriosissimo signore Sforza* in the vernacular, in which he dealt with Attendolo Sforza's actions (1369–1424).[48] Finally, it is worth keeping in mind that Antonio Cornazzano drafted in the vernacular his *Sforziade*, which nevertheless had limited success, whereas Lodrisio Crivelli wrote his *De vita rebusque gestis Francisci Sfortiae* in Latin, which remained unfinished.[49] Thus, in the Duke's entourage both languages were employed for the writing of literary works.

Therefore, in order to understand the reasons for Biondo's use of vernacular in these two letters, it seems necessary to extend our inquiry to the *corpus* of Francesco Sforza's letters held at the State Archives in Milan. Good reasons lead us to believe that Biondo's choice of using the vernacular is linked in some way to the practice of the Chancellery of the Duke. A survey on the letters of the Secret Chancellery during Francesco Sforza's duchy (1450–66), preserved in no fewer than 83 registers, each containing hundreds of official letters, shows that the documents in Latin are significantly less than those in the vernacular.[50] Moreover, we also have to consider that the letters of the Secret Chancellery were drawn up by several secretaries and then reviewed and approved by Francesco himself, who could have preferred the vernacular for such a demanding work. Thus, it is not surprising that one of the two letters addressed by Biondo to the Duke of Milan (Text C) has been written in

---

47   It is also worth remembering that Filelfo wrote a vernacular commentary to Petrarch's *Canzoniere*, commissioned by Filippo Maria Visconti in 1439. For Filelfo's vernacular production, see Verrelli 2012–2013, pp. 50–96.
48   Attendolo Sforza was the father of Francesco Sforza.
49   For this account, see Ianziti 1988, pp. 61–80; Zaggia 2014, p. 181.
50   This consideration is based on examination of the letters present in the registers I–XVI, whose transcription is now available on the internet site www.istitutolombardo.it/lamemoriadeglisforza.htm (last access: November 11, 2016).

the vernacular by "Cichus" (Cicco Simonetta) on 16 September 1451,[51] whereas the other (Text D), in an elegant Latin style, lacks both the date as well as the name of the secretary[52] and seems to have been written in answer to two other lost letters by Biondo.[53] In light of these data, we can therefore assume that Biondo's use of the vernacular was partially related in this case to a willingness to adapt to the practice of the Chancellery, which for practical reasons used primarily, although not exclusively, the vernacular language.

In conclusion, we can affirm that Biondo throughout his life questioned himself about the origins of the Italian vernacular language, its use in literature and its relationship with Latin. However, for him only Latin represented the language of culture. His literary training (which took place in the school of humanists at the forefront of the formal restoration of Latin), his career, and his cultural horizons led him to use the language of Cicero, who was considered, by most of the humanists of the 15th century, as an unquestionable model of eloquence.[54] In private correspondence, as we have seen, he sometimes used even the vernacular, though extant documents do not allow us to prove that this use exceeded the boundaries of the letters to the Duke of Milan, who seems to have fostered the colloquial language of that time within his Chancellery. In reality, Biondo did believe that only Latin could be the cultural language to link ancient and modern Rome together. During his life he was able to watch Leon Battista Alberti's and Leonardo Bruni's attempts to encourage the use of the vernacular in literature, but his admiration of these humanists was respectively related only to the ingeniousness of the former[55] and the

---

51   Text edited by Gabotto 1891, p. 7.
52   Text edited by Gabotto 1891, pp. 12–14. Nogara 1927, p. CV, dates it before 1453: "La lettera dello Sforza è senza data; ma poiché vi si accenna alla presa di Piacenza, avvenuta nel novembre 1447, come a cosa alquanto lontana, e poiché per altre speciali espressioni si lascia supporre che egli fosse già padrone di Milano, è logico riferirla agli anni posteriori al 1450, non oltre però il 1452, perché il 26 ottobre dell'anno seguente 1453 il Biondo stesso annunziava al Barbaro […] che la grande opera era compiuta e sparsa ormai in tutta l'Europa." For a detailed analysis of this letter, see Ianziti 1988, pp. 64–66.
53   See also Nogara 1927, p. CV and n. 129.
54   In *Italia illustrata*, he assigns a central role to his transcription of a manuscript containing Cicero's *Brutus*. Biondo, *Italy Illuminated* I, p. 306.
55   "nobili et ad multas artes bonas versatili ingenio" ("noble and versatile intelligence in many good arts." Biondo, *Italy Illuminated* I, p. 74). See also "nosterque Leo Baptista Albertus, geometra nostro tempore egregius, qui de re aedificatoria elegantissimos composuit libros, ad id operis est vocatus." ("My friend Leon Battista Alberti, the great mathematician of our age and author of a graceful work on the art of building, was summoned to help in the task," Biondo, *Italy Illustrated* I, p. 190, trans. White).

Latin eloquence of the latter.[56] When Biondo died in 1463, he probably could never have imagined that soon the fate of the Italian vernacular would take a completely different route with Cristoforo Landino, Angelo Poliziano, and Lorenzo de' Medici.

1 Appendix

1.1 *Biondo's Correspondence with Francesco Sforza*

The edition of the four following letters is based on the autographs held at the State Archives of Milan. All manuscripts have been autoptically examined. In letter *B*, in only one case, I distinguish the original reading from the subsequent correction by the same scribe. The notes to letter *D* provide information about the complex stratigraphy of the corrections, by distinguishing the different revisions made by a different scribe (Filelfo?) while drafting the document (M^1, M^2, M^3).

Text A) Biondo Flavio to Francesco Sforza; 16 January 1459.
Archivio di Stato di Milano, Archivio Visconteo Sforzesco, Potenze estere, Roma, 48.

Illustrissime princeps et excellen.me domine mi sing.me
post commendationem. Per la speranza chio ho grandissima in la v.s. che in qualunqua via et maniera possibile et honesta voi me adiuteresti sempre in governare la grave famiglia mia, ho preso confidentia de mettere una expectativa assai legiera, in la ghiesa de Parma per Jeronimo mio figliolo, doctore utriusque iuris, la vita et doctrina del quale spero non dispiacerà maj ad chi lo habbia ad havere subdito o collega. Et cum questa mando bolle, processi et procuratorij neccessarij ad ciò ch'el sia in arbitrio de la V.ra S. o de farle mettere ad exequtione, piacendovi, como spero, o retenerle. Et sempre ala V. S.mi recomando. Die XVI Januarij MCCCLVIIII Rome.
Illus[trissime] d[ominationis] v[estrae]
Servitor Blondus

[on the other side]

Illustrissimo principi et excellen.mo
dmo dmo Francisco Sfortiae vicecomiti
Mediolani Duci Dom.o
meo singulariss.

---

56 See Marcellino 2013, pp. 214–29.

Text B) Biondo Flavio to Francesco Sforza; 28 January 1463.
Archivio di Stato di Milano, Archivio Visconteo Sforzesco, Potenze estere, Roma, 54.

Illust.mo S. mio,
Per vostra virtute et de vostro padre site in questa etate molto exaltato et venite ad esser degno de gloria perpetua. La quale gloria sempre ha habuto questa conditione in ciascuno grande et virtuoso homo, che tanto è durata e amplificata quanto ha habuto bone et sollide historie scripte. Le quale historie se sum state particulare etiam facte da uno e più eloquentissimj, sono presto mancate, perché la natura de li homini è sempre stata de havere invidia et voluntiera supprimere laude d'altri, in tanto che fradelli l'uno dell'altro et fighioli, che li parà valere, de padri occultano la gloria. Perciò vedemo de niuno principe o altro homo antiquo romano o d'altra natione non esser durata historia particulare, salvi li commentarij de Caesare per la singulare eloquentia, singulare virtute et singulare grandeza, de principato de quello homo. Ma de altri molti imperadori et principi grandi de la cui vita et gesti fo scripte particulare historiae, non è remasta alcuna. Dove chi se trova in frotta con altri principi, popoli et valenti homini, in el corpo grande de Tito Livio, Suetonio, Tacito, Salustio, Amiano Marcellino et simili latini, o Plutarcho e altri greci, sono gloriosi et seranno longamente, quantunqua etiam in alcune de queste universale historie è stato già periculo. Gaio gallicula tertio imperadore romano viciosissimo per invidia ch'el haveva ali soi predecessori consuli et imperadori de molta fama, comandò per edicto pubblico che per tutto fossero brusate le deche de Livio, et seria stato exequito, se non che essendoli ricordato che Octaviano augusto, suo cio, veneva in dicto incendio molto offeso, retractò l'edicto. Adriano imperadore notabilissimo scrisse lui et fecie scrivere da soi amicissimi li soi gesti. Le quale historie adpena durarono quanto durò la sua vita. Et se non fusse una historia universale de circa LXXX principi scripta de Helio Spartiano et alcuni altri in uno corpo, non ci seria altro che la memoria del nome desso Adriano, come anco non è de Nerva et Traiano, molto più digni desso Adriano. Li quali dui habero ben boni scriptori particulari, ma per desgratia non intrarono in li corpi grandi de Suetonio o de Helio soi vicini. Ecelino da Romano mo' sum circa anni IIIC signorezò Ferrara, Padoa, Tarviso, Ceneda, Feltro, Cividale, Trento, Vicenza, Verona, Bressa, mantuano, cremonese et milanese contadi, et andando ad pigliar Milano fo morto. Del quale sono scripte alcune cronichette et historie particulare et perché non habe ventura de esser messo in qualche historia grande, come pur lo ho messo io, per uno crudele tiranno, non era cognosciuto; pur mo' sanno molti chi et como ello fo grande e tenuto in Italia. La mia prima deca longa de anni CCCC, vene fin ad VIIIC ab incarnatione. La seconda ariva al MCCCC. La tertia piena de gesti de anni XLII dal MCCCC vene fin a la pace facta per la vostra S. a Martinengo, et l'ultimo acto de dicta deca è scripto como la illust. ma Madonna Biancha vi mena in Cremona et doni quella Signoria. In dicta deca è qualche partesella de gesti del magnanimo Sforza vostro padre e de voi e tutto ciò che vi occurse mai fare da la morte del S. Braccio fin a la predicta pace de Martinengo, et

sono li vostri gesti con veritate, ordine e bono inchiostro narrati, cioè senza frappe vane, de le quale vi vogliono vestire alcuni. Et vedese per certa experientia che in le mia historie disseminate per Anglia, Spagna, Franza, quanto per Italia, da tutti li notabili principi[57] et homini litterati se lege la gloria vostra; sì che per certo modo io so et sanno molti in corte, el Serenissimo Re de Franza presente havere lette dicte mie historie, comparate in Roma dal Reverendissimo mio S. Arcivescovo de Milano per ducati 45. In le quale historie, ciò è in la terza Deca, habiando esso retrovato et relecto le guerre de Venetiani, cum lo S. Duca Philippo, in le quale el vostro nome è clarissimo, et veduto in longo tempo l'acquisto fece el re Alphonso del reame, cercò anche ancho et voleva trovare l'acquisto vostro de Milano et la venuta de re Renato a vostro alturio, et non possendo trovare dicte due parte, che non li sono et haveranno ad essere in la quarta deca, io ne sono stato domandato. Et ho resposto che quando questa quarta sia al mondo, la poranno comparare como le altre. Se io volesse esser più longo, poria assai bene mostrarvi cum reverentia et humilitade ch'el se sente più el vostro nome in scriptis per le mane mie che forsi per tutte l'altre scripte fin qui facte. Et del dover durare assai o no, ho pur uno argumento da extimare molto, ché per la christianitate in ogni natione e provintie sono molti volumi de mie historie, de quali oltra cinquanta sono gosti ad chi li ha voluti, oltra ducati quaranta per uno, et alcuni so io che non li dariali soi per ottanta; oltra che fra la mezzana gente ne sono moltissime copie et exempli. Dico tante cose per indure la S. vostra ad fare si ch'io possa scrivere la quarta deca, in la quale seria tutta la gloria vostra da Martinengo in qua. La quale deca ne altro più posso scrivere senza alturio de chi po et ad chi tocha. Altramente, se io debbo scrivere gratis, lo farò come ho facto da poi compita la terza, che ho scripto *Roma instaurata*, *Italia illustrata* et *Roma triumphante*, et molte altre operette. Recomandomi a la Vostra Signoria. XXVIII Ianuarii MCCCCLXIII. Rome.

Illu[stris] d[ominationis] vestrae
Servitor Blondus

[on the other side]

[illustrissimo] principi et excellen.mo domino
[F]rancisco Sfortiae Vivecomiti
[Medi]olani quarto duci dignissimo
[domino me]o inclyto

Text C) Francesco Sforza to Biondo Flavio; 16 September 1451.
Archivio di Stato di Milano, Registri delle missive, V, c. 170r.

---

57 notabili principi *B¹*: notabili homini principi *B*.

Domino Blondo de Forlivio

Como doveti recordarvi la S.ta del papa Eugenio ne concesse lo terreno de Barbiano per Cottignolla, per uno suo breve, et cossì noy stessi intrassemo alla possessione d'esso terreno; et perché esso breve ne bisognaria de presenti per certi respecti, quale non trovamo ne sappemo mai como haverlo, se non da vuy, quale ne recordiamo facesti quello altro et ne rendino certi habiati la copia presso vuy, ve scrivemo questo confortandovi et pregandovi in nostro servicio et singulare complacentia vogliati refare dicto breve in forma originale et auttentica, come fo lo primo et mandarcelo per lo presente portatore. Et de questo quanto più possiamo ve preghiamo certificandovi che de questo ad noy fareti singulare servicio et piacere. Et perché forse non ve pareria senza vostro incarico, vogliati saltem mandarci la copia del dicto breve, quale sia autenticata o de mano vostra o per quello modo meglio ve parera che ubique se gli possa dare fede.
Lade XVI Septembris 1451.
Cichus

Text D) Francesco Sforza to Biondo Flavio; *ante* 1453.
Archivio di Stato di Milano, Autografi: Biondo Flavio, Cart. 114, fasc. 7.

Spectatissime ac doctissime vir amice noster carissime,
Accepimus superioribus diebus binas[58] abs te litteras eadem fere materia ac sententia conscriptas[59] quibus si in presentem usque diem[60] in respondendo tardiores, quam volebas, fuerimus, non arrogantie, non ingratitudinis vitio,[61] non negligentie culpa, sed ingentibus occupatonibus nostris variisque curis in quibus diu noctuque versamur[62] factum velimus putes.[63] Et licet in dies,[64] quemadmodum decebat, litteris tuis omni quidem humanitate, suavitate, doctrina prudentiaque refertis respondere studuerimus, tamen si id absque iniuria facere licuisset perlibenter aliquandiu eas ipsas silentio[65] preterissemus, quo ea tu de re ad scribendum compulsus iterum atque iterum tuis nos ornatissimis epistolis et reviseres et demulceres.[66] Nam cum ob singularem doctrinam, virtutem ac dicendi gravitatem, tum etiam ob summam tuam erga nos

---

58 diebus binas *M¹*: diebus diversis tamen temporibus tres *M*.
59 sententia conscriptas *M¹*: sententia iisdemque verbis conscriptas *M*.
60 in presentem usque diem *M¹*: hucusque *M*.
61 ingratitudinis vitio *M¹*: ingratitudinis non vitio *M*.
62 sed ingentibus ... versamur *M³*: sed ingentium occupationum causa variisque curis in quibus diu noctuque versamur *M²*: sed ingentium occupationum variarumque curarum in quibus diu noctuque versamur causa *M¹*: sed occupationum permultarum variorumque laborum in quibus nocte dieque versamur causa *M*.
63 factum velimus putes *M¹*: velimus factum putes *M*.
64 licet in dies *M¹*: quamquam quottidie *M*.
65 ipsas silentio *M¹*: ipsas litteras silentio *M*.
66 epistolis et reviseres et demulceres *M¹*: scriptis reviseres et frequentares *M*.

affectionem[67] et caritatem, percipimus[68] exinde voluptatem[69] sane non mediocrem. Verum, ut ad ea veniamus que summo a nobis studio[70] petis, ut cronicha silicet que, ut scribis, aut Mediolani aut Papie esse debent,[71] continentia Vicecomitum originem resque per ipsos gestas,[72] ad te mitti curemus, licet nulla nobis neque ubi sint neque penes quem serventur sit cognitio, tamen, cupientes magnopere cum[73] in hoc, tum ceteris in rebus, tuo optimo desiderio satisfacere, ad ea summa cura summaque diligentia perquirenda iam operam indefessam dedisse[74] satis certo scias; que si usquam fuerint modo nobis facultas detur quamprimum[75] ad te transmittemus[76]. Id[77] etiam eo libentius facimus, quo magis[78] magisque Vicecomitum nomen famaque per orbem disseminetur atque propagetur ac posteritati tuis commentariis litterarumque monumentis studio diligentiaque tua mandetur.[79] Quod autem scribis, te animo previdisse preclarum facinus a nobis gestum,[80] idque capte Placentie urbis periculo comprobes, ac summus deinde nos laudibus in coelum extollas, queque ad honorem, dignitatem utilitatemque[81] nostram accedunt humaniter, prudenter amanterque in memoriam redigens[82] et ante oculos ponens, facis hoc, suavissime Blonde, singulari erga nos benivolentia precipuoque amore ductus.[83] Verum[84] nequaquam huic tue de nobis opinioni, quamvis ab optimo proficisci animo cognoscamus, volumus assentiri, quoniam contenti certe essemus si minimum earum rerum, quas nobis pro tua in nos humanitate attribuis, consequeremur. Quod vero humanitate ac potius pietate quadam commovearis[85] de Placentine civitatis dirreptione et captivitate animoque angeris,

---

67   summam ... affectionem *M¹*: summam erga nos tuam affectionem *M*.
68   percipimus *M¹*: capimus *M*.
69   voluptatem *M¹*: volutatem *M*.
70   que ... studio *M²*: que tanto a nobis studio *M¹*: que a nobis tanto studio *M*.
71   esse debent *M¹*: haberi debentur *M*.
72   continentia ... gestas *M¹*: continentia res gestas per vicecomitum prosapiam *M*.
73   magnopere cum *M¹*: magnopere tuo optimo desiderio satisfacere cum *M*.
74   operam indefessam dedisse *M¹*: operam dedisse *M*.
75   usquam ... quamprimum *M¹*: usquam repperta fuerint quamprimum *M*.
76   transmittemus *M¹*: transmittenda curaturos esse confidas *M*.
77   Id *M¹*: Quod *M*.
78   quo magis *M¹*: quo tuum magis *M*.
79   tuis ... mandetur *M¹*: tuis scriptis litterarumque memoriae tuo studio diligentiaque commendetur, tum etiam ut honeste petitioni tue pro voluntate respondere videamur *M*.
80   scribis ... gestum *M¹*: scribis illud quod non previdit preclarum facinus preclarum a nobis gestum esse *M*.
81   caelum ... utilitatemque *M²*: caelum extollens attingensque quae ad honorem dignitatem utilitatemque *M¹*: caelum extollens queque ad honorem dignitatemque [????] nostram utilitatemque *M*.
82   redigens *M¹*: reddis *M*.
83   ductus *M¹*: commotus *M*.
84   Verum *M¹*: sed *M*.
85   commovearis *M¹*: ductus *M*.

neque vel in hoc tibi cedere volumus cum[86] eadem, qua tu etiam, et ipsi misericordia afficiamur.[87] Nam etsi hec Placentie expugnatio non parvo sit nobis ornamento et glorie cumulo, tamen maluissemus profecto civitatem illam in voluntatem et potestatem nostram sua cum salute redegisse,[88] quam eam sua ex[89] vastitate et dissipatione victoriam retulisse, cum illius semper civitatis salutem et honori nostro privato et utilitati anteposuissemus. Nam omnis humanitas, omnis doctrina omnisque pietas nos plurimum hortabantur ac agere videbantur, ut multo pluris unius tanti populi conservationem quam nostri nominis fameque gloriam et utilitatem faceremus. Sed tamen et illius temporis et rei militaris conditiones ita tulerunt et illorum simul civium pertinatia et divinum forsan aliquod iudicium pro sue temeritatis penitentia, sic credimus voluerint. Quod novissime scribis, nihil te esse pretermissurum in describendis edendisque historiis, quod ad laudem nostram accedat et ad posterorum nostrorum memoriam et immortalitatem pertineat, audivimus non inviti. Sed de his non plura. Illud preter quod pro facultate industriaque nostra non destiterimus quin novam tibi in dies scribendi de nobis materiam preparemus; quod si minus erit, non negligentie, non ocio, sed repugnanti fortune asscripseris. Quibus omnibus de rebus magnas tibi gratias et habemus et referimus, et que in nostra sunt potestate grato quidem animo offerimus, quorum si quo pro voluntate et arbitrio tuo usus fueris, feceris nobis rem sane gratissimam et acceptissimam. Vale et te a nobis tum ob Flaminiam patriam, communem patriam, tum ob immensam virtutem tuam et diligi et quam vehementer amari tibi persuade.

Bibliography

Primary Sources

Alberti, Leon Battista. *Descriptio urbis Romae*, edited by Jean-Yves Boriaud and Francesco Furlan. Florence: Olschki, 2005.

Biondo, Flavio. *Italy Illuminated*, vol. 1, books I–IV, edited and translated by Jeffrey A. White. Cambridge, MA: Harvard University Library, 2005.

Biondo, Flavio. *Italy Illuminated*, vol. 2, books V–VIII, edited and translated by Jeffrey A. White. Cambridge, MA: Harvard University Library, 2016.

---

86   cum *M¹*: nam *M*.
87   afficiamur *M¹*: afficimur *M*.
88   salute redegisse *M¹*: salute ac incolumitate redegisse *M*.
89   ex *M¹*: cum *M*.

Biondo, Flavio. *Rome in Triumph*, edited by Maria Agata Pincelli. Introduction, English Translation and Notes by Frances Muecke. vol. 1, Cambridge, MA: Harvard University Library, 2016.

Blondus, Flavius. *De Roma triumphante libri decem, priscorum scriptorum lectoribus utilissimi ad totiusque Romanae antiquitatis cognitionem pernecessarii.* Basel: Froben, 1531.

Blondus, Flavius. *De verbis Romanae locutionis*, edited by Fulvio delle Donne. Rome: Istituto Storico Italiano per il Medio Evo, 2008.

Blondus, Flavius. *Ad Petrum de Campo Fregoso illustrem Genuae ducem*, edited by Clara Fossati. Rome: Istituto Storico Italiano per il Medio Evo, 2010.

Blondus, Flavius. *Italia illustrata*, edited by Paolo Pontari, vol. 1. Rome: Istituto Storico Italiano per il Medio Evo, 2011.

Blondus, Flavius. *Oratio coram serenissimo imperatore Frederico et Alphonso Aragonum rege inclito*, edited by Gabriella Albanese. Rome: Istituto Storico Italiano per il Medio Evo, 2015.

Flavio, Biondo. *Rome Restaurée (Roma instaurata)*, edited by Anne Raffarin-Dupuis. vol. 1, livre 1. Paris: Les Belles Lettres, 2005.

Flavio, Biondo. *Rome Restaurée (Roma instaurata)*, edited by Anne Raffarin-Dupuis. vol. 2, livres 2–3. Paris: Les Belles Lettres, 2012.

Pii II. *Commentarii rerum memorabilium que temporibus suis contigerunt*, edited by Adrianus van Heck, 2 vols. Vatican City: Biblioteca Apostolica Vaticana, 1984.

Valla, Lorenzo. *Orazione per l'inaugurazione dell'anno accademico 1455–1456. Atti di un seminario di filologia umanistica*, edited by Silvia Rizzo. Rome: Roma nel Rinascimento, 1994.

Secondary Sources

Albanese, Gabriella. "Mehrsprachigkeit und Literaturgeschichte im Renaissancehumanismus." In *Mehrsprachigkeit in der Renaissance*, edited by Christiane Maass and Annett Volmer. Heidelberg: 2005, pp. 23–56.

Baker, Patrick. *Italian Renaissance Humanism in the Mirror*. Cambridge, Eng.: Cambridge University Press, 2015.

Bertolini, Lucia. "Leon Battista Alberti." *Nuova informazione bibliografica* 1 (2004), pp. 245–87.

Bertolini, Lucia. "Fuori e dentro la *Grammatichetta* albertiana." In *Da riva a riva. Studi di lingua e letteratura italiana per Ornella Castellani Pollidori*, edited by Paola Manni and Nicoletta Maraschio. Florence: Franco Cesati Editore, 2011, pp. 55–70.

Campana, Augusto. "Biondo Flavio." In *Enciclopedia dantesca*, vol. 1. Rome, 1970, pp. 634–35.

Campana, Augusto. "Biondo Flavio da Forlì." *La Romagna* 16 (1927), pp. 487–97.

Campana, Augusto. *Ritratto romagnolo di Biondo Flavio*, edited by Michele Lodone. Cesena: Stilgraf, 2016.

Carpetto, George. *The Humanism of Matteo Palmieri*. Rome: Bulzoni, 1984.

Cardini, Roberto. *Ortografia e consolazione in un corpus allestito da L.B. Alberti. Il codice Moreni 2 della Biblioteca Moreniana di Firenze*. Florence: Olschki, 2008.

Defilippis, Domenico. "Biondo Flavio (1392–1463)." In *Centuriae Latinae: Cent une figures humanistes de la Renaissance aux Lumières. À la mémoire de M. de la Garanderie*, edited by Colette Nativel, vol. 2. Geneva: Droz, 2006, pp. 97–105.

Defilippis, Domenico. "L'ultima crociata. Biondo, Piccolomini e l'indagine corografica." In *Da Flavio Biondo a Leandro Alberti: corografia e antiquaria tra quattro e cinquecento. Atti del Convegno di Studi (Foggia, 2 febbraio 2006)*, edited by Domenico Defilippis. Bari: Adriatica, 2009a.

Defilippis, Domenico. "L'epistola ad Alfonso d'Aragona *De expeditione in Turchos* di Biondo Flavio." In *Oriente e Occidente nel Rinascimento: Atti del XIX Convegno Internazionale (Chianciano Terme-Pienza 16–19 luglio 2007)*, edited by Luisa Secchi Tarugi. Florence: Franco Cesati Editore, 2009a, pp. 127–38.

De Keyser, Jeroen. *Francesco Filelfo and Francesco Sforza. Critical Edition of Filelfo's Sphortias, De Genuensium deditione, Oratio parentalis, and his Polemical Exchange with Galeotto Marzio*. Hildesheim: Olms, 2015.

Della Schiava, Fabio and Marc Laureys. "La *Roma instaurata* di Biondo Flavio: censimento dei manoscritti." *Aevum* 87.3 (2013), pp. 643–65.

Della Schiava, Fabio. "La *Roma instaurata* di Biondo Flavio nella Biblioteca Vaticana." *Miscellanea Bibliothecae Apostolicae Vaticanae* 21 (2015), pp. 41–84.

Della Schiava, Fabio. "Per l'edizione nazionale della *Roma instaurata* di Biondo Flavio: indagini preliminari." In *A New Sense of the Past: The Scholarship of Biondo Flavio (1392–1463)*, edited by Angelo Mazzocco and Marc Laureys. Leuven: Leuven University Press, 2016, pp. 105–31.

Delle Donne, Fulvio. "Le fasi redazionali e le concezioni della storia nelle *Decadi* di Biondo: Tra storia particolare e generale, tra antica e moderna Roma." In *A New Sense of The Past: The Scholarship of Biondo Flavio (1392–1463)*, edited by Angelo Mazzocco and Marc Laureys. Leuven: Leuven University Press, 2016, pp. 55–87.

Finzi, Claudio. *Matteo Palmieri dalla 'Vita Civile' alla 'Città di vita'*. Rome: Giuffrè, 1984.

Fubini, Riccardo. "Biondo Flavio." In *Dizionario biografico degli Italiani*, vol. 10. Rome: 1968, pp. 536–59.

Fubini, Riccardo. "Biondo Flavio." In *Dizionario critico della letteratura italiana*, edited by Vittore Branca, vol. 1. Turin: UTET, 1986, pp. 339–44.

Furlan, Francesco. "*Nota al testo*." In *Leon Battista Alberti. I libri della famiglia*, edited by Ruggiero Romano and Alberto Tenenti, new edition by Francesco Furlan. Turin: Einaudi, 1994, pp. 429–78.

Furlan, Francesco. "Il bilinguismo albertiano." *Humanistica* 8 (2013), pp. 39–46.
Gabotto, Ferdinando. *Alcune idee di Flavio Biondo sulla storiografia, con documenti inediti*. Verona: Donato Tedeschi e figlio, 1891.
Griggio, Claudio. "Una lettera ufficiale di Francesco Barbaro in volgare." *Quaderni Veneti* 2 (2013), pp. 191–96.
Hankins, James. "Humanism in the Vernacular: The Case of Leonardo Bruni." In *Humanism and Creativity in the Renaissance: Essays in Honor of Ronald G. Witt*, edited by Christopher S. Celenza and Kenneth Gouwens. Leiden: Brill, 2006, pp. 11–29.
Hay, Danys. "Flavio Biondo and the Middle Ages." *Proceedings of the British Academy* 45 (1959), pp. 97–125.
Helmrath, Johannes. "Pius II. und die Türken." In *Europa und die Türken in der Renaissance*, edited by Bodo Guthmüller and Wilhelm Kühlmann. Tübingen: de Gruyter, 2000, pp. 79–137.
Ianziti, Gary. *Humanistic Historiography under the Sforzas: Politics and Propaganda in Fifteenth-Century Milan*. Oxford, Eng.: Clarendon Press, 1988.
Maraschio, Nicoletta. "Leon Battista Alberti, *De pictura*: bilinguismo e priorità." *Annali della Scuola Normale Superiore di Pisa*, s. III, 2 (1972), pp. 265–73.
Maraschio, Nicoletta. "Aspetti del bilinguismo albertiano nel *De pictura*." *Rinascimento* 12 (1972)a, pp. 183–228.
Maraschio, Nicoletta. "Il plurilinguismo italiano quattrocentesco e l'Alberti." In *Alberti e la cultura del Quattrocento. Atti del Convegno internazionale del Comitato Nazionale VI Centenario della nascita di Leon Battista Alberti (Firenze, 16–18 dicembre 2004)*, edited by Roberto Cardini and Mariangela Regoliosi. vol. 2. Florence: Polistampa, 2007, pp. 611–28.
Marcelli, Nicoletta. "Filelfo 'volgare'. Stato dell'arte e linee di ricerca." In *Philelfiana. Nuove prospettive di ricerca sulla figura di Francesco Filelfo*, edited by Silvia Fiaschi. Florence: Olschki, 2015, pp. 47–81.
Marcellino, Giuseppe. "Flavio Biondo lettore di Leonardo Bruni: Rileggendo il proemio del *De verbis Romanae locutionis*." *Albertiana* 16 (2013), pp. 214–29.
Marcellino, Giuseppe. "Lo studio delle antichità romane e la propaganda antiturca nella *Roma triumphans* di Biondo Flavio." *Studi Classici e Orientali* 60 (2014), pp. 163–86.
Marcellino, Giuseppe. "La disputa umanistica sulla lingua del volgo dell'antica Roma". In *Il latino e il 'volgare' nell'antica Roma Biondo Flavio, Leonardo Bruni e la disputa umanistica sulla lingua degli antichi Romani*, edited by Giuseppe Marcellino and Giulia Ammannati. Pisa: Edizioni della Normale, 2015, pp. 1–73.
Marcellino, Giuseppe. "Biondo Flavio e le origini del volgare: un riesame della questione (*De verbis* §§ 108–111)." In *A New Sense of The Past: The Scholarship of Biondo Flavio (1392–1463)*, edited by Angelo Mazzocco and Marc Laureys. Leuven: Leuven University Press, 2016, pp. 35–53.

Marcellino, Giuseppe. "Un excursus umanistico sulle letterature dell'antichità: Biondo Flavio e i classici (*Roma triumphans*, pp. 96–100)." In Muecke/Campanelli 2017, pp. 119–33.

Mazzocco, Angelo. "Some Philological Aspects of Biondo Flavio's *Roma triumphans*." *Humanistica Lovaniensia* 28 (1979), pp. 1–26.

Mazzocco, Angelo. "*Urbem Romam florentem ac qualem beatus Aurelius Augustinus triumphantem videre desideravit*: A Thorny Issue in Biondo Flavio's *Roma triumphans*." *Studi Umanistici Piceni* 30 (2010), pp. 133–41.

Mazzocco, Angelo. "A Glorification of Christian Rome or an Apology of Papal Policies: A Reappraisal of Biondo Flavio's *Roma instaurata* III. 83–114." In *Roma e il Papato nel Medioevo: Studi in onore di Massimo Miglio*, edited by Anna Modigliani, vol. 2. Rome: Storia e letteratura, 2012, pp. 73–88.

Mazzocco, Angelo. "Introduction." In *A New Sense of the Past: The Scholarship of Biondo Flavio (1392–1463)*, edited by Angelo Mazzocco and Marc Laureys. Leuven: Leuven University Press, 2016, pp. 9–34.

Muecke, Frances and Maurizio Campanelli, eds. *The invention of Rome: Biondo Flavio's Roma triumphans and its Worlds*. Geneva: Droz, 2017.

Nogara, Bartolomeo. *Scritti inediti e rari di Biondo Flavio*. Rome: Tipografia Poliglotta Vaticana, 1927.

Pincelli, Maria Agata. "La *Roma triumphans* e la nascita dell'antiquaria: Biondo Flavio e Andrea Mantegna." *Studiolo* 5 (2007), pp. 19–28.

Pittaluga, Stefano. "Biondo Flavio, Genova e i Turchi." In *Oriente e Occidente nel Rinascimento: Atti del XIX Convegno Internazionale (Chianciano Terme-Pienza 16–19 luglio 2007)*, edited by Luisa Secchi Tarugi. Florence: Franco Cesati Editore, 2009, pp. 557–668.

Raffarin, Anne. "La célébration des triomphes de Rome par Flavio Biondo dans la *Roma instaurata* et la *Roma triumphans*." In *Grecs et Romains aux prises avec l'histoire: Representations, récits et idéologie, Colloque de Nantes et Angers*, edited by Guy Lachenaud and Dominique Longrée, vol. 2. Rennes: Presses universitaires de Rennes, 2003, pp. 643–54.

Raffarin, Anne. *La langue des Romains. Débats humanistes sur le latin parlé dans l'Antiquité*. Paris: Les Belles Lettres, 2015.

Ramminger, Johann. "Humanists and the Vernacular: Creating the Terminology for a Bilingual Universe." In *Latin and the Vernaculars in Early Modern Europe*, edited by Trine Arlund Hass and Johann Ramminger. *Renæssanceforum* 6 (2010), pp. 1–22.

Regoliosi, Mariangela. *Nel cantiere del Valla. Elaborazione e montaggio delle 'Elegantiae.'* Rome: Bulzoni, 1993.

Rizzi, Andrea. "Leonardo Bruni and the Shimmering Facets of Languages in Early Quattrocento Florence." *I Tatti Studies in the Italian Renaissance* 16.1/2 (2013), pp. 243–56.

Rossi, Giovanni. "Reazioni umanistiche all'avanzata turca. L'appello di Biondo Flavio ad Alfonso d'Aragona (1453)." In *Oriente e Occidente nel Rinascimento: Atti del XIX Convegno Internazionale (Chianciano Terme-Pienza 16–19 luglio 2007)*, edited by Luisa Secchi Tarugi. Florence: Franco Cesati Editore, 2009, pp. 669–77.

Tomassini, Marina. "Per una lettura della *Roma triumphans* di Biondo Flavio." In *Tra Romagna ed Emilia nell'Umanesimo: Biondo e Cornazzano*, edited by Marina Tomassini and Claudia Bonavigo. Bologna: CLUEB, 1985, pp. 9–80.

Verrelli, Luca. "Filelfo volgare: *sermo familiaris*, eufemismi, trivialismi e proverbi nel commento al *Canzoniere* di Petrarca." *Interpres* 31 (2012–2013), pp. 50–96.

Zaggia, Massimo. "Culture in Lombardy, ca. 1350–1538." In *A Companion to Late Medieval and Early Modern Milan. The Distinctive Features of an Italian State*, edited by Andrea Gamberini. Leiden: Brill, 2015, pp. 166–89.

CHAPTER 3

Latin and Vernacular Interplay: Lazzaro Bonamico as Author and Character of Sperone Speroni's *Dialogo delle lingue*

Teodoro Katinis

1   Towards an Integration of Vernacular and Neo-Latin Studies[1]

Recent scholarly endeavours have focused on underlining the different identities of Neo-Latin and vernacular literature in the early-modern era instead of the interplay between them, with some remarkable but still few exceptions. Several editorial projects testify to a rebirth of the study of the Neo-Latin tradition and offer not only new tools for further research and teaching, but also new methodological approaches and perspectives for the future. In response to this increasing effort in the field of Neo-Latin Studies, a more recent research line has been promoted within Europe with the purpose of illuminating the knowledge and study of Italian vernacular literature of the Renaissance. Both research projects and publications have played a central role in this respect.[2]

On the one hand, all these initiatives risk stressing the competition between Latin and the vernacular beyond what may be necessary. On the other hand, these same initiatives simultaneously demonstrate important attempts at exploring the interplay between classical and modern languages in the hope of offering a comprehensive study of the early modern linguistic world. For example, in his exploration of the interplay between Neo-Latin and other languages, Demmy Verbeke recently pointed out that "an intentional and obvious form of polyglossia involving Latin and one or more vernaculars is found in

---

1   I would like to thank the organizers of the conference *Texts and Contexts VII: The Influence of Vernacular Discourses on Neo-Latin Literature*, Florian Schaffenrath and Alexander Winkler, for inviting me, and all the participants for their comments on my work. I wrote the first version while I was Marie Skłodowska-Curie Fellow at Ca' Foscari University Venice. The writing of this essay, therefore, was possible thanks to the funding from the European Union's Horizon 2020 research and innovation programme under the Marie Skłodowska-Curie grant agreement No 659644. The revised version I presented for publication was written during the first months of my current appointment as Research Professor of Italian Literature in the Department of Literary Studies at Ghent University (Belgium).
2   Among the most recent works, see Bianchi 2012; Sgarbi 2014; Lines 2015.

publications used for linguistic instruction."[3] The logic of competing languages, often assumed as the only way of studying the linguistic phenomenon of the Renaissance, does not apply to several significant literary cases, including such genres as grammar textbooks, dialogues, and medical works—among other genres—which require a different scholarly approach. A well-known example of collaboration between different languages in the same work is the *Hypnerotomachia Poliphili* (1499), attributed to Francesco Colonna, in which ancient Greek, Latin, and Italian vernaculars interact in narrating the allegorical story of Poliphilo who pursues his love between the worlds of reality and dreams. This text was published just before the beginning of a century when the so-called *questione della lingua* became a central issue in Italy and abroad. Particularly in Italy, the language debate over the identity and value of Latin and the vernacular took place in the 15th century and involved Leonardo Bruni and Flavio Biondo, among others, and continued to broaden, even in different forms, throughout the 16th century. In the first half of the 16th century, authors such as Niccolò Machiavelli, Pietro Bembo, and Sperone Speroni wrote on this subject from different perspectives, arguing for the use of different languages in different contexts, with regard, for example, to the evolution and legitimacy of Latin and the vernaculars, and the models to follow in each case.

In the context of this volume, my contribution aims at studying the linguistic arguments presented by Lazzaro Bonamico as a character and defender of Latin in Speroni's *Dialogo delle lingue* and comparing them with Bonamico's own writing and his intellectual profile. I will argue that one of Bonamico's Latin letters to a young prince confirms he claimed a close connection between the study of the classical literatures and the art of being a good ruler—a humanistic ideal, indeed. Nevertheless, the fact that Bonamico never wrote against the use of the vernacular does not confirm the strong condemnation of the Italian vernacular that Speroni attributed to him in his dialogue. Additionally, Bonamico's *Concetti della lingua latina*, a vernacular work on Latin grammar published in Venice in 1562, provides evidence that Speroni's representation of Bonamico as an old-fashioned Latin humanist is at least incomplete and confirms that, beyond the *mise-en-scène* built by Speroni for his readers, Bonamico was inclined to flexibility and willing to switch to the language required by his readers' needs.

As a best-seller within the *questione della lingua* and a most popular arena for the epic Renaissance conflict between ancient and modern languages, Speroni's *Dialogo delle lingue* will be our starting point for this short but

---

3 Verbeke 2015, p. 31. For an important overview on the subject, including relevant reflections on the methodological aspects, see Deneire 2014.

significant journey through the middle-earth of the interplay between Latin and Italian vernacular.

2   Bonamico in Speroni's *Dialogo delle lingue*

Sperone Speroni wrote his *Dialogo delle lingue* in the 1530s and Daniele Barbaro published it with Speroni's other dialogues in 1542, without the author's approval. In fact, we know very well that Speroni preferred to offer his works as a matter for discussion rather than publication. Given both the great influence that Speroni exerted over the next several generations of Renaissance scholars and the originality of his work, the collection of dialogues were republished at least nine times in the 16th century, while an edition of Speroni's (almost) complete works was published in Venice in 1740. Two modern editions were also published in 1996 and 1999.[4]

As usual, Speroni does not include himself in his dialogue and leaves it without a conclusion. The general subject of this open dialogue is not only a discussion of the value of vernacular languages compared to ancient Greek and Latin, but also a commentary on the nature and evolution of languages and the relation between linguistic issues and cultural identity.[5] As noticed by Valerio Vianello, Speroni's dialogue is the first early modern work to give a clear dramatic representation of the conflict among different positions on the value of ancient and modern languages.[6]

Speroni took part in the *questione della lingua* as a defender of the vernacular, which is clearly demonstrated in his work and life, including the fact that he wrote only in Italian. Additionally, when he played the role of 'principe' of the 'Accademia degli infiammati' in 1542, the Italian vernacular was the focus of this prestigious Academy in Padua.[7] Although there is no doubt

---

[4] Even an essential bibliography on Speroni and his works, especially the dialogues, would be too broad to be cited here. An excellent introduction is provided by Pozzi 1996, pp. 471–509. *Sperone Speroni* 1989 is a collection of essays on several aspects of Speroni's production and provides a bibliography of Speroni's published works and a catalogue of Speroni's manuscripts in the Biblioteca Capitolare of Padua. Speroni's dialogues were republished in 1543, 1544 (1545), 1546, 1550, 1552, 1558, 1560, 1564, and 1596. For the complete bibliographical references of the *editio princeps* and the editions of 1740, 1996, and 1999, see the Primary Sources of this article.

[5] On the evolution of the dialogical genre and its characteristics in the Renaissance, see Girardi 1989 and Cox 1992.

[6] "il primo a visualizzare scenograficamente con chiarezza di concezione le schermaglie antagonistiche." Vianello 1988, p. 108.

[7] Bruni 1967.

about Speroni's preference for the vernacular, what emerges from the dialogue is more a discussion among different interlocutors than Speroni's specific position on the matter, which makes the dialogue very interesting for our purpose.

The protagonists of the first part of the dialogue are Pietro Bembo, who defends the value of the Italian vernacular with the model of Petrarch's and Boccaccio's 14th-century writing style, and Lazzaro Bonamico, a humanist and very popular teacher (not only in Padua but also in other Italian cities and abroad), who defends the superiority of classical languages, especially Latin. A third character, called the Cortegiano—whose identity is unknown—plays the role of fostering the discussion. The second part of the dialogue is introduced by a new figure, the Scolare (an anonymous student) who reports the dialogue that occurred between Giovanni (Giano) Lascari and Pietro Pomponazzi, called Peretto, on the same subject regarding competition between ancient and modern languages during their life-times. At the end of the dialogue, Bonamico and Bembo, the same interlocutors who started the discussion, sum up some of their arguments while the author, Speroni, does not propose any reconciliation between the opponents.

The characters in the dialogue express different opinions over ancient and modern languages and their interrelationships within a variety of contexts. An overview of this variegated landscape of different perspectives will give us a better understanding of Bonamico's position in Speroni's work. The first argument is presented by Pietro Bembo who argues that one cannot be considered a philosopher if he does not know ancient Greek and Latin. There is evidence that this position also belonged to the actual author, Pietro Bembo.[8] The character Bonamico agrees and expresses his hatred of the vernaculars, which is refuted by Bembo who defends the 14-century Tuscan vernacular as a language that, although inferior to the classical languages, deserves legitimation. It is significant that in his reply, Bonamico, who insists on rejecting the vernaculars, is neither interested in differentiating among them nor in supporting the superiority of the Tuscan language.[9] This strict opposition to any form of the vernacular justifies, according to Bembo, the role that Bonamico should (and will) play as a defender of Latin. Indeed, Bembo's esteem for Latin does not bring him to scorn the Tuscan vernacular. Bonamico's attack on any use of the vernacular is so strong that the Cortegiano declares that Bonamico's ideal world, in which the vernacular would no longer exist, is impossible to realize given the actual use of the vernacular in daily life. To this pragmatic

---

8   Speroni, *Dialogo*, p. 589 and see pp. 587–88, n. 3 for the evidence brought by Pozzi and based on Bembo's biography (all the citations are from Pozzi's edition).
9   Speroni, *Dialogo*, p. 589.

argument Bonamico replies that the use of the vernacular should be avoided for intellectual purposes; consequently he in fact proposes a rigid dualism and boundary between Latin and the vernaculars.[10] In contrast, Bembo argues for the dignity of the vernacular as a language for literary and cultural purposes based on the model of Petrarch and Boccaccio. Furthermore, he defends the freedom of anyone to use the language one finds preferable, without the limitations imposed by Bonamico.[11] Before turning to the second part, the role of Bonamico decreases while the debate between Bembo and the Cortegiano intensifies. Their exchange focuses mostly on the issue of the best type of Italian vernacular. Bembo insists that the best candidate for intellectual subjects is the Tuscan vernacular used by Petrarch and Boccaccio, whereas the language of Dante ought to be avoided because of the Lombardian influence as should the Tuscan spoken by the "vulgo" in contemporary Italy. Therefore, according to Bembo, one should study Tuscan Italian as the only Italian language with a well-defined structure ("ben regolata").[12] The Cortegiano defends the right to express oneself in the type of Italian language that one prefers, and opposes those who would impose one specific vernacular on any prose writer, poet, or playwright. The Paduan comic playwright Ruzzante (Angelo Beolco), who wrote and acted in the Paduan vernacular, provides an example of an effective use of a non-Tuscan vernacular for cultural purposes.

In the second part of the dialogue, Peretto argues that in an ideal future, philosophy and science should be communicated in any vernacular language, and not only in the Greek, Latin, and Tuscan vernaculars. Peretto thus offers both a response to Bonamico and an extension of the Cortegiano's argument against Bembo's defence of Tuscan vernacular.[13] According to Peretto, any language is an artificial tool that serves to communicate the meaning of concepts and should not be considered an aim in itself. Ideally, we should not waste our time in learning a different language for studying and imparting knowledge. Lascari hopes that Peretto's dream will never come true and that Aristotle will never be translated and taught in any vernacular.[14] Bembo, who is the last speaker in the dialogue, points out that Peretto's arguments refer only to philosophical and scientific knowledge, whereas only the 14th-century Tuscan vernacular should be used for poetry and oratory.[15] Bembo, indeed, highlights

---

10   Speroni, *Dialogo*, p. 598.
11   Speroni, *Dialogo*, p. 600.
12   Speroni, *Dialogo*, pp. 612 and 614.
13   Speroni, *Dialogo*, p. 621 and passim.
14   Speroni, *Dialogo*, p. 630.
15   Speroni, *Dialogo*, p. 634.

the difference between the language of knowledge and that of the arts, which brings us back to the first part of the dialogue and leaves the reader without a conclusion.

Beyond the arguments presented in the dialogues, one can point out that in the *Dialogo delle lingue* Bonamico uses the vernacular to discuss a complex matter, despite arguing against the use of Italian as a language for intellectual discussion and reasoning. Speroni's irony in representing this contradiction demonstrates, on the one hand, that the vernacular is fit for conveying intellectual exchanges, while confirming, on the other hand, the reader's doubts regarding Bonamico's condemnation of the vernacular.

Having summarized the different positions presented by Speroni, we now will turn our attention specifically to the arguments used by Bonamico in the first part of the dialogue in defending the cultural and literary superiority of Latin, which, according to him, cannot be replaced by any Italian vernacular. His argument supporting the classical languages, summarized by Cesare Vasoli,[16] links the linguistic issue to relevant political and cultural factors. Investigating these factors will enable us to compare Bonamico as a character to Bonamico as an author.

Speroni's dialogue begins with Bembo asking Bonamico to present his arguments that demonstrate the superiority of Latin as well as of Greek. Bonamico is glad to have an opportunity to praise the classical languages:

> Lazzaro: [...] io n'ho pregato Domenedio che mi dia grazia e occasione una volta di far conoscere al mondo non quel poco ch'io so, ma il valore e l'eccellenzia di queste due lingue [greco e latino], le quali gran tempo sono state sprezzate da chi doveva adorarle.[17]

Bonamico condemns the vernacular because it does not bring any honour or glory; in fact, it is the language of the "vulgo" and the result of Latin's degeneration throughout the centuries:

> Lazzaro: Degna cosa da credere che 'l cielo abbia curato altre volte e curi ancora della greca e della latina, per la eccellenzia di queste lingue; ma di quelle altre [i vernacolari] né il cielo ne ha cura, né deeno averne i mortali: ai quali né onore né utile non può recare il parlar bene alla maniera del vulgo.[18]

---

16   Vasoli 1996, pp. 266–68.
17   Speroni, *Dialogo*, p. 587.
18   Speroni, *Dialogo*, p. 588.

> Lazzaro: [...] la [lingua] volgare non è altro che la latina guasta e corrotta oggimai dalla lunghezza del tempo e dalla forza de' barbari o dalla nostra viltà.[19]

Bonamico does not recognize any original identity of the vernacular and, to stress his devotion to the language and style of ancient oratory, claims that he would prefer to be able to speak as Cicero than have the power of a pope or emperor: "io vi dico che più tosto vorrei saper parlare come parlava Marco Tullio latino ch'esser Papa Clemente"[20] and "più istimo e ammiro la lingua latina di Cicerone che l'imperio d'Augusto."[21]

After praising Latin as a superior language, Bonamico condemns the Italian vernacular and its poetic style as a blend of foreign languages and, therefore, not at all Italian. According to Bonamico's argument, the Italian vernacular is a hybrid product in which different foreign linguistic terms blend to create a monster instead of a legitimate language. With a reference to the biblical Tower of Babel in the Book of Genesis, he prays that God will bring discord to the words of this monstrous language, so that Latin will be restored in Italy as the only language[22] of the peninsula:

> Lazzaro: [...] ella [la lingua volgare] mostra nella sua fronte d'aver avuto la origine e l'accrescimento da' barbari, e da quelli principalmente che più odiarono li Romani, cioè da' Francesi e da' Provenzali, da' quali non pur i nomi, i verbi e gli avverbi di lei, ma l'arte ancora dell'orare e del poetare sí si derivò. Oh glorioso linguaggio! Nominatelo come vi pare, solo che italiano non lo chiamate, essendo venuto tra noi d'oltre il mare e di là dall'Alpi, onde è chiusa l'Italia. [...] prego Dio che mandi ancora la sua discordia; la quale, separando una parola dall'altra [della lingua volgare] e ognuna di loro mandando alla propria sua regione, finalmente rimanga a questa povera Italia il suo primo idioma [il latino], per lo quale non meno fu riverita dalle altre provincie, che temuta per le armi.[23]

---

19 Speroni, *Dialogo*, p. 589. The conception of the vernacular as a degeneration of Latin was already argued by the humanists Biondo Flavio and Lorenzo Valla. For a recent summary of their arguments and sources, and of the broader 15th-century debate, see Marcellino 2015, pp. 60–73.
20 Speroni, *Dialogo*, p. 591.
21 Speroni, *Dialogo*, p. 592.
22 See the contribution by Marcellino in this volume.
23 Speroni, *Dialogo*, p. 596.

This passage also reveals the broader scope of Bonamico's speech, which, in fact, deals with the issue of how Italy's lack of cultural and political power was caused by the barbarian origin of vernacular expressions, a situation which can be resolved by revitalizing Latin—the only language that can restore the supremacy of Italian culture.

Bonamico thinks Latin is the only appropriate language for human beings when they interact with knowledgeable people. Indeed, vernacular ("volgare") should be permitted only in talking with people of the lower classes ("vulgo") and with slaves. We should speak only in Latin, in contrast, to communicate and reason among learned people and for academic purposes:

> Lazzaro: [...] se l'uomo è in piazza, in villa o in casa, col vulgo, co' contadini, co' servi, parli volgare e non altramente; ma nelle scole delle dottrine e tra i dotti, ove possiamo e debbiamo essere uomini, sia umano, cioè latino, il ragionamento.[24]

Moreover, the use of such a deplorable Italian vernacular is evidence of Italy's slavery and weakness, as well as its dependency and subjection to foreign cultures: "altro non essendo questa lingua volgare che un indizio dimostrativo della servitù degli italiani."[25]

The discussion between Bembo and Bonamico is politely interrupted by the Cortegiano who, despite his poor knowledge of the subject, makes an important contribution by pointing out how Bonamico's argument is quite out of context since he is arguing about the ruin of Italy, rather than complaining about the vernacular and praising Latin:

> Cortegiano: A me pare, messere Lazzaro, che questo non sia né lodar la lingua latina, né vituperar la volgare, ma più tosto un certo lamentarsi delle ruina d'Italia; la qual cosa come è poco fruttuosa, così è molto discosta dal nostro proponimento.[26]

Bonamico replies with a rhetorical question, suggesting that the link between the destruction of the Roman Empire and the decline of the Latin language actually *is* the point of the discussion: "parvi che il biasimo sia poco, quando io congiungo il nascimento di lei [la lingua volgare] alla destruzzione dell'imperio

---

24   Speroni, *Dialogo*, p. 598.
25   Speroni, *Dialogo*, p. 603.
26   Speroni, *Dialogo*, pp. 603–04.

e del nome latino?"[27] I believe this is a crux of the dialogue, since it reveals a major concern of Bonamico. Indeed, he is particularly focused on how the language, its nature and formation, can affect a specific cultural and political context. Similar to the critique of the vernacular, the link between the preservation of the ancient heritage and the political dimension can be recovered in other writings by Bonamico.

3   Bonamico's Authorship

The enormous renown that Speroni's *Dialogo delle lingue* has enjoyed since its publication might obscure the fact that some of the characters in his dialogue were first of all influential intellectuals and authors of their time. This is certainly the case for Pietro Bembo, Pietro Pomponazzi, and Lazzaro Bonamico. As Francesco Bruni did with Pietro Pomponazzi, one may question the degree to which the arguments expressed by the character of Bonamico correspond with the opinions that the humanist actually expressed in his works about language and related issues.[28] In other words, one may ask whether we can trust the intellectual portrayal of Bonamico made by Speroni. To verify Bonamico's position about language we need to turn our attention to his life and work. Unfortunately, unlike the case of Bembo and Pomponazzi, the primary sources on which we can rely to recover his intellectual position are not as copious as scholars would expect from such an influential humanist. Bonamico's life outside the academic field, on the contrary, can be traced with precision thanks to several documents in the Italian archives.

Lazzaro Bonamico (or Bonamici, Buonamici, Buonamico), born in 1477 or 1478, in Bassano del Grappa, studied Latin and Greek with rigorous teachers in Padua, such as Marco Musuro from Crete, the preeminent Greek humanist who eventually worked with Aldo Manuzio in Venice. Bonamico also studied philosophy with Pietro Pomponazzi (referred to in the dialogue by the nickname of Peretto), who served also as Speroni's mentor.[29]

We know Bonamico was esteemed by his contemporaries as a strong intellectual and a very distinguished professor. Students came not only from Italy but also from Europe to attend his lessons on classical languages in the University of Padua. According to Bernardino Tomitano's *Ragionamenti della lingua toscana* (Venice 1546), Bonamico participated in the meetings of the Accademia

---

27   Speroni, *Dialogo*, p. 604.
28   Bruni 1967, p. 43.
29   For an overview of Bonamico's biography and work see Avesani 1969.

degli infiammati at the beginning of the 1540s and had good personal and intellectual relations with supporters of both Latin and the vernacular.[30] He was mostly interested in ancient history as well as eloquence and rhetoric, as evidenced by his works on Thucydides, Livy, Demosthenes, and Cicero, but he never published his writings and, as far as we know, never wrote systematic works on language and rhetoric (unlike his competitor Pietro Bembo), or pamphlets against the vernacular.

Also, although he was referred to as "litterarum Graecarum et Latinarum lector excellentissimus," "utriusque linguae professor," and "eloquentiae lumen," he never engaged in translating, commenting, or editing any Greek or Latin work, and his preference for speaking instead of publishing was clearly stated in the name he was given: "novus Socrates."[31]

Loyal to Pietro Pomponazzi's teaching, Bonamico preferred Aristotle among the classical philosophers, and we know he intended to give a course on Aristotle's ethics. Although scholars have not found any information on his private library, one might argue, given his intellectual and personal profile, that practical disciplines, such as ethics, politics, oratory, and literary works, could have had a more relevant place than theoretical matters, such as metaphysics and mathematics, on his bookshelf. In his daily life as well he was a very practical man, according to the portrayal by Francesco Piovan, whose biography of Bonamico explores his business activities by analysing a good number of documents kept in a Paduan archive that are related to Bonamico's trading. Ironically, we do not have Bonamico's library, but we are well informed about his salary, goods, transactions, and negotiations in and out of the university. In short, he was a good mentor for his students and a skillful businessman.[32]

Considering the current state of the documentation and sources about Bonamico, it is hard to verify how much the actual humanist corresponds to the character depicted by Speroni in his *Dialogo delle lingue*. However, I believe one of Bonamico's Latin letters published after his death as well as his Latin grammar written in the vernacular can shed light on this matter.

The major part of Bonamico's published letters are in a collection entitled *Epistolae clarorum virorum, selectae de quamplurimis optimae, ad indicandam nostrorum temporum eloquentiam*, published several times in Italy and abroad from 1556 to 1586.[33]

---

30   See the pages on Bonamico in Girardi 1995.
31   Piovan 1988, p. 26.
32   Piovan 1988.
33   Venetiis, apud Paulum Manutium Aldi filium,1556; Parisiis, apud Bernardum Turrisanum, 1556; Venetiis, ex typographia Dominici Guerrei, 1568; Coloniae Agrippinae, apud Ioannem Gymnicum, 1586.

Even a quick look at Bonamico's list of letters can give us an idea of the variety of interlocutors the humanist had: there are cardinals and theologians, such as Gasparo Contarini, Iacopo Sadoleto, and Reginald Pole; there are publishers, such as Turrisano and Paolo Manuzio. However, the letter to which I would like to draw attention is the one to "Principi Melphitano iuniori,"[34] who was probably a young relative of Andrea Doria (1466–1560), the Italian statesman who was nominated Prince of Melfi by the emperor Charles V and established his power in Genoa in 1528 (six years before Bonamico wrote this letter). In his letter, dated 1534, possibly from the same period when Speroni was writing his *Dialogo delle lingue*, Bonamico praises the young prince and his relatives for their intellectual virtues and for being wise rulers. Furthermore, the letter presents advice about being a good ruler. Indeed, Bonamico suggests that the young man avoid the bad habits of their time, when the classical, ancient authors were unfortunately forgotten. Instead, he encourages him to appreciate the nobility of ancient texts that glorify the Romans, Greeks, and others who followed their examples. Indeed, he should not miss the opportunity of imitating ancient models.[35]

The letter presents the *studia humanitatis*, with a focus on the study of Latin and Greek as a foundation for wise ruling and as a necessary reference for statesmen. As in the *Dialogo delle lingue*, Bonamico's main concern is to highlight the relevance of keeping the classical languages alive and the messages they convey for the benefit of political order and cultural power in the Italian peninsula. In his letter, Bonamico shows concern about the political power and prestige of Italy; he is convinced they can be restored by establishing direct access to ancient literature; therefore, he advises recovering Latin and Greek as tools for achieving that purpose. Classical languages as an *instrumentum regni* and stable ground for attaining cultural supremacy is a vision that Bonamico set forth, both as a character in Speroni's dialogue and as author of the letter to the young prince. According to the humanist, given the origin and nature of the vernacular, this new language cannot replace Latin.

Scholars have pointed out that Bonamico's condemnation of the vernacular changed at some uncertain point after the 1530s. Evidence of a different position about the value of the vernacular appears in his *Concetti della lingua latina di un ualente huomo letteratissimo, per imparare insieme la grammatica, et la lingua di Cicerone, nuouamente a utilità commune posti in luce*, published in Venice for the first time in 1562, and then republished at least five times.[36]

---

34   *Epistolae clarorum virorum*, pp. 11–13.
35   *Epistolae clarorum virorum*, p. 12.
36   Venice: Bolognino Zaltieri, 1562 (1563, 1564, 1567 [twice], 1581).

In fact, the uncertain composition date of this work leaves us without any clue about when Bonamico decided to write in the vernacular. Even setting the 1530s as a *terminus post quem* for the composition of the *Concetti* relies on Speroni's description of Bonamico's opinions in the *Dialogo delle lingue*, a description that is not necessarily complete or totally reliable.

Bonamico's use of the vernacular as a language of instruction is not unique to the 16th century. In fact, at least three other works in this genre were published before the *Concetti della lingua latina*: Bernardino Donato's *Grammatica latina in volgare* (Verona 1529), which is also the first Latin grammar in vernacular in the Renaissance; Francesco Priscianese's *De primi principii della lingua romana* (Venice 1540); and Celio Magno's *Grammatica latina in volgare* (Venice 1544). But unlike the Latin grammars of Donato, Priscianese, and Magno, Bonamico's work was intended for advanced readers; indeed, it addresses individuals, including teachers and pupils, who already have at least a basic knowledge of the Latin language.[37]

Bonamico's *Concetti* seems to present a contrast with what the character Bonamico claims in Speroni's dialogue; indeed the character promotes using the vernacular only for non-academic purposes and not at all for conveying scholarly knowledge.[38] Furthermore, we discover at the beginning of the *Prologo* that Bonamico prefers to write his Latin grammar in the vernacular not only to avoid misunderstanding and to facilitate access to the subject for the public, but also because it was easier for him to discuss the matter; indeed, he claims to share with his readers a vernacular linguistic tool that has the power to facilitate communication on the topic of grammar:

> La lingua latina è corrotta in guisa che è gran pericolo che quelli che latinamente l'insegnano, non insegnino altra lingua che latina. Perilché volendo io communicare alcuni miei concetti, osservationi et regole, ho giudicato sia meglio che ciò io faccia con la lingua a voi e a me commune: che cosi fuggiremo questo pericolo: e a me sarà men fatica il dire i miei avisi, e a voi più facile l'intenderli.[39]

This is an extraordinary statement made in support of the vernacular by an author who is commonly considered an enemy of the use of this language for

---

37 I thank my colleague Claudia Crocco (Ghent University) for suggesting that I look at the works of Donato, Magno and Priscianese, and for pointing out the difference in the level of Latin taught in Bonamico's grammar.
38 Speroni, *Dialogo*, p. 598.
39 Bonamico, *Concetti*, p. 17.

reasoning, discussing, and teaching any type of intellectual subject. His position is even more striking when we consider that Bonamico's grammar skips basic notions, such as the Latin alphabet, and begins directly with advanced concepts. Indeed, Bonamico assumes his readers have already studied several topics:

> Già per l'istitutioni de' grammatici sapete quali articoli si giunghino a ciascheduna sorte de' nomi e quai sieno i numeri, quali i casi; e avete già imparato a concordare in ciascuno caso il nome adiettivo col sostantivo, il relativo con l'antecedente, il nominativo col verbo ...[40]

One may wonder if Bonamico had a complete conversion from his arguments against the vernacular in the *Dialogo delle lingue*, where he claims that no human being could use the barbarian language for intellectual purposes, to the *Prologo* of his work in which he esteems the vernacular for being capable of explaining Latin to knowledgeable people.

Of course, until scholars find additional documents, we cannot demonstrate whether Bonamico's opinion on the vernacular was the one shown by Speroni and eventually changed in such an extreme way in the *Concetti della lingua latina* (or sometime between the two works), or if Speroni's representation of Bonamico in his dialogue was very far from the positions that the actual author already held in the 1530s. The fact that the textual history and circulation of the *Concetti* is not documented and that no manuscript of this work has been discovered makes it impossible for scholars to determine when and under which circumstances Bonamico decided to write his grammar textbook.

As a result of this lack of evidence, the reception of Bonamico's opinion about the value of the vernacular has been compromised by Speroni's representation—or misrepresentation—of him and readers have tended to assume that Bonamico's position is reducible to the character in Speroni's dialogue.

4 Conclusion

Perhaps this work offers more questions than answers, and yet we can draw some conclusions. First, there is no evidence that Bonamico's esteem for Latin and Greek implied a condemnation of any intellectual use of the vernacular; on the contrary, the *Prologo* of the *Concetti della lingua latina* suggests quite

---

40 Bonamico, *Concetti*, p. 18.

an opposite position. Second, Bonamico's letter to the young prince confirms what Bonamico claims in the *Dialogo delle lingue*: his main concern was not condemning the vernacular but rather avoiding the political decline of Italy by keeping Latin and the messages it conveyed alive and circulating, which could also explain that the function of a Latin grammar in the vernacular was to disseminate the knowledge of classical literature to a broader public. Third, Bonamico shared with Speroni more than we might suspect: like Speroni, he was an Aristotelian devoted to the 'vita activa' more than the 'vita contemplativa' and to the disciplines related to it, such as rhetoric and oratory; moreover he chose not to publish his writings during his life; instead engaging in the linguistic and cultural debates of his time, which went far beyond the simplistic condemnation of a specific language.

These conclusions, I believe, bring us not only to reconsider the relationship between Bonamico and Speroni, and more generally between Speroni and the 15th-century humanists, but also to shed new light on the linguistic aspects of the Renaissance in Italy, at least in the area of Padua and Venice. In fact, I do not see the benefit in current scholarship of emphasising the competition between Latin and the vernaculars, which sometimes is assumed to be extremely strong in the Renaissance. We risk, indeed, radicalizing the terms of a conflict that certainly played a part in the Renaissance but was not necessarily as dominant as we might think. This assumption might bring about not only a misleading representation of the Renaissance but also a conflict between Neo-Latin studies and vernacular studies over how to determine what should be regarded as the legitimate language of culture in the Renaissance. This conflict could be replaced by a collaboration aimed at establishing an integrated approach that studies the different types of interactions among classical and modern languages during the Renaissance.

Verbeke claims that in the Renaissance "Latin was clearly still an important part [...] of the linguistic tapestry of this [Renaissance] polyglot world and continued to be used in a wide variety of contexts. It coexisted and interacted with the modern languages in any number of ways."[41] Latin played a flexible role in this "tapestry," along with the vernaculars, in a way that is very different from the one it takes on today.[42] We should, perhaps, look at the Renaissance

---

41 Verbeke 2015, p. 36.
42 Tom Deneire (2014, p. 276) stresses the difference between the Renaissance period and the present in the following terms: "The coexistence of Latin and the vernacular(s) in early modern times is a situation of *diglossia*, in which two languages (or dialects) are used by a single community [...] *diglossia* is a more accurate term to describe the specific linguistic situation of Neo-Latin and the different 'national' languages than *bilingualism*, which only refers to the mere use of two languages by individuals or communities. Most

"tapestry" of languages as a unique moment in Western history, a moment we are still attempting to understand in its specificity and which reveals a complexity that is not reducible to the category of "conflict" and "contest" between languages.

Bibliography

Primary Sources

Bonamico, Lazzaro. *Concetti della lingua latina di un ualente huomo letteratissimo, per imparare insieme la grammatica, et la lingua di Cicerone, nuouamente a utilità commune posti in luce.* Venice: Bolognino Zaltieri, 1562.

Bonamico, Lazzaro. *Epistolae clarorum virorum, selectae de quamplurimis optimae, ad indicandam nostrorum temporum eloquentiam.* Venice: Paulus Manutius Aldi filius, 1556; Paris: Bernardus Turrisanus, 1556; Venice: Dominicus Guerreus, 1568; Cologne: Ioannes Gymnicus, 1586.

Speroni, Sperone. *Dialogue des langues*, edited by Gérard Genot, Paul Larivaille and Mario Pozzi. Paris: Les Belles Lettres, 2001.

Speroni, Sperone. *Dialogo delle lingue*, edited by Antonio Sorella. Pescara: Libreria dell'Università Editrice, 1999.

Speroni, Sperone. *Dialogo delle lingue*. In *Trattatisti del Cinquecento*, edited by Mario Pozzi, vol. 2. Milan: Ricciardi, 1996, pp. 585–636.

Speroni, Sperone. "Di che si debba scrivere hoggidi in questa lingua volgare et a cui." In Speroni, *Opere* v, pp. 445–46.

Speroni, Sperone. *Dialogo delle lingue* [reprint from Speroni. Opere. I. Venice, 1740], with a German translation, edited by Helene Harth. Munich: W. Fink, 1975.

Speroni, Sperone. *I dialogi* [...], Venice: in casa de' figliuoli di Aldo, 1542.

Speroni, Sperone. *Opere* [...] *tratte da' mss. Originali*, edited by Natale dalle Laste and Marco Forcellini, 5 vols. Venice: D. Occhi, 1740 (reprint edited by Mario Pozzi. Rome: Vecchiarelli, 1989).

Secondary Sources

Avesani, Rino. "Bonamico." In *Dizionario Biografico degli Italiani*, vol. 11, Rome: Treccani, 1969, pp. 533–40.

Bianchi, Luca. "Volgarizzare Aristotele: per chi?" *Freiburger Zeitschrift für Philosophie und Theologie* 59 (2012), pp. 480–95.

---

people today, for instance, are bilingual [...] rather than diglossic [...] even if bilingualism is used as a general container-notion for all matters 'Latin and vernacular', we should remain aware of the variety of such bilingual situations."

Bruni, Francesco. "Sperone Speroni e l'accademia degli Infiammati." *Filologia e letteratura* 13 (1967), pp. 24–71.

Celenza, Christopher S. *The Lost Italian Renaissance. Humanists, Historians, and Latin's Legacy*. Baltimore: The Johns Hopkins University Press, 2004 (Italian translation: *Il Rinascimento perduto. La letteratura latina nella cultura italiana del Quattrocento*. Rome: Carocci, 2014).

Cox, Virginia. *The Renaissance Dialogue: Literary Dialogue in Its Social and Political Contexts, Castiglione to Galileo*. Cambridge, Eng.: Cambridge University Press, 1992.

Deneire, Tom, ed. *Dynamics of Neo-Latin and the Vernacular: Language and Poetics, Translation and Transfer*. Leiden: Brill, 2014.

Deneire, Tom. "Neo-Latin and the Vernacular: Methodological Issues." In Ford/Bloemendal/Fantazzi 2014, vol. 1, pp. 275–85.

Deutscher, Thomas Brian. "Lazzaro Bonamico of Bassano." In *Contemporaries of Erasmus: A Biographical Register of the Renaissance and Reformation*, edited by Peter G. Bietenholz and Thomas B. Deutscher. Toronto: University of Toronto Press, 1985, p. 166.

Ford, Philip, Jan Bloemendal and Charles Fantazzi, eds. *Brill's Encyclopaedia of the Neo-Latin World*, 2 vols. Leiden: Brill 2014.

Girardi, Maria Teresa. *Il sapere e le lettere in Bernardino Tomitano*. Milan: Vita e Pensiero, 1995.

Girardi, Raffaele. *La società del dialogo. Retorica e ideologia nella letteratura conviviale del Cinquecento*. Bari: Adriatica Eitrice, 1989.

Grata, Giulia. "Sperone Speroni." In *Apografi dei letterati italiani. Il Cinquecento*, edited by Matteo Motolese, Paolo Procaccioli and Emilio Russo, vol. 2. Rome: Salerno Editrice, 2013, pp. 327–43.

Knight, Sarah and Stefan Tilg, eds. *The Oxford Handbook of Neo-Latin*. Oxford, Eng: Oxford University Press, 2015.

Lines, David. "Beyond Latin in Renaissance Philosophy: A Plea for New Critical Perspectives." *Intellectual History Review* 25 (2015), pp. 373–89.

Marcellino, Giuseppe and Giulia Ammannati. *Il latino e il 'volgare' nell'antica Roma: Biondo Flavio, Leonardo Bruni e la disputa umanistica sulla lingua degli antichi Romani*. Pisa: Scuola Normale Superiore, 2015.

Piovan, Francesco. *Per la biografia di Lazzaro Bonamico: ricerche sul periodo dell'insegnamento padovano (1530–1552)*. Trieste: Lint, 1988.

Pozzi, Mario. "Nota introduttiva." In Pozzi 1996.

Pozzi, Mario, ed. *Trattatisti del Cinquecento*, 2 vols. Milan: Ricciardi, 1996.

Sgarbi, Marco. *The Italian Mind. Vernacular Logic in Renaissance Italy (1540–1551)*. Leiden: Brill, 2014.

Sperone Speroni. Padua: Editoriale Programma, 1989.

Vasoli, Cesare. *Civitas Mundi. Studi sulla cultura del Cinquecento*. Rome: Edizioni di Storia e Letteratura, 1996.

Verbeke, Demmy. "Neo-Latin's Interplay with Other Languages." In Knight/Tilg 2015, pp. 27–40.

Vianello, Valerio. *Il letterato, l'accademia, il libro. Contributi sulla cultura veneta del Contributi sulla cultura veneta del Cinquecento*. Padua: Editrice Antenore, 1988.

CHAPTER 4

Diserte Germanice loqui: the Cultural-Historical Status of the German Language in Franciscus Irenicus's *Germaniae Exegesis* (1518)

Ronny Kaiser

1   Prefatory Remarks

> Venio nunc ad extremam nomini Germano iniuriam ab Italo illatam, videlicet quia scriptorum quisque barbaros nostros dixit, sicuti Plutarchus in vita Marii, Florus li[bro] III, Herodianus et alii. Ut autem Germanis praesens sim, rogo, qua de re Barbari dicantur? Si enim linguae ratione barbari sumus, eo videlicet, quia non declinabilis nostra lingua est, nihil aliud respondebo, nisi Anaxarsis dictum ad Athenienses, quibus scripsit homines non linguis, sed virtute differre, et si linguis, melius tamen barbare loqui et obedientes esse quam contumaces et Attice dicere.[1]

In the above passage, the German humanist Franciscus Irenicus introduces a new section of the second book of his *Germaniae Exegesis* that broadly shapes his discussion of the verdict of barbarism against the Germanic-German nation passed by ancient authors and maintained by Italian humanists who continue to level a charge of cultural inferiority against them. According to Irenicus, this *extrema iniuria* against the Germans may be based on the assumption that the *lingua Germanorum* is a barbaric language. With such considerations, he joins a contemporary discourse shaped by certain Italian humanists who in particular stigmatise the North European nations and their national ancestors as cultural inferiors. The Germans were still struggling with their heritage from the

---

[1] "I now come to the greatest injustice, which was brought against the German name by the Italians, because each of their historians has said that our people were barbarians, such as Plutarch in his *Vita Marii*, Florus in the third book of his epitome, Herodianus, and others. In order to assist the Germans, I ask for what reason they are called barbarians. For if we are barbarians by the nature of our language—because our language is not declinable—I will answer nothing else but that which Anacharsis said to the Athenians. He wrote to them that people do not differ by their language, but in their *virtus*, and even if by language, then it would be better to speak barbarically and to be obedient than to speak stubbornly and in an Attic dialect." Irenicus, *Exegesis*, p. XXXVIIIr/g ii r.

Germanic tribes, to whom the ancient authors consistently imputed a barbaric state. An essential aspect of this supposed cultural inferiority of the Germans has been bound up with the question of their language. For example, Enea Silvio Piccolomini (1405–1464) and Giovanni Antonio Campani (1429–1477) consider the German language to be a barbaric relic left over from the uncultivated era of the Germanic tribes.[2]

Although Irenicus discusses the verdict of German barbarism exclusively on the basis of ancient authorities, he himself rejects this accusation. While he admits that the German language is not declinable at all (and probably therefore very simple in its nature), he states that 'language' by itself is not the right and decisive criterion for distinguishing between peoples culturally—and that this even extends to drawing a distinction between barbaric and non-barbaric people. Rather Irenicus argues, with reference to the Scythian Anacharsis, one of the Seven Wise Men of Greece, that the correct criterion for assessing the culture of a people should be *virtus*. Furthermore, if one did indeed use language as a criterion for distinguishing among cultures, a barbaric mode of speech and obedience would always be preferable to a stubborn attitude and pretentious way of speaking.

Two things become immediately obvious here: on the one hand, the semantic equation of 'Germanic' and 'German,' as is evidenced by the fact that if ancient authors write about the Germanic people, they thereby denote, according to the humanists, the early Germans in particular. On the other hand, there is a weighty verdict of barbarism rendered against the Germans and their ancient ancestors, with which the German humanists had to grapple again and again.[3] Against this background, Irenicus makes the question of language the object of this German humanist discourse on barbarism.

His reference to Anacharsis may indeed sound as if he were at least willing to recognise the cultural-historical status of the Germans as barbarians from the linguistic point of view, and as if he were going to meet this criticism by merely referring to their *virtus*. But in the argumentation that follows, he goes far beyond this basic position and takes the opportunity to discuss the question of the cultural-historical status of the *lingua Germanorum* in more detail. After providing a brief introduction to the author and his work, I will outline the image Irenicus draws of the cultural-historical status of the German language

---

2 For Piccolomini see Krebs 2005, p. 152; for Campani ibid, pp. 172–73. Even the German humanist Conrad Celtis (1459–1508) follows this verdict. Krebs 2005, p. 206. A very broad overview of the various opinions of the German humanists on the German language is provided by Tiedemann 1913, pp. 80–89.

3 See in particular Grünberger/Münkler 1998, pp. 210–33; Helmchen 2004, pp. 180–223; Krebs 2005, pp. 111–250; Hirschi 2005, pp. 243–49 and 302–19.

in the second book of his *Exegesis*, and consider the specific techniques and strategies characterising his treatment of this problem. My main focus will be on how Irenicus describes the relationship between German and Italian and on how he traces the history of German as an ancient language by referring to its influence on Latin and its indigenous origin.[4]

2   Irenicus's Career and the *Germaniae Exegesis*

Franciscus Irenicus, whose real name was Franz Fritz Friedlieb,[5] was probably born around 1495 in Ettlingen and attended the Latin school in Pforzheim. His most famous classmate was Philip Melanchthon, who was almost two years younger than him. Irenicus subsequently enrolled at Heidelberg University to study the *artes* on 10 October 1510.[6] He completed his studies successfully and graduated with the degree of *Baccalaureus* in the *via moderna* on 12 January 1512.[7] After a four-year period of travel, including stays in Strasbourg, Ansbach, and Nuremberg, he enrolled at the University of Tubingen on 16 May 1516,[8] where he again met his former classmate Melanchthon and deepened his knowledge of ancient Greek. But he did not stay in Tubingen for long, as he returned to Heidelberg at the beginning of 1517[9] and obtained the degree of *Magister artium* in the *via moderna* just three months later.[10] In that same year, he was accepted into the Katharinenburse of Heidelberg by Count Palatine Louis V (1478–1544). In August 1518, he was appointed its rector, and finally, in January 1519 he was even called into the council of the faculty of arts.[11] The further course of his life is first characterised by his reformist ambitions[12] and later, from 1531 on, also by his activity as a teacher and school rector at the Latin

---

4   Grünberger/Münkler 1998, pp. 220–27 and Helmchen 2004, pp. 202–03 provide a first and very broad overview of Irenicus's remarks on this topic.
5   Cordes 1975 provides a comprehensive biographical overview of Irenicus. At what time Franz Fritz Friedlieb took the Greek name 'Irenicus' cannot be ascertained. Cordes 1975, p. 353.
6   Toepke 1884, vol. 1, p. 477.
7   Cordes erroneously dated this to May 1512 and mentions that Irenicus obtained the degree of *Bacclaureus* in the *via antiqua*. Cordes 1975, p. 354. However, Toepke already contradicted this. Toepke 1884, vol. 1, p. 477, n. 8.
8   Hermelink 1906, p. 211.
9   A re-enrolment was not necessary. For this reason, there is no further entry in Toepke 1884, vol. 1.
10 Toepke 1884, vol. 2, p. 437.
11 Cordes 1975, p. 355.
12 For further details see Cordes 1975, pp. 359–68 and Müller/Worstbrock 2005, pp. 1248–49.

school of Gemmingen, established in 1521, where he worked until his death in 1553.[13]

In particular, his *Germaniae Exegesis* is an expression of his early interest in national history; however he did not devote himself further to this subject after the piece was published, perhaps owing to the sometimes devastating criticism of the *Germaniae Exegesis*, which began immediately after the work's appearance by high-profile humanists like Erasmus of Rotterdam, Johannes Aventinus, Beatus Rhenanus, Mutianus Rufus, and even—silently—Philipp Melanchthon.[14]

The *Germaniae Exegesis* constitutes an attempt at a historical study of Germany from the Germanic period to the present.[15] Of all the numerous paratexts that appear in this work, the *oratio protreptica* addressed to the Palatine Chancellor Florentius de Venningen and containing nearly 18 printed pages deserves to be emphasised.[16] In this *oratio*, Irenicus addresses the criticism of substantive inconsistencies and linguistic and stylistic deficits (obviously already made by Willibald Pirckheimer and Melanchthon before publication)[17] by referring to his youthful zeal and the lack of time at his disposal for writing his *Exegesis*. In this context, he also invokes his profoundly patriotic attitude as the fundamental *causa scribendi*.[18] His interest in patriotic historiography is also reflected in the fact that the work ends with an edition of the *Norimberga* written by Conrad Celtis (1459–1508), which connects the *Exegesis* to the *Germania illustrata* project inaugurated by Celtis.[19]

---

13   Cordes 1975, pp. 369–70.
14   For further details on the critical reception of Irenicus's *Exegesis*, see Cordes 1966, pp. 137–48 and Müller/Worstbrock 2005, pp. 1253–54.
15   Müller/Worstbrock 2005, p. 1251.
16   Irenicus, *Exegesis*, pp. Qiiii^r–Rvi^v: "Oratio protreptica eiusdem in amorem Germaniae, cum excusatione praesentis operis ad illustrissimi Principis Palatini Electoris Cancellarium Florentium de Phenningen utriusque censurae Doctorem."
17   Müller/Worstbrock 2005, p. 1253.
18   Irenicus, *Exegesis*, p. Riiii v. How long Irenicus worked on his *Exegesis*, we do not know, since he does not comment on the topic. However, he was present at the printing process in Haguenau with Thomas Anselm (see the colophon of the work, p. Vviii v), and obviously made some changes in the process. For the problematic question of the genesis of the work, see Cordes 1966, p. 3 and Müller/Worstbrock 2005, p. 1250.
19   Irenicus, *Exegesis*, pp. T[i]v–Vvii v. For Irenicus's attempt to embed his work in the *Germania illustrata* project, see also Müller 2001, pp. 473–75. For Conrad Celtis and his *Norimberga* (1502), see Arnold 2004; Orth 2004; and Robert 2008, pp. 395–97. A critical edition of Celtis's *Norimberga*, including his *Amores* and the *Germania generalis*, all of which belong to the core texts of his incomplete *Germania illustrata* project (Robert 2008, pp. 393–94), is provided by Celtis 1921. The project of the *Germania illustrata* was described for the first

Even in its concept and content, the *Exegesis* is loosely linked to the Celtis project. The 12 books, which contain almost 500 folio pages, fall into two parts:[20] whereas the first six books have a more ethnological-historiographical focus on the *traditio Germanorum*, the second hexade, which is summarised under the title of *patriae formatio*, illuminates geographical aspects.[21] Book I outlines the question of sources for Germanic-German history and gives an overview of the Germanic tribes and their settlements. Probably following Celtis,[22] Irenicus thus takes up the idea of the *Germania Magna*, under which he subsumes almost all the ethnic groups of Central, North, and Eastern Europe. Book II—the book at the heart of this essay—first focuses on the origin, nature, and culture of the Germans. Its central aim is to thoroughly disprove the verdict of cultural inferiority, which was pronounced against the Germans by the Italians.[23] Book III is devoted to the secular and spiritual elites of the empire and to their genealogies. Accordingly, it provides 22 illustrations of noble family trees.[24] Books IV–VI deal with Germanic warfare and wars in which, as Irenicus tries to show, the Germanic tribes were never defeated by any other nation. Books VII–XII comprise, as already indicated, mainly geographic phenomena, including discussion of the flora and fauna, waters, rivers, and cities, as well as reflections on the designation of Germania in ancient geography. Regarding conceptual classifications, it is worth mentioning that books XI–XII are constructed as a catalogue by listing and briefly explaining

---

    time and in detail by Joachimsen 1968, pp. 155–95. A basic overview of this topic is provided by Ridé 1979, pp. 99–111; Müller 2001, pp. 441–83; Muhlack 2002; Hirschi 2005, pp. 302–10; and Robert 2008, pp. 393–95. For comprehension of this project, it is important to recognise that it was not "ein generationenübergreifendes kollektives Gelehrtenunternehmen, sondern 'nur' [...] ein System diskursiver Referenzen," Hirschi 2005, p. 459, n. 86; nor did it include a fixed method or certain text types (Muhlack 2002, and Hirschi 2005, p. 459).

20   For a more detailed description of the *Exegesis*, see Cordes 1966, pp. 5–6 and Müller/Worstbrock 2005, pp. 1251–53.

21   Irenicus himself points out this compositional division of his work in the preface to book VII. Irenicus, *Exegesis*, pp. CLXIII^r/E[i]^r–CLXIIIV/E[i]^v, here: CLXIII^r/E[i]^r). A brief glance through the work shows that the ethnological-historiographical section (book I–VI: pp. Ir/a[i]r–CLXII^v/Dvi^v) is much more extensive than the geographical one (book VII–X: pp. CLXII^v/Dvi^v–CXCVIII^v [*recto* erroneously paginated as CC]/L[i]^v).

22   For Celtis's idea of the expansion of *Germania*, see esp. Müller 2001, pp. 366–70 and Robert 2003, pp. 411–14.

23   For the ancient barbarian discourse and its transformation in Italian humanism, see Hirschi 2005, 181–87. For the strategies used by German humanists in order to override the verdict of barbarism, see ibid., 302–19.

24   Kaiser 2016, 167–79.

the most important regions, cities, and tribes of the Germans *iuxta literarum seriem*.[25]

In writing his *Exegesis*, Irenicus consulted over 300 sources, most of which were printed,[26] but without eliminating or reflecting on inconsistencies and contradictions found among them.[27] He was unable to review the immense spectrum of sources adequately, as his numerous repetitions, substantive mismatches, and many incorrect quotations clearly show.[28] A further consequence, resulting from how numerous these sources were, is the fact that the *Exegesis* is more of a compilation[29] than a continuous narrative depiction. Indeed, it is an associative collection of material organised thematically,[30] and can therefore be placed in the genre of 'Buntschriftstellerei' with a decidedly historiographical and geographical focus. Nevertheless, Irenicus seems to have been aware that his diffuse and mosaic-like portrayal would demand a great deal from the reader. He therefore points out in his *oratio protreptica*, mentioned above, that he did not choose the term 'Exegesis' for the title of his book haphazardly; he uses the term in the sense of 'Commentarii,' signifying a genre in which no rhetorical claims of either a linguistic-stylistic or an otherwise conceptual nature are made, thus setting it apart in this respect from *historia*.[31]

---

25 Irenicus, *Exegesis* I, p. CXCIX^r. Book XI: pp. CXCVIII^v [*recto* erroneously paginated as CC]/L[i]^v–CCXV^v/Nvi^v; book XII: pp. CCXVI^r/O[i]^r–CCXXX^v [*recto* erroneously paginated as CCXXI]/Qiii^v. Book XII ends with a letter written by Irenicus to Margrave Philip I of Baden and his chancellor, Hieronymus Vehus (1484–1544). Irenicus praises their education and political abilities (pp. CCXXIX^v/Qii^v–CCXXX^v [*recto* erroneously paginated as CCXXI]/Qiii^v). For Vehus's life, see Immenkötter 1982, pp. 11–67. For his activity as chancellor, see ibid., pp. 18–20.
26 Cordes 1966, p. 76.
27 Müller/Worstbrock 2005, p. 1253. A first attempt to identify the literary and non-literary sources used by Irenicus, and to provide a concise explanation of them was made by Cordes 1966, pp. 12–75. For the question of how Irenicus used the sources, see ibid., pp. 76–93.
28 Cordes 1966, p. 76 and Müller/Worstbrock 2005, p. 1253.
29 Müller 2001, p. 476.
30 Müller/Worstbrock 2005, pp. 1252–53.
31 Irenicus, *Exegesis*, p. Riiii^v: "Multi praeterea ad id, quod elaboravimus, scribendi genus se composuerunt arduam tamen, quod scio, partem ipse obivi, et quae ad profectum Germaniae conferre vidi, non sub nomine Germaniae, verum potius operi huic ut occasionis aut ansae praebendae titulum τῆς ἐξηγήσεως i.<e.> commentariorum desumpsi. Nemo autem ignorat non ad eloquentiae lasciviam seu ad capiendas aures commentaria tradi, dum plus haec ad enodandos authores tempora et facta scribantur ac ab historia eo discrepent, quia licentius a stilo alioqui ieiuna facultate condita secedant. Ita Didymus Graecus volumina τῆς ἐξηγήσεως εἰς Πίνδαρον i.<e.> commentariorum in Pindarum reliquit. Et ut totam rem dicam, ad nullas eloquentiae leges me alligare volui ad obtinenda ea, quae modo tradidimus. Nam si facundiam spectassem, fuisset in me pariendorum

In order to compensate for these deficits, he provides each book, except for books XI and XII, with a detailed chapter overview.

3 The Relationship of the *lingua Germanorum* to the Italian (and Greek) Language

Irenicus discusses the verdict of barbarism against the Germanic tribes and Germans—he does not distinguish between the two, but rather subsumes them under the term *Germani*—in 19 of the 57 chapters of the second book. He strives to refute the verdict on three levels: first and foremost on a sociolinguistic level, second by tracing the historical change of the concept of barbarism in order to relativise its validity,[32] and third by extensively showing the high educational level and cultural significance of the Germans in the past and present, a demonstration that is included in 12 chapters and is strikingly oriented to Trithemius's *Cathalogus Illustrium virorum Germaniam* [...] *exornantium* (1495).[33]

Though at times referred to only implicitly, the Italians serve for Irenicus as permanent points of reference in discussing the charge of barbarism. Indeed, they constitute Irenicus's main challenge. The question of the cultural-historical status of the German language is, in this context, the first and probably most fundamental aspect of his argument against the charge of barbarism, as Irenicus attacks the Italian humanists in the area of their own core competence: the Latin language. He asks about the relationship of the *lingua*

---

aliorum usus multo locupletior uberiorque in aliis (quam commentariorum) studiorum ac operum generibus, ubi res ipsa materiae ingenium iuvasset, ac eloquentiae facultates ultor admisisset. In praesenti vero negotio potius voluntatem animi ac materiae recessum quam ambiendo prodigiosam eloquentiam nomina interpretari volui, et ut verba materiae vinculis solutae, non materia verbis serviret." See also Cordes 1966, pp. 149–50.

32 Irenicus, *Exegesis*, p. IXL^v/g iii^v: chap. XXXIII: *An Germani sint Barbari et quis dicatur Barbarus*. For more details see Grünberger/Münkler 1998, pp. 222–25.

33 Irenicus, *Exegesis*, pp. IXL^v/g iii^v–XLIX^r/ i [i]^r. E.g. chap. XXXV: *De Germanis antiquis illustribus*; chap. XXXVI: *Epilogus lectori de Germanis nostrae tempestatis illustribus*; chapters 37–44 contain extensive praise of numerous German scholars such as Desiderius Erasmus, Johann Reuchlin, Willibald Pirckheimer, Beatus Rhenanus, Philip Melanchthon, Martin Luther, and many others; chap. XLVII: *De inventione artis impressoriae*; and finally the highlight chap. XLVIII: *De inventione philosophiae a Germanis et Scythis, qui Germani sunt*. Especially chapters 37–44 commemorate Trithemius's *Cathalogus Illustrium virorum Germaniam* [...] *exornantium* (1495). See also Grünberger/Münkler 1998, pp. 226–27. For Trithemius's *Cathalogus* see Helmrath 2017.

Germanorum not only to the Italian language, but also to Greek—and in doing so he also refers to their ancient standard languages:

> Verum ut nil impensatum externorum iniuriae relinquamus, videamus, quae maiora incrementa vel Italorum vel Germanorum lingua sumpserit. Vulgaris Italiae sermo, qui olim comicos hauserat, quantum Dacorum, Langobardorum, Gotthorum irruptionibus deficit, ut profecto Italos iam nomen arguat. Simile iudicium de Graeco vulgari sermone est. Quantum vero incrementi Germanicae linguae rigor assumpserit, in propatulo est: propria enim lingua ipsi Germani inter se in tantum intersunt, quantum et Latina ac vulgaris. Non enim extremae laudationis elementum est scire diserte Germanice loqui. Si eorum linguam Itali dicant a vero fonte Latino originem habuisse, et Germani eorum linguam cum a Graeco tum a Latino fonte multum habere gloriantur [...]. [34]

Not willing to leave the *iniuria externorum* unexamined, Irenicus asks for the *incrementum*, the development and progress of the Italian and German languages. He thereby concludes that the Italian *volgare*, which he even relates unflatteringly to the Latin comedic language, has been influenced and defiled by the invasions of the Dacians, Lombards, and Goths—in other words, by the Germanic tribes.[35] He also passes the same judgement on the Greek vernacular, which, however, still remains a marginal phenomenon in his discussion. Irenicus differentiates between the ancient standard languages and their contemporary vernacular forms which, according to him, show a linguistic and cultural decline. In contrast, the *lingua Germanorum* has made some linguistic progress and is characterised at the same time by its strength. It includes both a standard language and a vernacular. The German language does not compete with any (classical) standard language, as the Italian and Greek vernaculars

---

34 "But lest any unjustness on the part of foreigners remain unpunished, let us see which has had the more important development: the language of the Italians or the Germans; how much was the common ('*vulgaris*') language of Italy, which once had drawn the comic playwrights, degenerated by the invasions of the Dacians, Longobards, and Goths, so that the name actually exposes the Italians to ridicule. Similar is the judgement on the common Greek language. But it is quite clear which important development the unbending quality of the German language has taken: for in their own language, the Germans differ from each other as much as the Latin language and the (Italian) *volgare* do. Being able to speak eloquently in German deserves great praise. If the Italians may say that their language originated from the true Latin source, the Germans too boast that their language possesses much from both the Greek and the Latin sources [...]." Irenicus, *Exegesis*, p. XXXVIII^r/g ii^r.

35 Grünberger/Münkler 1998, p. 222.

do with Latin and ancient Greek, respectively. It is able to do what both Latin and its contemporary *volgare* can only manage to do together. Therefore, the dichotomy of (ancient) standard and vernacular language is explicitly not applied to the German language by Irenicus.[36]

However, the differentiation from the Greek vernacular does not play any great role in his argumentation. Rather, Irenicus focuses mainly on the Italians and their *volgare*, as well as on the cultural-historical profiling of the German language. Specifically, he points out that Italian has its roots in Latin, and is therefore characterised by linguistic and cultural decline, while German itself has taken much from both Latin and ancient Greek and has not suffered any linguistic decline. Irenicus is therefore less interested in demonstrating the purity of the German language than its proximity to the two classical languages, Latin and ancient Greek, which explains why he points to its linguistic and cultural wealth, especially in contrast to the Italian language. The cultural-historical contrast between German and Italian could hardly be greater.

In his further discussion, Irenicus strives in particular to prove the *necessitas* and *vicinitas* of German and ancient Greek by citing select examples which all proceed with the same scheme: Greek word, German loanword.[37] Within these examples, phonetic proximity especially demonstrates the linguistic link between both languages. Irenicus also provides other linguistic proofs by referring to certain characteristics of both languages, such as the use of articles which Latin lacks. The overall aim of the examples cited is to show that the *lingua Germanorum* is closer to ancient Greek than Latin.[38]

In contrast, Irenicus hardly considers the influence of Latin on German worth mentioning, since it belongs, according to his argument, to the basic stock of almost every language.[39] In this way, he ostentatiously deprives the

---

36 Grünberger/Münkler 1998, p. 221.
37 Irenicus, *Exegesis*, pp. xxxviii^(r-v)/g ii^(r-v): "Quod Graeci θύρα dicunt, nos *thyr*, quod Graeci ἴκτις, nos *yltis* animal, quod illi φλεβότονον, nos *flieten*, ferrum, quo vena secatur, quod Graeci λαλεῖν, nos *lallen* dicimus et multa alia. Propria quoque nomina [...] easdem compositiones (ut et Graeci) habent, in quo nostra lingua proximior Graeco idiomati accedit quam Latina. Item terrarum nomina [...]."
38 Ibid., p. xxxviii^v/g ii^v: "Illud demum maxime est, in quo plus commercii lingua nostra cum Graeca habet quam vera et syncera Latinorum lingua. Germani enim articulis utuntur perinde ac Graeci. Hi enim τῆς μούσης, nos *diese* dicimus, quibus Latini supersederunt."
39 Ibid., p. xxxviii^v/g ii^v: "Quid vero a Latino habeat nostra lingua, vanum videtur dicere. Cuilibet enim linguae huiusmodi elementario id constat. Est ergo lingua illa nostra plurimum vel a Graeco vel Latino fontibus, aut a sono (sicut et ipse cum Graecus tum Latinus sermo) aut alia necessitate composita, quod Bebelius probat in eo, cum Gallicus sermo multum Graeci habuerit autore Caesare."

Italians' ancient standard language—even the language of those who judge German to be barbaric—of its cultural-historical significance. Irenicus thus ennobles the *lingua Germanorum*—especially in contrast to the Italian *volgare*—by a complex strategy in which he argues for the absent dichotomy of standard and vernacular forms of the German language, the meticulously elaborated *necessitas* and *vicinitas* of German and Greek,[40] the proximity of German and Latin, which is, at best, implied, and the implicit distance of the Italian and Latin languages to ancient Greek.

4 The Influence of the *lingua Germanorum* on Latin and Its Use in Antiquity

Irenicus's upgrading of the cultural-historical status of the German language is significantly shaped by his deflation of the status of Italian. He achieves this by referring to the influence of the German language on two famous authors of classical Latin literature:

> Si vero Itali dicant aptiorem linguam eorum carminibus, sicuti Guarinus Veronensis, Franciscus Petrarcha et alii, qui privatis Italorum linguis carmina struxerunt, sciant id et ante M annos in nostro sermone actum. Ovidius enim Getico idiomate librum Augusti laudis capacem scripsit, ut libro IV de Ponto: Et scripsi Getico sermone libellum structaque sunt nostris barbara verba modis. [...] Scriptores nomina etiam nostra ad Latinum saepissime verterunt, ut in Plinio libro decimo Ganzas latine, nominamus nos Gantz. Qui plura de iis legere cupit, Paulum Diaconum legat, qui pene omnibus Germanorum nominibus Latinum dat sonum.[41]

---

40 See also ibid., p. xxxviiiᵛ/g iiᵛ: chap. xxxi: "De perfectione linguae Germanicae, et quomodo Graece nomina eorum dicantur: Ex praemisso capite constat Germanicam linguam proximam Graecorum idiomati accedere ob articulorum communionem: alia quoque vicinitas est, quemadmodum Graecae linguae peculiare est, honesta compositione plures dictiones coaptare, ita et Germanico idiomati idem familiare est: in eo tamen longe Graecam quam Latinam linguam Germanicus tenor excedit. Nam omnis imperativus ac omnia pene Germanica vocabula monosyllaba sunt, ut *brot, fuzs, disch, der, dem, lisz, morn* etc. Et pene quicquid monosyllabam excedit, peregrinum ac non Germanicum est, sicuti *deller*, externorum est, qui *delir* dicunt, ita *wasser*, a peregrina lingua traductum, qua *wammesei* dicitur."
41 "But if the Italians were to say that their language is more appropriate for poems, such as Guarino da Verona, Francesco Petrarca, and others who have written poems in the ordinary Italian language, they should know that this was done even 1,000 years ago in our language. Ovid actually wrote a little book focusing on the praise of Augustus, in the Getic

Irenicus illustrates the influence of the German language on Latin by means of two well-known authors of classical Latin literature, Ovid and Pliny the Elder, thus stylising German as its own ancient language, on par with Latin. Its influence is expressed in certain Latinised loanwords as his reference to Pliny the Elder (Nat. Hist. 10.52) shows. But this is not limited only to classical antiquity: in the following centuries German also had an important influence on Latin, as Irenicus's reference to Paul the Deacon, who Latinised numerous German names, demonstrates.

Another argument, emphasising the influence of German on Latin, is especially evidenced by the Ovid example given above: by quoting from Ovid, *Epistulae ex Ponto* 4.13.19–20, Irenicus emphasises that even the ancient poet himself used the *sermo Geticus*[42] which Irenicus elsewhere in his *Exegesis* explicitly equates with the German language.[43] He thus believes that the classical Latin author Ovid wrote and versified in German. The fact that he did so in praise of Augustus ennobles the German language once again and confirms the high cultural-historical status it has enjoyed since Roman antiquity. However, Irenicus not only illustrates the influence of the German language on Latin and thus valorises its significance in this way; he also disproves the claim raised by famous Italian humanists such as Guarino da Verona and Petrarch, who themselves wrote poems in Italian, that the Italian language is, above all, suitable for poetry. Against this background, the Ovid reference seems to support the idea that the Germans are not only comparable to the Italian poets in linguistic and poetical terms, but also are actually superior to them in temporal terms.[44] That even one of the greatest poets of Roman antiquity, Ovid, had written in German is probably the strongest argument Irenicus could use to elevate the cultural-historical status of the German language. In this way he not only demonstrates the inconsistency of the Italian humanist position, but also reverses the alleged cultural prestige of the Italian language

---

phrases, as he wrote in the fourth book of his letters from the Black Sea: I have even written a poem in Getic tongue setting barbarian words to our measures [...]. Authors have very often translated our names into Latin, as we can see in Plinius, book 10 the 'Ganzas', which is Latin and what we call geese. Those who wish to learn more about it may read Paulus Diaconus, who gives almost all the names of the Germans a Latin sound." Ibid., p. xxxviii^v/g ii^v.

42   Ov. Epist. 4.13.19–23: "A! pudet et Getico scripsi sermone libellum / structaque sunt nostris barbara verba modis: / et placui—gratare mihi!—coepique poetae / inter inhumanos nomen habere Getas. / Materiam quaeris? Laudes: de Caesare dixi!"

43   Irenicus, *Exegesis*, p. xxxviii^v/g ii^v: "Ovidius nonnihil linguam Geticam, id est, vere Germanam cum Graecis habere asserit in Tristibus."

44   The idea 'the older the better' pervades Irenicus's *Exegesis* as his comments on the *origo gentis* of the Germans show, which he connects to Noah. Kaiser 2016, pp. 167–79.

over German. Furthermore, the influence of German on Latin makes the cross-fertilisation of the two languages clear and discredits the idea that the latter served above all as a model for the former.

Thus, perhaps the most important argument within the refutation of the verdict of barbarism is the discussion about the cultural-historical status of the German language and its influence on Latin as well as its general influence in Europe. Irenicus continues working on the theme of the German influence on the European cultural area, for example, by pointing out that Charlemagne gave the months and winds German names, and that he and his successors of course spoke German. In any case, there is no region in Europe, and especially not in Italy, where one does not hear German.[45] The influence of the German language on Latin, as well as its large-scale dissemination throughout the empire, as explained by Irenicus, also correlates with the more or less absent evaluation of the influence of the Latin language on German and emphatically underlines the immense cultural-historical significance of German. At the same time, Irenicus's explanations implicitly claim that German, with its influence on Latin, also had an indirect influence on the Italian language. This, in turn, correlates with his initial remarks about the development of the Italian vernacular corrupted by the Germanic invasions.

Moreover, the general cultural-historical influences of the German language repeatedly exposed by Irenicus, and the proof that German was even used in ancient literature, seem to react to a very definite aspect of the verdict of barbarism directed against the Germans as a result of the *Germania* reception that had recently begun: namely, the inability of Germanic men and women, mentioned by Tacitus, to avail themselves of the *litterarum secreta* (Tacitus, *Germania* 19.2). However, while Tacitus probably meant to apostrophise the Germanic *pudicitia* as a reflex against the Romans in order to implicitly hold up a mirror to Roman debaucheries and to explain the virtuous conduct of the Germanic tribes in part by citing their ignorance of both secret love letters

---

45 Irenicus, *Exegesis*, p. xxxviii^v/g ii^v: "Carolus Magnus, ut Wimphelingus scribit, Sigibertus Geblacensis Urspergenis et alii volunt mensibus inde et ventis nomina dedit. Lingua nostra tantum ita se extendit, ut nulla sit regio, ubi non Germanos audias. Zacharias Lilius in Geographia sua in pluribus Italiae civitatibus maiori imperio Germanorum quam Italorum linguam increbescere scribit. Id quoque Carolum maxime Germanum esse ac eius prosapiam argumentum est, quod hi plurimum in Germania habitantes Germanice locuti sunt, ut Einhardus Ludovici regis ac Caroli filii enarrator ostendit, dum scribit Ludovicum fata iam solventem dixisse Germanice uff uff, quod apud Latinos foras significat."

and literature,[46] the early modern reader apparently understood this passage as an indication of general illiteracy, as an indictment of the *inscientia* and uncultivated habits of the Germanic peoples. In humanist discourse, the lack of an ancient written tradition among the Germans is frequently explained with special reference to this Tacitean passage. Irenicus, by contrast, seems to reject this reading of the uncultivated German past. Instead, he claims German certainly was a cultured and coveted language in antiquity and that it never suffered any corruption, as did Latin and ancient Greek, in their vernaculars.[47] By making the influence of the German language in Latin literature recognisable, he provides evidence of the existence and the high cultural significance that German already had in Greek and Roman antiquity. In this way, he at least subverts the idea of Germanic illiteracy and instead attributes a long cultural continuity to the German language.

5 German as an Indigenous Language with Long Continuity

Despite emphasising the closeness of German to ancient Greek (and, although to a much lesser degree, to Latin), Irenicus does not go as far as to claim that German is descended from Greek or another language. Rather, he claims, as shown above, only that the German language possesses *cum a Graeco tum a Latino fonte multum*, but he does not refer to the question of its *origo*. Instead, he subsequently points out that the *lingua Germanorum* had its roots in no other language, but was established by Trebeta, the son of the Noahide Ninus and Semiramis, and the founder of Trier.[48] His recourse to Trebeta as the inventor of German—which raises the question in which language Irenicus imagines the Germanic-German ancestors to have conversed before this invention (but this aspect is not treated further by him)—ensures the very old age of the language with its roots deep in German history. In this way, Irenicus presents German as an indigenous language, as a genuine invention of the Germans themselves, which is, with respect to its origin, culturally and historically independent. Therefore, both the language's great age and its original autonomy

---

46 Lund 1988, p. 164 and Urban 1989, p. 89.
47 Irenicus, *Exegesis*, p. XL/g iiii[r]: "Itali ad hunc usque diem in nullo praeterquam inscientiae Germanos arguunt, quia Germani μήτε νεῖν μήτε γράμματα calleant. Ducuntur forsitan Cornelii Taciti dicto secreta literarum viros pariter et feminas Germaniae ignorare scribentis leberideque incultiores nos esse clamantis."
48 Ibid., p. XXXVIII[v]/g ii[v]: "Primus autem Germanicam linguam Trebeta composuit, filius Semiramis, ut Annales Novietensium dicunt."

are the two cornerstones of his argument on the cultural-historical status of German. This is precisely why it is not problematic for Irenicus to acknowledge the linguistic proximity of German to ancient Greek in particular and also—even if he hardly comments on this point—to Latin. Rather, this proximity and the mutual influences discussed above give the German language prestige and place it within the canon of the classical languages of antiquity.

Moreover, Irenicus's reflections on the age of German and its indigenous origins correspond well with his remarks on the *origo gentis* of the Germans that he makes in the third book of his *Exegesis*. Here, Irenicus outlines the Noachian origin of the Germans in order to present them with as ancient a history as possible. This history proves to be indigenous and thus competitive with other contemporary constructions of antiquity.[49] In this context, the most important person he portrays is Tuisco, father of the Germans and son of Noah. In the genealogical tree of the Germans designed by Irenicus in his third book, Trebeta himself appears a few generations after his German ancestor Tuisco, and thus in a direct Noachian tradition.[50] Against this background, Irenicus's comments on the cultural-historical status of the German language have to be understood as part of his concept of German history, which is also distinguished by the claim to an indigenous origin, its great age, and a tradition of national continuity leading to the present day. But his remarks on the German language are not seamlessly integrated into his concept of German history; if Tuisco is the father of the Germans and the German language has only been established by Trebeta, the question inevitably arises as to what language the Germans spoke in the period between Tuscio and Trebeta. This problem seems not to be considered by Irenicus—and is symptomatic of his entire work which shows numerous inconsistencies and contradictions.

Furthermore, Irenicus's detailed reflections in chapter 32 ('About German names and where they come from') also form an important part of his aim to demonstrate that German is not the descendent of another language but rather is indigenous.[51] In this chapter, he mentions a further characteristic of the German language, namely that almost all older German proper names, such as Dagobert, Lambert, Friedrich, Ulrich, or even Konrad, have an *origo Germanica* which, however, *ob linguae illius ignorantiam*, were appropriated by the Italians and presented as their own names.[52] Irenicus also complains

---

49 Kaiser 2016, 167–79.
50 See the illustration of the ancient German kings in Irenicus, *Exegesis*, p. LXII^r/k iii^r.
51 Irenicus, *Exegesis*, pp. lXL^{r-v}/g iii^{r-v}: "De nominibus Germanicis et unde emerserint, chap. XXXII."
52 Ibid., p. lXL^r/g iii^r: "Maxima necessitas, quam cum Graeco idiomate nostra lingua gerit, illa est, quod pene omnia antiquorum nomina Germanica Germanicam sapiunt originem

that the Germans themselves no longer know the etymological origins of the German tribes' ethnonyms and consider them Greek, because the Greeks and Romans have adopted and declined them.[53]

6   Conclusion: *Diserte Germanice loqui*?

The complex and interlinked strategies characterising Irenicus's discussion of the cultural-historical status of the *lingua Germanorum* have to be considered first and foremost in the context of his refutation of the verdict of barbarism imposed on the Germanic peoples and the Germans. Forming part of the elaborate historisation of the concept of barbarism, which includes relativising its validity, and of the high praise for the scholarship and cultural significance of German scholars (comprising 12 chapters), his discussion on the cultural-historical status of the German language lays the basis for his whole argument. Irenicus illustrates in great detail the persistence and continuity of German, beginning with its deepest past, showing in this way that a differentiation between a classical standard language and a separate *volgare*, as he argues happened for Italian and Greek, does not work for German. By elaborating upon the linguistic proximity of German to ancient Greek, the influences German and Latin exerted on each, as well as the German poetic potential already recognised in antiquity, he ennobles the German language and adds it to the canon of classical languages. This is an effective strategy since in humanist discourse the cultural-historical status of any group and its properties depends on how firmly it is anchored in antiquity. Thus, it is only logical that he evidences the Germans' own past, independent of Greco-Roman antiquity and endowed with an indigenous language, which underlines the cultural-historical independence of the Germans.

But Irenicus's complex strategies for re-evaluating the *lingua Germanorum* go far beyond the mere refutation of the verdict of barbarism levelled against the Germans. Rather, he also pursues an attack on the Italians themselves as advocates of this verdict and aims to curtail their own cultural-historical status. In fact, his remarks make clear that it is the Italians and their verdict of barbarism against both the Germanic peoples and the Germans that

ac significativa sunt, quemadmodum apud Graecos. [...] Haec omnia ideo adduximus, ut aequus lector agnoscat gentes illas vere Germanicas extitisse et nomina illa verissima Germanorum et ob linguae illius ignorantiam saepe ab Italis corrupta fuisse prolata."

53   Ibid., p. IXL^v/g iii^v: "Haec nomina Graeci perinde ut Latini ad declinationes traxerunt, unde et paululum variata sunt. Hinc est, ut multarum regionum civitatumque origines ignoramus et Graeca putamus, quae tamen Germanis debentur."

primarily provokes his reaction. He is, therefore, not content with appreciating the cultural-historical significance of the *lingua Germanorum*: he also endeavours to degrade the cultural-historical significance of the Italian *volgare* by diagnosing its linguistic decay and its derivation from other languages. His claim for the indigenous status, great age, and continuity of German corresponds well to his cultural-historical reduction of the Italian language. In the framework of this argumentation, it is, and has always been, an honour to use German—in contrast to the Italian *volgare*.

But *diserte Germanice loqui*? It may seem paradoxical that Irenicus, in discussing the cultural-historical significance of German, still uses the Latin language, i.e., the language to which his Italian opponents themselves refer. Irenicus does not draw any conclusions from his revaluation of German concerning the choice of language in terms of future textual production in Germany. As Latin is also the humanist *lingua franca*, his choice of language is first and foremost dependent on the discourse in which Irenicus's *Exegesis* participates. In order to bring his work to light successfully in the humanist discourse, he is dependent on readers understanding and receiving his work despite their vernacular language. Writing in German would surely be more consistent, but it would exclude from his potential circle of readers precisely the foreign-language humanists, such as the Italians, against whose verdict of barbarism he argues. An additional factor seems to be decisive for his choice of language: in the wake of the verdict of barbarism, German humanists seem to feel inferior to Italian humanists concerning their Latin language skills.[54] It is against this background that not only Irenicus's *Exegesis* but also the many other Latin writings by German humanists have to be understood. They all, despite their permanent rhetoric of modesty, claim to demonstrate that the Germans are also able to use Latin with great virtuosity and are therefore at the same level of Latin proficiency as the Italians. Irenicus's choice of language and his *Exegesis* serve thereby as a performative proof of his high humanist education. As a result, the cultural trauma of the verdict of barbarism, reflected in the sometimes more, sometimes less, subcutaneous feeling of cultural inferiority, as well as the rules of humanist discourse made it almost necessary for German humanists like Franciscus Irenicus to write their works not in the vernacular, but in Latin.

---

54 Müller 2001, pp. 213–16.

Bibliography

Primary Sources

Celtis, Conrad. *Conrad Celtis und sein Buch über Nürnberg*, edited by Albert Werminghoff. Freiburg: Julius Boltze, 1921.

Irenicus, Franciscus. *Germaniae Exegeseos volumina duodecim a Francisco Irenico Ettelingiacensi exarata. Eiusdem oratio protreptica in amorem Germaniae cum praesentis operis excusatione ad illustriss. Prinicipis Palatini Electoris Cancellarium Florentium de Pheningen, utriusque censurae Doctorem. Urbis Norinbergae descriptio, Conrado Celte enarratore*. Haguenau: Thomas Anshelm, 1518 [VD16 F 2815].

Secondary Sources

Arnold, Klaus. "Die 'Norinberga' des Konrad Celtis—ihre Entstehung und Aufnahme in Nürnberg." In *Konrad Celtis und Nürnberg. Akten des interdisziplinären Symposions vom 8. und 9. November 2002 im Caritas-Pirckheimer-Haus in Nürnberg*, edited by Franz Fuchs. Wiesbaden: Harrassowitz, 2004, pp. 100–16.

Cordes, Günter. *Die Quellen der Exegesis Germaniae des Franciscus Irenicus und sein Germanenbegriff*. Tübingen 1966.

Cordes, Günter. "Franciscus Irenicus von Ettlingen—Aus dem Leben eines Humanisten und Reformators." In *Festschrift für Günther Haselier aus Anlaß seines 60. Geburtstages am 19. April 1974*, edited by Alfons Schäfer. Karlsruhe: Braun, 1975, pp. 353–71.

Grünberger, Hans and Herfried Münkler. "Enea Silvio Piccolominis Anstösse zur Entdeckung der nationalen Identität der 'Deutschen'." In *Nationenbildung. Die Nationalisierung Europas im Diskurs humanistischer Intellektueller. Italien und Deutschland*, edited by Herfried Münkler, Hans Grünberger and Kathrin Mayer. Berlin: Akademie Verlag, 1998, pp. 163–233.

Helmchen, Annette. *Die Entstehung der Nationen im Europa der Frühen Neuzeit. Ein integraler Ansatz aus humanistischer Sicht*. Bern: Peter Lang, 2004.

Helmrath, Johannes. "Perception of the Middle Ages and Self-Perception in German Humanism: Johannes Trithemius and the *Cathalogus illustrium virorum Germaniam ... exornantium*." In *Biography, Historiography, and Modes of Philosophizing. The Tradition of Collective Biography in Early Modern Europe*, edited by Patrik Baker. Leiden: Brill, 2017, pp. 177–247.

Hermelink, Heinrich, ed. *Die Matrikeln der Universität Tübingen. Die Matrikeln von 1477–1600*, vol. 1. Stuttgart: Kohlhammer, 1906.

Hirschi, Caspar. *Wettkampf der Nationen. Konstruktionen einer deutschen Ehrgemeinschaft an der Wende vom Mittelalter zur Neuzeit*. Göttingen: Wallstein, 2005.

Immenkötter, Herbert. *Hieronymus Vehus. Jurist und Humanist der Reformationszeit.* Münster: Aschendorff, 1982.

Joachimsen, Paul. *Geschichtsauffassung und Geschichtsschreibung in Deutschland unter dem Einfluss des Humanismus.* Aalen: Scientia-Verlag, 1968 [reprint of Leipzig 1910].

Kaiser, Ronny. "Personelle Serialität und nationale Geschichte. Überlegungen zu den Herrschergestalten in Franciscus Irenicus' *Germaniae Exegesis* (1518)." In *Portraying the Prince in the Renaissance. The Humanist Depiction of Rulers in Historiographical and Biographical Texts*, edited by Patrik Baker, Ronny Kaiser, Maike Priesterjahn, and Johannes Helmrath. Berlin: de Gruyter, 2016, pp. 157–91.

Krebs, Christopher B. *Negotiatio Germaniae. Tacitus' Germania und Enea Silvio Piccolomini, Giannantonio Campano, Conrad Celtis und Heinrich Bebel.* Göttingen: Vandenhoeck & Ruprecht, 2005.

Lund, Allan A. *P. Cornelius Tacitus. Germania. Interpretiert, herausgegeben, übertragen, kommentiert und mit einer Bibliographie versehen von Allan A. Lund.* Heidelberg: Carl Winter Universitätsverlag 1988.

Muhlack, Ulrich. "Das Projekt der *Germania illustrata*. Ein Paradigma der Diffusion des Humanismus?" In *Diffusion des Humanismus. Studien zur nationalen Geschichtsschreibung europäischer Humanisten*, edited by Johannes Helmrath, Ulrich Muhlack, and Gerrit Walther. Göttingen: Wallstein, 2002, pp. 142–58.

Müller, Gernot Michael. *Die 'Germania Generalis' des Conrad Celtis. Studien mit Edition, Übersetzung und Kommentar.* Tübingen: Max Niemeyer Verlag, 2001.

Müller, Gernot Michael and Franz Josef Worstbrock. "Irenicus, Franciscus." In *Deutscher Humanismus 1480–1520. Verfasserlexikon*, edited by Franz Josef Worstbrock, vol. 1.1, Berlin: de Gruyter, 2005, pp. 1248–57.

Orth, Peter. "Rom an der Regnitz, Babylon an der Pegnitz. Beobachtungen zur ›Norimberga‹ des Konrad Celtis." In *Nova de veteribus. Mittel- und neulateinische Studien für Paul Gerhard Schmidt*, edited by Anreas Bihrer and Elisabeth Stein. Munich: K. G. Saur, 2004, pp. 809–22.

Ridé, Jacques. "Un grand projet patriotique Germania illustrate." In *XVIIIe colloque international de Tours. L'humanisme allemand (1480–1540)*, edited by Ernesto Grassi. Munich: Fink, 1979, pp. 99–111.

Robert, Jörg. *Konrad Celtis und das Projekt der deutschen Dichtung. Studien zur humanistischen Konstitution von Poetik, Philosophie, Nation und Ich*, Tübingen: Max Niemeyer Verlag, 2003.

Robert, Jörg. "Celtis (Bickel, Pickel), Konrad (Conradus Celtis Protucius)." In *Deutscher Humanismus 1480–1520. Verfasserlexikon*, edited by Franz Josef Worstbrock, vol. 1.1. Berlin: de Gruyter, 2008, pp. 375–427.

Tiedemann, Hans. *Tacitus und das Nationalbewußtsein der deutschen Humanisten Ende des 15. und Anfang des 16. Jahrhunderts.* Berlin: Ebering, 1913.

Toepke, Gustav. *Die Matrikel der Universität Heidelberg von 1386–1662*, 2 vols. Heidelberg 1884.

Urban, Ralf. "Aufbau und Gedankengang der *Germania*." In *Beiträge zum Verständnis der Germania des Tacitus. Teil 1: Bericht über die Kolloquien der Kommission für die Altertumskunde Nord- und Mitteleuropas im Jahr 1986*, edited by Herbert Jankuhn and Dieter Timpe. Göttingen: Vandenhoeck & Ruprecht, 1989, pp. 80–105.

CHAPTER 5

Ludvig Holberg's *Niels Klim* (1741) and the Irony of Reading and Writing in Latin

Thomas Velle

1   Introduction[1]

In scholarship, there are some persistent truisms circling around Ludvig Holberg's Latin novel, *Nicolai Klimii iter subterraneum* (henceforth referred to as *Niels Klim*), that have been stated at some point in the (sometimes distant) past and repeated ever since in prefaces, introductions, or footnotes. One of those commonplaces concerns the language in which *Niels Klim* is written. Not incorrectly but simplistically, scholars have always ascribed to Holberg the desire to write a work that had more international appeal than his Danish comedies. For example, Sven Hakon Rossel mentions that *Niels Klim* was "directed not merely toward a Danish public but toward the international, sophisticated reading public, for it was written in Latin," and Frederik J. Billeskov Jansen states that "[Holberg] chose to write in Latin, [...] not in order to conceal bold opinions behind a learned language, but to secure his book a wide dissemination."[2] Citing this attempt to gain an international audience often goes hand in hand with the observation that, despite the Latin original, *Niels Klim* has mainly reached the European public through translations.[3] As Karen Skovgaard-Petersen rightfully argues, Latin facilitated the translation process considerably: it "paved the way to a European vernacular readership."[4] The dissemination Billeskov Jansen speaks of was thus indirect.

Two formal elements of *Niels Klim* further complicate our understanding of Holberg's language choice. On the one hand, Holberg's book was published at least partly abroad, in Leipzig. This has been viewed as a strategic choice, not only in order to reach the international market but also to avoid rigid

---

1   The following study was made possible by the Research Foundation–Flanders (FWO). Additionally, I want to express my gratitude to Wim Verbaal for the support while preparing this text.
2   Rossel 1992, pp. 134–35; Billeskov Jansen 1974, p. 99.
3   Quantitative research on the diffusion and circulation of the editions of *Niels Klim*, however, is lacking and would shine new light on the language question.
4   Skovgaard-Petersen 2013, p. 186.

censorship in Holberg's home country.[5] According to Billeskov Jansen, *Niels Klim* "caused trouble" in Copenhagen immediately after publication, "and it was a borderline matter whether it should be confiscated or not."[6] On the other hand, the extensive use of prose and verse quotations of classical texts have led some to believe Holberg wanted to write a Menippean satire, a tradition that had past its highpoint over a century earlier. The strongest advocate of this theory, Sigrid Peters, argues that Holberg chose Latin because he wanted to be sure his readers would recognise quotations from a canonical literature and thus not pass over additional intertextual meanings.[7]

Although the publication strategies for *Niels Klim* that are repeatedly discussed seem strikingly self-evident, such factors as the desire for an international audience, the need to elude censorship, and the attempt to revive Menippean satire are not as unproblematic as scholarship hints at, especially when one tries to combine them. If Holberg mainly reached translators, was he aware that his book, published in 1741, would not primarily be read in the original version, but in the English, Dutch, French, and German translations that all followed within the same year? In other words, did he realise that his Menippean satire, in practice, would not be classified as such and thus entirely overshoot the mark that Peters has attributed to *Niels Klim*? Why would Holberg write a text that only works in Latin, for a public he reaches through translation? If Holberg wanted to connect with a traditionally Latin genre by writing in Latin, how should we explain the repeatedly stated influence of works that fall within the vernacular genre of imaginary voyages, the most prominent example of which is Jonathan Swift's *Gulliver's Travels*? As a Menippean satire, *Niels Klim* would seem to have been published long after the genre flourished, yet, as an imaginary voyage it would also be an anomaly, having been the only such work written in Latin out of more than two hundred published between 1700 and 1800.[8] Whereas the role of classical quotations has been the focus of many studies, the influence of *Gulliver's Travels* remains perhaps the most understudied commonplace in *Niels Klim* scholarship.[9] Symptomatic of this

---

5 As Cecilie Flugt argues, the reasons for publishing *Niels Klim* outside Denmark are not mutually exclusive. Flugt 2015, p. 144.
6 Billeskov Jansen 1974, p. 101.
7 Peters 1987, pp. 57–59.
8 The most extensive listing for this genre is still to found in Grove 1941.
9 I will briefly but concisely touch upon the problematic relation between *Niels Klim* and *Gulliver's Travels* later in this essay. For further reading on the relation between these two novels, see Sejersted 2005 and Skovgaard-Petersen/Zeeberg 2014, and the fourth chapter of Julius Paludan's work, which was the first and last monograph dealing with the influence of imaginary travel literature on *Niels Klim*. Paludan 1878, pp. 119–64.

entire language question of *Niels Klim*, as I will henceforth refer to the issue at the centre of this study, is Sven Hakon Rossel's description of *Niels Klim* as "quite simply a Danish *Gulliver's Travels*."[10] This not only reduces Holberg to one of Swift's many imitators, but also totally disregards the fact that *Niels Klim* was written in Latin, and not in Danish.

In short, Holberg-scholarship is in need of a renewed view on this issue, a view that de-familiarises what we have taken for granted in the countless introductions and references to *Niels Klim*. We need to consider these questions as stated above because they are crucial to gaining a better understanding of what puzzles scholars the most to this day, namely how to situate Holberg's novel within contemporary literary European literature (e.g., as a Latin or even Danish Gulliveriad, or as a novelistic Menippean satire) and how best to characterize Holberg himself (e.g., as an opportunistic modern writer or a skillful classicist).

In this essay, I will specifically consider a recent theory by Rebecca Walkowitz as a way to refresh our view of an old debate. In *Born Translated*, Walkowitz presents a view on literature that does not consider publication, dissemination, or translation and reprinting as part of the context but as an important part of the text itself.[11] As she is particularly concerned with contemporary novels, the speed by which texts are disseminated and translated in this digital age leads her to the assumption that some literature is "born-translated," originally existing as a group of texts, in several languages, and on several places. Many parts of her argument allow us to view *Niels Klim* in a new light.[12] Scholars today often readily speak of *Niels Klim* without specifying what referring to this text implies. Some, for example, refer to the first edition of 1741 while others to that of 1745, which includes only a few, though crucial additions. In other instances, scholars quote a Danish translation, not infrequently the one by the Danish poet Jens Baggesen (1789), or use anonymous translations in other languages, as *Niels Klim* is by no means only studied by Latinists. Without acknowledging it, many scholars already speak of *Niels Klim* as if naming that text were to refer

---

10   Rossel 1992, p. 134.
11   Walkowitz 2015. An older and more concise version of her theory was published in 2009. There she uses the term 'comparison literature' instead of 'born-translated literature.' Walkowitz 2009.
12   Walkowitz does not consider her theory to be applicable to periods earlier than the 20th century, arguing that a quick circulation of a book within Europe is not enough; it has to have global dissemination. Walkowitz 2015, p. 6. In the present essay, I consider this argument of Walkowitz as a matter of scale. In the 18th century, books indeed could not be published in, for example, Japan within a couple of years, but the aesthetics, dynamics, and strategies Walkowitz ascribes to born-translated literature were already seen within Europe.

to a group of editions and translations. Moreover, by repeatedly stating that *Niels Klim* mainly owes its European success to the almost immediate translations, scholars have already made way for the experiment of considering *Niels Klim* as a born-translated piece of literature.

Because of the prominent function of translation, both inside and outside the text, Walkowitz comes to the following definition of what "born-translated" means:

> In born-translated novels, translation functions as a thematic, structural, conceptual, and sometimes even typographical device. These works are *written for translation*, in the hope of being translated, but they are also often *written as translations*, pretending to take place in a language other than the one in which they have, in fact, been composed. Sometimes they present themselves as fake or fictional editions: subsequent versions (in English) of an original text (in some other language), which doesn't really exist. They are also frequently *written from translation*. Pointing backward as well as forward, they present translation as a spur to literary innovation, including their own.[13]

Walkowitz's theory interestingly sees the desire to reach a large audience as something that is not only part of an economic strategy, but also an aspect of literary innovation. Hereby, it can bridge the two extreme images of Holberg, namely, on the one hand, that of an opportunistic modern writer who seeks a wider audience, and, on the other hand, that of the skillful classicist. The extremely intellectual and seemingly classicist elements in *Niels Klim*, such as the quotations from classical authors, are a way to make the reader aware of the literary situation in contemporary Europe, a context in which the prestige of Latin, increasingly challenged by the rise of vernacular literature and translation, had, for many, become part of the experience of reading Latin literature.

One could argue that Walkowitz's theory has two sides: a text-internal part that focuses on fictional, narratological, and structural elements in the text that thematise translation, and a text-external part that treats the publication context and immediate translation history of the work.[14] Born-translated literature is unique in the fact that there is a dialogue between these two elements: on the one hand, the thematisation of language within the story becomes

---

13   Walkowitz 2015, p. 4.
14   The terms 'text-internal' and 'text-external' are my own. They enable me to concisely introduce and structure important elements of Walkowitz's multifaceted and often digressive theory.

externalised, a process through which the text is presented in a paratext as a translation or as an occasion for the reader to reflect upon language politics outside the text; on the other hand the external publication history becomes internalised as Walkowitz considers the immediate translations and following editions as a constructive part of the text itself. The present study will follow this structure and demonstrate that Holberg's text, like one of Walkowitz's born-translated texts, already prefigures or incorporates translation on many levels and reflects upon the contemporary, European context of publication, translation, and readership. The choice for Latin thus becomes a particularly ironical one: *Niels Klim* makes the reader aware of a world outside Latin literature while (s)he is reading a seemingly classicist piece. With this approach, this essay aims to do justice to the dynamics between vernacular literatures and Latin in Holberg's novel.

2 *Niels Klim* in Translation. Crossing National Boundaries

In the first part of this essay, I will consider the external part of Walkowitz's theory, i.e., the publication and translation history of *Niels Klim*. According to Walkowitz, modern-day born-translated novels are mainly written in English: "Anglophone novels are more likely than novels in other languages to appear in translation: more works are translated out of English than out of any other language."[15] The position of English in the present globalised market, makes one think of two languages in the 18th century, Latin and French. Latin was still the most dominant transnational or cosmopolitan language in Europe in the first half of the 18th century.[16] For over a century, however, Latin had been losing its position as the language of literature and moved to (or better: stayed strong in) the field of science. Partly due to considerations and reflections that were central to the Quarrel of Ancients and Moderns, authors had found ways to fit the strong inheritance of the classical tradition into their literary creations without having to write in the Latin language itself. For centuries, authors had been writing in a common language that was not their mother tongue *per se*, even though it still felt natural or 'native' to many of them. When Walkowitz discusses modern-day literature, she maintains that English has the

---

15   Walkowitz 2015, p. 20.
16   The intellectual historian Françoise Waquet convincingly argues in her monograph on Latin that through education, the Church, and the Republic of Letters, Latin could constitute a familiar universe that lasted even up to the 20th century. Waquet 1998.

"role as a mediator, within publishing, between other literary cultures."[17] Latin still had this role in the beginning of the 18th century.[18]

When it came to works of fiction, this mediating function had become particularly one-way, from Latin to the vernacular. The strongest two-way mediator for literary works in mid-18th-century Europe was French. It was through translations in this language, and not in Latin, that vernacular bestsellers reached other parts of Europe. A telling example is provided by the reception of Swift's *Gulliver's Travels*, which quickly spread out over Europe, but not in its original form. Due to an anonymous French translation and the rapidly-produced second version by Pierre François Guyot Desfontaines, both published within the same year, 1727, *Gulliver* could travel into other languages and language systems all over Europe. As Wilhelm Graeber notes, "there are signs everywhere to suggest that *Gulliver*, on its course from England to the Continent, was as shipwrecked as its protagonist on the coast of Lilliput."[19] However, the mediation was more than a verbal one. The translation of Swift's novel famously required—in the eyes of Desfontaines at least—a strong cultural translation, namely to French taste.[20] Vernacular languages such as English were still in a phase in which idioms and references to local culture required not only a linguistic mediation, but also a strong cultural one.

In a study of Holberg's translation-critique, Lars Eriksen shows that Holberg was very well aware that cultural differences impede translation. When it came to comical writings, the text had to be changed according to the expectations of the audience; otherwise the comical effect would be lost. A translator of comical works should be an author himself. Eriksen partly based this opinion on a previous experience he had with translations of his work.[21] In a French

---

17 Walkowitz 2015, p. 21.
18 There were, of course, regional differences in Europe. In the case of Denmark, the first half of the 18th century was a period in which the status of Latin was especially under review as a language of education within the monarchy. The turn to Danish seemed unavoidable when the Royal Danish Academy of Sciences and Letters was founded in 1742. Mortensen/Haberland 2012, 179–81. As an international language of academia, however, Latin would still be able resist its competitors German and French for some time.
19 Graeber 2005, p. 11. It is a subject for debate whether Holberg had read Swift's work in the original version or in a French (or even German) translation. In any case, Holberg was more comfortable reading French. He owned translations of several other works that were originally published in English. For a list of part of Holberg's private library, see Bruun 1869.
20 For a study of Desfontaines's translation, see Léger 2002.
21 Eriksen 1987, p. 103. Holberg expresses this opinion in an essay published in 1749, namely Holberg, *Epistles* IV.368. For all of Holberg's texts, I refer to the critical database of Holberg's oeuvre, *Ludvig Holbergs Skrifter* (LHS), which first appeared online in 2015. Holberg 2015. The numbers of volumes, chapters, and pages the database uses are kept;

introduction to a French translation of his comedies, *Le Théâtre Danois* (1746), Holberg had proclaimed quite the opposite concerning the task of a translator of comedy:

> Pour juger sainement du mérite de ce Théâtre Danois, il faut faire attention, que les Scènes ne sont pas à Paris, ni dans quelque autre Ville de France; mais la plupart à Copenhague. C'est la raison pourquoi le Traducteur n'a pas jugé à propos d'y faire de changemens; ce n'eût plus été peindre les moeurs de notre Septentrion, ni donner une Traduction, mais déguiser des Comédies du Nord en les habillant à la Françoise.[22]

Eriksen rightly states that Holberg shows himself to be an opportunist in this introduction. After the flop of *Le Théâtre Danois*, however, Holberg admits in his first autobiographical letter, *Ad virum perillustrem* (1728), that the translations of his comedies did not suit the Parisian public, as they were too Danish.[23] Holberg thus learned his lesson: the translations were not sufficiently tuned in to French culture to successfully translate a comical text from one culture to the other.

What Holberg's translation-critique demonstrates is that the loss of something that is typical for the original text does not lead to a corresponding loss of effect on readership, at least if the translator is skilled and inventive enough. The original work is not sacred, but the spirit of the text must be kept in translation. As Eriksen concludes, the translation must answer to the expectations of its audience, which for Holberg is clearly bound not only to the genre, but also to the literature and culture of the target audience.[24]

In writing *Niels Klim* Holberg had only one real option when it came to the choice between Latin and French—or for any vernacular language that could reach Europe for that matter. Besides the fact that he was more comfortable writing a novel in Latin than in German or French,[25] Holberg's language choice was also determined by an attempt to reach Europe in a different way. Though

---

only the Danish titles of Holberg's works are anglicised. English translations of Holberg's texts are my own, unless stated otherwise.

22   Holberg, *Preface* to Fursman's *Le Théâtre Danois*, p. 11.
23   For Holberg's remark on the reception of his plays in Paris, see Holberg, *Ad virum perillustrem* I, p. 143.
24   Eriksen 1987, p. 106.
25   Beside the introduction to the French translation of his comedies, there are three texts by Holberg in French, published at the very end of his career: *Conjectures sur les causes de la grandeur des Romains* (1752), the short *Lettre qui contient quelques remarques sur les mémoires concernant la Reine Christine* (1752) and *Remarques sur l'esprit des loix* (1753), a commentary on the work of Montesquieu.

written in Latin, *Niels Klim* had to be translated, as an increasing number of people were more comfortable reading in the vernacular; however, it was also the case that the culture was not in need of translation as much as French or Danish were; Latin covered a cosmopolitan language system that was European in nature, not bound to nations, and thus detachable and movable.

An author's decision to write in a dominant language in order to "mitigate the need for translation" is what Walkowitz calls "preemptive translation."[26] She admits that this strategy can already be found in late medieval and early modern times, but downplays these early forms of preemptive translation, arguing that there is not a clear division between writing and speaking a language: "writing in Latin while speaking in French is only a species of translation, or second-language use, if writing in French is the norm."[27] I believe that when writing in the vernacular became the norm in the first half of the 18th century, arguably even a bit earlier, preemptive translation was already a pressing reality for authors from small language areas. They constantly turned to German, French, and also Latin to make themselves known, which inevitably had become a form of self-translation.

Writing in Latin as a Danish writer was particularly useful to Holberg as his work would not be bound to a geographical place, only to a mental place, one to which Holberg, like so many others all over Europe, had visited since childhood. As Walkowitz argues, born-translated literature is not made in one country, after which it travels to others; it is often written by a migrant who is not bound to a specific country.[28] Eighteenth-century authors who wrote in Latin, a language that was not their mother tongue, were all migrants in a sense. Especially when a European-minded author like Holberg wrote a Latin travelogue, his text was not meant to stay at one place or in one language. It was "designed to travel" across national boundaries and in different language systems at the same time.[29]

But what exactly does it mean to be 'designed to travel' in *Niels Klim*'s case, or to be 'a migrant' in the case of Holberg? First of all, we need to reconsider the place and context of publication from this new perspective. On the title page of the first edition both Copenhagen and Leipzig (*Hafniae et Lipsiae*) are mentioned as the place of publication, and the publisher is Jacob Preuss (*Iacobi Preusii*), an autodidactic bookseller who was at the beginning of a period in Copenhagen's book history in which both cities were joined together in

---

26   Walkowitz 2015, p. 11.
27   Ibid., p. 11.
28   Ibid. et passim. See also Walkowitz 2009, pp. 573–76.
29   Walkowitz 2009, p. 570.

the publication process.[30] As Harald Ilsøe has shown, Copenhagen booksellers frequently visited the biannual book fair in Leipzig, but Preuss must have had local contacts that allowed him to print and stock at least part of his issues in Leipzig.[31] If we may believe Holberg himself, Preuss repeatedly asked him to sell him the manuscript of *Niels Klim* because he could make a great profit from it.[32] The reluctance Holberg claims to have had, however, must be read with skepticism. Preuss was Holberg's ideal business associate for *Niels Klim*. He was an upcoming man, a new purveyor of the Court, who already had one foot in an international book market, thus providing Holberg with a contact that would allow him to bypass Danish censorship.[33]

Although Holberg's hand in the actual distribution of *Niels Klim* remains unclear, it was definitely not his test piece. In an excellent and thorough study of the book history of Holberg's *Peder Paars* (1719/20), Jens Bjerring-Hansen shows that Holberg was strongly committed to the marketing and distribution of his poetical debut. The piece took shape along the way: within only a two-year period, four books were published in three serial editions, with changing titles and publishers. The complex publication history of *Peder Paars* provides both an early and extreme illustration of how Holberg played with and mocked the book market.[34] Reader responses and criticisms were immediately countered or parodied in following editions—a practice he repeatedly used throughout his career, as in *Niels Klim* which Holberg made into a lively and ever-shifting piece of literature. With *Peder Paars*, Holberg showed two faces for the first time: "the entrepreneurial actor with an eye for profit maximising in an eighteenth-century reality and the critical observer of the book market and the literary commercialising and commoditization."[35] In *Peder Paars*, Holberg thus already internalised the book market by making different editions part of what we now know as *Peder Paars*. He also used paratexts, such as the critical footnotes of the fictional academic Just Justesen, in order to internalise different reading publics. Holberg thus already sowed the seeds for born-translated

---

30   Whether the copies of *Niels Klim*, or some of them, were actually printed in Leipzig is not certain though plausible, since production costs were much lower in Germany. Ilsøe 2001, p. 20.
31   Ibid., p. 21.
32   Holberg, *Ad virum perillustrem* III, p. 9.
33   Ilsøe 2001, p. 8.
34   Holberg always had strong opinions about the book market and the quality of its goods, but is most open about it in his *Moral Thoughts* (1744) and *Epistles*. For a discussion of Holberg's criticisms, see Bjerring-Hansen 2015, pp. 53–84.
35   Ibid., p. 82.

literature in his poetical debut, but he would only reap the harvest when he turned to his Latin travelogue.

Jacob Preuss was not only the man who published *Nicolaus Klimius*, but he was for Holberg also a gateway to translations of some of his works. Holberg gave him the right to publish Klim's *Voyages* in French and *Reise* in German, both of which appeared in 1741. The German edition remained anonymous, but the translator of the French edition was printed on the front page: Eléazar Mauvillon, a Huguenot who at the time was residing, not coincidentally, in Leipzig.[36] Even the anonymous Dutch edition, also published in 1741, but not by Preuss, could have had a German connection as it could have been translated by a German residing in the Netherlands.[37] As Yanick Maes notes, "Holberg is lucid enough to understand that the use of Latin excludes the majority of the public. The success of his novel will be measured, not by the copies sold, but by the number of translations made."[38] The choice for Preuss was thus not one out of charity—although Preuss needed it as he went bankrupt later that year, despite *Niels Klim*'s success.[39] It allowed Holberg to publish a work that immediately existed in different places, initially Copenhagen and Leipzig, and in different languages. Preuss could get his text around Europe, and so *Niels Klim* was born, that is, born-translated.

3   *Niels Klim* as Translation: a Vain Quest for the Original

For Walkowitz, being born-translated means more than the almost simultaneous existence of a work in different languages and places.[40] Translation goes much deeper: it is not only written *for* translation, but also written *as* translation.[41] Especially in imaginary travel literature in the 17th and 18th centuries, a

---

36   Flugt 2015, p. 69.
37   According to the editor of *Niels Klim*'s most recent reprint in Dutch, André Hanou, the translation of 1741 was written in a "peculiar kind of Dutch," more specifically "a sort of 'eastern' Dutch." Hanou 1995, p. 20.
38   Maes 2009, p. 8.
39   Harald Ilsøe extensively describes the turbulent history of the auction of Preuss's stock. Ilsøe 2001.
40   In Walkowitz's view only post-Holocaust literature is eligible in this sense as the distribution of books was greatly facilitated by globalisation and the upcoming digital age. As Bjerring-Hansen shows, however, the book market at the beginning of the 18th century greatly expanded, with increasing levels of differentiation. Bjerring-Hansen 2015, p. 53. The book markets in both periods are thus not comparable in absolute numbers but in the scale by which they grew compared to previous periods.
41   Walkowitz 2015, p. 4.

simulated translation of the original work was very common. Between *The Man in the Moone* of Francis Godwin (1638), which was supposedly written by a Spaniard, and the bulky *Icosaméron* (1788), supposedly translated from English into French by Casanova, numerous examples are to be found of travel reports that originated from another language. Daniel Defoe's *The Consolidator* even claims to be a translation from a lunar language, in imitation of Godwin's work. However, few have used this literary conceit to its full potential.

Holberg plays with this tradition in the second edition of his novel, published in 1745. By this time, *Niels Klim* had already appeared in a Swedish, English, and Danish version, in addition to the German, French, and Dutch editions discussed earlier in this essay. In the third letter *Ad virum perillustrem* (1743), Holberg is not shy about repeatedly boasting that *Niels Klim*, is a "much celebrated work which is already being read in various languages."[42] Inspired by imaginary travel literature, Holberg saw the fictional potential of the immediate translation boom, a recognition he internalizes in a *Praefatio apologetica* added in 1745. Here, the grandsons of Klim ambiguously confirm the veracity of the story of their grandfather and add that the text of the first edition was a Latin translation from the original manuscript. The effect of this preface is that the reader of the second edition is invited to reread the book and adjust his image of the protagonist and supposed author, Klim, according to this new information.[43] As in *Peder Paars*, Holberg thus uses editions as a way to alter and renew his text. Unlike *Peder Paars*, however, Holberg also draws the translation history into the fiction. As a consequence, when talking about *Niels Klim* we cannot just refer to one text but rather to a virtual group of texts.

The addition of this supposed translation apparently caused some confusion in later periods and gave rise to a myth that *Niels Klim* was originally written in Danish and even predated the publication of Swift's *Gulliver's Travels*. The most famous example of this theory is provided by Henry Weber, editor of an English translation of *Niels Klim* in 1812.[44] As absurd as this might sound, it could demonstrate two things that are not mutually exclusive: namely, that Holberg was very effective in manipulating his reading public, and that a 19th-century readership was out of touch with the idea of born-translation. In a

---

42   "Hinc celebratissimum istud Opus, qvod variis jam lingvis legitur." Holberg, *Ad virum perillustrem* III, p. 8.

43   In another article, I focus precisely on the consequences of this supposed translation for the characterisation of Klim as a narrator. Velle 2016.

44   Flugt 2015, pp. 156–57. For the original version, see Weber 1812, pp. xxix–xxxi. In his autobiography, Holberg indeed mentions that he had written *Niels Klim* "some years before" (*ante aliqvot annos*). Holberg, *Ad virum perillustrem* III, p. 8. However, it is improbable that this would cover the long period between Swift's publication in 1726 and 1741.

study on the translation history of *Niels Klim*, Cecilie Flugt draws attention not only to a significant decrease of interest in translating *Niels Klim* in the 19th century, but also a tendency towards a process of adaptation, in which translators shaped their work in part to meet the specific needs and sensitivities of the target culture.[45] This illustrates both a key characteristic of 19th-century nationalism, and the loss of something that previously existed; during the 18th century Latin still was easily *relatable* to a European public in different countries—forming something like a cosmopolitan collective memory, even though it was not always *readable* in this very language by everyone. The 19th-century reader lost touch with the cosmopolitan aspect of literature, or—to use Walkowitz's terms—the 'translatability' of texts and the 'migrating' identity of Latin. As translators increasingly felt the need to adjust Latin to the target culture, Latin in a sense became German, French, or English, and stopped being simply European.

If we return to the *Praefatio apologetica* in the second edition, it becomes clear that Holberg saw the potential lying in his first text and in the following translation history. He dramatises translation much more prominently and invites the reader to an ongoing act of translating. We have already seen that Klim's manuscript was apparently translated into Latin. In addition, the grandsons of Klim invoke a Finnish shaman, Peyvis, as the ultimate source that supports their truth claims. Peyvis transforms himself into an eagle, flies to the underground world, and reports back in Bergen what he has seen in his subterranean journey. Before departing, Peyvis praises his magical powers to the citizens of Bergen "with words expressing a Danish idiom."[46] As the commentators of *Niels Klim* note, the narrators of the preface hereby point out to their readers that they will read something that is translated from Danish to Latin.[47] What follows is ironically a verse quotation from Petronius's *Satyricon*:

> *Quicquid in orbe vides, paret mihi: Florida tellus,*
> *Cum volo, spissatis arescit languida succis:*
> *Cum volo, fundit opes; scopulique ac horrida saxa*
> *Limosas iaculantur aquas: Mihi Pontus inertes*
> *Submittit fluctus: Zephyrique tacentia ponunt*
> *Ante meos sua flabra pedes: Mihi flumina parent.*

---

45 Flugt 2015, pp. 144–46.
46 "verbis Danico idiomate expressis." Holberg, *Praefatio apologetica*, p. 5v.
47 Skovgaard-Petersen/Zeeberg/Flugt 2015, p. 5v.

Whatever thou seest in the world is obedient to me. The flowery earth, when I will, faints and withers as its juices dry, and, when I will, pours forth its riches, while rocks and rough crags spurt waters wide as the Nile. The great sea lays its waves lifeless before me, and the winds lower their blasts in silence at my feet. The rivers obey me [...].[48]

In the *Satyricon*, the Priapus-priestess Oenothea commends herself as a sorceress to Encolpius, who suffers from erectile dysfunction.[49] The healing ritual of Oenothea, however, fails completely, first after a series of accidents and later even more so when Encolpius kills a goose without knowing that the animal was a guardian of Priapus. The reader thus never sees the great powers Oenothea claims to possess.

Within the context of the *Praefatio apologetica*, the self-praise of Peyvis does not help to convince the reader either. When he returns to Bergen, he reports how Klim's other grandson (he also had a wife during his reign in Quama), now rules the subterranean world. Instead of reinforcing the truth claim of Klim's superterranean grandsons, the excessive fantasy of Peyvis's metamorphosis has quite the opposite effect. Petronius thus does not support Peyvis's story, which rather only highlights the absurdity and ineffectiveness of his claim.

The irony of Peyvis's use of quotations prefigures how the reading of *Niels Klim* is suddenly changed. That is, quotations in the text remind the reader that they are not reading the original, but a translation. All the quotations the reader comes across in the following 16 chapters of *Niels Klim* thus suddenly receive an entirely different status. Klim might not have been the writer of these quotations after all, for often a similar kind of ambiguity or irony is voiced in a text that is not from Klim's hand. The translator, Abeline, has not only translated the words of Klim; he has translated Klim's text entirely into another language system and culture, the kind of transposition that for Holberg was necessary to bring humour to a different audience.

In the next part of this essay, we will come back to the issue of the quotations, but let us for now go a bit deeper into the difference between reading *Niels Klim* from 1741 and the edition published in 1745, which amounts to more than just reading *Niels Klim* with or without the preface. For the attentive reader, these are two different texts. Holberg has amplified specific topics from the first edition in the second, and has done this with a specific goal.

---

48 Holberg, *Praefatio apologetica*, p. 5v, and Petronius, *Satyricon* 134, 12. The English translation is by Michael Heseltine, a volume appearing in the Loeb Classical Library series.
49 Skovgaard-Petersen/Zeeberg/Flugt 2015, p. 5v.

When discussing *Niels Klim* in his third autobiographical letter *Ad virum perillustrem*, published in 1743, in-between *Niels Klim*'s two editions, Holberg presents himself as being most concerned with bringing across the right morals to his reading public. He speaks of a "whole moral system" (*totum systema morale*) that is hidden within the "enjoyable fiction" (*festiva fictio*) of *Niels Klim*. He uses a simile of a fisherman who changes his bait to the taste of little fishes, to explain why he opted for an imaginary voyage to teach his readership morals. He arms himself against petty critics "who find everything that is enjoyable and attractive nauseating, [...] and unworthy of a Christian."[50] The entire passage exudes frustration with those readers who remained fixated on the story itself, something Holberg seemingly considered only as a "vehicle for [expressing] moral precepts and meditations."[51] Moreover, as Holberg portrays them, the readers of *Niels Klim*'s first edition are not only blinded by the light-footed story when assessing the novel; some are also hindered by their insufficient language skills. For this last group of readers, Holberg delayed the publication of the Danish translation. As Holberg claims himself, most of the Danes he wanted to reach with *Niels Klim* could also read it in German. The rest were just not ready to interpret his *systema morale*.[52]

The way Holberg presents the readership of *Niels Klim* in this letter is, however, an ironic marketing trick. The flagrant misinterpretations of his work by unskilled readers, and sometimes by people who did not even read the text, are cited as ways to rouse the interest of the readers of his autobiography for *Niels Klim*. He even warms his readers up for an upcoming second edition, two years later, for, in the third letter, Holberg already speaks of "two prefaces" (*binae Praefationes*) that explain the scope of *Niels Klim*. At the time the public reads this, in 1743, there is no single preface to be found in *Niels Klim*. The impatient reader has to wait two years to be able to read only one of them.[53]

Holberg thus already prefigures the *Praefatio apologetica* of the second edition in 1743. In that preface, Holberg highlights those themes that seemingly presented the greatest obstacles for the hack critics of the first edition: unreliability and fictionality, multilingualism, and translation. Through the amplification of these themes and the irony that surrounds them in the *Praefatio apologetica*, Holberg offers caricatures of *Niels Klim*'s readership in a fashion similar to what he does in the autobiographical letter: they seem to have been

---

50 "qvi qvicqvid festivum ac amœnum est, nauseant [...] ac christiano homine indignum judicant." Holberg, *Ad virum perillustrem* III, p. 9. For the entire passage on *Niels Klim*, see ibid. III, pp. 8–25.
51 "vehiculum [...] praeceptorum ac meditationum moralium." ibid. III, p. 12.
52 Ibid. III, p. 25.
53 It remains unclear whether the second preface Holberg speaks of is a fictional one or not.

outraged about the fantastical elements of the story and unable to penetrate its intellectual language and style. Holberg thus not only incorporates the immediate translations of *Niels Klim* into his text, but also establishes a dialogue between *Niels Klim* and his commentary of *Niels Klim* in his Latin memoirs. The translations, editions, and commentary, were all part of Holberg's plan to make *Niels Klim* into a travelling novel.

4 Niels Klim Translating? The Failure of Latin in a Multilingual Environment

That the second edition of *Niels Klim* explicitly foregrounds the issues at stake in this essay does not mean, however, that the *Niels Klim* of 1741 does not address issues such as multilingualism and translation. In various ways, the first edition already suggests that the reader is confronted with a translation, or to use one of Walkowitz's terms, with a 'dramatization of translation'; the text "registers the presence of foreign languages without representing them directly."[54] *Niels Klim* constantly reminds readers that the text they have before them has emerged out of a long process, through which it has undergone multiple translations.

The entire journey of Klim is one that passes through an environment which is extremely multilingual, perhaps even more so than in Europe. The inhabitants of the planet of Nazar speak just one language—which might be connected to the utopian status of Potu—but the different races on the Firmament speak languages such as Martinian and Quamitian. Others communicate through their rear ends, or by the help of a bow and strings. Holberg explores the entire range of imaginary languages that the rich tradition of imaginary travel literature has to offer. The Potuan, Martinian, and Quamitian languages primarily differ in their function or purpose in society, while the fantastical languages of the Pyglossians and the Musical Instruments stretch the range of possible answers to the age-old question, 'what is language?' As often occurs in imaginary travel literature, Holberg thus explores both the cultural and formal implications of multilingualism.[55] He also upholds the tradition of imaginary travel literature by making his protagonist into one of the genre's notorious

---

54 Walkowitz 2015, p. 40.
55 The space limitation on this essay does not allow me to expand here on the way Holberg incorporates and parodies the common theme of imaginary languages in travel literature, which I will leave for another place. The most extensive treatments of this theme until now can be found in Cornelius 1965 and Ducet 2006.

polyglots, of which Gulliver is perhaps the most infamous precursor.[56] They pick up exotic languages like no other and gladly show off their knowledge of different European languages as well.

In sharp contrast with the multilingualism of the subterranean world and of Klim, however, stands the status of Latin. After a long wandering through many subterranean countries, Klim is washed ashore in Quama, the first country he sees that is inhabited by humans. Expecting he would be able to converse with them in European languages, Klim tries to speak German, Danish, and Latin, but these seem to be unknown languages for the Quamitians (*ignotas linguas*).[57] The order of languages in which Klim tries to communicate with the locals is particularly telling. Klim is not an intellectual but an opportunistic, multilingual European who first tries German and Danish, before reaching for Latin. For Klim, Latin is not a living language that feels natural; it is reduced to a facade that can help you claim a specific social status in Europe. Klim is not a Latin author, but a caricature of the multilingual European. As some kind of pseudo Latinist, Klim is unable to convince inhabitants of the underground world of the value of Latin and its culture that originated and somehow survived for ages in the superterranean world. When Klim tries to establish an educational institute in Quama as one of his first acts as the new monarch, he quickly realises that his subterranean subjects have no use in learning a European language. Klim thus reconciles himself with the failure of Latin in the subterranean world, and takes over Quamitian as the medium of communication of his new monarchy.

Holberg goes one step even further and explicitly transfers this negative status of Latin to the superterranean world, to Europe. Later in the novel, Klim reads a book, written by a further unknown creature, Tanian, who managed to travel to Europe. He describes how arrogant, inconsequential, and corrupt Europeans are. This *Itinerarium Taniani* is the culminating point to which the previous reflections on language, including Latin evolve. When Tanian speaks about Latin in the Catholic Church, he mentions it is forbidden for the faithful to honour God, except in an unknown dialect (*ignota dialecto*). Tanian thus alludes to Catholic liturgy in which all prayers and rituals were in Latin, a language that the lion's share of the faithful could not understand. In just a couple of remarks, an unknown, fictive subterranean author, whose voice lacks any authority, reduces Latin from an *ignota lingua* in Quama to an *ignota dialectus* in Europe. As Yanick Maes states when referring to this passage, "we are

---

56 For Gulliver's language knowledge and linguistic adventures, see Kelly 1978 and Wyrick 1988. *Gulliver's Travels* is repeatedly discussed in the latter.
57 Holberg, *Niels Klim* XII, p. 274.

witnessing not a splendid resurgence of a vitalized Latin literature—no, this is some sort of *Götterdämmerung*."[58] Latin is knocked off of its pedestal.

Tanian's harsh criticism, moreover, is itself mediated multiple times; for example, it is translated for Klim by a befriended tiger, called Tomopoloko. He, in his turn, translated it from an unknown subterranean language in which the text had been written by Tanian. Criticism of the use of Latin in Europe—in this case by the Church—is thus communicated to the reader through a subterranean text, interpreted into a subterranean language (Quamitian or Tanachitian), and eventually written down by Klim. In 1745, when Holberg adds the aspect of Latin translation, Tanian's criticism is suddenly mediated once more, and, ironically, by the language he initially criticised, Latin.

The characterisation of Klim as a naïve, multilingual European that we already find in the first edition of *Niels Klim* makes one wonder if such a character is able to insert so many Latin quotations into his travelogue. In Swift's novel, the polyglot Gulliver at least chose to write in the language in which he could reach the public he wanted. That is still doubtful in the case of Klim. Within the fictional world of Holberg's text, however, Klim did not reach the public he initially intended to reach; his allegedly Danish work was published in Latin. However, outside that fictional world, his work did not reach Europe in Latin, but through translations. By adding mediating layers of translation, Holberg invites readers to reflect upon multilingualism in Europe, and more specifically the status of Latin in society, education and literature. As has become clear by now, it is not fruitful to stay within the fictive world of the text while interpreting *Niels Klim*, nor is it helpful to focus upon the historical context to which the narrative refers. According to Walkowitz, born-translated literature asks for a "close reading from a distance."[59] Only by adopting such an approach can the reader play along with Holberg's metafictional game: he encourages his readers, as he also did in *Peder Paars*, to continually pass back and forth across those boundaries while reading.

5 Reading *Niels Klim* as Translating: the Translatability of the Classics

As I demonstrated in an earlier part of this essay, the countless quotations from classical texts play an important role within the fiction of *Niels Klim*, not least of all given the doubtful authorship of these digressions in both the first and second editions. The question remains: how this affects the actual reading

---

58 Maes 2009, p. 8.
59 Walkowitz 2015, p. 90.

experience? Let us therefore step out of the fictional world once more and look at how *Niels Klim* externalises not only the problem of translation and multilingualism, but also the problem of quotations.

Multiple scholars have shown that the effects of these quotations are varied and often far-reaching, from a subtle sense of irony to a tone that characterises an entire part of the novel.[60] They are a crucial part of Holberg's Latin text, especially for the characterisation of Klim as a narrator and foreign observer.[61] If one follows the reasoning of Sigrid Peters, one could argue that this use of quotations in particular provides a perfect example of the untranslatability of Holberg's text. The effect of the quotations in a Menippean satire can only come across in Latin, in the original language of the reference frame that is being used, namely that of the classics. This traditional idea behind Peters's entire study offers an example of what Walkowitz critiques in her monograph when she discusses the 'untranslatability' of born-translated texts:

> It is conventional to distinguish between works that impede translation ('untranslatable') and those that invite it ('translatable'). But what would it mean for a work both to impede and to invite at the same time? The work that is difficult to translate is celebrated for its engagement with a specific national language and for its refusal to enter, or enter easily, into the pipeline of multinational publishing. The portable work, for its part, is vilified for having surrendered to that pipeline, exchanging aesthetic innovation for commercial success, eschewing the idiosyncrasy of the local for the interchangeability of the global.[62]

Walkowitz thus fights the idea that a work is valued more when it seems to be inextricably linked to one specific nation or language system due to its difficulty. Considering what we have seen so far—that multilingualism and translation are important aspects of Klim's journey and that Holberg's text conquered Europe not in Latin alone but as a group of editions and translations—, we may have to look at the use of quotations from a different perspective than that of Peters: what if *Niels Klim* is a text that both impedes and invites translation?

---

60   Besides Karen Skovgaard-Petersen and Sigrid Peters, there is one scholar in particular who needs to be mentioned here, namely Aage Kragelund. He spent a lifetime editing Holberg's Latin oeuvre and studying Holberg's use of quotations. For his edition of *Niels Klim*, see Holberg 1970.
61   For a case study on the implications of quotations for Klim's characterisation, see Velle 2016.
62   Walkowitz 2015, p. 31.

From the study of *Niels Klim*'s translation history by Cecilie Flugt, two concluding observations need to be mentioned in this respect. In general, the translations that were published at the same time as the Latin first edition are quite faithful to the original. Part of this 'faithfulness' is evidenced by the fact that they generally translate the poetic quotations from classical authors, but in a manner that stays quite close to the text and yet still remains separate from the prose text, as is the case in the Latin original:

> The cause of the early tendency towards faithful translation can be that *Niels Klim* is linked to classical literature in Latin and is therefore regarded as a part of the joint European literary history in the middle of the eighteenth century, which entailed that *Niels Klim* did not appear strange to the target culture and that quotations from Roman authors are incorporated in the same work, which was considered at this time as the standard after which everything else should be moulded.[63]

In the earliest translations of *Niels Klim*, translators did not feel the need to change the poetic or literary function of the quotations in the text. The first English translation even kept the poetic quotations in Latin.[64] Another remarkable, though less surprising, conclusion Flugt makes is that in later translations, especially from the turn of the century onwards, there is an increasing tendency towards either omitting these quotations or translating them freely in the prose text.[65]

This periodical difference is again telling. While European culture became increasingly nationalistic, the classics changed from being part of a common, cosmopolitan tradition to a culture in which the use of classics brings discomfort and interrupts the reading process. Returning to Walkowitz's concepts of 'translatable' and 'untranslatable,' one could argue that, indeed, both terms apply to *Niels Klim* when it comes to the quotations. The references to classical authors are not translatable in the strictest sense; they constitute a manifest break in tone, style, and register that invites translators to change their way of translating accordingly. It impedes translation in the sense that it complicates

---

63   "Årsagen til den tidlige trofaste oversættelsestendens kan være, at *NK* knitter sig til en klassisk latin-sproget litteratur og dermed opfattedes som del af en fælleseuropæisk litteraturhistorie i midten af 1700-tallet, hvilket bevirkede, at *NK* ikke fremstod fremmed for målsprogskulturen, og at der i selve værket er indarbejdet citater fra romerske forfattere, som på dette tidspunkt blev anset for målestokken, efter hvilken alt andet skulle måles." Flugt 2015, p. 141.
64   For a discussion of this first, anonymous English translation, see ibid., pp. 40–43.
65   Especially in the German tradition, this is very clear. Ibid., p. 141.

the practice of the translator. At the same time, they are translatable in the contemporary European context as they carry out a reference frame that is known by the reader from other texts, not only in Latin, but also in translation and vernacular texts. Readers of the first translations of *Niels Klim* would not be interrupted in their reading process when coming across poetic forms in their prose text, for they refer to an 'interchangeable' European culture.

The quotations from classical authors are, of course, a trigger for the reader to look for more intertextual references. Karen Skovgaard-Petersen, for example, demonstrated the importance of Livy and Virgil in the characterisation of Klim as a ruler in the last part of *Niels Klim*.[66] When these quotations are translated into French, German, or Dutch, and therefore become less recognisable, this part of Klim's characterisation becomes blurred. Traditionally, this unavoidable loss of meaning that was couched in Holberg's Latin text is considered to be the main reason why *Niels Klim* seems untranslatable. To some extent this is true; quotations from Petronius or Cicero skilfully hidden in the prose text will almost never be noticed by readers of translations. However, the poetic quotations that were separate from the prose text are still recognisable as quotations. In this vein, *Niels Klim* is one of Walkowitz's untranslatable texts that "find ways to keep translation from stopping" and "invite translation rather than prohibit it."[67] The translation process of *Niels Klim* does not stop when it is published in another language, but continues during the reading process. In search for what the separate quotations refer to, readers translate again to Latin, not literally, but to the cosmopolitan realm of Latin. Whether they fail to recognise them or to attach an extra meaning to the quotation (which could as a matter of fact also happen when reading in Latin) is of secondary importance. *Niels Klim* invites readers to keep on translating and incites the awareness that they are in fact reading a translation.

The ongoing act of translation makes *Niels Klim* into a versatile text that is not, as often is plainly stated, directed to the intellectual audience of Latin readers, but rather to multiple audiences. European intellectuals formed a very heterogeneous, polyglot group, with varying abilities to read Latin. To cite Walkowitz once more:

> [B]orn-translated works block readers from being 'native readers', those who assume that the book they are holding was written for them or that

---

66   Skovgaard-Petersen 2013, pp. 186–89.
67   Walkowitz 2015, p. 44.

the language they are encountering is, in some proprietary or intrinsic way, theirs.[68]

Here lies the irony of reading *Niels Klim*. Holberg holds up a mirror and makes his readers aware of the fact that they are not native readers. When the readers have Latin skills sufficient to understand the extra levels of meaning of the quotations, they perceive themselves to be reading either a translation by someone else or a text written by someone with insufficient Latin skills. When reading *Niels Klim* in translation, readers are reminded by Klim's extolling of classical culture and by the translated verse quotations that their reading skills are insufficient to read it in Latin. From the moment these quotations are left out of the translations, there is no longer any reason to expect the original was written in Latin except for a statement on the front page which enables mistakes like the one made by Henry Weber and ultimately reduces Holberg's novel to one of the many imaginary voyages that use this element of fictional translation only on the front page. Nineteenth-century readers and translators lost touch with the way *Niels Klim* was composed; as a work that was born-translated, not only in the sense that it immediately existed at several places in Europe, but also in that the reader was confronted with a narrative inviting her/him to reflect upon the function and place of translation in European literature. It is a work that both impedes and invites translation. The quotations of classical authors are as much part of Holberg's idea as the effect on the reader of starting to reflect upon the language in which it is written.

6 Conclusion

Irony had always been Holberg's favourite way to issue critiques or present moral teachings. In a Danish essay published seven years after *Niels Klim*, he warns an anonymous reader not to take his writings too literally because he often uses irony, "which is the most powerful means by which one can fight people's faults and ignorance." After linking this writing method to Socrates and Erasmus, Holberg also notes that "this age has produced a great master in the English Doctor Swift."[69] The way Holberg treats Latin, as demonstrated in this essay, makes Latin more than a functional language choice. Functionality or even opportunism becomes part of Holberg's aesthetics.

---

68 Ibid., p. 6.
69 Holberg, *Epistles* II.157, p. 321.

Although Holberg praises Swift for his ironical style, he manages to deviate from his example in the way his text conveys irony towards the very language in which it is written. To understand the innovation of Holberg compared to Swift, Walkowitz can be of use perhaps one last time: "[p]ointing backward as well as forward, [born-translated writings] present translation as a spur to literary innovation, including their own."[70] Swift only points backward by inviting the reader to reflect upon ideals and problems concerning the language in which it is written, English. Swift's work reached Europe almost immediately, but was never actually European, which is perhaps why *Gulliver's Travels* survived the age of 19th-century nationalism (and its rigid determinations of what constitutes a properly 'nationalist' literature) better than Holberg's novel has. Swift's travelogue was in essence born-English. It travelled afterwards from Dublin into several remote nations of the world, but always returned to the canonical lists of *English* literature.

Niels Klim, by contrast, fits uneasily within every literary history: the Danish or the Neo-Latin, the one of imaginary voyages or the one of Menippean satire. One of the reasons behind this is that Holberg not only points backward by asking his reader to reflect upon Latin, but also points forward, enforcing this reflection by anticipating *Niels Klim*'s translation and existence in other languages as an arguably fortunate, yet inevitable fate. Holberg prefigures a reader who is not just Danish, French, German, or Dutch, etc. His reader is part of a cosmopolitan culture that is increasingly heterogeneous and increasingly endangered because of both external factors, such as the rise of the vernacular, and internal factors, exemplified by the humanistic translating style of Abelinus. Before *Niels Klim* was turned into "simply a Danish *Gulliver's Travels*" in the 19th century onwards, *Niels Klim* had neither a place of birth nor a resting-place. Holberg's travelogue was designed to be translated as well as to prevent translation from stopping, but perhaps most importantly it was designed to travel.

Bibliography

Primary Sources

Holberg, Ludvig. *Le Théâtre danois, traduit du danois par Mr. G. Fursman*. Copenhagen: Mengel, 1746.

Holberg, Ludvig. *Niels Klims Underjordiske Rejse: 1741–1745*, edited by Aage Kragelund. Copenhagen: Gad, 1970.

---

70   Walkowitz 2015, p. 4.

Holberg, Ludvig. *Ludvig Holbergs Skrifter*. Bergen/Copenhagen: University of Bergen/ Society of Danish Language and Literature, version 1.0, first appeared online 2015, accessed 30 November 2016, http://holbergsskrifter.dk.

Secondary Sources

Billeskov, Jansen, Frederik J. *Ludvig Holberg*. New York: Twayne, 1974.

Bjerring-Hansen, Jens. *Ludvig Holberg på bogmarkedet: Studier i Peder Paars og den litterære kultur i 1700- og 1800-tallet*. Copenhagen: Museum Tusculanums Forlag, 2015.

Bruun, Christian. *Fortegnelse over en del af Ludvig Holbergs bibliothek*. Copenhagen: Lynges, 1869.

Cornelius, Paul. *Languages in Seventeenth- and Early Eighteenth-Century Imaginary Voyages*. Geneva: Droz, 1965.

Ducet, Priscille. *Le monde souterrain et ses origines dans la littérature française du XVIIIe siècle*. Unpublished PhD-thesis, Paris IV-Sorbonne, 2006.

Eriksen, Lars H. "Ludvig Holbergs Übersetzungskritik. Ein Beitrag zur Übersetzungssituation im Nordeuropa der Aufklärung." *Skandinavistik* 17.2 (1987), pp. 93–108.

Flugt, Cecilie. *Niels Klims Europæiske rejse. En oversættelseshistorisk undersøgelse af Nicolai Klimii iter subterraneum*. Unpublished PhD-thesis, Copenhagen University, 2015.

Gove, Philip Babcock. *The Imaginary Voyages in Prose Fiction. A History of Its Criticism and a Guide for Its Study, with an Annotated Check List of 215 Imaginary Voyages from 1700 to 1800*. London: The Holland Press, 1941.

Graeber, Wilhelm. "Swift's First Voyages to Europe. His Impact on Eighteenth-Century France." In *The Reception of Jonathan Swift in Europe*, edited by Hermann J. Real. London: Thoemmes Continuum, 2005, pp. 5–16.

Hanou, André. "Inleiding." In Holberg, Ludvig. *De Onderaardse Reise Van Claas Klim (1741)*. Leiden: Astraea, 1995, pp. 1–27.

Ilsøe, Harald. "Et forlag til salg. Jacob Preusses lager af forlagsskrifter 1743." *Fund og Forskning* 40 (2001), pp. 7–47.

Kelly, Ann Cline. "After Eden. Gullivers (Linguistic) Travels." *English Literary History* 45.1 (1978), pp. 33–54.

Léger, Benoit. "Les notes du traducteur des Voyages de Gulliver. Détonation et «détonnement»." *Lumen* 21 (2002), pp. 179–98.

Maes, Yanick. "Continuity through Appropriation? By Way of Introduction." In *Latinitas Perennis*, edited by Wim Verbaal, Yanick Maes, and Jan Papy. Leiden: Brill, 2009, pp. 1–13.

Mortensen, Janus and H. Haberland. "English—the New Latin of Academia? Danish Universities as a Case." *International Journal of the Sociology of Language* 216 (2012), pp. 175–97.

Paludan, Julius. *Om Holbergs Niels Klim med saerligt hensyn til tidligere satirer i form af opdigtede og vidunderlige reiser.* Copenhagen: Wilhelm Prior, 1878.

Peters, Sigrid. *Ludvig Holbergs Menippeische Satire. Das 'Iter Subterraneum' und seine Beziehungen zur antiken Literatur.* Bern: Peter Lang, 1987.

Rossel, Sven Hakon. *A History of Danish Literature.* Lincoln, NE: University of Nebraska Press, 1992.

Sejersted, Jørgen Magnus. "Reflections on Peer Gynt's Forefathers Niels Klim and Lemuel Gulliver." In *Ibsen on the Cusp of the 21st Century. Critical Perspectives*, edited by Pål Bjørby, Alvhild Dvergsdal, and Idar Stegane. Laksevåg: Alvheim & Eide Akademisk Forlag, 2005, pp. 153–69.

Skovgaard-Petersen, Karen. "The Interplay with Roman Literature in Ludvig Holberg's *Iter Subterraneum*." In *Der Neulateinische Roman als Medium seiner Zeit*, edited by Stefan Tilg and Isabella Walser. Tübingen: Narr Verlag, 2013, pp. 185–92.

Skovgaard-Petersen, Karen and Peter Zeeberg. "Verdensfjerne matematikere, blodtørstige anatomer og sexhungrende hustruer: Swifts *Gulliver* og Holbergs *Klim*." AIGIS supplementum III (2014), pp. 1–11, accessed 30 November 2016, http://aigis.igl.ku.dk/aigis/CMT80/KSP-PZ.pdf.

Skovgaard-Petersen, Karen, Peter Zeeberg, and Cecilie Flugt. "Kommentarer til *Niels Klim, Forsvarende Fortale* 1745." In *Ludvig Holbergs Skrifter*. Bergen: University of Bergen/Society of Danish Language and Literature, first appeared online 2015, accessed 30 November 2016, http://holbergsskrifter.dk/holberg-public/view?docId=niels_klim%2FPraefApol.page&toc.depth=1&brand=&chunk.id=start&show.second=komm.

Velle, Thomas. "Telling True Lies. Metanarration, Intertextuality and (Un)Reliability in Holberg's *Iter Subterraneum*." *European Journal of Scandinavian Studies* 46.2 (2016), pp. 215–33.

Walkowitz, Rebecca L. *Born Translated. The Contemporary Novel in an Age of World Literature.* New York: Columbia University Press, 2015.

Walkowitz, Rebecca L. "Comparison Literature." *New Literary History* 40.3 (2009), pp. 567–82.

Waquet, Françoise. *Le latin, ou, l'empire d'un signe: XVIe–XXe siècle.* Paris: Albin Michel, 1998.

Weber, Henry William. "Introduction." In *Popular Romances: Consisting of Imaginary Voyages and Travels.* Edinburgh: J. Ballantyne and company, 1812, pp. xvii–xliii.

Wyrick, Deborah Baker. *Jonathan Swift and the Vested Word.* Chapel Hill: University of North Carolina Press, 1988.

CHAPTER 6

Neo-Latin and Vernacular Translation Theory in the 15th and 16th Centuries: the 'Tasks of the Translator' According to Leonardo Bruni and Étienne Dolet

Marianne Pade

In general linguistics a vernacular is opposed to a *lingua franca*, a third-party language through which persons speaking different vernaculars not understood by each other may communicate. In this way, the relation of Latin and the vernacular is an issue innate to Renaissance society, which used Latin as a common ground for cultural, educational, diplomatic, and even economic interchange. At the same time, however, it seems somewhat ironic that the cultural movement that tried to restore Latin would coincide with the rise of the vernacular languages of Europe, which gradually left the linguistic muck to be appreciated grammatically, literarily, and culturally. Indeed, it was the rediscovery of Cicero's discussion on Rome's native refinement, the *sapor vernaculus* that led to the mother tongue being considered not as a depreciated *lingua vulgaris* but as a *sermo vernaculus* steeped in national and cultural pride.[1]

This is how Tom Deneire begins to define the complicated relationship between Neo-latin and the vernacular in his article in *Brill's Encyclopaedia of the Neo-Latin World*. He goes on to point out that "the coexistence of Latin and the vernacular(s) in early modern times is a situation of *diglossia*, in which two languages (or dialects) are used by a single community, i.e. an everyday or vernacular variety and a second, 'high' variety, only used in literary, educational, or other specific settings."[2] The question I want to address in this essay is how humanists, especially in the Italian Quattrocento, saw this situation of

---

[1] Deneire 2014a, p. 275.
[2] Deneire 2014a, pp. 275–76. Charles A. Ferguson coined the term 'diglossia' in 1959. The concept denotes a linguistic situation where two distinct varieties of the same language are used by the same individual in a complementary fashion dependent on circumstances. Ferguson 1959. I would also like to draw attention to Deneire's useful remarks in the concluding article on methodology in Deneire 2014b, pp. 302–14, and Jan Bloemendal's Introduction in Bloemendal 2015, pp. 1–14. See also the Introduction to this volume, pp. 3–5.

diglossia, and whether their understanding of it can be seen in contemporary theory of translation.[3]

Fifteenth-century Italy witnessed an explosion both in the production of Latin translations from the Greek and in theoretical writings on translation. Surprisingly, humanist translation theory is largely ignored by modern translation studies, perhaps because it repeatedly refers to the *loci classici* of ancient translation—(Ps.) Cicero's *On the Best Kind of Orator* (§14), Horace's *Art of Poetry* (vv. 133–34) and Jerome's letter to Pammachius—and so does not seem to add anything new. However, humanist theoreticians did in fact develop a well-articulated translation theory, subtly attuned to the exigencies of a trilingual translator who was a non-native speaker of the target language, and, moreover, a theory that took into account the literary and rhetorical expectations of the target culture, as well as societal developments.

1   *Diglossia* in Ancient Rome?

Around 1435, one of the most famous debates about *la questione della lingua* began in Florence, among members of the papal chancery. The question was whether the Romans in classical antiquity had one language common to all, or whether they, like contemporary Italians, lived in a situation of *diglossia* with two ways of speaking—one for men of letters, and the other for common people. It may have been the discovery of Cicero's *Brutus* some years previously that inspired the discussion about the *volgare* and its origin.[4] The main

---

3   Silvia Rizzo also argued that in Italy in the late Middle Ages, Latin and the vernacular were probably felt as variants of the same language. Rizzo 2004, pp. 51–52.

4   "Tum Brutus: Quid tu igitur, inquit, tribuis istis externis quasi oratoribus? Quid censes, inquam, nisi idem quod urbanis? Praeter unum, quod non est eorum urbanitate quadam quasi colorata oratio. Et Brutus: Qui est, inquit, iste tandem urbanitatis color? Nescio, inquam; tantum esse quendam scio. Id tu, Brute, iam intelleges, cum in Galliam veneris; audies tu quidem etiam verba quaedam non trita Romae, sed haec mutari dediscique possunt; illud est maius, quod in vocibus nostrorum oratorum retinnit quiddam et resonat urbanius. Nec hoc in oratoribus modo apparet sed etiam in ceteris. Ego memini T. Tincam Placentinum hominem facetissimum cum familiari nostro Q. Granio praecone dicacitate certare. [...] Tincam non minus multa ridicule dicentem Granius obruebat nescio quo sapore vernaculo." Cicero, *Brutus*, 170–72. ("Then Brutus: 'What status do these non-Roman orators have?' 'What do you think', I say, 'not the same as the ones from the city? Except that their speech lacks a certain tinge of urbanity.' And Brutus: 'What is this colour of urbanity?' 'I don't know. But it does exist. You will understand this when you come to Gaul; you will hear words not used in Rome—but these you will be able to forget again. The other is more important: In the voices of our orators there is simply a more urban ring or sound, and this is recognizable not in orators only but in others, too. I recall hearing Titus Tinca of Piacenza, a very amusing man,

protagonists in the debate were Leonardo Bruni and Biondo Flavio, but there were contributions by a number of other humanists, among them Antonio Loschi, Poggio Bracciolini, and Cencio de' Rustici.[5]

In a letter addressed to Leonardo Bruni, Biondo gives his version of the debate:

> There is a huge discussion in learned circles nowadays, and one which I have often taken part in, as to whether Romans delivered their speeches in our mother-tongue, i.e., the idiom common in our days in the ignorant masses without learning, or employed a regularized manner built on the use of grammar which we call Latin.[6]

According to Biondo the Romans had a monoglossic culture, but of course with variations depending on social status and other factors. Therefore public speeches, which needed to be comprehensible to everyone, could have been delivered in Latin. Bruni answered with a letter on "Whether the common people and the men of letters spoke the same language in the times of Terence and Cicero." Here he talks about language use in general and maintains that "just as now, also then there was a *volgare* different from the language of literature."[7] So at least by the mid-1430s, Bruni was convinced that some kind of *volgare* existed in ancient Rome, though not necessarily the same as in his own time. This view of the linguistic situation in ancient Rome is of course very similar to Dante's, but it is still arguable whether Bruni actually knew the *De vulgari eloquentia* that apparently was only rediscovered in the 16th century.[8]

---

engaged in a competition of wit with my friend, the herald Quintus Granius. [...] Tinca, although being quite hilarious, was overwhelmed by Granius with a sort of native refinement.") Translation in Ramminger 2010, p. 7.

5   There are two very recent editions of the relevant texts. See Biondo et al. 2015 and Marcellino/Ammanati 2015. For discussions of the implications of the debate see also Mazzocco 1993, Part One, and Ramminger 2010.

6   "Magna est apud doctos aetatis nostrae homines altercatio et cui saepenumero interfuerim contentio, maternone et passim apud rudem indoctamque multitudinem aetate nostra vulgato idiomate, an grammaticae artis usu, quod latinum appellamus, instituto loquendi more, Romani orare fuerint soliti." Biondo, *De verbis Romanae locutionis*, 1.1; English translations of the various contributions to the debate are all from Ramminger 2010. For Biondo's viewpoints, also see Marcellino 2016.

7   "Ego autem, ut nunc est, sic etiam tunc distinctam fuisse vulgarem linguam a litterata existimo." Bruni, *Epistulae*, 6.15 [6.10 M.].

8   Mazzocco 1993, pp. 30–38 and 214 n. 1. On the basis of internal evidence present in Bruni's *Vita di Dante*, Mazzocco thinks it likely that Bruni did know the *De vulgari eloquentia* directly.

Though Biondo and Bruni used the traditional *maternus* and *vulgaris* to designate the mode of speech of the uneducated, the newly discovered *Brutus* provided the term *vernaculus*, which was useful in describing both classical and contemporary urban Roman eloquence. Biondo used it when he argued "that the often-mentioned written Latin was the only idiom of the Roman population, who could feel long and short syllables in verse and were able to distinguish urban sound and native-tasting words from the small-town way of speaking."[9] Remnants of the old eloquence could still be heard in Roman women who greeted each other "in rather refined words and showing [...] a greater elegance, urbanity and typical Roman way of speech than even a few of our own townswomen could master."[10] So it was unnecessary to maintain that Latin grammar was too complicated for the ordinary people. For Biondo the refined words used by Roman women and the vernacular elegance of Roman speech show the descent of present-day *volgare* from the Latin of antiquity. Bruni too admired the eloquence of Roman women;[11] to him the *volgare* heard in the streets of Rome was an attractive and regionally established way of speaking, but it was not evidence that the *sermo maternus* once had been the sophisticated language we know from Latin literature.

The implication of this is that Bruni, the most important 15th-century Italian writer of translation theory, must have felt that he lived in a linguistic situation similar to that of ancient Rome. Like many of his contemporaries, he wrote about the decline of Latin and good letters in the centuries leading up to his own time, but he also celebrated the cultural reawakening he had witnessed during his lifetime. For instance, in *An Account of the Events of his Own Time* (*Rerum suo tempore gestarum commentarius*, after 1440), he wrote about the blossoming of letters in his youth:

---

9   "Latinitatem litteratam, de qua totiens dixi, unicum fuisse idioma romanae multitudini, quae et syllabarum brevitatem longitudinemque in versu sentiret ac urbanitatis sonum saporemque vernaculum et oppidanum genus dicendi internoscere posset." Biondo, *De verbis Romanae locutionis*, 20.5.

10 "Eas [*sc.* mulieres Romanas] saepenumero adverti, mutua salute obvianti data redditaque, bonam valetudinem ceterasque domus condiciones verbis magna ex parte litteratis vicissim interrogantes, maiorem, ut existimo, quam quae a nostrorum paucis servari possit, urbanitatis et gentis romanae vernaculi saporis proprietatem elegantiamque adhibere." Biondo, *De verbis Romanae locutionis*, 22.98.

11 "Haec illa [*sc.* matrona Romana] puro nativoque romano proferebat sermone, ita ut admodum sim equidem delectatus, cum et verba nitorem gravitatemque sententiae et pronunciatio ipsa vernaculam quandam haberet suavitatem." Bruni, *Epistulae*, 6.15 [6.10 M.].

When there was a pause in this war, the study of letters, too, flourished wonderfully, because then for the first time people became acquainted with Greek literature, which had ceased to be familiar to us as long as seven hundred years ago.[12]

Bruni repeatedly praised the richness of Latin, and he and other humanists confidently encouraged their readers to aim at the highest linguistic registers when writing in Latin. The fact that it was not their mother tongue, and therefore had to be learned, was no hindrance—as obviously it hadn't been for the ancient Romans who had lived in a similar situation of *diglossia*.

2 Bruni's Trilingual Translator

Bruni wrote about translation, in letters about his own translations and those of others, in letters of dedications, and then of course in his treatise *De interpretatione recta* (*On the correct way of translating*). Bruni was a pupil of Manuel Chrysoloras and adhered to the *ad sententiam* method of translation advocated by his revered teacher. In an often-quoted letter to Niccolò Niccoli (a. 1404), he explains the method he had followed in his recent translation of Plato's *Phaedo*. First, he describes *how* Plato is in Greek—that is, he talks about Plato's style, not the factual content of the work. Among other things he mentions his *charis*, his grace and elegance. Then Bruni explains how he goes about rendering this and formulates his golden rule:

> I stay with Plato—I have imagined him knowing Latin, so that he can form his own judgement, and I use him as authoritative witness of his move [*sc.* into Latin]; and I lead him over as I understand pleases him best. [...] Plato himself asks me to do that, for a man with a most elegant way of expressing himself among the Greeks surely does not want to appear crude and clumsy among the Latins.[13]

---

12 "Litterae quoque per huius belli intercapedines mirabile quantum per Italiam increvere, accedente tunc primum cognitione litterarum graecarum, quae septingentis iam annis apud nostros homines desierant esse in usu." Bruni, *Rerum suo tempore gestarum commentarius,* p. 431. For the humanists' own descriptions of cultural developments during the early Quattrocento, see Pade 2014.

13 "ego autem Platoni adhereo quem ego ipse mihi effinxi et quidem latine scientem, ut iudicare possit, testemque eum adhibeo traductionis sue, atque ita traduco ut illi maxime placere intelligo [...] Hoc enim ipse Plato presens me facere iubet, qui cum elegantissimi

We notice that while Plato's original audience or readers were the Greeks, the new audience to whom Bruni will present him and whom he will wish to please, are the Latins. Both groups are mentioned without any chronological indications, though in the case of the Latins Bruni must necessarily mean his own contemporaries. The juxtaposition *apud Graecos—apud Latinos* implies that Bruni expects the readers of his translation to have linguistic competences in Latin similar to those of Plato's original readers in Greek—regardless of the fact that it was not their mother tongue.

In the roughly contemporary preface to his translation of Plutarch's *Life of Marc Antony*, Bruni more explicitly discusses linguistic competences. The translation is dedicated to Coluccio Salutati. Bruni first laments the great loss of Latin literature that had described the deeds of those who had made Italy famous all over the world. Bruni promises to try to remedy this loss by translating all of Plutarch's lives, now that he knows some Greek and now that his Latin translations are on a level that even *bene litterati homines* do not despise some of his writings. This, Bruni stresses, he has only achieved after much work and with the help of Salutati—who himself strove assiduously to perfect his Latin style.[14] Bruni here openly acknowledges that to write Latin in a way that would please the *bene litterati* requires hard work.

In Bruni's terminology the adjective *litteratus* is invariably connected with Latin; in his *Life of Dante* Bruni discusses why Dante had chosen to write in Italian. Like any other language, Italian has a polished and scientific register, but still this register is not *litterato*, as becomes clear from the following passage:

---

oris apud Grecos sit, non vult certe apud Latinos ineptus videri." Bruni, *Epistulae*, 1.8 M. [1.1 L.]; translation based on that of Johann Ramminger in Ramminger 2016, p. 38.

14 "Nam cum apud Plutarchum, summae auctoritatis hominem, res gestas clarorum uirorum legeremus, quos ille praestantissimos e Graecis Romanisque delectos in paria et contentiones distribuit, doluimus profecto animaduertentes tantam apud nos scriptorum factam esse iacturam, ut nec facta maiorum nostrorum nec nomina iam eorum teneremus, per quos Italia in uniuerso orbe gloriosissime nominata esset. Nos igitur, quoniam et Graecis litteris ita operam dedimus, ut illarum non admodum simus ignari, et in Latinis ita laborauimus, ita a te adiuti sumus, ut quaedam iam a nobis transcripta etiam bene litterati homines non omnino aspernarentur, habemus quidem in animo hos omnes Plutarchi uiros, si per occupationes nostras licebit, in Latinum conuertere et famam ac gloriam summorum uirorum renouare, ut simul cum utilitate nostra, quam ex Graecorum cognitione percepimus, nostrorum quoque hominum sit coniuncta utilitas." Bruni, *praefatio in Plutarchi vitam Marci Antonii*, 22.2.2–3. For Bruni's use of *transcribere* for 'to translate,' see Ramminger 2016, pp. 37–38.

> Ciascuna lingua ha sua perfezione, e suo suono, e suo parlare limato e scientifico; pur, chi mi domandasse per che cagione Dante più tosto elesse scrivere in vulgare che in latino e litterato stilo, risponderei quello che è la verità: cioè che Dante conosceva sé medesimo molto più atto a questo stilo vulgare e in rima, che a quello latino o litterato.[15]

Later in the *Antonius* preface, Bruni answers the objection—made by some—that Latin could not match the charm and elegance of Greek. Bruni here clearly compares the Greek of the authors he translates, i.e., ancient Greek, with both contemporary and ancient Latin, or rather he does not make a distinction though he admits to feeling humbled whenever he reads Cicero. His point is that Latin is perfectly able to match Greek, if written by *homines bene litterati*. Perhaps things can be expressed in more ways in Greek, but if one translates not *ad verbum* like a school boy, but rather aims at rendering meaning, Latin will be perfectly adequate. The richness of Greek amounts to an almost excessive superabundance, whereas Latin has grace and ornament without levity.[16] Thus, according to Bruni, it is possible to acquire, also in his day and age, what amounts to a complete mastery of Latin, one that equals that of the ancient Greeks in their own language. We also notice that even though Greek and Latin have different lexical characteristics, the two languages are equally powerful. There is absolutely no need to change or develop Latin to make it match Greek as a target language. Later in the century, Lorenzo Valla went a step further than Bruni: he compared the Greek dialects to factions within the state, stating that the Latins were much better off, using one and the same language.[17]

---

15   Bruni, *Vita di Dante,* p. 12. For Bruni's *Vita di Dante*, see Gualdo Rosa 1995.
16   "At non potest—quis inquit—ea uenustate in Latinum referre, qua scriptum est Graece. At id ipsum non intelligo, cur non possit. Primo equidem non uideo, qua in re Latinae litterae a Graecis superentur, nec, si qui nostrorum hominum bene litterati fuerunt, non satis uim dicendi Graecorum aut facundiam adaequauerunt. Deinde, etsi uberiores sunt Graecae quam nostrae, quid tamen uetat, si non uerba, ut pueri in ludo, sed sententias dictorum sequamur, posse cum elegantia id ipsum Latine dicere, quod dictum sit Graece? Nam si pluribus modis illi quam nos quidlibet exprimere possunt, est illa quidem superabundantia quaedam atque luxuries. Latinitas uero nostra ut non ambitiosa neque leuis matrona mundum certe habet et supellectilem suam, non luxuriosam quidem, sed tamen opulentam et quae ad omnem usum abunde sufficiat." Bruni, *praefatio in Plutarchi vitam Marci Antonii,* 22.2.19–24.
17   "Eant nunc Greci et linguarum copia se iactent! Plus nostra una effecit, et quidem inops, ut ipsi volunt, quam illorum quinque, si eis credimus, locupletissime; et multarum gentium, velut una lex, una est lingua romana: unius Grecie, quod pudendum est, non una sed multe sunt, tanquam in republica factiones." Valla, *Elegantie,* 1 *praef.* 24.

In 1416–17 Bruni translated the *Nicomachean Ethics*. All his earlier translations had been of texts not previously translated, but the *Nicomachean Ethics* was widely known in the 13th-century version by Robert of Grosseteste. Moreover, in his preface Bruni made abundantly clear why he had undertaken a new Latin version of Aristotle's work: not because it had not been translated previously, but because it had been translated in a way that seemed barbarous and a desecration of proper Latin.[18] He criticizes the style of the old version and its lack of philological correctness that had led to factual errors of content. The old translator—whom Bruni does not name and whom he believed to be identical with the medieval translator of Aristotle's *Politics*—had repeatedly transcribed Greek words, instead of translating them, as if Latin wasn't rich enough. In general he had betrayed Aristotle's style, as we know from Cicero that his books were in fact written with great eloquence.[19] In Bruni's strictures with regard to transliteration we recognize the theme of rivalry between two prestige languages that he also took up in the preface to the *Antonius*.[20]

Bruni's translation of the *Nicomachean Ethics* and the harsh criticism of his predecessor caused quite an uproar.[21] As his final contribution to the ensuing debate, Bruni eventually wrote *De interpretatione recta* (*On the correct way of translating*, 1424–26). He first defends himself against the accusation that he had been too hard and unfair in his critique of the medieval translator, i.e., Grosseteste:

> So what did I accuse him of? Simply of not knowing Latin well enough. But, by God, what kind of censure is that? Cannot a man be honourable and at the same time have no knowledge of Latin, or not a very extensive one? I did not call him dishonourable, just a bad translator.[22]

---

18 "Aristotelis Ethicorum libros Latinos facere nuper institui, non quia prius traducti non essent, sed quia sic traducti erant, ut barbari magis quam Latini effecti uiderentur." Bruni, *praefatio in Aristotelis ethicam Nicomacheam,* p. 157.

19 Bruni, *praefatio in Aristotelis ethicam Nicomacheam,* p. 158. On Bruni's critique of the practice of transliterating Greek terms in translations and on his own vocabulary in the *Ethics* translation, see Pade, 2017.

20 Bruni's reference to Cicero for an authoritative judgement of Aristotle's style, used as an argument for his own choice of style in the translation, is part of a trend. I know a number of 15th-century translators who explain their choices by referring to ancient literary criticism, such as Cicero or Quintilian. Pade 2016b, pp. 11–16.

21 On the so-called '*Ethics* controversy,' see Hankins 2003, with earlier literature.

22 "Quid igitur in illo reprehendi? Imperitiam solummodo litterarum. Haec autem, per deum immortalem, quae tandem vituperatio est? An non potest quis esse vir bonus, litteras tamen aut nescire penitus aut non magnam illam, quam in isto requiro, peritiam

We notice that Bruni again emphasizes the knowledge of *litterae* which is the equivalent of, or the precondition for, a mastery of Latin.

Bruni then goes on to describe the *curae interpretis*, the tasks of the translator. First he must have a thorough knowledge of the source language, in this case Greek, of both lexicon and idioms. The second requirement is that the translator should have a complete command of the target language, stemming from wide and close reading of philosophers, orators, poets, and other writers, a reading that would ensure a thorough comprehension of the texts.

Up to this point, the knowledge required of the translator with regard to source and target language seems quite similar, but there are subtle differences in the vocabulary Bruni's uses in describing the first and the second "cura" ("task"), respectively. He uses the passive *peritissime scire* (be thoroughly acquainted with) with regard to source language, and the more active "tenere," "dominari," and "in potestate habere" ("comprehend, master, have in one's power") with regard to the target language. Moreover, in what follows, Bruni's advice to the translator becomes very detailed and explicit. In fact the part that deals with the target language, i.e., Latin, is much longer than the preceding part on the linguistic competence necessary in the source language. Bruni stresses that the translator should not borrow or leave a word in Greek out of ignorance of Latin ("ob ignorantiam Latini sermonis"). We remember that he criticized the old translation for the many transliterated Greek words, and that, in general, Bruni was opposed to the practice: translation from Greek into Latin was not regarded by him as a movement from a fully developed language to a less developed one; rather the process consisted of a translation between two languages with equal possibilities.[23] Another piece of specific advice he provides is that the translator must be familiar with idioms and figures of speech used by the best *auctores*; he should imitate them and avoid verbal and grammatical novelties.[24]

Bruni's phrasing thus shows that his ideal translator will write in a language that has to be learned, as would be the case with a person not writing in his mother tongue. His detailed instruction specifying that the translator must have mastery over Latin shows that such was not always the case. The very term Bruni uses to signify a person with the required linguistic proficiency, i.e., *litteratus*, indicates that the target language here is not the everyday *volgare*;

---

habere? Ego hunc non malum hominem, sed malum interpretem esse dixi." Bruni, *De interpretatione recta*, p. 83.

23   Bruni, *De interpretatione recta*, pp. 84–85.

24   "Consuetudinis vero figurarumque loquendi, quibus optimi scriptores utuntur, nequaquam sit ignarus; quos imitetur et ipse scribens, fugiatque et verborum et orationis novitatem, praesertim ineptam et barbaram." Bruni, *De interpretatione recta*, p. 86.

only if the translator is *litteratus*, if he has studied the best writers and is able to imitate them, will he be up to the task.[25]

In addition to possessing these basic requirements the translator must have a sound ear in order to discern the fullness and rhythmical qualities of the original and conserve them in the new language. Bruni uses a lot of imagery to convey this sensitive part of the translator's task; for instance, he emphasizes that the best translator considers how he may express the shape, attitude, and stance of speech of the original author, along with all his lines and colours. These elaborate specifications are followed by a long passage detailing how difficult it is to meet them if the original author had written with a sense of prose rhythm and literary polish. This is evidently a subject that greatly interested Bruni, and he shows his own attempts at meeting the tasks of the translator, some of them rather elegant.[26] Viewed in this light, it becomes especially apparent that the tract was not written for translation into the vernacular, as Italian did not have quantities and a prose rhythm to match Greek. Moreover, as Ronald Witt has shown, from Bruni's generation onwards there is a growing tendency to avoid the accentual patterns of the medieval *cursus* and a preference for a quantitative prose rhythm that has been seen as a key factor in the genesis of classicizing prose.[27] The chapter in *De interpretatione* is clearly part of the humanist attempt to recuperate that part of classical prose style.

To sum up: Bruni's advice to the translator with regard to the target language shows that he is aware that it is a language one needs to study in order to achieve the required mastery. However, although he does not refer to the relationship between the translator's mother tongue and the language used in the translation, it is clear that there is no limit to the proficiency he could achieve in that language—if only he were *bene litteratus*. I do not know if Bruni had already formed his opinion on the *diglossia* of ancient Rome when he compiled the *De interpretatione*: that is, if he already believed that in antiquity Romans lived in a situation of *diglossia* with two ways of speaking—one for men of letters, and the other for common people. By the mid-1420s he could have known Cicero's *Brutus*, which, as we saw, was probably the point of departure for the Florentine debate ten years later (and it has been suggested that the *De interpretatione* is, in fact, an attempt to systematize Cicero's thoughts as found in *Brutus, Orator*, and *De oratore*).[28]

---

25 Den Haan shows how Gianozzo Manetti, who was very much influenced by Bruni, objected to translation into the vernacular. Den Haan 2014, pp. 171–75.
26 Bruni, *De interpretatione recta*, pp. 87–89.
27 Witt 2002, pp. 509–14.
28 Norton 1981, p. 185.

If Bruni had started to think about the two languages of ancient Rome at the time he composed the *De interpretatione*, then he could have envisaged his translator as being in a position not materially different from that of ancient Roman writers. Like them, the 15th-century humanist translator used a language he had acquired, rather than his mother tongue, for cultural, educational, diplomatic, and even economic interchange.

3   Outside Italy

Outside Italy we also meet the *questione della lingua*; however when humanism crossed the Alps, the central issue more often became the hierarchy of Latin versus the vernacular. Italian humanists had been eager to point out that they—as descendants and heirs to the culture of ancient Rome—were the only true heirs to the linguistic supremacy of Rome, i.e., that only they could hope to achieve true mastery of Latin. The rest of the world was barbarian.[29] Transalpine humanists raged at the slight—and would for instance say that their language descended from one even worthier than Latin, namely Greek[30]—but the fact remains that Latin was perceived as an essentially foreign language. The choice between Latin and the vernacular entailed different arguments, and in France, for instance, a general opposition to the literary use of Latin developed during the 16th century.[31]

This dispute over the use of Latin or the vernacular also affected writings on translation theory. In the following section, I shall concentrate on Étienne Dolet's *La manière de bien traduire d'une langue en une aultre*, printed with Dolet's two small pamphlets on punctuation and accents in French, *D'advantage de la punctuation de la langue francoyse* and *Des accents d'ycelle* (Lyons, 1540).[32] Dolet was a French humanist printer and a controversial figure throughout his lifetime. His scientific scholarship aroused suspicions concerning his religious views and he was eventually arrested and burned with his books on orders of the theological faculty of the Sorbonne. In view of his championing the use of the vernacular, it is interesting that he became the opponent of Erasmus in the 'Ciceronian controversy' in which he took an ultra-Ciceronian stance, publishing in 1535 a *Dialogus de imitatione Ciceroniana*.[33]

---

29 Pade 2016a.
30 For this, see Cowling 2012, pp. 78–81 and the contribution by Ronny Kaiser to this volume.
31 Cowling 2012.
32 For Dolet's treatise, see Norton 1974 and Worth 1988.
33 For Dolet, see now Clément 2012.

According to Susan Bassnett, one of the leading modern translation scholars, Dolet was one of the first writers to formulate a theory of translation.[34] I hope that I have already shown that this is not entirely accurate; I also hope that I shall be able to demonstrate that Bruni not only formed a coherent theory of translation more than 100 years before Dolet (albeit in Latin), but also must have served as Dolet's prime source. In fact, one might say that Dolet's treatise constitutes a piece of cultural translation: Bruni's work was written for an audience that expected to hear about translation between the two prestige languages, i.e., from Greek into Latin; Dolet translated Bruni's work into a culture that had begun to reject the literary use of Latin and wanted to promote the use of the vernacular.[35]

It could be objected that Bruni's treatise apparently did not have an overwhelming diffusion. As it is, I know of only 11 manuscripts and no early prints survive. However, two of the known manuscripts are now in France, and I think that the similarities between Bruni's and Dolet's texts are too many to be incidental.[36]

In the prefatory dedication to Guillaume du Bellay, seigneur de Langey, Dolet explains his reason for having undertaken the work: his patriotic zeal was such that he would do anything to make his country famous, and there was no better way to do that than celebrating its language, as the Greeks and Romans had done.[37] For Dolet the Greeks and Romans remained models, even though he purportedly rejected their language. He goes on to make a more pointed defence of the vernacular: he follows in the footsteps of the ancients, who all wrote in their mother-tongue; Homer, Plato, Aristotle and Thucydides [...] among the Greeks, and among the Romans Cicero, Caesar, Sallust, Vergil, etc. None of them would abandon their mother tongue to achieve fame in another language. Among modern writers, a number had undertaken something similar [to Dolet's enterprise]: Bruni, Sannazaro, Petrarch, Pietro Bembo (among the Italians), and in France, Guillaume Budé, Charles de Bovelles, and Jacques Dubois (Sylvius).[38] A common effort was required; it had taken more

---

34 Bassnett 2014, p. 53.
35 For the concept of cultural translation, see Burke/Po-chia Hsia 2009.
36 Also see Norton 1984, p. 203.
37 "Mais à cecy je donne deux raisons: l'une, que mon affection est telle envers lhonneur de mon païs que je veux trouver tout moyen de l'illustrer. Et ne le puis myeulx faire que de celebrer sa langue, comme ont faict Grecs et Rommains la leur." Dolet, *Manière*, p. 3.
38 "L'autre raison est, que non sans exemple de plusieurs je m'addonne à ceste exercitation. Quant aux antiques tant Grecs que Latins, ilz n'ont prins aultre instrument de leur eloquence que la langue maternelle. De la Grecque seront pour tesmoing Demosthene, Aristote, Platon, Isocrate, Thucydide, Herodote, Homere. Et des Latins je produis Ciceron, Cæsar, Salluste, Virgile, Ovide, lesquelz n'ont delaissé leur langue pour estre renommez

than one man to make Greek and Latin into languages "reduced to technique" ("reduire la langue Grecque et Latine en art," Dolet, *Manière*, p. 4), an expression that Glyn B. Norton explains as "analytical in structure and generated in artificial clausal patterns."[39] However, by the work of learned men, French could gradually reach the same state of perfection.[40]

Though Dolet does not dwell upon it, it is clear that he is on Biondo's side in the language question (whether he knew it or not). The admired writers of Greece and Rome composed their immortal works in their mother tongue ("langue maternelle"). Only by the accumulated efforts of the learned did their respective languages develop into regulated, cultured languages. Thus, Dolet does not imagine that a situation of *diglossia* had existed in ancient Rome or Athens, nor is that what he wished for in France. Instead he hoped that French would acquire the registers possessed by the two prestige languages, and one way to achieve that was through translation. Hence, *La manière de bien traduire*.

Dolet's tract is much shorter than Bruni's *De interpretatione*, but, *mutatis mutandis*, it treats the same subject matters in the same order. Translation, Dolet says, requires five things:[41] the first is a perfect understanding of the sense and subject matter of the original. As an example, Dolet cites a complicated passage from Cicero's *Tusculans*; Bruni had shown how the medieval translator's philological mistakes led to a misunderstanding of Aristotle's text. The second point is that the translator must have perfect comprehension of the source language and a perfect command of the target language, with regard to vocabulary, figures of speech, etc. The same requirements are, as shown above, found in the *De interpretatione*. Like Bruni, Dolet dislikes word-for-word translation, which he finds a sign of poor intellect. Instead, the translator must be faithful to the author's intention; he should translate meaning and observe the *proprietates* of both languages ("gardant curieusement la proprieté de l'une et l'autre langue," *Manière*, p. 13). We remember the many images used by Bruni

---

en une autre. Et ont mesprisé toute autre sinon qu'aucuns des Latins ont apris la Grecque afin de scavoir les arts et disciplines traictées par les autheurs d'icelle. Quant aux modernes, semblable chose que moy a faict Leonard Aretin, Sannazare, Petrarque, Bembe (ceux cy Italiens), et en France Budée, Bouille, et maistre Jacques Sylvius." Dolet, *Manière*, pp. 3–4. In the margin opposite the passage there is a note in the 1540 edition: "Aulcuns autheurs modernes illustrateurs de leur langue, tant en Italien qu'en Francoys."

39 Glyn 1984, p. 212.
40 "par le moyen et travail des gens doctes elle pourra estre reduicte en telle parfection que les langues dessudictes." Dolet, *Manière*, p. 4.
41 Dolet, *Manière*, pp. 11–16.

to explain how one should be faithful to the intentions of the original author and preserve the *proprietates* of both languages.

Bruni repeatedly criticized linguistic borrowing, i.e., transliterations of Greek words in Latin translations. According to him it was not only regrettable, but also completely unnecessary, as Latin was as rich a language as Greek. In the parallel passage in *Manière*, Dolet must use different arguments, and it is here where we perhaps most clearly see the cultural translation of Latin humanist translation theory into a vernacular context. For, says Dolet, when the target language is not "reduced to technique" (i.e., analytical in structure and generated in artificial clausal patterns)—as Italian, Spanish, German, English and even French were not—and the source language (for instance Latin), is, the translator must take care not to borrow from it and or to use words not previously used in the target language.[42]

Bruni's tract ended with a discussion about translation of prose rhythm and figures of speech, and so does *Manière*. This may be yet another instance of the vernaculars being described and analysed with a terminology and in categories that pertain to the ancient prestige languages, first and foremost Latin. French does not and did not have prose rhythm based on quantity. However, this hallmark of elegant Latin prose, which had been reintroduced by 15th-century Italian humanists, was, so to speak, a *sine qua non* of a cultured language, and it seems that Dolet wanted to claim it for French. According to Carine Skupien Dekens, he was not the only one; in his *Défense et illustration de la langue française* (1.9). Du Bellay also maintained that prose rhythm based on quantity was applicable to French.[43]

To my mind there is no doubt that Dolet was deeply influenced by Bruni's translation theory; as already noted, the two treatises discuss the same points in roughly the same way and in the same order. The main differences stem from their different language situations and their stances towards these situations.

---

42 "La quatriesme reigle que je veulx bailler en cest endroict, est plus a observer en langues non reduictes en art, qu'en autres. J'appelle langues non reduictes encores en art certain et repceu: comme est la Francoyse, l'italienne, l'Hespaignole, celle d'Allemaigne, d'Angleterre, et autres vulgaires. S'il advient doncques que tu traduises quelque livre Latin en icelles, mesmement en la Francoyse, il te fault garder d'usurper mots trop approchans du Latin, et peu usitez par le passé: mais contente toy du commun, sans innover aucunes dictions follement, et par curiosité reprehensible." Dolet, *Manière*, pp. 16–17. For the attempts at Latinization of French syntax, see Skupien Dekens 2009, pp. 148–50.

43 Skupien Dekens 2009, pp. 141–43. By the time of François de Fénelon (1651–1715) this idea was no longer pursued. In his *Lettre à l'Académie*, printed only after his death in 1716, he mentions the lack of quantities in French as a characteristic that necessarily made French poetry different from that of Greece or Rome. For this, see Florian Schaffenrath's essay in this volume.

Bruni—who saw Italian Quattrocento humanist culture as being in a situation of *diglossia* similar to that of ancient Rome—could use his treatise as yet another call to adhere to the linguistic standards of ancient Latin, the standards of the *homines bene litterati*. Dolet's treatise is also about the target language, but it was not yet "reduced to technique" or *litterata*. That had yet to happen—or, in the words of Tom Deneire, French was only beginning to leave "the linguistic muck to be appreciated grammatically, literarily, and culturally."[44]

Bibliography

Primary Sources

Biondo Flavio. *De verbis Romanae locutionis*, edited by Fulvio Delle Donne. Rome: Istituto Storico Italiano per il Medio Evo, 2008.

Bruni, Leonardo. *An vulgus et literati eodem modo per Terentii Tulliique tempora Romae locuti sint*. In idem., *Epistolarum libri VIII*, edited by Laurentius Mehus, vol. 2. Florence: Bernardus Paperinius, 1741, pp. 62–68.

Bruni, Leonardo. *De interpretatione recta*. In *Leonardo Bruni Aretino, Humanistisch-Philosophische Schriften*, edited by Hans Baron. Leipzig: Teubner, 1928, pp. 81–96.

Dolet, Étienne. *La manière de bien traduire d'une langue en une aultre. D'advantage de la punctuation de la langue Francoyse, Plus. Des accents d'ycelle*. Lyon: Dolet, 1540.

Secondary Sources

Bassnett, Susan. *Translation Studies*, 4th ed. London: Routledge, 2014.

Bloemendal, Jan, ed. *Bilingual Europe. Latin and Vernacular Cultures. Examples of Bilingualism and Multilingualism c. 1300–1800*. Leiden: Brill, 2015.

Burke, Peter and R. Po-chia Hsia, eds. *Cultural Translation in Early Modern Europe*. Cambridge, Eng.: Cambridge University Press, 2007.

Castor, Grahame and Terence Cave. *Neo-Latin and the Vernacular in Renaissance France*. Oxford, Eng.: Clarendon Press, 1984.

Cowling, David. "Constructions of Nationhood in the Latin Writings of Henri Estienne." In *The Role of Latin in the Early Modern World: Linguistic identity and nationalism 1350–1800*, edited by Alejandro Coroleu, Carlo Caruso, and Andrew Laird. *Renæssanceforum* 8 (2012), pp. 71–86.

Clément, Michèle, ed. *Étienne Dolet 1509–2009*. Geneva: Droz, 2012.

---

44 Deneire 2014a, p. 275.

Deneire, Tom. "Neo-Latin and the Vernacular: Methodological Issues." In *Brill's Encyclopaedia of the Neo-Latin World*, edited by Philip Ford, Jan Bloemendal, and Charles Fantazzi, vol. 1. Leiden: Brill, 2014a, pp. 275–86.

Deneire, Tom, "Conclusion: Methodology in Early Modern Multilingualism," in *Dynamics of Neo-Latin and the Vernacular. Language and Poetics, Translation and Transfer*, edited by Tom Deneire. Leiden: Brill, 2014b, pp. 302–14.

den Haan, Annet. "Translation into the *Sermo Maternus*: The View of Gianozzo Manetti (1396–1459)." In *Dynamics of Neo-Latin and the Vernacular. Language and Poetics, Translation and Transfer*, edited by Tom Deneire. Leiden: Brill, 2014, pp. 163–76.

Ferguson, Charles A. "Diglossia." *Word* 15 (1959), pp. 325–40.

Gualdo Rosa, Lucia. "Leonardo Bruni e le sue 'vite parallele' di Dante e del Petrarca." *Lettere Italiane* 47.3 (1995), pp. 386–401.

Hankins, James. "The *Ethics* Controversy." In *Humanism and Platonism in the Italian Renaissance*, edited by James Hankins, vol. 1. Rome: Edizioni di storia e letteratura, 2003, pp. 193–239.

Marcellino, Giuseppe. "Biondo Flavio e le origini del volgare." In *A New Sense of the Past. The Scholarship of Biondo Flavio 1392–1463*, edited by Angelo Mazzocco and Marc Laureys. Leuven: Leuven University Press, 2016, pp. 35–53.

Marcellino, Giuseppe and Giulia Ammanati. *Il latino e il 'volgare' nell'antica Roma. Biondo Flavio, Leonardo Bruni e la disputa umanistica sulla lingua degli antichi Romani*. Pisa: Edizioni della Normale, 2015.

Mazzocco, Angelo. *Linguistic Theories in Dante and the Humanists. Studies of Language and Intellectual History in Late Medieval and Early Renaissance Italy*. Leiden: Brill, 1993.

Norton, Glyn P. "Translation Theory in Renaissance France: Étienne Dolet and the Rhetorical Tradition." *Renaissance and Reformation / Renaissance et Réforme* 10.1 (1974), pp. 1–13.

Norton, Glyn P. "Humanist Foundations of Translation Theory (1400–1450): A Study in the Dynamics of Word." *Canadian Review of Comparative Literature—Revue Canadienne de Littérature Comparée* 8.2 (1981), pp. 173–203.

Norton, Glyn P. *The Ideology and Language of Translation in Renaissance France and their Humanist Antecedents*. Geneva: Droz, 1984.

Pade, Marianne. "From medieval Latin to neo-Latin." In *Brill's Encyclopaedia of the Neo-Latin World*, edited by Philip Ford, Jan Bloemendal, and Charles Fantazzi. Leiden: Brill, 2014, pp. 5–19.

Pade, Marianne. "In Gallos: Renaissance Humanism and Italian Cultural Leadership." In *Latin and the Early Modern World. Linguistic Identity and the Polity from Petrarch to the Habsburg Novelists*, edited by Trine Hass, Noreen Humble, and Marianne Pade. *Renæssanceforum* 10 (2016a), pp. 35–47.

Pade, Marianne. "Translating Thucydides: the Metadiscourse of Italian Humanist Translators." In *The Metadiscourse of Italian Humanism*, edited by Annette den Haan. *Renæssanceforum* 11 (2016b), pp. 1–22.

Pade, Marianne. "Popular Government Revisited: New Texts on Greek Political History and Their Influence in Fifteenth-Century Italy." *Neulateinisches Jahrbuch* 19 (2017), pp. 313–38.

Raffarin, Anne, ed. *Flavio Biondo, Leonardo Bruni, Poggio Bracciolini, Lorenzo Valla. Débats humanistes sur la langue parlée dans l'Antiquité*. Paris: Belles Lettres, 2015.

Ramminger, Johann. *Neulateinische Wortliste. Ein Wörterbuch des Lateinischen von Petrarca bis 1700* (2003–; http:www.neulatein.de).

Ramminger, Johann. "Humanists and the Vernacular. Creating the Terminology for a Bilingual Universe." In *Latin and the Vernaculars in Early Modern Europe*, edited by Trine Arlund Hass and Johann Ramminger. *Renæssanceforum* 6 (2010), pp. 1–22.

Ramminger, Johann. "Language Change in Humanist Latin: the case of *traducere* (to translate)." *Analecta Romana Instituti Danici* 40–41 (2015–16), pp. 35–62.

Rizzo, Silvia. "I latini dell'umanesimo." In *Il latino nell'età dell'umanesimo. Atti del Convegno Mantova, 26–27 ottobre 2001*, edited by Giorgio Bernardi Perini. Florence: Olschki, 2004, pp. 51–95.

Skupien Dekens, Carine. *Traduire pour le peuple de Dieu. La syntaxe de la phrase française dans la traduction de la Bible par Sébastien Castellion, Bâle, 1555*. Geneva: Droz, 2009.

Steiner, George. *After Babel: Aspects of Language and Translation*. London, Eng.: Oxford University Press, 1975.

Witt, Ronald G. *'In the Footsteps of the Ancients.' The Origins of Humanism from Lovato to Bruni*. Leiden: Brill, 2000.

Worth, Valérie. *Practising Translation in Renaissance France. The Example of Étienne Dolet*. Oxford, Eng.: Oxford University Press, 1988.

CHAPTER 7

Ariosto *Latine Redditus*: Early Modern Neo-Latin Rewritings of the *Orlando Furioso*

Francesco Lucioli

> La popolarità ch'ebbe in Italia il poema ariostesco nel secolo in cui fu composto, è attestata, oltre che dal numero stragrande delle edizioni [...], da sei ordini di fatti, che sono: i versi in lode dell'opera [...]; il lavoro degli editori e degl'interpreti [...]; il lavoro degl'incisori [...]; le traduzioni in latino e i travestimenti in dialetto od in istile burlesco; i pezzi di musica su parole di esso; e finalmente le innumerevoli aggiunte, continuazioni ed imitazioni.[1]

According to Francesco Foffano, the success of Ludovico Ariosto's *Orlando furioso* in the 16th century is attributable, among other reasons, to its translations into Latin and its rewritings in dialect or parody. This statement is rather intriguing; not only because Foffano considered Latin translations and parodies of the *Furioso* (in both dialect and the vernacular) at the same level, but also because he admitted that: "i bibliografi citano una sola versione in latino del *Furioso* nel Cinquecento, opera di un tal Visito Maurizi da Montefiore (Osimo, 1570), sebbene il Ferrazzi asserisca essere state vane le sue ricerche per scoprirne un esemplare."[2] Foffanno was referring to the *Bibliografia ariostesca* by Giuseppe Jacopo Ferrazzi, where the translation by Visito Maurizio (which Ferrazzi could not read first hand) was presented as the only 16th-century Latin rewriting of the *Furioso*.[3] This same translation, made "in versi esametrici latini da Visito Maurizi da Montefiore,"[4] is further listed in both the *Annali delle edizioni e delle versioni dell'* Orlando furioso, published in 1861 by Ulisse Guidi, and in the *Annali delle edizioni ariostee*, published in 1933 by Giuseppe Agnelli and Giuseppe Ravegnani.[5] However, none of these bibliographers had the opportunity to consult this work directly. In her *La fortuna dell'* Orlando furioso

---

1 Foffano 1897, p. 60.
2 Ibid., p. 73.
3 Ferrazzi 1881, p. 165.
4 Guidi 1861, p. 169.
5 Agnelli/Ravegnani 1933, vol. 2, p. 317.

in Italia nel secolo XVI, published in 1912, Giuseppina Fumagalli also stated that she could not find any copy of this translation, "per la sua grande rarità."[6] Nevertheless, she mentioned another Neo-Latin rewriting of the *Furioso*: namely, the *Metaphorae ex Ludovico Ariosto sub numeris Latinitati redditae*.[7] Fumagalli published one of these *Metaphorae* in order to offer an example of this text, "per la sua gran rarità, non perché abbia alcun valore letterario."[8]

This is all we know so far about 16th-century Neo-Latin translations of the *Orlando furioso*. Bibliographers and scholars presented these Latin versions of the poem as rarities similar to parodic rewritings, rather than literary texts that could offer fascinating insights into the canonization of Ariosto's work.[9] It is, therefore, necessary to reassess the Neo-Latin reception of the *Furioso*, in order to understand not only the value and meaning of its translations, but also the function of these texts in contemporary debates about chivalric and epic poetry. For this reason, the present analysis will focus on booklets containing extended examples of Neo-Latin adaptations of the *Furioso*, rather than single poems or short examples of translation by different authors, with the aim of highlighting not only the strategies employed by the translators in rendering the poem into Latin, but also the links between these texts and contemporary rewritings of and commentaries on the poem in the vernacular.[10]

In 1574, Guy du Faur de Pibrac published his *Cinquante quatrains, contenans préceptes et enseignemens utiles pour la vie de l'homme*,[11] a book which had an immediate success. It was republished several times, rewritten in enlarged editions, and even translated into both Greek and Latin, for example, by Florent Chrestien (1584), Augustin Prévost (1584), Jean Richard de Dijon (1585), and Volrad von Plessen (1588). The latter is the author of a translation printed in

---

6   Fumagalli 1912, p. 207.
7   This text was also mentioned by Ferrazzi 1881, p. 148, among the anthologies of lines or octaves of the *Furioso*.
8   Fumagalli 1912, p. 207; this example is published in Appendix I, pp. 1–11.
9   On this topic see Javitch 1991.
10 Among the short examples of translation of the *Furioso* there are two anonymous octaves preserved in ms. Ashb. 436 (fol. 271v), Biblioteca Medicea Laurenziana, Florence (I would like to thank Marco Faini for his help), and two other stanzas (attributed to Niccolò d'Arco and Annibale Cruceo) published in the collection of *Delitiae CC Italorum poetarum*, vol. 1, respectively pp. 257 and 861. A free translation "ex Ariosti materno carmine" ("from Ariosto's mother tongue") in 53 Latin hexameters of Ariosto's invective against fire-arms (in canto IX) was written by Achille Bocchi and preserved by Rota, *De tormentariorum vulnerum natura*, pp. 4–6. Kristeller also mentions the "fragments of a Latin version of the *Orlando furioso*, attributed to Raffaele Fagnani," preserved in ms. V 44 sup at the Biblioteca Ambrosiana in Milan. Kristeller 1992, vol. 6, p. 61. These texts will be the topic of another contribution on the reception of the *Orlando furioso*.
11 Pibrac, *Cinquante quatrains*.

Herborn by Christoph Rab with the title *Praecepta ethica, sive regulae vitae*.[12] Nevertheless, on the front page of this edition we can read that the text by Guy du Faur de Pibrac is followed by a curious work by Plessen: *Moralia quaedam Ludovici Ariosti celeberrimi apud Italos poetae in versus heroicos Latinos conversa*.[13] This text, published with continuous pagination except for its title page, offers a Neo-Latin version of some octaves from the *Furioso*, in which "singulis octonariis Italicis (vulgo Italice *octave* sive *stanze* vocantur) singuli octo versus heroici Latini et numero et sensu respondent."[14]

Plessen did not simply translate Ariosto's octaves in stanzas of eight hexameters; rather, he made an accurate selection of the original text, in order to present the *Orlando furioso* as a collection of moral precepts (*Moralia*). For this reason, he did not translate the poem in its entirety, but only a few stanzas from some specific cantos: IV, 1; V, 1–3; VI, 1; XV, 1; XVII, 1; XVIII, 1–2; XIX, 1; XXI, 1–2; XLIII, 1–3; XXIII, 1; XLIV, 1; XXX, 1; XXIX, 1. Plessen chose only the first octaves of 13 selected cantos, which offered him the opportunity to discuss topics such as simulation, envy, violence, human and divine justice, faith, greed, generosity, instinct, and reason. Plessen stressed the moral function of the proems of Ariosto's cantos, and omitted all the other proems not related to this moral perspective; namely, the stanzas focused on myth, history, or chivalric matter (I, III, VII, VIII, XII, XIII, XIV, XXXII, XXXIII, XXXIV, XXXV, XXXVI, XXXIX, XL, XLV, XLVI), as well as the octaves dedicated to hendiadys love (II, IX, X, XI, XVI, XXIV, XXV, XXXI, XLI, XLII) and women (XX, XXII, XXVI, XXVII, XXVIII, XXXVII, XXXVIII), a topic which is present in the *Orlando furioso* from its first line ("Le donne, i cavalieri, l'arme, gl'amori").

A case in point is Plessen's *Morale* XIII, which is a translation of the first octave of Ariosto's canto XXIX:

O degli uomini inferma e instabil mente!	O infirmam hominum mente, o variabile pectus!
come siàn presti a variar disegno!	Quanta consilium levitate inceptaque mutant!
Tutti i pensier mutamo facilmente,	Quod placuit modo post momentum displicet horae;

---

12   Pibrac, *Praecepta ethica*.
13   Plessen, *Moralia*. I quote from the copy preserved in the Universitäts- und Landesbibliothek Sachsen-Anhalt (VD16 P 2559). On Plessen see Wieden 2001.
14   "the single stanzas in the Italian vernacular (which are called *ottave* or *stanze* in Italian) are translated in stanzas which consist of eight Latin hexameters." Plessen, *Moralia*, p. [28].

più quei che nascon d'amoroso sdegno.	praecipue si intus Veneris cor roditur igni.
Io vidi dianzi il Saracin sì ardente	Adversus muliebre genus paulo ante flagrabat
contra le donne, e passar tanto il segno,	ira odioque dolo impulsus Saracenus amicae.
che non che spegner l'odio, ma pensai	Nunc illum intuitu sic movit Olympia solo,
che non dovesse intiepidirlo mai.[15]	irarum ut flammae flammis vincantur amoris.[16]

In this stanza, Ariosto laments the feeble and unstable minds of men in order to criticize Rodomonte, the Saracen knight who blames women at the beginning of canto XXVIII, but then falls in love with Isabella at the end of the same canto. In the proem to canto XXIX, Ariosto writes in praise and defence of women, inverting the words against female nature and behaviour that we can read in the previous canto. This is a characteristic of Ariosto, who "closely reproduces a variety of well known arguments from the *querelle* [*des femmes*] tradition in the octaves of his poem."[17] If Ariosto dissimulates his own opinion, assuming an "ambiguous position in terms of gender-related issues,"[18] Plessen's translations seem completely unrelated to this debate. In his version this stanza, which is also the final one in this short collection of Neo-Latin octaves, becomes a much more general reflection on human inconstancy, with no references to women or feminist topics.

Moreover, in order to make these lines understandable to his readership, Plessen had to directly refer to the protagonists of the episode: namely, the *Saracenus* Rodomonte but also Olimpia, who can change the feelings of the pagan knight with a simple look. We do not find this reference in the original stanza, though it is not an invention by Plessen; rather, it is a translation from another octave of the same proem, where Ariosto states, referring to Rodomonte's sudden change of mind: "poi d'Issabella un sguardo sì l'ha tocco, / che

---

15   Ariosto, *Orlando furioso*, XXIX, 1.
16   "O feeble and unstable minds of men! / How easily our intentions change! / After a few moments we dislike what we used to like before, / particularly if our hearts burn for love. / So wroth I saw the Saracen with the woman, / so outrageous in his hate for his friend. / And now Olimpia with a simple glance can move him so much / that the flames of his anger are won by amorous flames." Plessen, *Moralia*, p. 34.
17   Shemek 1989, p. 69.
18   Schiesari 1991, p. 125.

subito gli fa mutar sentenzia."[19] However, as is evident, the female protagonist of this canto is not Olimpia (named in the Latin translation, but absent from the poem since canto XI), but Isabella. This detail confirms that Plessen is not interested in a philological interpretation of Ariosto's text and plot. He rather aims to use the poem and its proems as outlines for his personal rewriting of the text in a moral perspective.

The *Moralia quaedam Ludovici Ariosti* can thus be considered something more than a simple exercise of translation, from the vernacular into Neo-Latin. It is intended as a complex rewriting of Ariosto's poem, following two tendencies that characterize the reception of the *Orlando furioso* in the Italian vernacular in the second half of the 16th century: on the one hand, the strong interest in the proems of the poem; on the other, the need for a moralization of Ariosto's work. These two tendencies are deeply interconnected because the *Orlando furioso* from its first appearance was included in a debate characterized by both a moral and a poetic perspective.[20] After its publication, the poem was frequently used as a source of moral precepts, as shown by a collection of *Versi morali et sententiosi di Dante, del Petrarca, di m. Lodovico Ariosto*, published in Venice in 1554, in which lines from the *Furioso* are used as mottos or proverbs. However, as stressed by Daniela Delcorno Branca, the presence of sententious and moral proems is a characteristic of Ariosto's style that differentiates his poem from previous epic and chivalric traditions.[21] Therefore, the proems of the *Furioso* were frequently considered to be expressions of Ariosto's ethics. A case in point is Laura Terracina's *Discorso sopra tutti li primi canti d'Orlando furioso*, first printed in 1549.[22] In this poem, for long read as a cento, Terracina shows a great debt "to the Neapolitan tradition of the *glosa* or *tramutazione*, an originally Hispanic form," which "consisted of a short ottava rima poem incorporating lines from a source text".[23] However, if centos aim to hide their sources, which are reassembled into new texts endowed with different meanings, Terracina's *Discorso* imports the context of Ariosto's proems together with his stanzas and lines. This means that the *Discorso* is not just a form of rewriting; rather, it is a real gloss of the *Furioso*, aimed at offering a range of critical, moral, and allegoric interpretations of the poem.

Terracina's work had an immediate and enormous success. It was repeatedly republished in the 16th century, and even read in some Venetian schools in the

---

19 Ariosto, *Orlando furioso*, XXIX, 3, 5–6.
20 Jossa 2009, p. 127.
21 Delcorno Branca 2011.
22 Terracina, *Discorso* (see also the recent modern edition, Terracina, *Discorsi*). On this text see Cosentino 2005, and Lucioli forthcoming.
23 Cox 2008, p. 110.

second half of the century.[24] Because it revealed a strong commitment to offering moral readings of the poem, which precede much more erudite works—such as Simon Fornari's *Spositione sopra l'Orlando furioso* (1549) and Orazio Toscanella's *Bellezze del Furioso* (1574). It often popularized the rich paratextual material that accompanied the editions of the *Furioso* and included comments on the text and allegories designed to explain the meaning of Ariosto's verses. The same interest also characterizes Plessen's poetic version, in which Neo-Latin is adopted as a means to further stress and legitimize the moral nature of the proems of the *Furioso*. It is exactly this ethical perspective that explains the reason why both the Catholic Terracina and the Protestant Plessen focused on the same portions of the poem; although working independently of one another, both authors intended to offer a moral interpretation of the *Furioso* based on all (Terracina) or some of (Plessen) the first octaves of the poem. Therefore, a very similar approach characterizes the reception and rewriting of the proems of the *Orlando furioso* in both the vernacular and Neo-Latin; and these publication histories provide a significant example of the extraordinary success of these parts of the texts, which were also frequently translated not only into other dialects, but also into music.[25]

Terracina's *Discorso* and Plessen's *Moralia quaedam Ludovici Ariosti* are not simple comments on the *Furioso*; rather, they are original texts that use Ariosto's poem as a common basis for creating different poems. We can thus include both these works in that 'productive' or 'creative' reception of the poem, which Klaus Hempfer has described as the creation of new texts on the basis of a common source (that is, Ariosto's poem).[26] According to Hempfer, this kind of reception must be distinguished from the so-called 'explicit' reception of the work, which deals instead with the commentaries and the paratextual apparatus of the *Orlando furioso*. Nevertheless, these two lines of reception are not completely independent but are strongly interconnected, particularly in the case of the Neo-Latin rewritings of the poem.

The above-mentioned work by Visito Maurizio da Montefiore, frequently quoted (though never read) by bibliographers and scholars, represents another example of this 'creative' reception of the *Orlando furioso*. Teacher and author of an *Epitome in Publii Ovidii Nasonis Metamorphoses* printed in Rimini in 1562, Maurizio published in 1570 two different Neo-Latin versions of the *Orlando furioso: Rolandi Furiosi liber primus Latinitate donatus*, which is a translation in hexameters of the first canto of the poem, with a dedication to Angelo Ferretti

---

24   Grendler 1989, p. 299.
25   See, for example, Di Cataldo, *Tutti i principii*.
26   Hempfer 1997, p. 11.

from Ancona;[27] and *Rolandi Furiosi cantus cuiusque principia Latinitate donata*, which is a translation of all the first octaves of all the cantos of the poem, with a dedication to the senate of Ancona.[28]

Both Plessen and Maurizio used the hexameters to translate Ariosto's hendecasyllables. While Plessen created stanzas of eight lines, however, Maurizio composed stanzas with a different number of lines, from four to nine. The first canto of the *Furioso*, for example, which originally consists of 648 hendecasyllables, is translated into 590 hexameters. Moreover, compared to the *Moralia quaedam Ludovici Ariosti*, the translations by Maurizio demonstrate a stronger attention toward classical literature, as shown by the rewriting of the first octave of the *Furioso* (which is identical in both poems by Maurizio):

Le donne, i cavallier, l'arme, gli amori,	Arma virosque cano fortes et maxima gesta,
le cortesie, l'audaci imprese io canto,	ingenuosque hominum primatum tempore amores,
che furo al tempo che passaro i Mori	Aphrica quo fervens iuvenilibus excita curis
d'Africa il mare, e in Francia nocquer tanto,	Regis Agramantis traiecit classe parata
seguendo l'ire e i giovenil furori	ad gelidas Arctos, ubi Gallia littora pandit,
d'Agramante lor re, che si diè vanto	Gallia dives opum studiisque, asperrima belli,
di vendicar la morte di Troiano	Troiani cupiens ulcisci funera patris:
sopra re Carlo imperator romano.[29]	hic iuvenis Carolo bellum iam indixerat atrox,
	Romanum imperium Gallus rex iste gerebat.[30]

---

27   Maurizio, *Rolandi Furiosi liber primus*.
28   Maurizio, *Rolandi Furiosi cantus cuiusque principia*. Both poems are preserved in the Vatican Library (Stamp.De.Luca.v.51, respectively int. 3 and 4).
29   Ariosto, *Orlando furioso*, I, 1.
30   "I sing of arms and the strong men, the great feats / and the pure loves of noble men, / at the time when Africa, led by the juvenile rage / of its king Agramante, crossed with its fleet / the sea and reached the shore of France / (which is rich in wealth, and savage in pursuit of war), / in order to avenge the death of Agramante's father Troiano; / the young

As in the *Moralia* by Plessen, we do not find any reference to women in this first stanza, while the *amori* ("loves") are placed at the end of the second line. Nevertheless, the goal of Maurizio is different from Plessen's: Maurizio aimed to offer a classical rather than a moral reading of Ariosto's poem. Considering this simple octave, we can recognize *tesserae* and *iuncturae* from Virgil's *Aeneid*[31] but also from Ovid's *Metamorphoses*,[32] and Justin's *Historiae Philippicae*.[33] It is evident that Maurizio intended to present the *Orlando furioso* as an epic rather than a chivalric poem. This was the same goal of some contemporary editors and printers of Ariosto's poem, who frequently promoted the *Orlando furioso* as a classical poem in the lively debate on literary genres stimulated by the translation of Aristotle's *Poetics* and the publication of both Ariosto's work and Torquato Tasso's *Gerusalemme liberata*.[34] The difference between the *Moralia* by Plessen and the two *Rolandi Furiosi* by Maurizio is therefore the same difference that we find in the commentaries to Ariosto's poem written by Girolamo Ruscelli (for the edition printed by Vincenzo Valgrisi in 1556) and by Lodovico Dolce (for the edition printed by Giovanni Giolito in 1542).[35] While the allegories and the *annotationi* by Ruscelli aimed to present the *Orlando furioso* as a moral poem, Dolce's annotations instead were meant to describe the text as a classic.[36] For both Dolce and Maurizio, the 'classicity,' rather than the morality of the *Furioso* is at the basis of its canonization; and in Maurizio's text the choice of the Neo-Latin language is a further way to stress this reading of the poem.

Moreover, Maurizio's attempts to promote the *Orlando furioso* as a classic rather than a modern poem reminds us not only of Dolce's editions, but also his translation in *ottava rima* of Ovid's *Metamorphoses*, published in Venice in 1553. As stressed by Daniel Javitch, the translation of the *Metamorphoses* published by Dolce (together with Giovanni Andrea dell'Anguillara) in the second half of the 16th century revealed the influence of Ariosto's poem in both "the verse form and the editorial presentation"[37] of the book. In Lodovico Dolce's and Giovanni Andrea dell'Anguillara's works, Ovid is translated into the

---

king waged a dreadful war against Charlemagne, / the French king of the Roman empire." Maurizio, *Rolandi Furiosi liber primus*, 1, 1, fol. A3r.

31 Maurizio, *Rolandi Furiosi liber primus*, l. 1, and Virgil, *Aeneid* 1.1; Visito, *Rolandi Furiosi liber primus*, l. 5, and Virgil, *Aeneid* 6.16; Visito, *Rolandi Furiosi liber primus*, l. 6, and Virgil, *Aeneid* 1.14.
32 Maurizio, *Rolandi Furiosi liber primus*, l. 3, and Ovid, *Metamorphoses* 2.179.
33 Maurizio, *Rolandi Furiosi liber primus*, l. 7, and Justin, *Historiae Philippicae* 26,1.
34 On this see Sberlati 2001.
35 Ariosto, *Orlando furioso* 1542 and 1556.
36 On this topic see Acucella 2013; Iorio 2013; Lo Rito 2013.
37 Javitch 1991, p. 78; on the topic see also Bucchi 2011.

vernacular as was Ariosto, which meant that such works followed the model (and the mode) of contemporary successful editions of the *Orlando furioso*, in order to mark a connection between the two texts. In Maurizio's work, in contrast, Ariosto's *Orlando furioso* is translated into Neo-Latin with the insertion of quotations from Latin (and particularly epic) authors, in order to legitimate its status as a classic.

If the *Rolandi Furiosi cantus cuiusque principia Latinitate donata*, which aimed at translating only the proems of the poem, reminds us of the work by Terracina (as does Plessen's text), the *Rolandi Furiosi liber primus Latinitate donatus* perfectly follows another trend that characterizes the reception of the *Furioso* in the vernacular, namely, the success of the first canto as the focus of different forms of rewriting. Usually, both spiritual versions of the *Furioso*,[38] such as *Primo canto del Furioso traslatato in spirituale* by Goro da Colcelalto (1589), *Primo canto dell'Ariosto tradotto in rime spirituali* by Cristoforo Scanello (1593), and *Il primo canto dell'Ariosto tradotto in spirituale* by Giulio Cesare Croce (1622), and its translations and parodic adaptations into different dialects[39]— among others, *Orland furius de misser Lodovic Ferraris. novament compost in buna lingua da Berghem* (1553), *La prima parte de le rime di Magagnò, Menon e Begotto in lingua rustica padovana con una tradottione del primo canto de M. Ludovico Ariosto* (1558), *Il primo canto d'Orlando furioso ridotto in lingua genovese* (1588)—focus merely on the first canto, which is therefore a real testing ground for the rewriting of the *Orlando furioso*. Once more, the Neo-Latin versions of the poem show a deep relationship with the contemporary reception of the poem in the vernacular.

However, the first canto or the first octaves of the *Furioso* were not the only parts of the poem to be translated into Neo-Latin during the 16th century: for example there is the other work cited by Giuseppina Fumagalli in her study on the reception of Ariosto's poem, namely, the *Metaphorae ex Ludovico Ariosto, sub numeris Latinitati redditae*, published by the Veronese nobleman Antonio Dionisi in 1599.[40] An author of pastoral eclogues in the vernacular, printed in Verona in 1588, and a collection of Latin odes published the following year, Dionisi translated some of the numerous metaphors and similes used by Ariosto in his poem into Neo-Latin. Dionisi's collection, addressed to his brothers Ottavio and Iacopo Dionisi, consists of 18 metaphors: the first 16 are taken from the *Furioso*, while the last two metaphors come from, respectively, a *Lamento*

---

38 Torre 2010.
39 D'Onghia 2010.
40 Dionisi, *Metaphorae*. I quote from the copy preserved in the Biblioteca Civica Aprosiana in Ventimiglia (CINQ M-3-22). I would like to thank Dr Ruggero Marro for his help.

di Figeno, that is, 19 octaves from Dionisi's own pastoral poem *Figeno*,[41] and a sonnet on the tempest ('Sembra a l'incontr'al ciel l'inferno accenda') by the Veronese Aurelio Prandini, a friend of Tasso and Marino.

According to a recent study on figurative language in the *Furioso*, Ariosto included 956 similes in his poem, more than his predecessors. Moreover, many of these figures consist of more than four lines, which is a characteristic of epic rather than chivalric poetry.[42] In his collection Dionisi included metaphors of different length, from one single octave (*metaphora* 3) to 36 stanzas (*metaphora* 7). He chose passages from the entire poem, although with particular attention to very specific portions of the text, as shown by the *Index metaphorarum* printed at the end of the book: 'In lamentatione Sacripantis' (1; *OF* I, 41–44); 'In pulchritudine Alcinae' (2; *OF* VII, 11–15); 'In deformitate Alcinae' (3; *OF* VII, 73); 'In lamentatione Olympiae' (4; *OF* X, 25–34); 'In amore Angelicae et Medori' (5; *OF* XIX, 27–36); 'In notione Bradamantis et Rugerii' (6; *OF* XXII, 32–33); 'In furore Orlandi' (7; *OF* XXIII, 100–135); 'In lamentatione Isabellae' (8; *OF* XXIV, 77–86); 'In amore Fiorispinae et Rizardeti' (9; *OF* XXV, 60–69); 'In lamentatione Rodamontis' (10; *OF* XXVII, 117–121); 'In lamentatione Doralicis' (11; *OF* XXX, 32–37); 'In lamentatione Bradamantis' (12, 13, 14, 16; *OF* XXXII, 18–25; XXXII, 37–43; XXXVI, 32–34; XLIV, 57–66); 'In lamentatione Bradamantis in suo tractatu matrimonii cum Leoneae' (15; *OF* XLIV, 39–50). It is evident that Dionisi's translation focuses in particular on the *lamentationes* ("lamentations") of Ariosto's characters and especially on those of Bradamante, who is the second character of the poem for number of lines after Melissa.[43] In this way, Dionisi shows perfect awareness of the elegiac function that Ariosto attributed to this character in his poem.[44]

The presence of texts of lamentation in Dionisi's collection is another element that enables associations to be made between Neo-Latin rewritings and the vernacular reception of the *Furioso* in early modern culture. The year before her *Discorso*, Terracina published a collection of *Rime*, which included some examples of *tramutazioni* presented as "lamenti" (of Sacripante, Rodomonte, Isabella, and Bradamante, namely, the same characters chosen by Dionisi).[45] A couple of them (precisely the lamentations of Isabella and Rodomonte)

---

41   Dionisi, *Figeno*, fols. 9r–12r.
42   Copello 2013.
43   Guidicetti 2010, p. 220.
44   On this see Ferretti 2008.
45   Terracina, *Rime*, fols. 16v–18r; 18r–19r; 19v–20v; 22r–23r. Terracina also published lamentations of characters taken from the *Orlando furioso* in other collections of *Rime*: Terracina, *Rime seconde*, pp. 28–31; Terracina, *Quarte rime*, fols.. 39v–40v; Terracina, *Le seste rime*, pp. 197–227, 233–37.

were also republished autonomously and anonymously (on the front page appears the same portrait of Terracina that we find in some editions of her *Rime*, although without the indication of her name) in booklets published in the second half of the century.[46] Moreover, numerous other short books, in both dialect and the vernacular, that were printed between the 16th and the 17th century, offer excerpts or rewritings of Ariosto's lamentations: *Lamento d'Isabella della morte di Zerbino* (1579); *Lamento de Olimpia abbandonata da Bireno* (1593); *Lamento d'Isabella et di Zerbino tratto dal Furioso de l'Ariosto et più diffusamente in ottave ridotto* (c. 1595); *Lamento di Bradamante cavato dal libro dell'Ariosto al suo canto, e tradotto in lingua bolognese dal già Giulio Cesare Croce* (1617). Dionisi's *Metaphorae* are influenced by the same interest in Ariosto's lamentations that characterizes the reception of these scenes in the vernacular. The Neo-Latin translation of these specific parts of the text represents, therefore, an attempt to ennoble an editorial product (the lamentations) that was particularly successful at a popular level.

Dionisi's translations are quite literal, as shown by the shortest of his metaphors, the octave dedicated to Alcina's ugliness:

Pallido, crespo e macilente avea	Pallidus et gracilis, rugis contractus et horrens
Alcina il viso, il crin raro e canuto:	frons erat Alcinae, raraque et alba coma,
sua statura a sei palmi non giungea:	corpus et exiguum sex intra cedere palmas:
ogni dente di bocca era caduto;	exuta et penitus dentibus ora suis;
che più d'Ecuba e più de la Cumea,	plusquam Hecuba et plusquam senior Cumae sibilla
et avea più d'ogn'altra mai vivuto.	vixerat, et plusquam quaeque sub axe poli.
Ma sì l'arti usa al nostro tempo ignote,	Talibus at nobis ignotis artibus uti
che bella e giovanetta parer puote.[47]	praestitit, ut potuit pulchra puella coli.[48]

---

46   *Lamento de Isabella*.
47   Ariosto, *Orlando furioso*, VII, 73.
48   "Pale, skinny, wrinkled, horrible / was Alcina's face, and her hair sparse and white, / her stature did not surpass six spans: / from her mouth her teeth had fallen away; / she had lived more than Hecub, more than the Cumaean Sybills, / more than any other ever lived

The original octave is faithfully translated by Dionisi into a stanza of eight lines, using elegiac couplets instead of the hexameters that we found in the versions by Visito Maurizio and Plessen. Moreover, compared to previous instances of Neo-Latin translation of Ariosto's poem, Dionisi does not seem interested in enriching his work with quotations from classical authors, as we have seen in the case of *Rolandi Furiosi cantus cuiusque principia Latinitate donata*. The *iuncturae* used in the collection of *Metaphorae* are pretty ordinary (*alba coma, ignotis artibus, pulchra puella*), and the quality of these lines appears very far from that of other translations, which try to ennoble both Ariosto's poem and its Neo-Latin versions through classical quotations. Dionisi's word-for-word translation of the *Furioso*, in contrast, legitimizes the adoption in Neo-Latin poetry of figures of speech that belong to a poem in the vernacular.

Dionisi's work offers a further significant example of the practices of rewriting that characterize the reception of the *Furioso* in both Latin and the vernacular. In his *Metaphorae* Ariosto's poem is not only translated into a different language but also is presented in a different form and genre: namely, it is transformed into a useful catalogue of metaphors. Once more, the text by Dionisi reminds us of the editions of the *Orlando furioso* that were repeatedly published, particularly in Venice, between 1540 and 1560. Among the great amount of paratextual material that enriched these editions (i.e., comments on the text, allegories designed to explain the meaning of Ariosto's verses, biographies of the author, indexes of characters and episodes in the poem, collections of sources used by Ariosto, tables listing the changes made from one edition to the next), we also find a "Dimostratione delle comparationi et altre annotationi [...], con le citationi de' luoghi dall'autore imitati,"[49] which thus consists of a collection of Ariosto's similes and the classical sources at their basis. The book of the *Metaphorae ex Ludovico Ariosto, sub numeris Latinitati redditae* published by Antonio Dionisi therefore reveals a strong connection with the contemporary editorial strategies that influenced the early modern reception of the *Orlando furioso* (as we have already seen in the case of the works by Plessen and Visito).

From the 17th century there are two partial examples of Neo-Latin translation of the *Orlando furioso* that deserve to be mentioned, and both are significantly short exercises included in collections of poems, rather than autonomous booklets. The first one, listed by Ulisse Guidi in his bibliography,[50] is the translation of the first canto written by Bernardo Filippino and included in a

---

on the earth. / But she practised arts unknown to our age, / so that she could appear a lovely young woman." Dionisi, *Metaphorae*, 3, p. 15.
49   Ariosto, *Orlando furioso*, 1553, fols. Aa7r–Bb3v.
50   Guidi 1861, p. 169.

collection of *Versi e prose* by Filippino and other authors, published in Rome in 1659.[51] However, as stressed by Giuseppe Jacopo Ferrazzi, this version is not in Latin hexameters, as stated by Guidi, but in Italian hexameters.[52] This curious example of rewriting in 'barbarian metrics' is quite interesting, not only because Filippino focuses once again only on the first canto of the *Furioso*, but also because in the collection this adaptation follows the similar translations of the first cantos of Homer's *Iliad*, Virgil's *Aeneid*, Petrarch's *Africa*, Bargeo's *Syrias*, and Tasso's *Gerusalemme liberata*. It is clear that, from Filippino's perspective, the *Orlando furioso* is considered an epic rather than a chivalric poem.

The second 17th-century example of Neo-Latin translation of the *Furioso* was published 40 years after Filippino's exercise, and exactly one century after the *Metaphorae* by Dionisi, in 1699. This is the year when the Jesuit Tommaso Ceva published the *editio princeps* of his *Sylvae*. In this collection of Neo-Latin poems, we can also find a text that Tommaso wrote in praise of his brother Cristoforo and 'De eiusdem versione latina Torquati Tassi,' the Neo-Latin translation of the *Gerusalemme liberata* which Cristoforo was writing.[53] Tommaso compared Cristoforo's ability to convey Tasso's poetics with his personal inability to finish a project of Neo-Latin translation of some parts of the *Orlando furioso*. In order to demonstrate his incompetence, Ceva included in this poem an essay on his translation of Ariosto's text (28 lines containing his rewriting of the invective against the murderers of the Duke of Sora that we can read in *Furioso*, XXXVI, 7, 2–10, 4.)[54] Once again the hendecasyllables are translated with hexameters, respecting the number of lines, rather than that of the stanzas. However, these lines are neither a *proemio* which can be easily moralized, nor a metaphor which can promote a canonization of the *Furioso* as a model; rather, Tommaso Ceva chose to translate one of the poet's direct interventions into the poem, in other words, Ariosto's own voice. Nevertheless, the failure of Ceva's enterprise testifies to the risks of a translation that aimed to offer a simple reproduction of the words and the form of the text, rather than a clear moral or exegetical interpretation of it.

In the history of the early modern reception of the *Furioso* there are no Neo-Latin translations of the poem as a whole: the first complete translation is published only in 1756 by Torquato Barbolani, a member of the Arcadia Academy.[55] Rather, we have a series of experiments that we should consider, in a much

---

51   Filippino, *Versi e prose*, pp. 134–52.
52   Ferrazzi 1881, p. 165.
53   Ceva 1699, pp. 49–51.
54   On this see also Milani 2003, p. 427.
55   Ariosto, *Orlando furioso*, 1756.

more correct and appropriate way, as Neo-Latin rewritings rather than translations of the *Orlando furioso*. These texts are constantly connected to contemporary editions, their paratextual apparatus, and vernacular rewritings of the *Furioso*. They contribute, from the Neo-Latin side, to the canonization of Ariosto's poem as a classic, often following the same editorial and ideological strategies that characterized this process on the other side, the side of the vernacular. These rewritings represent, therefore, an interesting example of the reception of the *Orlando furioso* not only from both a 'creative' and an 'explicit' point of view, but also from one that illuminates the interplay between Neo-Latin and vernacular literature in early modern Europe.

Bibliography

Primary Sources

Ariosto, Ludovico. *Orlando furioso di M. Ludovico Ariosto novissimamente alla sua integrità ridotto et ornato di varie figure, con l'espositione di tutti i vocaboli et luoghi difficili che nel libro si trovano raccolte da M. Lodovico Dolce, e da lui stesso corrette et ampliate*. Venice: Gabriel Giolito, 1542.

Ariosto, Ludovico. *Orlando furioso di M. Lodovico Ariosto, ornato di nove figure et allegorie in ciascun canto, aggiutovi nel fine l'espositione de' luogi difficili et emendato secondo l'originale del proprio authore*. Venice: Giovanni Andrea Valvassori, 1553.

Ariosto, Ludovico. *Orlando furioso di M. Lodovico Ariosto, tutto ricorretto et di nuove figure adornato. Al quale di nuovo sono aggiunte le annotationi, gli avvertimenti et le dichiarationi di Girolamo Ruscelli, la vita dell'autore descritta dal signor Giovambattista Pigna, gli scontri de' luoghi mutati dall'autore doppo la sua prima impressione, la dichiaratione di tutte le favole, il vocabolario di tutte le parole oscure, et altre cose utili et necessarie*. Venice: Vincenzo Valgrisi, 1556.

Ariosto, Ludovico. *Orlando furioso di messer Lodovico Ariosto tradotto in versi latini dall'illustrissimo signor marchese Torquato Barbolani dei conti di Montauto*, 2 vols. Arezzo: Michele Bellotti, 1756.

Ariosto, Ludovico. *Orlando furioso*, edited by Cesare Segre. Milan: Mondadori, 1976.

Ceva, Tommaso. *Sylvae*. Milan: Giuseppe Pandolfo Malatesta, 1699.

Delitiae CC Italorum poetarum huius superiorisque aevi illustrium, collectore Ranutio Ghero, 2 vols. [Frankfurt]: Jonas Rosa, 1608.

Di Cataldo, Salvatore. *Tutti i principii de' canti dell'Ariosto posti in musica*. Venice: Girolomo Scotto, 1559.

Dionisi, Antonio. *Figeno egloghe pastorale*. Verona: Sebastiano Dalle Donne e Camillo Franceschini, 1588.

Dionisi, Antonio. *Metaphorae ex Ludovico Ariosto, sub numeris Latinitati redditae.* Verona: Angelo Tamo, 1599.

Filippino, Bernardo. *Versi e prose di Bernardo Filippino e d'altri.* Rome: Angelo Bernabò dal Verme, 1659.

Lamento de Isabella, con il lamento di Rodomonte, et un sonetto, et il dialogo di Caronte, et con alcune napolitane bellissime. Venice: in Frezzaria al segno della Regina, 1590.

Maurizio, Visito. *Rolandi Furiosi cantus cuiusque principia Latinitate donata.* Osimo: Astulfo Grandi, 1570.

Maurizio, Visito. *Rolandi Furiosi liber primus Latinitate donatus.* Osimo: Astulfo Grandi, 1570.

Pibrac, Guy du Faur de. *Cinquante quatrains, contenans préceptes et enseignemens utiles pour la vie de l'homme.* Paris: Gilles Gorbin, 1574.

Pibrac, Guy du Faur de. *Praecepta ethica, sive regulae vitae. [...] Interprete Volrado a Plessen Megapolitano. [...] Accesserunt moralia quaedam Ludovici Ariosti celeberrimi apud Italos poetae in versus heroicos Latinos conversa, pauca item poemata Latina eodem interprete et auctore.* Herborn: Christoph Rab, 1588.

Plessen, Volrad von. "Moralia quaedam Ludovici Ariosti celeberrimi apud Italos poetae in versus heroicos Latinos conversa." In Pibrac, *Praecepta ethica,* pp. 27–34.

Rota, Giovan Francesco. *De tormentariorum vulnerum natura et curatione liber.* Bologna: Anselmo Giaccarelli, 1555.

Terracina, Laura. *Rime.* Venice: Gabriel Giolito, 1548.

Terracina, Laura. *Discorso sopra tutti li primi canti d'Orlando furioso.* Venice: Gabriel Giolito, 1549.

Terracina, Laura. *Rime seconde.* Florence: [Lorenzo Torrentino], 1549.

Terracina, Laura. *Quarte rime.* Venice: Giovanni Andrea Valvassori, 1550.

Terracina, Laura. *Le seste rime.* Lucca: Vicenzo Busdraghi, 1558.

Terracina, Laura. *Discorsi sopra le prime stanze de' canti d*'Orlando furioso, edited by Rotraud von Kulessa and Daria Perocco. Florence: Franco Cesati Editore, 2017.

Versi morali et sentenziosi di Dante, del Petrarca, di m. Lodovico Ariosto et de molti altri autori, per utilità comune insieme raccolti, perché in essi si può imparare molte cose utili et virtuose. Venice: al segno della Speranza, 1554.

Secondary Sources

Acucella, Cristina. "'Le perfettioni di un autor profano.' Ruscelli e le allegorie dell'edizione Valgrisi (1556) del *Furioso.*" In Caracciolo/Rossi 2013, pp. 55–73.

Agnelli, Giuseppe and Giuseppe Ravegnani. *Annali delle edizioni ariostee,* 2 vols. Bologna: Zanichelli, 1933.

Bolzoni, Lina, Serena Pezzini, and Giovanna Rizzarelli, eds. *"Tra mille carte vive ancora." Ricezione del* Furioso *tra immagini e parole.* Lucca: Pacini Fazzi, 2010.

Bucchi, Gabriele. *"Meraviglioso diletto."* La traduzione poetica del Cinquecento e le Metamorfosi d'Ovidio di Giovanni Andrea dell'Anguillara. Pisa: ETS, 2011.

Caracciolo, Daniela and Massimiliano Rossi, eds. *Le sorti d'Orlando. Illustrazioni e riscritture del Furioso*. Lucca: Pacini Fazzi, 2013.

Copello, Veronica. *Valori e funzioni delle similitudini nell'Orlando furioso*. Bologna: I libri di Emil, 2013.

Cosentino, Paola. "Sulla fortuna dei proemi ariosteschi: il *Discorso sopra al principio di tutti i canti d'Orlando furioso* di Laura Terracina." *Collection de l'E.C.R.I.T.* 10 (2005), pp. 133–52.

Cox, Virginia. *Women's Writing in Italy, 1400–1650*. Baltimore, MD: The Johns Hopkins University Press, 2008.

D'Onghia, Luca. "Due paragrafi sulla prima fortuna dialettale del *Furioso*." In Bolzoni/Pezzini/Rizzarelli 2010, pp. 281–98.

Delcorno Branca, Daniela. "Ariosto e la tradizione del proemio epico-cavalleresco." *Rassegna europea di letteratura italiana* 38 (2011), 2, pp. 117–48.

Ferrazzi, Giuseppe Jacopo. *Bibliografia ariostesca*. Bassano: Tipografia Sante Pozzato, 1881.

Ferretti, Francesco. "Bradamante elegiaca. Costruzione del personaggio e intersezione di generi nell'*Orlando furioso*." *Italianistica* 37.3 (2008), pp. 63–75.

Foffano, Francesco. *Ricerche letterarie*. Livorno: Tipografia di Raffaele Giusti, 1897.

Fumagalli, Giuseppina. "La fortuna dell'*Orlando furioso* in Italia nel secolo XVI." *Atti e Memorie della Deputazione ferrarese di storia patria* 20.2 (1912), pp. 135–497.

Giudicetti, Gian Paolo. *Mandricardo e la melanconia. Discorsi diretti e sproloqui nell'Orlando furioso*. Bern: Peter Lang, 2010.

Grendler, Paul F. *Schooling in Renaissance Italy: Literacy and Learning, 1300–1600*. Baltimore, MD: The Johns Hopkins University Press, 1989.

Guidi, Ulisse. *Annali delle edizioni e delle versioni dell'Orlando furioso e d'altri lavori al poema relativi*. Bologna: Tipografia in via Poggiale n. 715, 1861.

Hempfer, Klaus W. *Diskrepante Lektüren. Die Orlando-Furioso-Rezeption im Cinquecento. Historische Rezeptionsforschung als Heuristik der Interpretation*. Stuttgart: Steiner, 1997.

Iorio, Giuseppe. "*Inventio* e *dispositio* nelle allegorie delle edizioni Giolito (1542) e Valvassori (1553)." In Caracciolo/Rossi 2013, pp. 39–53.

Javitch, Daniel. *Proclaiming a Classic: The Canonization of Orlando Furioso*. Princeton, NJ: Princeton University Press, 1991.

Jossa, Stefano. *Ariosto*. Bologna: il Mulino, 2009.

Kristeller, Paul Oskar. *Iter Italicum*, 6 vols. London/Leiden: The Warburg Institute/Brill, 1992.

Lo Rito, Claudia. "Due contendenti nell'agone del *Furioso*. Ludovico Dolce e Girolamo Ruscelli curatori del poema ariostesco." In Caracciolo/Rossi 2013, pp. 75–86.

Lucioli, Francesco. "Riscrittura come esegesi: Laura Terracina lettrice ed interprete dell'*Orlando furioso*." *Romanische Studien* (forthcoming).

Milani, Felice. "Il modello latino del Ceva nella *Gerusalemme Liberata* milanese di Domenico Balestrieri." In *Sul Tasso. Studi di filologia e letteratura italiana offerti a Luigi Poma*, edited by Francesco Gavazzeni. Rome/Padua: Antenore, 2003, pp. 415–532.

Sberlati, Francesco. *Il genere e la disputa. La poetica tra Ariosto e Tasso*. Rome: Bulzoni, 2001.

Schiesari, Juliana. "The Domestication of Woman in *Orlando Furioso* 42 and 43, or A Snake is Being Beaten." *Stanford Italian Review* 10 (1991), pp. 123–43.

Shemek, Deanna. "Of Women, Knights, Arms, and Love: The *Querelle des Femmes* in Ariosto's Poem." *Modern Language Notes* 104.1 (1989), pp. 68–97.

Torre, Andrea. "Orlando santo. Riusi di testi e immagini tra parodia e devozione." In Bolzoni/Pezzini/Rizzarelli 2010, pp. 255–79.

Wieden, Helge. "Plessen, Volrad von." In *Biographisches Lexikon für Mecklenburg* vol. 3. Lübeck: Schmidt-Römhild, 2001, pp. 186–89.

CHAPTER 8

Rewriting Vernacular Prose in Neo-Latin Hexameters: Francisco de Pedrosa's *Austriaca sive Naumachia* (1580)

Maxim Rigaux

In the preface to the *Relación de la guerra de Cipre, y sucesso de la batalla Naval de Lepanto* (1572) of Fernando de Herrera, the young poet Cristóbal Mosquera de Figueroa, born in Seville and disciple of the humanist Juan de Mal Lara, considers at length why Fernando de Herrera chose to write a historical account and not an epic to celebrate the victory at Lepanto.[1] Figueroa's reasoning is as follows:

> Porque si su intento fuera dilatarse, y hazer largos discursos, podia el autor hazerlo en verso Heroico, tan grave y numeroso, que viniera a ygualar su estilo con la grandeza del sujeto. Pero el quiso tomar esta empresa y escrevirla en oracion desatada, por huyr de las ficciones de la poesia. Porque como el fin della sea la delectacion, el fin de la historia es la pura verdad. Y para el ornato del verso por fuerça avia de aver partes que con sus fabulosas digressiones quitarian a la verdad aquellas fuerças que en la historia son tan necessarias, y le dan tanta calidad.[2]

---

1 The following study was made possible by the Research Foundation – Flanders (FWO). I also want to express my gratitude to Elizabeth Amann and Wim Verbaal for their support during the preparation of this essay.
2 "For if his intention was to expand, and to write elaborate speeches, the author could have done it in heroic verse, so solemn and numerous, that it would equate his style with the majesty of its subject. But he wanted to take this venture and write it in a free style, in order to escape the fictions of poetry. Because just as the final goal of poetry is pleasure, so the end of history is pure truth. And for the ornamentation of verse one is obliged to introduce parts that with their fabulous digressions would take away from the truth those forces that are so necessary in history and grant it so much quality." Figueroa, "Prefación," in: Herrera, *Relación*, 4–A3. The English translation from the Spanish original is mine. I have made use of the edition printed by Alonso Escrivano (BNE R. 3794), which has a slightly extended preface compared to the other known edition of the text, printed by Alonso Picardo (BNE U-2524). For more information on the two editions of Herrera's *Relación*, see Montero 2007.

It is significant that Figueroa feels he has to defend Herrera's choice of history instead of epic poetry.[3] According to Figueroa, the main difference between writing history and writing epic is one of intention: the purpose of history is absolute truth ("pura verdad") without any fantastical digressions whereas epic poetry seeks first of all to amuse the reader. "Fabuloso" is defined in the early modern Spanish dictionary of Sebastián de Covarrubias as "that which does not have any truth."[4] This does not mean that epic poetry is devoid of all truth, but rather that it requires a style appropriate to the importance of its subject. Thus, the epic genre needs fabulous digressions, which serve to give the subject its 'heroic' gravity, whereas history is characterized by a greater brevity of style. Figueroa mentions the authoritative authors of classical historiography—Herodotus, Thucydides, Sallust, and Tacitus—to illustrate the importance of concision in writing history. The fictitious digressions in poetry, however, are not to be understood as false and irrational additions to the pure truth of history, but rather as plausible (although, in the end, unreal) events that correspond to the heroic style and order of the epic poem.

As I will demonstrate in the following pages, the elaboration of this kind of fiction differs from one poet to another. A telling example of the tension between fiction and non-fiction is Luis Zapata's *Carlo Famoso* (Valencia, 1566), one of the first vernacular heroic poems written and published in early modern Spain. In a brief note to the reader ("Al lector"), the printer Joan Mey explains that he has added an asterisk next to passages that are 'ficciones.' Here, the 'ficciones' refer to the episodes that bear no direct relation to the historical sources used by the poet and are thus to be considered as clear digressions with respect to the historical source text. In this essay, I will reconsider the idea of fiction in Francisco de Pedrosa's *Austriaca sive Naumachia*. This six-book Neo-Latin epic poem on the battle of Lepanto draws on the vernacular source text of Herrera, but restructures the historical material and invents a series of 'ficciones.' In modern scholarship, the fictions are often taken for granted as

---

3 Although Spain seems to lack any serious poetic theorization until Alonso López Pinciano's 1596 *Philosophía antigua poética*, recent scholarship has pointed to conscious theoretical considerations in the Iberian peninsula as early as the mid-16th century. See, for example, Vega and Vilà 2010, which takes into account the paratexts of Iberian epic poems as a means to explore the theoretical reflections on the epic genre in Golden Age Spain.

4 "lo que no contiene verdad." Covarrubias, *Tesoro*, 394. However, the Spanish lexicographer ends his discussion of the word 'fabula' with the observation that sometimes true and truthful things are called 'fables' because of the enormous variety and apparent inventiveness. Covarrubias gives the example of the *Corónicas de las Indias*, which surpass in content what has been written in chivalric literature.

humanist syncretism or mere adornment.[5] As an alternative to the strict division between fact and fiction, I suggest that we keep in mind the classical triad of rhetorical narration: 'historia' for what has truly happened, 'argumentum' for what did not happen but might have happened, and 'fabula' for what never happened and could never happen.[6] In the Renaissance period, 'historia' came to stand for what it more or less means today; by contrast, the realm of fiction was more elusive and not considered simply the opposite of non-fiction.[7] In order to gain a better insight into Pedrosa's poetics of fiction, I will compare his epic with two vernacular texts from the same period that also take Herrera's vernacular history as their point of departure.

The *Relación* was published in Seville in the first year after the decisive naval victory of the Holy League against the Ottoman Empire, which took place on 7 October 1571.[8] The work almost immediately acquired authority as the model text for at least three Iberian epic poems: Jerónimo Corte-Real's *Felicíssima Victoria* (Lisbon, 1578), which was completed and sent as a manuscript to Philip II in 1575; Juan Rufo's *La Austríada*, printed first in Madrid in 1584, and subsequently in Toledo (1585) and Alcalá de Henares (1586); finally, Francisco de Pedrosa's *Austriaca sive Naumachia*, which was sent as a manuscript from Guatemala to the Spanish king in 1580 but never published, despite the author's fervent plea in the prologue of his work, as well as in a memorial written three years later as a reminder and promotion of the epic poem.[9] All three had to deal with the problem of reconciling historical truth with the epic form,

---

5   See Fernández de la Cotera Navarro 2003, who lists examples of pagan and Christian elements divided into two separate categories. The pagan fictions are used to cover the Christian messages.

6   This classical triad is developed in several ancient rhetorical treatises. See, e.g., Cicero, *De inventione*, 1.19.27 and Quintilian, *Institutio Oratoria*, 2.4.2. Isidore of Seville, *Etymologiae*, 1.44.5, offers three definitions that would become the standard throughout the Christian Middle Ages. For its importance in the poetics of the 12th and early 13th centuries, I refer to Mehtonen 1996. Although this classical triad is no longer repeated in early modern treatises, I believe that the triad continued to influence rhetorical thinking about fiction in the Renaissance.

7   See Bietenholz 1993, pp. 147–57, for the renewed discussion and terminology of fiction in the early modern period.

8   The license for publication is 20 September 1572. For an extensive study of Herrera's account of the naval battle, see Gaylord Randel 1970, 7–111.

9   Rufo's poem was finished earlier, in 1582, as we infer from the dedicatory letter to Maria of Austria, Holy Roman Empress and sister of Philip II. Little is known about the life of Pedrosa, except for the facts that the author gives himself in the manuscript of 1580 and in a memorial of 1583, of which we have the transcription copied in the CODOIN, vol. III, pp. 289–91. For more information on these three authors as poets of Lepanto, see the classic work of López de Toro 1950, pp. 63–66, 80–93, 99–102.

which required fabulous digressions and ornamentation. How, then, should we read the fictions in these three epics? What are the functions and implications of Pedrosa's use of Latin? And how do they compare to the use of fictions in Corte-Real's and Rufo's vernacular poems?

In the first part of this essay, I will consider the vernacular texts, which are extremely different from one another. While Jerónimo Corte-Real opts for classical 'fabulae,' Juan Rufo pointedly takes a different road, avoiding pagan mythology as the inspiration for his fabulous digressions. On several occasions in his poem, Rufo alludes to ancient myths but eventually decides not to relate them. In the second part of the essay, I will critically reassess Pedrosa's theoretical considerations on the fictions of his poetry, which he expresses in the prologue to his *Austriaca*. Pedrosa proposes an allegorical reading that draws on Lactantius and Erasmus and does not seem to apply to most of the digressions in his epic. As a case in point, I will explore the differences between Pedrosa and Rufo in their staging of the Demon and other hellish forces. I will argue that in these and other fictions of Pedrosa's Neo-Latin epic, the suggestion of reading allegorically may not have completely satisfied the early modern reader, thus causing serious tension with respect to the theoretical explanations on 'fabula' in the prologue.

1   Vernacular Fictions

The Portuguese poet Jerónimo Corte-Real incorporates classical mythology in order to give his epic the gravity of heroic poetry. In many episodes, the reader recognizes the poet's ancient and modern epic models.[10] In contrast, Rufo keeps his distance from mythological 'fabulae.' The digressions in his epic veer instead towards the realm of 'historia.' The interventions of the Demon (XX and XXI) and the fabulous digression with the magician Xiloes (XXII) provide the two examples that most clearly show Rufo's interpretation of the fictions that epic poetry requires. These fictions, however, are very different from Corte-Real's pagan 'fabulae.' At the beginning of canto XXI, Rufo confesses that he does not need the fictions of his ancient and modern predecessors. For Rufo, the truth of the Lepanto events is in itself so fabulous that he will not draw on fictions from the literary tradition. Therefore, Rufo explicitly dissociates his epic fictions from the 'fabulae' written by poets such as Corte-Real.[11]

---

10   The two primary models are Vergil and Camões, though certainly not the only ones. For more information on Corte-Real's poetics, see Alves 2001.
11   Rufo, *La Austríada*, XXI.1–4.

In the prologues to their works, both poets emphasize the truth of what they narrate in verse. Corte-Real's prologue consists of a letter to Philip II, in which the author humbly offers a work of "poorly polished verses" ("mal pulidos versos") and "low style" ("baxo estilo"), but with an enormous degree of veracity. The poem's "rigidity" ("dureza") and its "dryness" ("sequedad") are counterbalanced by the painterly skills of the author:

> Por estos y por otros mil inconvenientes he passado, y a todos facilmente ha resistido el deseo de presentar a V. M. este libro *debuxado de mi mano*, para que la variedad de las colores, y la invencion de la pintura a que V. M. es inclinado, haga facil aquel peso y molestia de una lectura falta de invencion, y de aquel ornamento y polido estilo que en los grandes ingenios, solo se hallan.[12]

Indeed, the 1578 edition printed in Lisbon contains 15 engravings preceding the cantos, illustrating a remarkable amount of detail in each one.[13] These illustrations, however, are not part of the 1575 manuscript, which Philip had in front of him when he wrote his enthusiastic response, praising the poet's achievement. The fine manuscript has rich colours, which are used to adorn the initials of each canto, and another set of illustrated drawings (that are unfortunately not conserved in the original manuscript, except for one or two). If we understand the fictions of poetry metaphorically as the brushstrokes of a painter, we may more easily comprehend why Corte-Real represented his epic poem as a "rigid" and "dry" narrative of the factual truth. The fabulous digressions in the form of mythological allegories are used to impart a light-hearted quality to the historical narrative.

Rufo, for his part, writes a letter to Philip's sister Maria of Austria, the Holy Roman Empress, who is the dedicatee of his work, and a second prologue to the reader to emphasize the reliability of his poem. In the latter, Rufo strategically anticipates criticism on his work:

---

12 "I have experienced these and a thousand other inconveniences, and the wish to offer this book to Your Majesty has withstood all of them. *It is painted by my hand*, so that the variety of the colours and the invention of painting, to which Your Majesty is inclined, facilitate the burden and discomfort of a reading without the invention, ornament and polished style that one can only find in the real talents." Corte-Real, *prologo*, n. pag. Italics and translation are mine. For a critical approach to the word 'invention' in the early modern period, I refer to Greene 2013, pp. 15–40, especially p. 18: "it may be more challenging to absorb a notion of invention that encompasses many senses from discovery to adaptation to application to conception."

13 For a discussion of these engravings, see Cacheda Barreiro 2012, who interprets these words from the prologue as an explicit reference of the author to these drawings.

> Aunque pudiera escusarme con dezir que esta obra es una curiosidad escripta en verso, y que no esta obligada a ser historia general, digo q[ue] quien con razon pudiere quexarse sea a mi, y no de mi, que en otra impression quedara sin quexa, como yo sin culpa.[14]

Rufo defines his poem as "a carefully elaborated product in verse" ("una curiosidad escripta en verso"), instead of a "general history" ("historia general"). He uses this concept of 'curiosidad' to defend possible lacunae in his poem that would constitute elementary material in a general history. The term, however, also raises the question of truth, which the author believes to be inevitably a relative one because of the many different possible opinions about certain events that took place during the naval battle. He presents his poetic procedures as a compromise between factual truth and verisimilitude:

> Lo que yo pude hacer fue en las evidencias estar a lo cierto, y en las dudas atenerme a lo verisimil, porque si esta no fuera mi intencion mas espacioso campo hallara para escribir, y mas oportunidad pa[ra] esplicarme en otros sujetos de invencion que en el de historia y tan moderna.[15]

Rufo's choice of contemporary history as the subject for poetry limits his freedom to include poetic material or fictions as he might have done in a heroic poem. This restriction on Rufo's poetics, I believe, concerns the realm of mythological 'fabulae' but leaves enough space for digressions in what I have called the realm of 'argumentum.' While writing his own poem, Rufo read the mythological epic of Corte-Real and clearly sought to distance his work from this example.

Indeed, Corte-Real fills in the narrative gaps of the historical narrative with mythological 'fabulae,' which can be read allegorically. The pagan figures of Morpheus, Alecto, and Neptune, among others, change the course of history with their interventions. Although Pedrosa seems to follow this model at the beginning of his poem (Alecto, for example, stirs up the emotions of the Ottoman sultan Selim II), he soon switches to the infernal powers of Satan and his minions in order to explain two narrative events on a supernatural

---

14   "Although I could excuse myself by saying that this work is a carefully elaborated product (*curiosidad*) written in verse, which is not obliged to be a general history, I ask that the person who justly complains will do so to me and not about me so that in another edition he will have no complaints and I will be without blame." Rufo, *Al lector*, n. pag. English translations of the prologue as well as the epic are mine.

15   "What I could do was be indisputable in certainties, and hold to the verisimilar in case of doubt. For if this were not my intention, I would have found more space to write, and more opportunities to explain myself in other subjects of invention than in this one of a history so modern." Rufo, *Al lector*, n. pag.

level, namely, Selim II's decision to assault Cyprus and the unending disputes among the members of the Holy League. Intermingled with these two supernatural interventions are the prophetic speeches of the hero's guardian angel, the Virgin Muse, and the emperor Augustus, which interrupt the narrative of the Holy League's voyage to Lepanto.[16] In Corte-Real's epic, the League's journey has been extended with the fabulous digressions of Venus imploring first her husband, Vulcan, whom she asks to forge new weapons for the Austrian hero (canto VI), and next her brother, Neptune, who has to influence the winds in favour of the Holy League (canto VIII).

Like the diabolic forces in books one and three of Pedrosa's epic, Rufo's Lucifer is introduced in canto XX to delay the Holy League enterprise. As soon as the Christian fleet has left the Sicilian shores, the Demon moans and groans for five octaves (XX.58–62). First, he refers to his previous efforts to thwart the formation and success of the Holy League. Pope Pius V had attempted to form the alliance as early as 1565 after the Turkish siege of Malta. Eventually, the Christian delegates signed the Holy League contract on 25 May 1571. The fleet was detained for some time on Candia because of bad weather, for which the Demon claims responsibility. Nevertheless, Lucifer perceives how the Christian League continues its voyage and decides to convoke the hellish forces. In contrast to Pedrosa's Satan, who speaks directly to his minions in the first book, Rufo's Lucifer only anticipates the discord this will sow among the Christian members of the Holy League. The monologue ends with a revealing reference to a historical episode involving Charles V, an event which is mixed up with a fabulous digression recounted in another epic of the period. The rhetorical question at the end of the Devil's monologue seeks to show Lucifer's self-assurance through a 'fabula':

> Pudieron de una maga los conjuros,
> turbando el mar con tempestad terrible,
> assegurar de Argel los altos muros
> de la furia de Carlos invencible;
> y ¿piensan navegar de muy seguros
> los que van con su hijo a lo impossible,
> llevando en contra de su mal govierno
> la tierra, el agua, el viento y el infierno?[17]

---

16   I have used the manuscript conserved in the Biblioteca Nacional de España, ms. 3960. For the episode of Alecto, see I.82–105; for the two interventions of Satan, I.214–65 and III.596–629; for the prophetic speeches, see II.85–135 (the guardian angel), III. 546–95 (the Virgo Muse), III.630–76 and IV.265–308 (Augustus).

17   "The invocations of a magician, which disturbed the sea with a terrible tempest, managed to preserve the high walls of Algiers from the fury of the invincible Charles. Do the ones

Rufo's Lucifer ends his lamentation with a reference to an exemplary event of the recent past: Charles's failed attempt to conquer Algiers in 1541. The argument Lucifer utters to convince himself that his actions will succeed refers to the fabulous episode in Zapata's epic *Carlo famoso* (XLV.8–12, 48–115), in which the nymph Espio seeks the help of Neptune to avenge the harm done to her by Charles's ships. Rufo does not call her a nymph but a witch ("maga"). In doing so, the author rewrites the 'fabula' of his predecessor, Luis Zapata, as a fiction that is all the more verisimilar and in line with Xiloes's appearance later on in his own poem (canto XXII). This small but decisive change in the use of fictions assures Rufo's authority as epic poet and his claim of verisimilitude.

The introductory octaves of the next canto (XXI) attest once again to the tension between fiction and history. The poet presents the hypothesis that six illustrious predecessors—both ancient (Homer, Vergil, Lucan) and modern (Petrarch, Ariosto, Juan de Mena)—would have chosen the naval battle of Lepanto as their sole subject had they been aware of it (1–4). The reason is obvious: the pure truth of this history provides so much admirable and diverse material "that there is no need of *other* fictions" ("que no hay necessidad de *otras* ficciones").[18] Surprisingly, for a modern reader at least, Rufo's metanarrative comment is followed by two cantos with episodes of a nature that we would today call fictional. The interventions of Lucifer and the appearance of the magician Xiloes do not seem to belong to the "*other* fictions" Rufo refers to in the opening of canto XXI. The speeches of both Lucifer and Xiloes rather form part of the realm of 'argumentum' to which the direct speeches of John of Austria and other characters of his poem likewise belong. Rufo must have considered pagan fictions too close to the realm of 'fabula,' in spite of their function as allegories. Rufo's choices, therefore, must be seen as a conscious attempt to distance his epic from those of his predecessors such as Zapata and Corte-Real who wrote allegorical epic fictions.

2   Pedrosa's Prologue to Philip II

At this point, we turn to Pedrosa's concept of fiction in the prologue of his work and consider to what extent he follows these precepts in the epic poem itself. A humanist born in Madrid, Pedrosa sent his work in manuscript to the Spanish King Philip II with the aid of García de Valverde, president of the Royal

---

who go with his son toward the impossible think they sail safely, having against their bad government the earth, the sea, the wind and hell?" Rufo, *La Austríada*, XX.62.

18   Rufo, *La Austríada*, XXI.4.8. Italics are mine.

Audience of Guatemala at the time.[19] The Neo-Latin epic includes preliminary vernacular poems written by illustrious people (among them, the dean of the cathedral of Guatemala and two relatives of Eugenio de Salazar), a prologue-letter dedicated to King Philip in both Spanish and Neo-Latin, and a letter by the Franciscan friar Martín de la Cueva, which all attempt to promote Pedrosa's epic. In the prologue from 1580, Pedrosa writes that he has been teaching Latin and rhetoric for 25 years at the cathedral school in the city of Guatemala. He longs to return to his native city where once as a child he was in the royal entourage of Prince Philip. Pedrosa claims to have 12 children in Philip's royal service. Apart from such biographical details, the author fashions himself as a distinguished man ("vir aliquis"), fit to celebrate and eternalize in epic verse the heroic deeds of Philip II and his half-brother, John of Austria.[20] According to Pedrosa, the historian writing in prose—that is, Fernando de Herrera, author of the vernacular source text, although Pedrosa does not name him directly—badly fails in his literary ambition to confer immortality and eternal glory on Philip II and John of Austria. The next passage may have been written in response to Figueroa's ideas about the advantages of writing history versus epic:

> Hic etenim versus eam venustatem, eum leporem, eam gratiam, et autoritatem habet, ut si viri, quem laudat, meritis par extiterit, non solum gratiam et autoritatem afferat, atque plus splendoris addat, et optimae imaginis instar atque pinturae, quae nempe quo propius aspiciatur, melior, ac magis pulchra videtur, plusque ad sese allicit, et invitat, verum etiam longiorem multo vitam praestat, quam Historia soluto sermone conscripta.[21]

---

19   No modern edition of Pedrosa's manuscript exists. All English translations are mine.
20   "Aequum esse arbitratus sum virum aliquem literis insignem praesertim apud Hispanos exoriri, ubi sane bonae literae tantopere tuo favore atque patrocinio florescunt. Qui tuae maiestatis praeclarissima gesta, animi dotes atque virtutes heroico carmine celebraret, ut tam clarum inclytum ac famosum nomen ut tuum, charissimi atque fortunatissimi fratris Domini Ioannis ab Austria, nullo non carminum genere celebrata immortalitati comendentur. Hoc praesertim scribendi genere omnium optimo atque gravissimo." Pedrosa, *Austriaca*, preface, n. pag., "I believe it fit that a distinguished man strong in letters would rise, especially among the Spaniards, where high literature is flourishing because of your enormous goodwill and benevolence, in order to celebrate in heroic verse your outstanding deeds, as well as the gifts and virtues of your soul. In doing so, a most notable and famous name like yours and that of your most beloved and fortunate brother don John of Austria, would be immortalized in every single genre of poetry, especially in that excellent and most grave genre."
21   "The [heroic] verse indeed has that refinement, that charm, that grace and authority, by which—if equal to the deeds of the man praised—it not only brings grace and authority, but even adds more splendour to it. Just like the effect of an excellent image or painting, the closer one looks to it, the better and more beautiful it appears. It attracts and invites

The heroic hexameter has the gravity and authority required to narrate the victory of Lepanto. The effects of poetry are compared to those of painting, which likewise invite the reader to have a closer look and absorb a work's beauty. The subtle brushstrokes of the painter, Pedrosa suggests, are similar to the fictions invented by the poet. This metaphor reminds the reader of Corte-Real's language in his letter to Philip II and in the first place the classical allusion to Horace's well-known phrase "ut pictura poesis."

Pedrosa indeed presents the fictions of poetry as essential for seducing the reader to the truth of history and its everlasting memory. To corroborate his argument, Pedrosa refers to the ideas of both Lactantius and Erasmus. The early Christian writer Lactantius is used to underscore the idea that the fictions (or *figmenta*) of poets are not meant to tell lies instead of truths. In his *Divine Institutions*, Lactantius argues that the so-called fictions of poets are intended to veil the deeds of the characters in the narrative:

> Sed dicet aliquis ficta haec esse a poetis. Non est hoc poeticum sic fingere, ut totum mentiare, sed ut ea quae gesta sunt figura et quasi velamine aliquo versicolore praetexas.[22]

Pedrosa then immediately and explicitly turns to Erasmus's explanation of the four types of allegory in his rhetorical treatise *De copia rerum*. Erasmus distinguishes between allegories that are either theologically, historically, physically, or morally based. The examples are taken from the epics of Homer and faithfully reproduced by Pedrosa:

> Quamquam autem non ubique perinde obvia est allegoriae ratio, tamen illud extra controversiam est apud antiquitatis peritos, in omnibus veterum poetarum figmentis subesse alegoriam: vel historicam, velut in pugna Herculis cum Acheloo bicorni: vel theologicam, ut in Proteo se vertente in omnis formas, aut Pallade e Iovis cerebro nata: vel physicam ut in fabula Phaetontis: vel moralem, velut in his quos Circe poculo et virga sua verterat in bruta animalia.[23]

---

one more, it even guarantees a much longer life, than a history written in free style." Pedrosa, *Austriaca*, preface, n. pag.

22 "But someone will say that these legends are poets' fictions. It is not the function of poetry so to compose things as to turn all to falsehood, but to clothe actions in due shape—so to say, with a parti-coloured veil." Lactantius, *Epitome*, chapter XI. The Latin text and English translation are from Ibid., pp. 8 and 67 respectively.

23 "Although the principle of the allegory or hidden meaning is not equally obvious in every case, experts in antiquity are agreed that under all the inventions of the ancient poets

In fact, the only change Pedrosa makes in his text is to invert the order of the historical and theological types of allegory. The examples taken from Homer are exactly the same ones given in Erasmus and represent metamorphoses in the ancient world of paganism. The allegorical character of the pagan fictions is clearly recognized and its use highly praised in Pedrosa's prologue.

3   Pedrosa's Neo-Latin Fictions

The difficulty for both the modern and contemporary reader, however, is that a major part of the fictions in Pedrosa's epic are neither pagan fables nor metamorphoses. Although the key to the allegory offered in the prologue seems to resolve all further questions, the passages from Lactantius and Erasmus concern pagan mythology alone. How, then, must we read, for example, the divine council between God and three patron saints in book 1? Or what about the prophetic (dream) visions of the hero John of Austria, in which he sees his guardian angel, the virginal Muse, and the Roman Emperor Augustus? Finally, how does the prophetic speech of Protheus relate to the previous visions? Pedrosa's allusion to the ideas of Lactantius and Erasmus on allegory serves in the first place to stress the highly rhetorical style of his epic poem. At the same time, it protects him against possible charges of heresy. Allegory is considered here as one of the many 'ficciones de la poesía' that Figueroa says the historian has to avoid. The introduction of allegorical reading in the prologue also has a social function. It means that Pedrosa writes for an audience that is able to read the 'ficciones' on a higher level that will not affect the pure truth of the history.

Pedrosa's aim is to write a *'Vergilio cristiano'* in line with two highly influential texts in Neo-Latin from the first half of the 16th century, as he clearly expresses his admiration for Marco Girolamo Vida's *Christiad* (Cremona, 1535) and Álvaro Gómez de Ciudad Real's *On the Military Order of the Prince of Burgundy* (Toledo, 1540).[24] The use of pagan allegory is syncretised with fictions related to the sacred world. The few examples of metamorphosis in

---

there does lie a hidden meaning, whether historical, as in the story of Hercules fighting the twin-horned Achelous; or theological, as in that of Proteus turning into all kinds of shapes or of Pallas springing from the head of Jove; or physical, as in the story of Phaëthon; or moral, as in the case of the men whom Circe turned into brute beasts with her cup and wand." Erasmus, *Copia*, p. 611. I have used the translation of Betty I. Knott, which is included in volume 24 of the series *Collected Works of Erasmus*.

24   Antonio de Nebrija called Álvaro Gómez de Ciudad Real the Spanish Vergil in the prologue of the *Thalichristia*, a religious epic poem of 16,400 hexameters published in Alcalá in 1522. For the status of Vida's *Christiad* as a *'Vergilius Christianus,'* see Vida 2009, p. ix.

Pedrosa's epic poem are not to be found in the pagan world. On the contrary, it is Satan, the "lemurum princeps," who changes form twice in the narrative. First, he transforms himself into an old man in the senate of Venice so that he can thwart the agreements of the Holy League, and later on, in the third book, he assumes the shape of the Christian captain, Andrea Doria, in order to convince John of Austria to withdraw from the battle.[25] From a theological viewpoint, however, these two transformations are 'probable' actions as the Devil and Demons were thought to be able to use human bodies as tools.

The final part of this essay tackles the problem of Pedrosa's seeming failure to define accurately the poetic fictions that he introduces in his epic poem. The rhetorical concept of 'argumentum'—i.e., what did not but might have happened—serves as a supplementary reading tool in my analysis of several examples of digression and amplification in Pedrosa's poem. Some of Pedrosa's inventions lean more towards an idea of 'historia'—we may think of John of Austria's invented speeches in the course of the poem—while others veer toward the realm of 'fabula.' In the first book of his epic, Pedrosa introduces the classic epic topos of the divine council converted in a Christianised form, which is clearly inspired by Vida's successful epic, the *Christiad*. First, we encounter Satan who speaks to his minions in hell in order to convince them to thwart the "latest agreements" ("nova foedera") among the Christian parties. A short description of the 'first among the demonic souls' is followed by the character's direct speech.[26] Satan promises great rewards ("praemia magna") to the demon who manages to undermine the *nova foedera*. Immediately after the speech we see the infernal powers heading toward the senate in Venice. There is no way to fit the allegory of Satan into one of the four types discussed by Erasmus. However, reading this passage as an example of the rhetorical mode of 'argumentum' may solve the problem. For Satan's performance and that of his minions are undoubtedly a fiction invented by the poet's imagination; yet at the same time, the Devil might have been at work in disturbing the formation of the Holy League. In contrast, the allegorical fictions of ancient mythology never happened at all.

The threat to the agreements of the Holy League leads Pedrosa to narrate the zealous efforts of Pope Pius V as providing a counter-example to the council of hell. The prayer of the pope to Saint Peter is likewise represented with a direct speech that originates from the poet's mind, as do the speeches of John of Austria and Satan. However, we do not read the digression of the pope's prayer as a fabulous digression. The gradual transition towards the speech of

---

25   See, respectively, *Austriaca*, I.251–65 and III.596–629.
26   Pedrosa, *Austriaca*, I.214–31.

Saint Peter to the saints Jacob and Mark, and subsequently towards the divine council in heaven with God as ultimate authority, shows the vague boundaries between our modern dichotomy of fiction and non-fiction. In the gravity of epic poetry, I believe that the direct speeches are an example of 'argumentum' that alternately verges on 'historia' or 'fabula.'

4 Repeated Prophecies

In John of Austria's first dream vision, an angel who resembles the Archangel Gabriel in almost every physical aspect appears to the hero and delivers a prophetic speech to encourage the Holy League:

> Ecce secans liquidum caelum delapsus ab arce
> Aetherea, vultum similis, vocemque colorem
> Incessumque habitum iuveni, qui nuntia caeli
> Detulit ad Mariam sacram, qui foedera iunxit
> Caelica, sed genius fuerat vultu venerando,
> Qui datus haerebat custos, mentemque regebat
> Ipsius a vitae exortu, atque a lumine primo.[27]

The introduction of a supernatural being is made explicit to the eyes of the reader ("constitit ante oculos iuvenis").[28] The angel's exhortation that follows the description of the apparition continues for more than 20 hexameters and serves to assure the hero of divine help in the battle. This pattern is repeated in books III and IV, that is, as long as the journey to Lepanto lasts and whenever the Holy League pauses. The other prophetic speakers are the Virgin—although she introduces herself as a Muse—and the Roman emperor Augustus, who appears twice to the hero. The digressions are invented by the poet's imagination, but their style fits perfectly in the epic journey of the hero. As the general goal of the four speeches is somewhat similar, that is, to encourage John of Austria and to obtain divine help, the digressions do not undermine the pure truth of the history but rather enhance the higher spiritual meaning of the poem. The

---

27 "Look, an angel is flying down through the clear sky! His face, his voice, and his appearance overall are similar to that young boy, who delivered the sacred messages to Holy Mary and who concluded the heavenly pacts. But it had been a genius with a venerable face, John of Austria's guardian angel, who looked after him from the moment he first saw light." Pedrosa, *Austriaca*, II.89–95.

28 Pedrosa, *Austriaca*, II.99.

narrative frame of the dream vision likewise gives authority to the passage and enhances the admissibility of the use of fiction in this context.

Even the pure mythological appearances of Protheus in the third book or Neptune later in the poem do not harm the narrative truth of the work. Although these digressions are to be considered as clearly 'fabulosa,' they are appropriately introduced in the unity of the epic story. The direct speech of Protheus is almost identical to the ones delivered to the hero in the prophetic dream visions. The intervention of Neptune is equally limited to a direct speech and to affirm God's providence. In the rhetorical structure of the poem, these appearances serve to deliver direct panegyric speeches, which in turn have to be read as 'argumenta' that incline to 'fabula.' Generally, the fictions in Pedrosa's poetry, particularly the digressions, whether in effect closer to 'historia' or to 'fabula,' thus serve as a means to evoke the higher meaning of Habsburg imperialism and to represent the 'gesta' of Philip II as divinely inspired.

However, these seemingly harmless allegorical fictions, invented to seduce the reader into the narrated history and to give the picture greater splendour, are not without risk. Precisely because of the short temporal distance between the historical events and the epic, the fictions that are introduced into the historical narrative may bring discomfort to the contemporary reader, as Torquato Tasso would explain in his *Discorsi*.[29] That is why Tasso advised poets to choose a past that was far enough removed from their own times. Indeed, the fictional digression in the third book of Pedrosa's epic, which represents Satan in the shape of Doria attempting to dissuade John of Austria from fighting, was undoubtedly an uneasy read for Philip II, the poem's first intended reader. As we know from private letters of the Spanish king addressed to the more experienced commanders of the Holy League, it was Philip II who strongly advised the Genoese admiral Doria to discourage John of Austria from fighting.[30] Although structurally the episode fits into the epic narrative, the explanation of Doria's unwillingness to fight by introducing Satan is an unfortunate literary invention of the author. In staging Satan's ruse as an allegorical fiction, Pedrosa

---

29   See, for example, Tasso 1964, p. 9, for the relevant passage in Discorso primo. Tasso published first the *Discorsi dell'arte poetica* in 1587 and later the *Discorsi del poema eroico* in 1594. His epic poem, *La Gerusalemme liberata*, was published earlier in 1581, although already completed in April 1575.

30   For more information, see Crowley 2013, p. 319–26. The Spanish fraction was heavily opposed to risking their ships and men in a naval battle against the Ottoman Empire. Not only Doria, but also Requesens tried to dissuade John of Austria from fighting. As late as 28 September, Philip II wrote a letter to his half-brother with the order to hibernate in Sicily and restart the military expedition the following year.

unconsciously equates Philip II's intentions with the hellish forces of the underworld. We do not know whether this awkward coincidence was one of the reasons for not publishing the poem, but it does suggest the risks involved in adding fabulous digressions to the narrative of recent history.

5 Final Remarks

While Figueroa in his prologue to Fernando de Herrera's *Relación* adamantly argues that historians have to avoid the fictions of poetry ("ficciones de la poesia") and represent the factual truth ("pura verdad"), he also affirms that epic writers need the fabulous digressions as an essential part of the genre in which they chose to compose their narrative. Pedrosa continues this reasoning in his prologue addressed to Philip II where he states that the fictions are necessary to guide the reader to a truth different from the pure and factual one of historians, a truth that must last for eternity. That is why Pedrosa repeats the theories of Lactantius and Erasmus in the prologue to Philip. The authority of allegorical reading is used to affirm that 'fabulae' do not diminish the truth of the epic poem but rather enhance it, giving it a higher, spiritual truth. Therefore, the concept of 'argumentum' as a means of understanding the fictions of Pedrosa's poetry is a useful way to account for the poet's invention of direct speeches by historical or other characters in the epic universe. This rhetorical concept allows us to understand how Christian religion and humanist erudition are combined in Pedrosa's epic. Furthermore, according to Pedrosa, Latin is the sole language in which the epic of Lepanto can be written because of the correspondence between the gravity of the subject and the Latin hexameter. The 'fabulae' achieve their allegorical significance only in relation to the poet's Neo-Latin epic models.

In contrast, we have seen how the Portuguese poet, Jerónimo Corte-Real, retained the 'fabulae' of classical mythology and the possibility of an allegorical reading of them. Juan Rufo, in turn, consciously avoided the introduction of mythological 'fabulae' and chose to limit the digressions of his epic to direct speeches of historical characters, the intervention of a Demon to disturb the Holy League forces, and finally, the episode of the magician Xiloes, which is clearly modelled after Erichtho in Lucan's historical epic. Pedrosa's choice of Neo-Latin to write the epic poem of Lepanto and especially his wish to write as a '*Vergilio Cristiano*' convinced him to syncretize two of Vergil's pagan mythological figures, Alecto and Neptune, which were easily interpreted as allegories in the scheme of Erasmus, with the sacred world and characters he found in the religious epic model texts of Vida and Gómez de Ciudad Real. Such an appropriation of Vergil surely demonstrates the wide array of fabulous digressions that Pedrosa believed could be syncretized in Neo-Latin epic poetry, while his vernacular counterparts Corte-Real and Rufo clearly restricted their use of fictions to one specific mode of writing poetic 'fabulae.' The allegorical syncretism typical of Pedrosa's Neo-Latin predecessors, Vida and Gómez de Ciudad Real, as elaborated in their Christian epics, became somewhat awkward when used for contemporary history.

Bibliography

Primary Sources

Corte-Real, Jerónimo de. *Felicíssima victoria*. Lisbon, 1578. [Madrid: Biblioteca Nacional de España, ms. 3693].

Covarrubias, Sebastián de. *Tesoro de la lengua castellana, o española*. Madrid: Luis Sánchez, 1611.

Erasmus, Desiderius. *The Collected Works of Erasmus*, vols. 23–24: *Literary and Educational Writings*, edited by Craig Thompson. Toronto: University of Toronto Press, 1978.

Herrera, Fernando de. *Relación de la guerra de Cipre, y sucesso de la batalla Naval de Lepanto*. Seville: Alonso Escrivano, 1572.

Lactantius, Firmianus. *Epitome of the Divine Institutions*, edited and translated with a commentary by Edward Henry Blakeney. London: S.P.C.K., 1950.

Pedrosa, Francisco de. *Austriaca sive Naumachia*. [Madrid: Biblioteca Nacional de España, ms. 3960].

Rufo, Juan. *La Austríada*. Madrid, 1584 [Toledo, 1585; Alcalá de Henares, 1586].

Tasso, Torquato. *Discorsi dell'arte poetica e Discorsi del poema eroico*, edited by Luigi Poma. Bari: Laterza, 1964.

Vida, Marco Girolamo. *Christiad*, translated by James Gardner. Cambridge, MA: Harvard University Press, 2009.

Zapata, Luis. *Carlo famoso*. Valencia: Joan Mey, 1566.

Secondary Sources

Alves, Hélio. *Camões, Corte-Real e o Sistema da Epopeia Quinhentista*. Coimbra: Biblioteca Geral da Universidade de Coimbra, 2001.

Bietenholz, Peter. *Historia and Fabula. Myths and Legends in Historical Thought from Antiquity to the Modern Age*. Leiden: Brill, 1994.

Cacheda Barreiro, Rosa Margarita. "Las naves de Lepanto. Las glorias de Jerónimo Corte-Real." *Quintana. Revista de Estudos do Departamento de Historia da Arte* 11 (2012), pp. 125–38.

Crowley, Roger. *Imperios del Mar. La batalla final por el Mediterráneo, 1521–1580.* Barcelona: Ático de los Libros, 2013.

Fernández de la Cotera Navarro, Patricia. "Paganismo y Cristianismo en la *Austriaca sive Naumachia* de Francisco de Pedrosa." *Calamus Renascens* 4 (2003), pp. 49–65.

Gaylord Randel, Mary. *The Historical Prose of Fernando de Herrera.* London, Eng: Tamesis, 1970.

Greene, Roland. *Five Words. Critical Semantics in the Age of Shakespeare and Cervantes.* Chicago, ILL: The University of Chicago Press, 2013.

López de Toro, José. *Los poetas de Lepanto.* Madrid: Instituto Histórico de Marina, 1950.

Mehtonen, Päivi. *Old Concepts and New Poetics. Historia, Argumentum, and Fabula in the Twelfth- and Early Thirteenth-Century Latin Poetics of Fiction.* Helsinki: Societas Scientiarum Fennicza, 1996.

Montero, Juan. "Fernando de Herrera, Relación de la guerra de Cipre y sucesso de la batalla naval de Lepanto (Sevilla, 1572): dos ediciones." In *Geh hin und lern. Homenaje al Profesor Klaus Wagner*, edited by Piedad Bolaños Donoso, Aurora Dominguez Guzmán, and Mercedes de los Reyes Peña. Santander: Secretariado de Publicaciones de la Universidad de Sevilla, 2007, pp. 339–53.

Vega, María José and Lara Vilà, eds. *La teoría de la épica en el siglo XVI (España, Francia, Italia y Portugal).* Vigo: Editorial Academia del Hispanismo, 2010.

CHAPTER 9

Neo-Latin Epic Poetry on Telemach after Fénelon

Florian Schaffenrath

If we consider a text within the framework of its editions, translations, critical reviews, etc., one of the most popular French novels was *Les Aventures de Télémaque*, published in the early 18th century and written by François de Salignac de la Mothe-Fénelon (usually abbreviated to Fénelon).[1] This novel, a prototypical *Bildungsroman*), consists of 24 books in its definitive form.[2] It deals with the adventures of young Telemachus, Ulysses's son, protagonist of the first four books of Homer's *Odyssey*. Fénelon starts his narrative at the point where Homer's story ends, with Telemachus's departure from Pylos and Sparta.

Together with his tutor Mentor—who is in fact the disguised Pallas Athena—Telemachus is cast ashore in various Mediterranean locations; after surviving a storm he reaches Sicily, before travelling to Egypt and Tyre.[3] In each place, he gets to know different types of rulers, presented to him as positive or negative models. In Cyprus, he struggles with the temptations of wine and Venus. In Crete, he encounters citizens who have just expelled their king Idomeneus, and are on the lookout for a new one; they light upon Telemachus himself, who refuses, continues his journey, gets drawn into another storm, and finally lands on Calypso's island, narrowly missing Ulysses, who has just departed for Ithaca. Telemachus falls in love with a beautiful servant, and Calypso jealously forces Telemachus and Mentor to leave her island quickly without a boat. Rescued by a Tyrian ship, they reach Salento in southern Italy. Here Idomeneus, expelled from Crete, attempts to found his new city, but comes under attack from indigenous tribes. Mentor conducts peace negotiations for Idomeneus and helps

---

1 For this essay, the novel is quoted from the classic edition of Albert Cahen. Cahen 1920. The latest edition is by Jacques Le Brun. Le Brun 1983–97.
2 Fénelon wrote his novel during the years 1694–96. The original manuscript is still preserved. Bibliothèque Nationale de France, fond français 14944. Cahen, *Fénelon*, pp. LXXXIII–XCV. In 1699, an unauthorised edition of the novel, in five volumes, was published by the widow of Claude Barbin. Cahen, *Fénelon*, pp. CIV–CVII. Following this publication, several more unauthorised editions appeared in France and abroad. Only in 1717, did Fénelon's great-nephew, Marquis Gabriel-Jacques Fénelon (1688–1746), publish an edition advertised on the title page as the "première édition conforme au manuscrit originale." This edition became the basis for the future reception of the text. Cahen, *Fénelon*, pp. LXXXII and CXIV–CXVIII.
3 A summary of the content and structure of the *Télémaque* is given by Dédéyan 1991, pp. 61–64.

him to establish a sound constitution for his new city, while Telemachus is sent out to help Philoctetes, Idomeneus's new ally, in a military campaign. He gets involved in fierce battles, but nevertheless finds time to pay a visit to the underworld, where he learns more about the future destiny of good and bad kings. In a final *aristeia* he puts an end to the war and establishes peace through wise negotiations. Back in Salento, he falls in love with Antiope, Idomeneus's chaste daughter, whom he saves from a boar during a hunting trip. Mentor urges Telemachus to travel back to Ithaca, but, just before they land, Mentor is revealed as the goddess Pallas and disappears. Finally, Telemachus comes home and meets his father.

1 Fénelon and French Poetics

Fénelon (1651–1715) was a Catholic priest who came from a prominent French noble family.[4] During his career, he gained recognition as an educational theorist and Catholic missionary working within France. In August 1689, Louis XIV nominated him as tutor of the Duc de Bourgogne, Louis de France (1682–1712), the seven-year-old son of the dauphin.

It is clear from Fénelon's correspondence[5] that exemplary figures, such as Charlemagne, played an important role in his pedagogical theory. In a letter addressed to the Duc de Beauvillier (1648–1714), dating from between 1690 and 1695, Fénelon discusses Charlemagne and his importance for his pupil:

> Je ne crois pas même qu'on puisse trouver un roi plus digne d'être étudié en tout, ni d'une autorité plus grande pour donner des leçons à ceux qui doivent régner. Aussi suis-je très persuadé que sa vie pourra beaucoup nous servir pour donner à Mgr le duc de Bourgogne les sentiments et les maximes qu'il doit avoir.[6]

The chief purpose of Fénelon's educational program was to shape a future ruler, and the use of exemplary figures was included among his methods of education. The experience Fénelon acquired as tutor to this boy is reflected in the

---

[4] For Fénelon's biography see Cahen, *Fénelon*, pp. XV–XXVIII; Dédéyan 1991, pp. 33–40; Delon/Malandain 1996, pp. 51–52; Reichenberger 2016, p. 222.

[5] Fénelon's letters were edited by Jean Orcibal in 1972–2007 in 18 volumes in Paris and Genf (from vol. 6 in the series *Histoire des idées et critique littéraire*). The letters from the period when Fénelon was teaching are contained in vol. 2 (*Les lettres antérieures à l'épiscopat 1670–1695*).

[6] Fénelon, *Correspondance*, p. 320.

novel *Les Aventures de Télémaque*, where the relationship of its protagonists—
the wise Mentor teaches his young student Telemachus how to become a good
king—reflects that of Fénelon and Louis. The wisdom of Fénelon's decision
not to publish the novel during his own lifetime is clear from the hostile reception of the unauthorised versions, which were read as critical of the king or of
the true faith.[7]

During his lifetime, Fénelon published several texts and was involved in a
number of academic discussions, notably a famous debate on quietism.[8] Especially relevant to this essay are Fénelon's ideas about French poetics, which
he addressed at length in his *Lettre à l'Académie*.[9] In 1713, the French academy
consulted its members as to its next project. In essence, Fénelon's letter provides an answer to this question, suggesting that the academy turn its attention to poetics. Opening the chapter, *projet de poétique*, with a general statement about the importance of poetics, Fénelon states that all the great poets
called on the people to strive after wisdom and virtue with vivid pictures and
splendid figures of speech. Turning his attention to French literature, however,
Fénelon argues that poetic perfection was impossible in French versification:
rhymed verse is incompatible with clear and natural expression:

> Me sera-t-il permis de représenter ici ma peine sur ce que la perfection
> sur la versification française me paraît presque impossible? [...] Notre
> versification perd plus, si je ne me trompe, qu'elle ne gagne par les rimes.
> Elle perd beaucoup de variété, de facilité et d'harmonie. Souvent la rime
> qu'un poëte va chercher bien loin, le réduit à allonger et à faire languir
> son discours. [...] les vers heroïques, qui demanderaient le son le plus
> doux, le plus varié et le plus majestueux, sont souvent ceux qui ont le
> moins cette perfection. [...] Nous n'avons point dans notre langue cette
> diversité de brèves et de longues, qui faisait dans le grec et dans le latin la
> règle des pieds, et la mesure des vers. Mais je croirais qu'il serait à propos
> de mettre nos poëtes un peu plus au large sur les rimes, pour leur donner
> le moyen d'être plus exacts sur le sens et sur l'harmonie.[10]

In France, the problem of rhyme had already been identified by Joachim Du
Bellay (1522–60) in his *Deffence et illustration de la langue francoyse* as one of

---

7   See note 2.
8   Kraus/Calvet 1953; Pellegrini 1959, pp. 246–51; Grimm/Hartwig 2014, pp. 193–95.
9   The letter was edited by Ernesta Caldarini (Geneva 1970). Goré 1957, pp. 520–26.
10 Fénelon, *Lettre*, pp. 64–66.

the most challenging problems for poetic translations.[11] Just like Du Bellay, Fénelon notes the further problem that modern French, unlike the ancient languages Latin and Greek, lacks an independent, free word order. This is the second main obstacle for poetic perfection:

> On voit toujours venir d'abord un nominatif substantif, qui mène son adjectif comme par la main; son verbe ne manque pas de marcher derrière, suivi d'un adverbe qui ne souffre rien entre deux, et le régime appelle aussitôt un accusatif, qui ne peut jamais se déplacer. C'est ce qui exclut toute suspension de l'esprit, toute attention, toute surprise, toute variété et souvent toute magnifique cadence.[12]

While Fénelon's points of criticism in this letter are very specific and precise, his solutions are general and superficial. He does not, for instance, attempt to answer questions of rhyme or word order, beyond the oblique solution provided by the *Télémaque*, on which he was working at the time. In his epic poetry—and his novel is explicitly ascribed to this genre (see below)—he renounces metrics and tries to use expressions that were as natural and simple as possible.

2   The Edition of 1717 and Ramsey's *Discours*

Fénelon started writing his novel during his time as a tutor (probably between 1694 and 1696). Before its final publication in 1717, Fénelon made a number of alterations to the text, a process studied by several scholars of the novel. It is clear from Fénelon's correspondence that he did not authorise the 1699 publication of parts of the novel, which appeared in five booklets under the title *Suite du quatrième Livre de L'Odyssée ou Les Aventures de Télémaque fils d'Ulysse*. This fragmentary edition had already provoked a number of reactions, including translations, fierce criticisms, and even satirical replies.[13]

The most important edition for the reception of the *Télémaque* was the one prepared by Fénelon's grandnephew in Paris 1717. This edition was dedicated to the son of the Duc de Bourgogne, Louis XV, and is based on a manuscript found among Fénelon's effects. From this edition on, the novel is divided

---

11   Ford 2013, pp. 23–53, esp. pp. 25–30; for general information about the so-called 'Reimstreit der Neuzeit' see Asmuth 2005, pp. 1137–43.
12   Fénelon, *Lettre*, pp. 71–72.
13   See note 2.

into 24 books, a division reminiscent of the 24 books of Homers *Odyssey* and *Iliad*. According to the *avertissement* of the book, this division originated with Fénelon himself.[14]

This Homeric division into 24 books emphasises the epic character of the work. It was perceived as a heroic poem and as a poetical product rather than simply as a work on education or as a political statement.[15] Its epic character is further underlined by a paratext at the beginning of the edition, the *Discours de la poésie épique et de l'excellence du poème de Télémaque*.[16] André Michel Ramsay (1686–1743), a Scot who became a close friend of Fénelon in the final years of his life, writes in this text about the epic genre in general and about the *Télémaque* as representative of this genre.

For Ramsay, poetry is important because the ideas of truth always require imaginative realisation in order to reach people who normally do not feel affected by beauty alone. With this theoretical background, Ramsay looks at the *Télémaque* as a text that is intended to teach and to please, and which in this respect surpasses the traditional epic poems of Homer or Virgil. Poems by Lucan, Silius Italicus, and Statius are emphatically excluded, while Claudian and others are not even mentioned. Underlying these omissions is Ramsay's definition of the epic genre:

> Une fable racontée par un Poete pour exciter l'admiration et inspirer l'amour de la vertu, en nous représentant l'action d'un Heros favorisé du Ciel, qui execute un grand dessein malgré tous les obstacles qui s'y opposent.[17]

Ramsay then picks out a couple of typical features of epic poems and compares them in Homer or Virgil with the *Télémaque*, such as the use of the gods. Finally, Ramsay discusses the international meaning and timelessness of Fénelon's work, not without a certain self-contradiction:

---

[14] "Toutes les Editions qu'on en a vû jusqu'à présent ont été tres défectueuses, & faites sans l'aveu de l'Auteur. C'est une justice qu'on lui rend en faisant paroître son Ouvrage tel qu'il est sorti de ses mains. Il l'avoit partagé en 24 Livres à l'imitation de l'Iliade." Fénelon, *Les avantures*, p. IV.

[15] For the role of the *Télémaque* in the general discussion about (French) epic poetry see Hepp 1961; Goupillaud 2005, pp. 195–98.

[16] Fénelon, *Les avantures*, pp. vii–lviii; Dédéyan gives the text of the *Discours* in his Appendix IV, Dédéyan 1991, pp. 231–46.

[17] Ramsay, *Discours*, p. ix.

> Dans le Telemaque tout est raison, tout est sentiment. C'est ce qui le rend un poeme de toutes les Nations, et de tous les siecles. Tous les Etrangers en sont également touchez. Les traductions qu'on en a faites en des langues moins délicates que la Langue Françoise, n'effacent point ses beautez originales. La savante Apologiste d'Homere nous assure que le Poete Grec perd infiniment par une traduction, qu'il n'est pas possible d'y faire passer la force, la noblesse, et l'ame de la Poesie. Mais on ose dire que Telemaque conservera toûjours en toutes sortes de Langues sa force, sa noblesse, son ame et ses beautez essentielles. C'est que l'excellence de ce Poeme ne consiste pas dans l'arrangement heureux et harmonieux des paroles, ni même dans les agréments que lui prête l'imagination, mais dans un goût sublime de la vérité, dans les sentimens nobles et élevez, et dans la maniere naturelle, délicate et judicieuse de les traiter. De parailles beautez sont de toutes les Langues, de tous les temps, de tous les Païs, et touchent également les bons esprits, et les grandes ames dans tout l'Univers.[18]

At the very end of his *Discours*, Ramsay discusses a series of criticisms of the *Télémaque*, chief among them the fact that this epic poem was not written in verse. For Ramsay, versification is not necessary for poetry. Moreover, the fixed syntax of modern European languages is an obstacle to natural poetry, in contrast to the free word order of Greek and Latin, which renders versification much easier—a point we have already seen in Fénelon's *Lettre*. Ramsay continues as follows:

> De plus, je ne sçai pas si la gêne des rimes et la regularité scrupuleuse de notre construction Européenne jointe à ce nombre fixe et mesuré de pieds, ne diminueroient pas beaucoup l'effort et la passion de la Poesie heroïque. Pour bien émouvoir les passions, on doit souvent retrancher l'ordre et la liaison. Voilà pourquoi les Grecs et les Romains, qui peignoient tout avec vivacité et goût, usoient des inversions de frases; leurs mots n'avoient point de place fixe: ils les arrangeoient comme ils vouloient. Les Langues de l'Europe sont un composé de Latin, et des Jargons de toutes les Nations barbares qui subjuguérent l'Empire Romain. Ces peuples du Nord glaçoient tout, comme leur climat, par une froide regularité de Syntaxe. Ils ne comprenoient point cette belle varieté de longues et de bréves, qui imite si bien les mouvements délicats de l'ame. Ils prononçoient tout avec le même froid, et ne connurent d'abord d'autre harmonie

---

18 Ramsay, *Discours*, pp. xlv–xlvi.

dans les paroles, qu'un vain tintement de finales monotones. Quelques Italiens, quelques Espagnols ont tâché d'affranchir leur versification de la gêne des rimes. Un poete Anglois y a réussi merveilleusement, et a commencé même avec succès d'introduire les inversions de frases dans la Langue. Peutêtre que les François reprendront un jour cette noble liberté des Grecs et des Romains.[19]

Ramsay marshals all the rhetorical power at his disposal in an attempt to present the *Télémaque* as a genuine French epic text. Had he known the collected correspondence by Fénelon, published only later, he could have quoted the following passage, addressed to the Jesuit Michel Le Tellier in 1710:

Pour Télémaque, c'est une narration fabuleuse en forme de poème héroique, comme ceux d'Homère et de Virgile, où j'ai mis les principales instructions qui conviennent à un prince que sa naissance destine à régner.[20]

At least since the edition of 1717, Fénelon's *Télémaque* has been considered not so much in the light of educational discourse or political opposition but rather in the context of current discussions on French (i.e., national) epic poetry.

3   Latin Translations

The novel soon became immensely popular and was translated into several languages, even including Greek.[21] I focus here on the Latin translations.

Vernacular texts were often translated into Latin, in order to make them available to an audience unfamiliar with the language of the original.[22] There were, however, further reasons for translation into Latin. The *Télémaque*, written in the important cultural and diplomatic language of French, could already command a wide potential audience; translation into Latin could also represent an attempt to compete with the original as literature (*aemulatio*), as indicated most clearly in the case of verse translations, which attempt to outdo the prose of the original.

---

19   Ramsay, *Discours*, pp. xlvii–xlviii.
20   Quotation after Fénelon, *Les avantures* (1987), pp. 39–40.
21   The Greek translation came out in Venice with Antonio Bertalo in 1742. It was dedicated to Athanasios Joanaqui. *Nouveau Dictionnaire Bibliographique*, vol. 2, p. 194.
22   This aspect of modern translations into Latin is stressed by Korenjak 2016, pp. 142–48.

It is these verse translations that provide the focus of what follows in this essay. I exclude from consideration here the subgroup of partial translations, written by teachers who used the *Télémaque* as a starting point for the translations of their students into Latin. These translations have received some attention in scholarship on the history of the study of the classics.[23] I also exclude those Latin translations which, like the *Télémaque* itself, are written in prose.[24]

Georg Trautwein uses modern poetics (in Latin or in the vernacular) to criticise poetic translations of the *Télémaque*. When he discusses his own translation, he is much more interested in the success of his imitation of the style of certain classical models. The reader is asked to compare his text with Sallust, Caesar, Nepos, Livy, Velleius, Florus, Tacitus, Curtius, and (the only Neo-Latin author of this catalogue) John Barclay, author of the famous novel *Argenis*. It is for the reader to find out which qualities of which author Trautwein was able to imitate (or even surpass). In brief, prose translations like Trautwein's are judged by completely different criteria.

I focus now on complete translations from French prose into Latin verse. After the anonymous *Fata Telemachi* (1743), later translations were produced by Joseph Claude Destouches (1759) and Etienne Bernard Alexandre Viel (1808). The Spanish brothers José and Joaquín Hernandez de Luna y Roja published their *Telemachi peregrinationes* in Madrid between 1760 and 1775 (the book appeared without date). While at first glance this seems to be another complete translation, closer inspection reveals that they only translated the first six books and could not finish their work.[25]

4   Anonymous, *Fata Telemachi* (1743)

An anonymous translation of the *Télémaque* appeared in Berlin in 1743 in two volumes under the title *Summi viri Francisci Salignac de la Motte Fata Telemachi filii Ulyssis regis Ithacae*. The first volume consists of books 1–12, the second, of books 13–24.[26]

The anonymous translator, who addresses the reader at the beginning in a short letter, asks the reader's forgiveness for a style that falls short of an author as important as Fénelon. He apologizes by quoting the famous lines in René

---

23   Köpeczi 1969; Tarnai 1979; Briesemeister 1985, pp. 211–12; Manchón Gómez 2005, pp. 61–64.
24   For instance, Georg Trautwein (1711–85) from Ulm published in 1744 in Frankfurt his prose translation *Telemachus*. Sacré 2014, p. 902. For the late 1819 prose translation of De Bussy see Manchón Gómez 2005, p. 60.
25   Briesemeister 1985, p. 212; Manchón Gómez 2005.
26   Manchón Gómez 2005, pp. 57–58.

Rapin's didactic poem[27] that offer an excuse for following or imitating Virgil. Immediately after these brief remarks, the first book starts. At the beginning of each book, a short prose abstract of about ten lines informs the reader of the book's content. Each book also exhibits one copper engraving.

It seems that this translation was not highly regarded. In 1839, the *Nouveaux Dictionnaire Biographique* states: "On estime peu cette traduction en vers latins" (vol. 2, p. 194). However, a more sympathetic assessment of the *Fata* can be found in the preface to Trautwein's (1711–85) Latin prose translation of 1744, written shortly after the publication of the *Fata* and similarly titled (*Francisci Fenelonii Fata Telemachi filii Ulyssis captui iuventutis recte accomodata, oder: deutliche und nach dem Begrif* [sic] *der Jugend eingerichtete Erklärung der in die lateinische Sprache übersetzten Begebenheiten des Telemachs*).[28] In his preface, Trautwein tells his readers how he became acquainted with the *Fata* just after finishing his own translation:

> I had already finished the preface, when, behold, I was presented a printed *Telemachus*, written in Latin and in heroic verse. I did not expect this at all, and at the beginning I was worried. With both my hands I pounced upon the work: I wanted to know who the author was. I found out that he was a very famous anonymous author, and therefore I presumed he was a plagiarist. [...] I pored over the book, once and again, I tasted the beginning, the middle, the end, and the rest. [...] I was then able to easily absolve the author from the suspicion of being a plagiarist.[29]

After this very detailed personal story of his first encounter with the *Fata*, Trautwein assesses the poetical quality of the translation:

> People required from me—the things Jouvancy and the other French theorists request from an epic poem—clarity, sweetness, accurate expression, and correct metrical feet. But I proceeded, reminding myself

---

27 "Fas mihi divini tantum vestigia vatis / Posse sequi; summoque volans dum tendit Olympo, / Sublimen aspicere, et longe observare tuendo", Rapin, *Hortorum libri IV*, 1.11–13; Monreal 2010, pp. 78–83.
28 See note 24.
29 "Iam praefationi statueram finem, cum ecce Telemachus mihi offertur latino et heroico carmine expressus impressusque. Alia omnia expectaveram, movebarque initio. Involabam in opus ambabus manibus. Cupido erat noscendi auctoris. Celeberrimum Anonymum esse inveni, suspicabar propterea plagiarium esse [...] Volvo itaque, revolvo: libo prima, media, finem, cetera. [...] Facile tum auctorem istum plagii suspicione absolvi." (Trautwein, *Fata Telemachi*, preface, no pagination).

that even the best horses sometimes misbehave at the beginning: [...] But then I started to embark on the thought that because of ostentatious expression or artificial embellishment the famous Gottsched will never have this poet forwarded to the madhouse. And may God prevent me from forwarding him! That man did a great job who transformed the whole Télémaque into a poem, indeed an even greater one, as he translated it into Latin. I came to think that he could do the best job because of the wealth of poetic, especially Virgilian parlance, and because of his acuteness of mind, so that also his suaveness, accurate expression, metre, and all the other aspects rendered this epic translation (like that of Neukirch) worthwhile and corresponding to its model.[30]

The benchmark Trautwein uses for the poetic translation is modern literary criticism. First, he quotes Joseph de Jouvancy SJ (1643–1719) and his *Institutiones poeticae* from 1718. In chapter ten of the first book, Jouvancy discusses poetic language, citing three criteria of quality: "clarity" ("perspicuitas," §1), "grandeur" ("maiestas," §2) and "metrical accuracy" ("numerus," §3). Trautwein argues that the *Fata Telemachi* fails to exhibit these qualities. Furthermore, with the phrase "ad moriotrophium" ("to the madhouse"), he alludes to a passage of the *Versuch einer critischen Dichtkunst* of Johann Christoph Gottsched (1700–66), in which contemporary poets are compared to the inhabitants of a madhouse.[31]

5   Joseph Claude Destouches

The next Latin verse translation was produced in Munich. The lawyer, Joseph Claude Destouches (1726–95), was counsellor of the court chamber of

---

[30]   "Desiderabatur a me, quam Iuvencius cum Gallis suis in Epopoea requirit, perspicuitas, suavitas, accurata dictio, numerus poeticus. Pergebam tamen, memor, equos etiam optimos subinde initio peccare incessus: 'Tristia squalebant [...] intrabat at udis.' At ego tum in eam ingrediebar cogitationem, ob tumorem aut affectatum decus numquam fore, ut poetam hunc ad moriotrophium clarissimus Gottschedus amandet. Et absit, ut amandem ego. Rem magnam vir praestitit, quod totum Telemachum pertexuit carmine, maiorem, quod Latino. Imo tum ob sparsam passim copiam poeticae et Virgilianae dictionis, tum ob vim satis acrem cogitandi rem mihi videbatur praestare maximam potuisse; ut et suavitas et accurata dictio et numerus ceteraque heroicam translationem eius, ut illam Neukirchii, dignam plane et aequalem exemplari suo reddidissent." (Ibid., n. pag.).

[31]   "dieser Helikon ist wie ein Narrenhaus." Gottsched, *Versuch*, appendix 3, chap. 6.

the Bavarian elector (kurfürstlicher Hofkammerrat).[32] In 1759, he published in Munich his Latin translation of the *Télémaque* under the title *Telemach* [!] *Ulyssis filius seu exercitatio ethica moralis* (reprint Augsburg 1764). The following subtitle to the publication gives an initial sense of the whole project: *ex lingua Gallica in carmen heroicum translata*. Skipping one logical step, Destouches tells us that he not only translated the *Télémaque* from French into Latin but also changed the literary genre and made it into a real epic poem, a *carmen heroicum*.

The dedicatee of this translation is Maximilian III Joseph, elector of Bavaria (1727–77). Inaugurated in 1745, he initially leaned towards Austria, but from the middle of the 1750s attempted to approach France. During his reign, the Bavarian Academy of Science and the Academy of Fine Arts in Munich were founded. This personal background has an important bearing on the translation of the *Télémaque*. In his dedication, Destouches explains that Fénelon's novel was written while he was tutor of a (potential) future ruler, the Duc de Bourgogne. Maximilian Joseph's interest in the promotion of education and science in his electorate made him the perfect addressee of this translation.

In the dedication letter, Destouches writes about his way of working and the methodology he applied. He did not translate everything in a garrulous way ("garrulitate"), but carried out a process of selection. He wanted to focus on the most elegant and most useful passages ("elegantissima, utilissima"), on those passages which were especially able to touch people's minds ("sententias animos pro varietate affectuum moventes").[33] Perhaps because the text itself begins *in medias res*, without any explanatory proem, Destouches proceeds to give a very short summary of his poem's content:

> This will be my task: I will show you a prince who out of love for his country accomplishes a long journey, buffeted by fate and destiny, condemned to death on the altar, prevailing over passion and enemies, who finally after so many disasters returns home as the best model of a prince.[34]

---

32 For his biography see Koppe 1793, pp. 133–34; Meusel 1802–15, vol. 2, p. 338; Baader 1804, pp. 232–33; Stepf 1820–25, vol. 2, p. 191; Killy/Vierhaus 1995–99, vol. 2, p. 499.

33 For translations of selected passages of an epic poem, see the contribution of Lucioli in this volume.

34 "Hoc opus est nostrum: Principem patriae amore ad longa itinera evocatum, fatis obluctantibus circumactum, mortis discrimine ad aras destinatum, voluptatis hostiumque triumphantem et denique post tot adversa specimen principis probatissimum in patriam revertentem exhibeo." Destouches, *Telemach*, fol. b[1]$^{r\text{-}v}$.

In the following *praefatio*, Destouches addresses his readers and asks them to read the following story (which he calls *ethica*) again and again. Everybody, even peasants ("civi ac nobili, rustico ac civi"), can learn something. Destouches will try to imitate Virgil's style ("metrum, dictionem et artem"). Then the work itself begins. Instead of the 24 books of Fénelon's original, it is divided into 12 books just like Virgil's *Aeneid*. However, Destouches has not simply combined two of Fénelon's books into one of his own. Destouches's style is obscure and difficult. Without Fénelon's model, Destouches's text would be very hard to understand. Moreover, it appears that Destouches himself did not always understand Fénelon's text (for an example, see below).

6   Etienne Bernard Alexandre Viel

The last translation under consideration in this essay was published at the beginning of the 19th century and brings us, at least to some extent, into the New World. The translator, Etienne Bernard Alexandre Viel, was born in New Orleans in 1736.[35] He became a member of the Oratory Congregation, which appointed him prefect of studies at the Collège de Juilly, approximately 30 km from Paris. When he returned to America in 1791, he left the manuscript of his translation with his friend, Father Dotteville, who passed it on to a group of Viel's students. They then prepared the edition of the manuscript (Paris 1808), and when Viel came back to France, he even helped them to finish a second edition of his poem (Paris 1814) before he died in 1821.

One of his students, the famous politician Eusèbe Baconnière de Salverte (1771–1839), was responsible for the first edition (Paris 1808). Salverte addresses the reader at the outset of the volume in an *avertissement*: the pictures delivered by even the best prose texts can only become more beautiful when expressed in verse. Fénelon's *Télémaque* consists of such beautiful pictures that it deserves versification for the sake of poetic perfection. Moreover, this versification is not French, but Latin:

> Cette langue qui, quoi qu'on en ait dit, ne peut cesser d'être classique parmi les modernes sans appauvrir d'une maniere irréparable le domaine de la littérature, la langue des Romains, s'offroit naturellement aux admirateurs du chef-d'oeuvre de Fénelon. Télémaque était digne des chants d'un Virgile.[36]

---

35   For his biography see *Annuaire nécrologique* 1821; A. Fr. 1822; Blair 2014, p. 842.
36   Salverte, *avertissement*, pp. v–vi.

NEO-LATIN EPIC POETRY ON TELEMACH AFTER FÉNELON 159

Salverte knows about earlier efforts to translate the *Télémaque* into Latin and quotes them. But he cannot say whether Father Viel knew these precursors. He reproaches the anonymous *Fata Telemachi* for sometimes having added certain elements that cannot be found in the original. He professes himself frequently unable to understand the meaning of Destouche's version. The *avertissement* ends with a biography of Father Viel, commenting on the similarity of Viel's situation to that of Fénelon: both were tutors, and neither edited their own versions of the *Télémaque*.

7 Comparison of the Translations

The different methods of composition and the contrasting functions of these various translations are illuminated by their respective handling of one particular passage from the first book, which reveals how the different translators coped with the challenge of bringing the message into Latin hexameter. In this passage, Telemachus, wanting to sail to Sicily, is caught up in a storm, the very same storm that every educated reader knows from the beginning of Virgil's *Aeneid* (1.81–156). During this storm, Telemachus manages to keep his ship apart from Aeneas's fleet, but once the wind drops, Telemachus finds himself in the middle of the hostile Trojan fleet. In this crucial situation Mentor recognizes that one Trojan ship is sailing at some distance from the others:

> Dans le moment où le ciel commençoit à s'éclaircir et où les Troyens, nous voyant de près, n'auroient pas manqué de nous reconnoître, il [*sc.* Mentor] remarqua un de leurs vaisseaux presque semblable à celui des nôtres que la tempête avoit écarté, et dont la poupe étoit couronnée de certaines fleurs, il se hâta de mettre sur notre poupe des couronnes de fleurs semblables; il les attacha lui-même avec des bandelettes de la même couleur que celles des Troyens; il ordonna à tous nos rameurs de se baisser le plus qu'ils pourroient le long de leurs bancs, pour n'être point reconnus des ennemis. En cet état, nous passâmes au milieu de leur flotte: ils poussèrent des cris de joie en nous voyant, comme en voyant des compagnons qu'ils avoient crus perdus.[37]

The three translations render this episode as follows:

---

37 Fénelon, *Les avantures*, pp. 30–32, ll. 322–36.

Diffugere polo nox spissa atraeque tenebrae. [...]
Mentor at adversa cernit de classe carinam
Forte unam, a reliquis saevis quae fluctibus acta, et
Non nostrae absimilis, paribus numerosaque remis.
Illi puppis erat florum redimita coronis.
Est mora nulla, senis moderamine nostra vetusti
Flore etiam simili navis stat vincta; colore
Loramenta pari renitent cum Troïbus, ipse
Serta senex subito puppi queis florea iungit.
Tum vero nautis, remos impellere pronis
Vultibus et tergo demisso, praecipit, audax
Ne Tros agnoscat populum nos esse Pelasgum.
Sic totam timidi Teucrorum verrimus aequor
Per classem. Socios illi Troasque putantes,
Quos timuere feris absorptos aequoris undis,
Nos plausu excipiunt et magna voce salutant.
    Fata Telemachi, 1.412; 416–30

Fulgebat caelo stellîs lux clara fugatis
Et vultu coràm classem Trojanus agebat,
Ludit fraude piâ Mentor, fuit una virenti,
Quae nostrae similis, sertô circumdata navis.
Observans Mentor nostrae figebat olivam,
Dùm veniunt, magno plaudunt clamore viámque
Cedebant mediis Teucri, de gente putantes.
    DESTOUCHES, *Telemach*, 1.298–304

Cùm primâ sed enim coelum clarescere luce
Coeperat, et jam nos propiori agnoscere visu
Aeneadae poterant, reliquis e navibus unam
Advertit nostrae similem, quam turbidus auster
Dispulerat, certis redimitam floribus esse.
Illico florenti puppim de fronte coronat,
Et paribus nectit vittis, similique colore.
Tum nautas, ne quis vultum malè proderet hosti,
Quàm poterant per transtra jubet demittere corpus.
Sic medii vehimur. Socios ceu fortè revisant
Amissos, Teucri laeto clamore sequuntur.
    VIEL, *Telemachiados libri*, 1.309–19

The presentation of this episode in the *Fata Telemachi* comprises 16 lines and is quite extensive. The anonymous author did understand the content and followed his model step by step. Not one single element of Fénelon's story was omitted: (1) Mentor recognizes the danger; (2) he detects the single vessel and its garlands of flowers; (3) he turns Telemachus's ship; (4) asks the sailors to hide away; (5) they pass the Trojan fleet; (6) and the Trojans even wave their hands in joy. In order to make his narrative as clear as possible, the anonymous author even provides additional information. While the original describes the Trojan ship as "un de leurs vaisseaux presque semblable à celui des nôtres," the Latin translation further specifies this resemblance by explaining that it was propelled by the same high number of oars ("Non nostrae absimilis, paribus numerosaque remis," 418).

With only seven lines, the presentation in Destouches's translation is much shorter, and modifies the original in a way which suggests that the translator may not have understood Mentor's stratagem. Rather than adorning the ship with flowers in the manner of the separated Trojan ship, Destouches has Mentor apply an olive branch, the classical symbol of peace (see Virgil, *Aeneid* 8.116), which enables the ship to sail through the Trojan fleet unharmed. Also omitted is any reference to the hiding sailors, which would make no sense on a boat protected by an olive branch. Using the expression "fraude pia," Destouches alludes to Ovid's use of the phrase to denote Iphis's disguise as a boy (*Metamorphoses* 9.711, "inde incepta pia mendacia fraude latebant"). The intertextual relationship between the two passages is based on the common idea that something precious must be disguised in order to be protected.

Viel's 11 lines lie between the 16 of the *Fata Telemachi* and Destouches's seven. He observes the original order of events as well, but in contrast to the *Fata*, his depiction seems to be more compact, made clearer by avoiding the use of two expressions for one idea. On the other hand, Viel uses diction that assumes his audience is made up of highly-educated readers; for instance, "les troyens" become "Aeneades," "la tempete" becomes "auster." Such nuances create a more Virgilian atmosphere.

These microcosmic observations also hold true for the overall structure of the three texts. The following chart compares the structure of the first book in the three different versions:

Content of the first book	*Fata*	Destouches	Viel
Calypso mourns.	1.1–18	1.1–13	1.1–13
She finds two shipwrecked men at the beach.	19–42	14–32	14–28
Calypso addresses Telemachus.	43–49	33–38	29–36
Telemachus. explains the reasons for his trip.	50–75	39–63	37–58
Calypso invites Telemachus to her palace.	76–84	64–71	59–65
The nymphs proceed to Calypso's grotto.	85–95	72–83	66–76
Description of the grotto	96–125	84–107	77–99
Description of the island	126–152	108–124	100–120
Telemachus gets new clothes.	153–167	125–136	121–134
Mentor reminds Telemachus to focus on his mission.	168–205	137–169	135–162
Banquet	206–248	170–194	163–189
Calypso tells Telemachus about his father.	249–291	195–218	190–217
Telemachus wants to mourn his father.	292–302	219–224	218–225
Telemachus narrates his trip: Mentor warned against sailing to Sicily.	303–364	225–266	226–273
Storm	365–437	267–304	274–324
Landing on Sicily; Telemachus is arrested and brought to Acestes.	438–459	305–323	325–349
Telemachus says who he is and is condemned to death.	460–507	324–350	350–376
Mentor predicts a barbarian attack in three days.	508–525	351–377	377–396
The town prepares for the attack.	526–547	378–388	397–412
The Himerians attack on the third day, and Telemachus is reprieved.	548–567	389–407	413–426
Mentor and Telemachus fight together with Acestes.	570–591	408–432	427–440
Telemachus kills the son of the king and carries off his armour.	592–614	433–448	441–457
After the battle Acestes sends them back to their homeland.	615–636	449–465	458–473

The first book of the *Fata Telemachi* comprises 636 lines while Destouches needs only 465 lines (which is one third of his first book) and Viel 473 lines. Destouches does not leave out any important elements of the plot, but often his terseness makes it difficult for the reader to follow the text. Viel, who needs approximately as many lines as Destouches, handles his material more adroitly: consistently clear, he takes care to remain intelligible to the reader.

8 Conclusion

Whereas modern readings of Fénelon's *Télémaque* focus on the pedagogical qualities of the text, none of the three translations under discussion addresses contemporary educational issues or the genre of 'mirror of princes' in their respective paratexts, rather they reflect on their position within the contemporary discourse on poetics. They all raise questions as to the appropriate style and imitation of Virgil and the definition of the epic genre, the *carmen heroicum*. It does not come as a surprise that these texts position themselves in such a (poetological) context, given that the most important early edition of Fénelon's novel, the 1717 text, presents the work in the context of poetological or generic discussions.

All the translations discussed here were produced more or less in the second half of the 18th century. This period saw the composition of a significant number of Latin translations of vernacular epic poems. William Dobson translated Matthew Prior's didactic poem, *Solomon*, in 1734. Joachim Gottlob translated Alexander Pope's *An Essay on Man* in Wittenberg in 1743. Domenico Zanni published a translation of Tasso's *Gerusalemme liberata* in Cremona in 1743. Raymundus Cunichius, famous for his translations of Homer, began a translation of Torquato Tasso in 1760. Ludwig Bertrand Neumann translated Milton's *Paradise Lost* in Vienna in 1768 and Klopstock's *Messias* in 1770. Cappeval published a translation of Voltaire's *Henriade* in Zweibrücken in 1772. Many of these works were already studied in the context of the 'battle of the languages' (*contentio de primatu linguarum*), a war in which Latin's last victories were won in the 18th century.[38] Our translations of Fénelon must also be seen in this context. Before the breakdown of the production of Neo-Latin literature and its retreat into small niches in the 19th century, Latin poets of the late 18th century tried to appropriate vernacular epics to themselves via translation, and as a result of this process, these texts remain a part of the poetic discourse of the time.

---

38 Briesemeister 1985.

Bibliography

Primary Sources

Destouches, Joseph Claude. *Telemach Ulyssis filius seu exercitatio ethica moralis ex lingua Gallica in carmen heroicum translata*. Munich: Thuille, 1759.

Fénelon, François de Salignac de La Mothe. *Les avantures de Telemaque*. Paris: Jacques Estienne. 1717.

Fénelon. *Les aventures de Télémaque*, edited by Albert Cahen. Nouvelle édition. Paris: Hachette, 1920.

Fénelon. *Les aventures de Télémaque*, edited by Jeanne-Lydie Goré. Paris: Garnier, 1987.

Fénelon. *Œuvres*, edited by Jacques Le Brun, 2 vols. Paris: Gallimard, 1983–1997.

Fénelon. *Lettre à l'Académie, avec les versions primitives*, edited by Ernesta Caldarini. Geneva: Droz, 1970.

Fénelon. *Correspondance de Fénelon. Tome II: Les lettres antérieures à l'épiscopat 1670–1695*, edited by Jean Orcibal. Paris: Klincksieck, 1972.

Fénelon. *Télémaque: Die Begebenheiten des Prinzen von Ithaca [...] aus dem Französischen des Herrn von Fénelon in deutsche Verse gebracht*, translated by Benjamin Neukirch, 3 vols. Ansbach: Lüders, 1727–39.

Gottsched, Johann Christoph. *Versuch einer critischen Dichtkunst vor die Deutschen*. Leipzig: Breitkopf, 1730.

Trautwein, Georg. *Francisci Fenelonii Fata Telemachi filii Ulyssis captui iuventutis recte accomodata, oder: deutliche und nach dem Begrif der Jugend eingerichtete Erklärung der in die lateinische Sprache übersetzten Begebenheiten des Telemachs*. Stuttgart: Erhard, 1758.

Viel, Stephanus Alexander. *Telemachiados libri XXIV*. Paris: Didot, 1808.

Secondary Sources

A. Fr. "Nécrologie." *Apis Romana* 3 (1822), pp. 122–29.

Annuaire nécrologique ou complément annuel et continuation de toutes les biographies ou dictionnaires historiques 2 (1821), pp. 302–03.

Asmuth, B. "Reim." In *Historisches Wörterbuch der Rhetorik*, edited by Gerd Ueding, vol. 7. Tübingen: Niemeyer, 2005, pp. 1115–44.

Baader, Klement Alois. *Das gelehrte Baiern, oder Lexikon aller Schriftsteller, welche Baiern im achtzehnten Jahrhunderte erzeugte oder ernährte*. Nürnberg: Seidel, 1804.

Blair, Ann M. "Neo-Latin in North America." In *Brill's Encyclopaedia of the Neo-Latin World*, edited by Philip Ford, Jan Bloemendal, and Charles Fantazzi. Leiden: Brill, 2014, pp. 833–48.

Briesemeister, Dietrich. "Französische Literatur in neulateinischen Übersetzungen." In *Acta Conventus Neolatini Bononiensis*, edited by Richard Schoeck. Binghamton, NY: Center for Medieval and Early Renaissance Studies, 1985, pp. 205–14.

Dédéyan, Charles. *Télémaque ou la liberté de l'ésprit*. Paris: Nizet, 1991.

Delon, Michel and Pierre Malandain. *Littérature française du XVIIIe siècle*. Paris: Presses Universitaires de France, 1996.

Ford, Philip. *The Judgement of Palaemon. The Contest between Neo-Latin and Vernacular Poetry in Renaissance France*. Leiden: Brill, 2013.

Goré, Jeanne-Lydie. *L'itinéraire de Fénelon. Humanisme et spiritualité*. Paris: Presses Universitaires de France, 1957.

Goupillaud, Ludivine. *De l'or de Virgile aux ors de Versailles. Métamorphoses de l'épopée dans la seconde moitié du XVIIe siècle en France*. Geneva: Droz, 2005.

Grimm, Jürgen and Susanne Hartwig, eds. *Französische Literaturgeschichte*. 6th ed. Stuttgart: Metzler, 2014.

Hepp, Noémi. "De l'épopée au roman. L'Odyssée et Télémaque." In *La Littérature narrative d'imagination. Actes du colloque de Strasbourg, 23–25 avril 1959*. Paris: Presses Universitaires de France, 1961, pp. 97–113.

Killy, Walther and Rudolf Vierhaus, eds. *Deutsche Biographische Enzyklopädie*, 10 vols. Munich: Saur, 1995–1999.

Köpeczi, Béla. "Fénelon Telemachosànak elsö magyarországi forditàsi kisérlete." *Filológiae Közlöny* 15 (1969), pp. 1–18.

Koppe, Johann Christian. *Lexicon der jetzt in Teutschland lebenden juristischen Schriftsteller und akademischen Lehrer*. Leipzig: Kummer, 1793.

Kraus, Johannes and Josef Calvet, eds. *Fénelon. Persönlichkeit und Werk*. Baden-Baden: Verlag für Kunst und Wissenschaft, 1953.

Manchón Gómez, Raúl. "Telemachi, Ulyssis filii, peregrinationes. Una desconocida versión poética neolatina del Telémaco de Fénelon en la España del siglo XVIII." In *Silva. Estudios de humanismo y tradición clásica* 4 (2005), pp. 51–71.

Mazure, Adolphe, ed. *Lettre à l'académie française sur la grammaire, la rhétorique, la poétique et l'histoire, par Fénelon*. Paris: Eugène Belin, 1879.

Meusel, Johann Georg. *Lexikon der vom Jahr 1750 bis 1800 verstorbenen teutschen Schriftsteller*, 15 vols. Leipzig: Fleischer, 1802–1815.

Monreal, Ruth. *Flora Neolatina. Die Hortorum libri IV von René Rapin S. J. und die Plantarum libri VI von Abraham Cowley. Zwei lateinische Dichtungen des 17. Jahrhunderts*. Berlin: de Gruyter, 2010.

Pellegrini, Carlo. *Storia della letteratura francese*. 3rd ed. Milan: Principato, 1959.

Reichenberger, Kurt. "Fénelon." In *Kindler Klassiker Französische Literatur*, edited by Gerhard Wild. Stuttgart: Metzler, 2016, pp. 222–23.

Sacré, Dirk. "Neo-Latin Prose in the Twilight Years (1700–Present)." In *Brill's Encyclopaedia of the Neo-Latin World*, edited by Philip Ford, Jan Bloemendal, and Charles Fantazzi. Leiden: Brill 2014, pp. 879–903.

Stepf, Johann Heinrich. *Gallerie aller juridischen Autoren von der ältesten bis auf die jetzige Zeit*, 4 vols. Leipzig: Lauffer, 1820–25.

Tarnai, Andor. "Lateinische Übersetzungen französischen Schrifttums im Ungarn des 18. Jahrhunderts." In *Acta Conventus Neolatini Amstelodamensis*, edited by Pierre Tuynman, Gerdien C. Kuiper, and Eckhard Kessler. Munich: Fink, 1979, pp. 976–82.

CHAPTER 10

Coexistence and Contamination of Vernacular and Latin in Alessandro Braccesi's Bilingual Tribute to Camilla Saracini: the Literatures of Siena and Florence between Illustrious Women and Neoplatonism

Federica Signoriello

In October 1491 the Florentine envoy to Siena, Alessandro Braccesi (1445–1503), composed and dedicated two sonnets in the vernacular and one Latin *carmen* to Camilla Saracini, the most beautiful girl in the city, who had recently and suddenly become blind.[1] While this may seem only occasional poetry by a lesser-known figure of 15th-century Tuscany, a closer look at both the texts and their context reveals that these poems mirror the social and artistic ambitions embedded in Florentine society and the cultural trends of two cities and two languages employed for different purposes. In Siena, where the poems were written, vernacular poetry was the norm, and the production of literary texts in Latin was progressively dying out. Braccesi, however, brought with him a multifaceted Florentine heritage; in his hometown, during the same century, the endorsement of the Tuscan vernacular as the language of literature, culture and philosophy, followed a tortuous path.

Braccesi's work did not stand out among those of his renowned contemporaries. Despite not achieving great success as an intellectual, both his prose and poetry are of great interest, especially in relation to the contamination of Latin and the vernacular. In the specific episode related to Camilla Saracini, it is worth looking into the reasons that moved him to communicate in both languages, at a time when the status of the vernacular was changing side by side with a flourishing Neo-Latin literature.

In this essay, my aim is to first shed light on Braccesi's background and literary ambitions and then to examine the poems for Camilla. In the third and

---

1 I would like to acknowledge the help of the Renaissance Society of America whose grant allowed me to conduct my research for six weeks in Florence, Italy, and find the archival documents relevant to this essay.

fourth sections I offer my own interpretation of the texts, within the cultural context of Florence and then that of Siena.

1   Alessandro Braccesi, Background and Ambitions

According to Paul Oskar Kristeller, Braccesi "occupies an important, if not a leading, position among the Florentine humanists of the second half of the 15th century,"[2] nevertheless the study of his literary works and letters has so far lacked depth. Braccesi, or, as he signed his letters, Alexander Braccius, was born in Florence, became a notary and worked for the Florentine government in a number of temporary offices. He travelled to Rome, Siena, Perugia, and Lucca, serving first the Medici family and then the chancery of the Florentine Republic. Thanks to his prominent employers, he became personally acquainted with many well-known officials and intellectuals of the age, such as Bartolomeo Scala, Marsilio Ficino, Angelo Poliziano, Cristoforo Landino, Naldo Naldi, and Ugolino Verino. Special mention should be made of his friendships with Benedetto Dei, the eclectic chronicler and traveller, and Nicolò Michelozzi, son of the renowned architect Michelozzo and personal secretary to Lorenzo de' Medici.[3] Braccesi corresponded widely and his letters are held in a number of libraries.[4]

Braccesi's life was eventful, as Alessandro Perosa wrote in his entry for the *Dizionario biografico degli italiani*, but has not been duly studied.[5] His origins could not have been humbler: his father, Rinaldo Braccesi, had, at the age of sixteen, lost his father, Sandro, and been entrusted with the care of his mother Pippa, aged thirty-six. Rinaldo lived in the quarter of San Giovanni, Gonfalone of Drago, popolo of San Leo. This information is found in his first *catasto* record (an early Florentine version of a tax return) that dates back to 1427, which also reveals that Rinaldo's family name was not yet Braccesi, but Uccellini.[6] The Uccellini family appears in another *catasto* record from 1451. Rinaldo, now

---

2   Kristeller 1964, vol. 2, p. 311.
3   For more on Niccolò Michelozzi and his correspondence, see Isenberg 1982; on Benedetto Dei, see Orvieto 1969. The most interesting letters that Braccesi wrote to Dei, commenting on events and foreign affairs, are in Florence, Biblioteca Medicea Laurenziana, Ashb. 1841, cass. I, 52–59, cass. II, 37–38.
4   For a full list of his letters, see Viti 1984.
5   A brief volume on this humanist was published by Bice Agnoletti in 1901 but is now outdated. The most complete information on Braccesi, although relying sometimes on Agnoletti's inaccurate archival research, was collected by Perosa and Kristeller; Perosa 1943, p. 138 and 1971; Kristeller 1964, pp. 311–15.
6   Catasto, 79, fol. 555v.

a forty-year old servant (*famiglio*), lived in the house of the family for whom he worked in the popolo of San Lorenzo near the church of San Barnaba, with his mother (aged sixty-five), his wife, Sandra (aged twenty-four), his son Alessandro or Sandro (aged five).[7] The family still lived in San Barnaba in 1458, when Alessandro appears again, now aged thirteen and with a three-year-old brother, Giovanbattista. Their father is listed simply as "Rinaldo di Sandro" without any reference to the surname, Uccellini, and is now aged forty-seven, his wife Sandra is thirty-four and his mother, Madonna Pippa, is seventy.[8]

Having followed the members of the family record by record, we can now safely assume that the Uccellinis became the Braccesis at some point between 1458 and 1480. Their ambition and talent drove them to rent a house near piazza San Giovanni and the cathedral of Santa Maria del Fiore, next to the "canto dei pupilli" (corner of the orphans). This name might refer to what is nowadays known as the Loggia del Bigallo, where, when this *catasto* record was written, abandoned children were left for the charitable Compagnia del Bigallo to take into custody and guardianship. The 1480 *catasto* record begins with these words: "[I], Rinaldo of Alexandro of Sancti Braccesi, live in the popolo of Sancta Maria del Fiore in Florence [...]"[9] (albeit this document is clearly in Alessandro's handwriting). It lists Rinaldo, his wife Sandra, Alessandro, Alessandro's brother, Alessandro's wife, Lisabetta, and their daughters, notably named after two classical heroines, Camilla and Lucrezia. The family owned some land in the outskirts of the city and, most importantly, both Alessandro and his brother had done well for themselves and became notaries.[10]

Braccesi held a series of temporary positions for the Florentine government from his early twenties, working as a notary all his life. In the 1490s he was appointed, replacing Andrea da Foiano, as "secretary-notary" with a hybrid function of facilitating Florence's various businesses, including recruiting teaching staff for the Studio (the University of Florence) and, more importantly, of acting as Lorenzo de' Medici's eyes and ears in Siena.[11] After the fall of the Medici he was employed in other cities, such as Perugia and Lucca, and as an informer for Savonarola in the papal curia, where he assisted the Florentine ambassador Ricciardo Becchi and his successor Domenico Bonsi. Braccesi was elected secretary of the chancery, preceding the appointment of Niccolò Machiavelli.

---

7   Catasto, 714, fol. 177.
8   Catasto, 822, fol. 439.
9   "[Io] Rinaldo di Alexandro di Sancti Braccesi habito nel popolo di Sancta Maria del Fiore di Firençe [...]."
10 Catasto, 1017, fol. 419. This record and that of 1457 are mentioned by Perosa 1971 who quotes Agnoletti.
11 Brown 2011, p. 41.

However, when Savonarola died, Braccesi presumably resumed his post as notary, even though we have no letters from this period to confirm this. On 7 July 1503, he died of a sudden fever in Rome, where he had returned to assist the new Florentine ambassador, Giovan Vittorio Soderini in 1502.

Despite his efforts and wide literary production, which is listed in detail below, Braccesi struggled to gain recognition as a poet even when he attempted to find patrons other than the Medici. The drive to emerge socially and artistically that belonged to Braccesi and his family affected him even after death, when his grandson, the poet Agnolo Firenzuola, commissioned a gravestone for his burial place in the church of Santa Prassede in Rome, which included a bas-relief depicting the coats of arms of the noble and prestigious Florentine Bracci family, completely unrelated to the Braccesi except for the sound of their name.

Braccesi's literary production seems divided equally between Latin and the vernacular. He wrote a collection of *carmina*, which were further divided into *amorum libellus, secundus liber epistolarum ad amicos* and *epigrammatum libellus*, which went through several revisions.[12] The first version of this collection, published by 1473, was dedicated to the Florentine merchant Francesco Sassetti and the last version, released some 13 years later, was dedicated to Guidobaldo da Montefeltro, the Duke of Urbino.[13] His vernacular poems can be divided into two main genres, love poetry and comic poetry. The love poems were composed and organized into a *canzoniere* entitled *amorum libellus*, a sylloge that imitates Petrarch's *Rerum vulgarium fragmenta*, while adding some original features.[14] The comic production, however, is mostly *alla burchia*, i.e., the poems are modelled on the poetry of the 15th-century master of comic-realism, Domenico di Giovanni, also known as Burchiello. Despite the disparaging words we find in the *epigrammatum libellus* ("Burchiello, who writes truly empty poems"),[15] Braccesi wrote more than 200 poems *alla burchia*, often achieving excellent results.[16] A collection that joined the first version of the love and comic poems, transcribed in a parchment manuscript now kept at

---

12   For the full ecdotic analysis, see Perosa 1984.
13   Perosa 1984, pp. 139–49.
14   Braccesi 1983, pp. IX–XXX.
15   Braccesi followed a similar statement by Cristoforo Landino, who deeply influenced his poetic style in Latin. "I send you the numerous poems of Burchiello" he writes in his *Carmina, liber secundus*, XXVIII, "read them. And what are they? You will read nothing." See Landino 1939, p. 70: "Plurima mitto tibi tonsoris carmina Burchi; / haec lege. Sed quid tum? Legeris inde nihil." Braccesi 1943, p. 105: "Burchius Aoniis migravit collibus alter/ qui quoque nimirum carmen inane facit [...]."
16   Signoriello 2014, pp. 118–40.

the Vatican Library, was a gift to Giovanni, Count of Carpegna, the feudal lord of an area in Montefeltro under the protection of the Medici in the second half of the 15th century.[17] However, the second version of the *amorum libellus*, dated around 1487, is dedicated to Guidobaldo da Montefeltro, as are the Latin poems from the same period.

What Braccesi managed to print in his lifetime were only his translations of others from Latin into the vernacular, volumes that enjoyed wide circulation and stayed in print for nearly two centuries: Pius II's *Historia de duobus amantibus* and Appian's *Roman history* from Pier Candido Decembrio's translation from the Greek. A translation of the tale of two lovers, the *Historia*, written in Vienna in 1444 by the illustrious Sienese Enea Silvio Piccolomini, is set in the hometown of the future Pope Pius II. This translation went through two revisions, the first dated around 1478–79, and the second printed between 1481 and 1483 in Milan by Leonardus Pachel and Uldericus Scinzenzeler.[18] Braccesi's is no mere translation, but a fresh rendition of the tale of Euryalus and Lucretia in which the form is changed into a *prosimetrum*, as the prose is interspersed with many of Braccesi's Petrarchan poems, while the content is also affected, especially by the gift of a happy ending. This approach to translation from Latin into the vernacular is the sign of a mentality that went beyond the intention of making a text available to those who could not afford to learn Latin, as was the case with some intellectuals of the age (e.g., Marsilio Ficino with his *De amore* and *De Christiana religione*), who translated their own works for this purpose.[19] Braccesi's *Historia* bears the noble heritage of Piccolomini's Latin, but it is a work in its own right, an entirely new tale.[20]

Finally, Braccesi's favourable attitude towards the coexistence and contamination of Latin and the vernacular is very clear from the fact that he translated one of his own poems from the vernacular *canzoniere*, "Come incaúto pesce correr sòle," into Latin, and included it in his *amorum libellus* (VI, "Ut solet incautus fatales piscis ad escas"). The fact that there are only a few occurrences of self-translation in 15th-century Florence—and those deal only with prose—clearly puts Braccesi into a category of his own.[21]

The poems written to honour Camilla Saracini, which have never been studied, are another case in point. Braccesi had been in Siena for two months when he seized an *occasio caecitatis*, so to speak, and composed two poems in

---

17 Rome, Biblioteca Apostolica Vaticana, 10681.
18 Viti 1982, pp. 49–50.
19 Bertolini 2015, pp. 206–07.
20 Viti 1982, pp. 67–68.
21 See the list drafted in Bertolini 2015, pp. 213–14.

lamentation of Camilla's blindness. These he included in four letters to four different people, correspondences that explained the circumstances of the event: letters were sent on 28 October 1491 to Lorenzo de' Medici;[22] on 29 November to Bartolomeo Scala, the chancellor of Florence;[23] to Niccolò Michelozzi, the personal secretary of Lorenzo, on 28 November;[24] and to Francesco Gaddi, the secretary of the Otto di Pratica and Braccesi's direct supervisor in this mission, on 4 December.[25] The poems were allegedly sent to each of them, and the two vernacular sonnets were written in response to one dedicated to Camilla by Bartolomeo Scala, now lost, as we can infer from the letter written to the chancellor:

> I know you will wonder and perhaps also barely tolerate the fact that I put off until today replying to these letters, which you wrote to me so kindly and intimately, with some poems that you wrote for Camilla Saracini. This undoubtedly happened because of the weakness of my intellect and the poverty of my native language, as I could barely find and explain what I think to you, such an authoritative and learned man, or barely do the minimum, and I strongly doubt it would be enough, lest I offend your very delicate ears with my incompetence and ignorance.[26]

---

22   SDO, 27, fols. 38v–39.
23   SDO, 27, fols. 56–56v; L, fols. 71–72, transcribed by Perosa in Braccesi 1943, p. 156.
24   L, fols. 76–76v (this copy of the letter is not mentioned in the list by Viti 1984, p. 392); SDO, 27, fols. 53r–54v; New York, Pierpont Morgan Library, F. 132. This is the copy of the letter that Michelozzi actually received and that Viti mentions as "Coll. Bocchi Bianchi (aut. datata «28 nov. 1491»)". This letter belonged to a corpus owned by the baroness Maria Clorinda De Franceschi Bocchi Bianchi, who gave them to the bibliophile Tammaro de Marinis in 1970. De Marinis published the letters and his heirs gave the letters back to the Bocchi Bianchi family. De Marinis-Perosa 1970, p. 43. The letters, however, were scattered and found partly at the Pierpont Morgan Library in New York and partly in London at Christie's, where they were impounded and given to the Biblioteca Nazionale Centrale in Florence. See *De Franceschi, famiglia*, ed. E. Insabato, S. Trovato, first appeared online 2012, accessed 26 November 2016 http://siusa.archivi.beniculturali.it/cgi-bin/pagina.pl?TipoPag=comparc&Chiave=126948.
25   SDO, 27, fols. 58–58v; L, fol. 75, transcribed by Perosa in Braccesi 1943, pp. 158–59. This manuscript is described by Perosa in Braccesi 1943, pp. XVII–XXII.
26   "Scio miraberis et forte etiam moleste feres quod distulerim ad hanc usque diem respondere his litteris quas ad me una cum rithmis a te editis in Camillam Saracinam scripsisti tam humaniter tamque familiariter. Primum quidem accidit hoc imbecillitate ingenii mei deinde inopia sermonis patrij cum vix potuerim et invenire et explicare quod putarem homini tibi gravissimo doctissimoque vel minima in parte posse facere, satis addubitans vehementer, ne delicatissimas aures tuas meis ineptijs ac ruditate offenderem." (L, fol. 71).

In his daily life and duties, Braccesi, like all functionaries of his time, used both Latin and the vernacular for specific purposes, reserving Latin for notarial documents[27] while utilizing the vernacular in both personal and professional correspondence. Most of his few letters in Latin were addressed to Michelozzi, but the vernacular was his default choice for all others, even his employer, Lorenzo de' Medici, in 1491. In writing the letters about Camilla's illness, however, Braccesi chose ornate Latin. In doing so was he trying to impress his superiors and peers back in Florence? In his letter to Francesco Gaddi, Braccesi mentions that he had written to Lorenzo de' Medici in October, perhaps implicitly asking him if there had been any reaction:

> I am delighted that I wrote to Lorenzo de' Medici that, Camilla Saracina having lost her sight, there is hope that at some point she will fully recover her vision; the same happens to the sun when it undergoes an eclipse, once it overcomes the eclipse's gloom, it appears the same as it was before, and it shines on us with its usual brightness.[28]

On the one hand, the use of Latin, so uncommon in his secretarial duties and employed only in the letters about Camilla, sets a specific register for Braccesi's illustrious interlocutors in Florence. On the other hand, this small corpus of texts includes two vernacular sonnets that are more than just a reply to Bartolomeo Scala; they pay homage to the Sienese tradition of vernacular poetry. I will now explore these two sides of the matter and the interaction between two languages, two cities, and their cultural legacies in the Quattrocento.

2   The Poems

Braccesi first wrote the letters about Camilla in a draft version, now at the Archivio di Stato in Florence (SDO), and then transcribed three of them, leaving out the first one to Lorenzo de' Medici (the latter is preserved in an autograph codex now in Florence, Biblioteca Medicea Laurenziana, Laur. Plut. 91

---

27   Florence, Archivio di Stato, Notarile antecosimiano 3331–39. Note that Perosa 1971 still quotes the old classmark, Notarile B 2317–25.
28   "Gaudeo quod, ita scripserim ad Laurentium Medicem Camillam Saracinam oculorum visum amisisse, ut spe non careas futurum esse quin illa possit aliquando videndi recuperare vim pristinam, quemadmodum etiam soli defectum patienti evenit, qui sublato eclipsis incommodo, idem qui ante eclipsim fuerit appareat, atque ad nos consuetum splendorem emittat." SDO, fol. 75.

sup. 41, (fols. 72v–73), henceforth referred to as "L."[29] One version of the poems for Camilla survived in this manuscript, following the letter to Gaddi. Another version of the poems is in the copy of the letter to Michelozzi that was actually sent (now in New York, Pierpont Morgan Library, F. 132), henceforth referred to as "N."[30] L was written and kept for personal use by the author, and we can therefore assume that the very last variations to the texts are found here. Below, I transcribe the texts as found in L, and N's variations in the apparatus.

I

> Ponat Amor pharetram moestus frangatque sagictas,   1
> ac tenera plangat pectora nuda manu,
> et doleat tristis passis Citherea capillis,
> delitias ploret casta Minerva suas;
> cesset et omnis honor, cultus valeatque Senensis,   5
> et matrona simul lugeat atque nurus,
> usque puellarum coetus, quin tota iuventus,[31]
> certatim lachrymis abluat ora gemens:
> heu, Saracina, decus splendorque et gloria formae,
> pulchrius in vestra qua fuit urbe nihil,   10
> infoelix visu capta est, miserabile dictu;
> sic ne vacare deos, heu, pietate decet?
> Quidnam erat in terris oculis formosius huius?
> Quid magis his poterat par fore syderibus?
> Hos obscura tamen caligo ac densa recondit,   15
> nec caelum aut terras posse videre sinit.
> Quod scelus auditum maius, quod saevius isto?
> Quid Sena, quid potuit tristius esse tibi?
> Sed maior iactura fuit tua, saeve Cupido:
> huius erant oculi retia nanque tua.   20
> Nil tibi nunc superest, quo vincula nectere possis,
> ut prius, in iuvenes, quos Sena pulchra fovet.
> Nunc et abest omnis penitus iucunda venustas,
> nunc reliqua est Veneri gratia nulla deae,
> nunc quoque moeret iners, artes quae docta Minervae   25

---

29   Fols. 72v–73, transcribed by Perosa in Braccesi, *Carmina*, pp. 140–41 and 157–58.
30   Transcribed in De Marinis-Perosa 1970, pp. 47–49.
31   Unlike Perosa, who transcribed "inventus," I read "iuventus" as in MS N.

callet, quod tenebrae lumina clausa tenent.
Ergo, Cupido simul Venus et Bellona parenti
fundite devotas, heu, sine fine preces,
lumina restituat donec formosa Camillae,
hanc, prius ut poterat, posse videre sinat.   30

15   Hos ... recondite: N Corripit obducta tamen hos ceu nocte caligo
25   Minervae: N Minerva
26   quod ... clausa: N at heu tenebrae lumina diva
28   heu: N nunc
29   formosa: N purgata
30   posse: N queque

II

Piangete donne belle, et chon voi Amore   1
poi chè perduto havete il vostro sole
de duo begli ochi, onde 'l mondo si dole
e 'l celo anchora par ne mostri dolore,

poi che la luce che faceva honore   5
all'altre stelle, più chome far sole,
non illustra la terra et la suo mole
chon la virtù del suo grande splendore.

Manchati sono a Phebo e' raçi suoi;
Amore ha perso l'arme e la baldanza;   10
Invidia ha spento il fior d'ogni belleça.

Pietoso Giove, adunque, se tu vuoi
in una opra mostrare ogni possanza
rendi a' begli ochi la sua gran dolceça.

N   Senensibus puellis
3   de: N ne'
4   anchora: N anchor

III

> Ben puoi dolerti, Siena, del mal fato 1
> che 'l terreste tuo sole ha in te spento
> et privo ti ha d'un sì bello ornamento
> che chi el vedie se ne tenea beato.
>
> Chome esser può che tanto mal sie nato 5
> che duo begli ochi quai sença fomento
> d'amor nissun potie ghuardare intento
> chondocti sieno in sì misero stato?
>
> O la lor luce Phebo ha convertito
> ne' raçi suoi per duplichar suo força 10
> che se gli è vero ha da temer la terra.
>
> O per suo dignità s'è risentito
> che vedendo suo lume in terra amorça
> un altro sole in tenebre lo serra.

N   Ad Senensem urbem
9   lor: N suo
13 lume: N luce

Predictably, the author places emphasis on every figure of speech related to Camilla's eyes. In terms of metaphor, her eyes were like the Sun that shone over Siena and the whole world, especially in the vernacular texts (II.3, II.7, III.2, III.15), or like the most beautiful stars that, fading, left darkness in the sky—in the Latin *carmen* (1.14–16). In both vernacular and Latin poetry, comparing a woman's eyes to the sun and the stars is topical and needs no further exploration here. What is far less common is finding literary sources describing blindness with metaphors or similes. Blindness as a metaphor, however, is not uncommon in philosophy, which is the point of departure for investigating Braccesi's bond with Florence.[32]

---

32 "Blindness is not a central theme in Renaissance imagery. Neither in literature nor in the visual art is much attention paid to the sightless person. To the student of Renaissance culture, particularly of Italy during the fifteenth and sixteenth centuries, this seeming lack of interest in the blind and their world shaped by this defect, remains a puzzle. We

3 Florence and Neoplatonism

In his letters, Braccesi offers a sort of self-commentary to his poems. The letter to Lorenzo de' Medici, possibly the most interesting, is unfortunately the least readable. It has survived only in its draft copy, with scribbled notes and crossed out words making it almost illegible except in isolated sentences, such as the following marginal note: "The Sienese sun suffered an eclipse."[33] This simile also appears as a metaphor in the letter to Gaddi, in which Braccesi expresses the wish that Camilla's condition would resemble that of an eclipse, whereby the sun is only temporarily obscured by the moon:

> I would not have denied that you were moved by an excellent reason, when it is obvious that the sun itself during an eclipse does not suffer, but cheats our sight, because the moon, drawing close to the sun, blocks the light of the sun from our eyes with its mass. The sun endures the eclipse for as long as the moon covers it.[34]

This very unusual metaphor is in fact a quotation from Macrobius's *Commentarii in somnium Scipionis*, in a passage explaining first a lunar and then a solar eclipse I, 15, 13–14:

> For it happens that when the moon borrows from the sun the usual light, being opposite to the sun, its trajectory meets the cone [of shade] of the earth; while in the other case, when the moon overtakes the sun, by its interposition it deprives the earth of the sun's light. Therefore, during the eclipse, the sun itself does not suffer but our sight is cheated and, in fact, the moon suffers, not receiving the sun's light, by which it colours the night.[35]

---

hardly know of a period in which vision was so highly valued as in the Renaissance." Barasch 2001, p. 115.

[33] "Senensis sol eclypsim patitur."

[34] "Non negaverim fuisse te optima ratione adductum, cum manifestum sit solem ipsum in defectu nil pati, sed nostrum fraudari aspectum, cum luna, soli succedens, obiectu suo lumen eius ab oculis nostris repellat: et quamdiu soli adversa sit, tamdiu ille patiatur eclipsim." (L, fols. 75–75v).

[35] "Sic enim evenit ut aut lunae contra solem positae ad mutuandum ab eo solitum lumen sub eadem inventus linea terrae conus obsistat aut soli ipsa succedens obiectu suo ab humano aspectu lumen eius repellat. In defectu ergo sol ipse nil patitur sed noster fraudatur aspectus, luna vero circa proprium defectum laborat non accipiendo solis lumen, cuius beneficio noctem colorat."

The eyes of Camilla might still be rescued by divine intervention and indeed might not have been hurt at all, just as the sun is only temporarily obscured by the shadow projected by the moon during an eclipse. The precision of this description is not common in lyric poetry and this could be the very reason why Braccesi decided to leave it in the letters. Comic poetry, nonetheless, was an entirely different matter. As a comic poet, Braccesi did not restrict himself to a satirical style and clearly felt at ease with many other subjects and styles, expressing interest in such things as the explanation of natural phenomena when he quotes Macrobius. In his corpus of comic poems in the vernacular, for example, *Grandine è pioggia in aer congelata* ("Hailstones are rain frozen in the air"), he explains in only 14 lines the nature of hailstones:

> Grandine è pioggia in aer congelata
> dalla forza del vento, e è vapore
> humido e freddo, o vogliam dire umore,
> dal caldo spinto in nube più gelata.
>
> Questa cagione dal Philosopho è data:
> che 'l freddo, in aer fuggendo il calore,
> alla parte ricorre interiore
> della nube, dov'è più condensata.
>
> E quello humor, che nella nube trova,
> in tondi serra di tanta freddeza
> che ciò che toca da morzar[36] fa prova.
>
> La state più che l'inverno si impeza[37]
> perché del freddo allor la virtù nova
> chiamata dal calor s'unisce en treza.[38]

---

36 "morzar": Battaglia, vol. 10, p. 976: "ant. spegnere, smorzare (la luce); estinguere (il calore)."
37 "impeza": for an alternative form of *impecia* from *impeciare*, see Battaglia, vol. 7, p. 420, s.v. "impeciare": "invischiarsi; restare impaniato, irretito."
38 "Trezza" is *treccia*, "plait." Other examples of the affrication occur in Braccesi 1983, I.37–38, p. 4 and 71.7–8, p. 73: "Son le sue treze bionde / l'esca della mia fiamma"; "quella bionda treza / e 'l bel volto ch'a morte mi conduce" "presto mutare / suolsi in altro color la bionda treza."

> E nel verno si speza
> e per l'aer si sparge disunita,
> che fa la neve spesso a poggi unita.³⁹

In this sonnet, Braccesi employs Aristotle's theory from the *Meteorology* quite literally, without adding any metaphor, which produces a dry and didactic effect. This genre was not new: Dante's *Commedia* inspired a large number of didactic poems written in *terza rima* during the 13th century. Although it was never coupled with the sonnet form prior to Braccesi, didactic poetry remained popular during the 15th century, often as an encyclopaedic mode of displaying curiosity about natural philosophy.⁴⁰

An interest in natural philosophy alone might not fully justify the presence of Macrobius's *Commentarii in Somnium Scipionis* in Braccesi's letters, especially considering the time (second half of the 15th century) and the place (Florence) where these letters were read. The choice of Macrobius is not as clear as that of Aristotle; Macrobius's commentary was a Neoplatonic text that had been read and referred to by Marsilio Ficino, who, in 1491, was still the most prominent philosopher in Italy and beyond the peninsula. Even though the poems for Camilla do not have a Neoplatonic message *per se*, the significance of her eyes and the unusual eclipse metaphor might hint at something that goes beyond a literary description about a woman's eyes that uses traditional figures of speech.

Before exploring the Neoplatonic aspect of the texts, it is useful to compare them to a sonnet by Braccesi in order to appreciate the difference between a Petrarchan, indeed almost standard, lyric poem and the verses for Camilla. Braccesi was not averse to using traditional metaphors to describe the eyes, the look, and the effects that these produced on him, as evidenced by a sonnet included in his love *canzoniere* that touches upon the theme of blindness (VI):

---

39 Florence, Biblioteca Riccardiana, 2725, fol. 105v. See my commentary in Signoriello 2014, p. 122. This explanation is presented in Aristotle, *Meteorology*, 1.12, and could have been found by Braccesi in several commentaries, for example, those of Albertus Magnus, Thomas Aquinas, and Themon Judaeus. See Martin 2011, p. 18. See also the vernacular version by Cecco d'Ascoli in his poem *Acerba*: Stabili 2002, I, 7.13–24, p. 40: "Ma qui pò dubitar[e] l'alma gentile: / nel tempo caldo com[o] si forma il ghiazzo, / e sprivase nel suo tempo simìle. / La spera che ten[e] focho in sua virtute / dico che fuga il fredo col suo brazzo / e tienlo in unità con sue ferute. / Così de focho li raggi reflessi / inverso l'aire de la nostra terra / per l'orizonte essendo conessi, / e quando regie Chancro e poi Leone, / assai più fredo nel mezo se serra:/ però il gh<i>azo piove la stagione."

40 Ciociola 1995–2005, p. 413.

> Phebo, da invidia preso e maraviglia, 1
> veggendo in terra una sì chiara luce
> che più che 'l sole a mezzo dì reluce
> quando tra nube e nube s'assottiglia,
>
> da ira tinto e con turbate ciglia, 5
> avanti a sì belli ochi si conduce
> e con inganno pose un ferro truce
> in quella man ch'al marmo s'assomiglia.
>
> Poi nella adorna veste un nodo strinse
> tal che col ferro bisognando sciorre, 10
> la man transcorsa già l'occhio feriva;
>
> se non ch'allor Dïana pietà vinse
> tanto della sua amata nynpha diva,
> che 'l ferro dal suo corso fece tòrre.[41]

This sonnet and those for Camilla share the image of the envious Phoebus and emphasise the description of light. No attention, however, is drawn here to the eyes themselves and there is no mention of the rays of light coming directly from the eyes of the woman saved by Diana, who is almost a secondary figure compared to the gods who decide her fate.

Camilla's eyes receive an entirely different treatment. In those texts there is an oddity that stands out; the idea that a young woman might not be virtuous or beautiful, even if blind, considering that Camilla was after all still alive and presumably honourable. From a Ficinian perspective however, having lost her sight, Camilla has lost her chance to reach for the divine. In his treatise, *De amore*, a commentary on Plato's *Symposium* completed by 1469 and translated into the vernacular in 1474, Ficino explained at length, in particular in the sixth oration, how love is nothing but desire for beauty and how the first step to reach for the divine is always taken via the observation of physical beauty, which is seen through the eyes:

> The gates of the soul are the eyes and the ears, because many things pass to the soul through them, and the emotions and habits of the soul clearly show in them. Lovers spend most of their time in looking and listening

---

41 Braccesi 1983, p. 7.

to their loved one, and they are rarely attentive, and their mind wanders often to their eyes and ears.[42]

In Ficino's metaphorical system, it is the sun, i.e., God, which both generates the eyes and allows them to see beauty. To describe this process, Ficino uses the concept of the rays of the sun, which originate from God, reach the lover, and then go back to God:

> This great gift is generated from the richness that is the origin of Love, because the ray of beauty, which is the richness and origin of Love, has this power to reflect back to the place from whence it came, and by reflecting pulls back the lover. Certainly this ray, coming down first from God, and then going through the angel and the soul as if they were glass, and from the soul into the body, which is ready to receive this ray, passing easily, from this full body shines brightly outside through the eyes as if they were clear windows, and immediately flies through the air, and penetrating the eyes of the attentive man, it hits his soul, generating desire.[43]

Braccesi might have referred to this concept when mentioning Phoebus's rays, "razi" (II.9, III.10): rays that Camilla has lost. This would not be new to Neoplatonism, as Ficino himself wrote in a letter to thank him for an epigram in his honour:

> Our Plato, in the dialogue entitled Ion, considers as divine music and deeply imbued with the frenzy of Muses only songs which are accompanied by the music of men and somehow incite into frenzy the singer himself and those listening. Yesterday, Alessandro wrote some songs to

---

42 "Le porte dell'animo sono gli occhi e gli orecchi, perché per questi molte cose entrano nell'animo, e gli affecti e costumi dell'animo chiaramente per gli occhi si manifestano. Gl'innamorati consumano el più del tempo nel badare con gli occhi e con gli orecchi intorno allo amato, e rade volte la mente loro in sé si raccoglie, vagando spesso per gli occhi e per gli orecchi." Ficino 1987, p. 140.

43 "Questo tanto dono nasce dalla copia che è padre dello Amore, perché el razzo della bellezza, che è copia e padre d'Amore, ha questa forza, che'e' si riflecte quivi ond'e' venne, e riflectendosi tira seco l'amante. Certamente questo razzo, disceso prima da Dio, e poi passando nell'angelo e nell'anima come per materie di vetro, e dall'anima nel corpo, preparato a ricevere tale razzo, facilmente passando, da esso corpo formoso traluce fuori maxime per gli occhi come per transparenti finestre, e subito vola per aria, e penetrando gli occhi dell'uomo che bada ferisce l'anima, accende l'appetito." Ficino 1987, p. 143.

Marsilio that were truly of this kind, and soon my cithara proved it to many listeners.[44]

Moreover, in his love *canzoniere* Braccesi had already focused on Neoplatonic themes filtered through Lorenzo de' Medici's *Comento de' miei sonetti*. For instance, Braccesi developed in his poems the theme of the lover becoming the object of his love (LIII). Although this theme had been developed in courtly poetry, Ficino described it in his *De amore* (II, VIII) and Lorenzo repeated it in his *Comento* (XXX). Another theme used by Braccesi (LIV), one that has a resonance with Lorenzo's work (III, XXXI, XXXVII), is the lover's intense experience of both pain and pleasure. There are more deeply rooted ties to Lorenzo, such as the distance of the loved one experienced as deprivation by absence (LXIII–LXX), a Petrarchan theme that later became humanistic, and an overlap between erotic and theological themes—a trope common to both Lorenzo's *Comento* and the final section of Braccesi's collection (LXX–LV).[45] According to the scholar Franca Magnani, Braccesi at some point had been a student of Cristoforo Landino but, as this cursory survey of his works might suggest, Neoplatonism in the works of Lorenzo de' Medici and Ficino may well have been an important influence.

---

44 "Plato noster in dialogo, qui Ion inscribitur, carmina illa solum divina musica Musarumque furore infusa penitus existimat, quae cum musica humana cantantur et cantorem ipsum et audientes quodammodo concitant in furorem. Alexandri vero carmina heri ad Marsilium scripta esse talia, mox cithara mea plurimis audientibus comprobavit." A more explicit admiration for Ficino and his philosophy is found in Braccesi's *Epigrammatum libellus* (XII). One of these letters is addressed to Ficino, who is described in quite flattering words: "[...] you shall have, believe me, everlasting fame. This is because Britons read your works, which have already reached them; people from Tomi and Sabaeans read your works, and I do not even mention our people: your name is constantly in their mouths and they bring you to heavens with their praises. But why do I attempt to praise you with such a weak pen? Why do I sing this with hoarse verses? For this topic needs a sweeter and greater speech, and it must be better celebrated by a refined lyre. Nevertheless, I have written these things inflamed by a great love: grant indulgence, if you do not read a worthy poem." (Braccesi 1943, p. 85, "[...] ac tibi, crede mihi, fama peremnis erit; /scripta legunt quoniam tua iam vulgata Britanni, / illa thomitani gensque Sabaea legunt, / ut taceam nostros, quorum versaris in ore / et qui te in caelum laudibus usque ferunt. / Ast ego cur tenui calamo tibi dicere laudes / tento? Quid haec raucis versibus ipse cano? / Dulcius eloquium nanque haec maiusque requirunt, / et magis exculta sunt celebranda lyra; / haec ego sed magno succensus amore notavi: / da veniam, nisi te carmina digna leges.").

45 Braccesi 1983, pp. XXXII–XXXIX.

4 Siena and Its Illustrious Women

Despite his attempts to promote his poetry in Florence, Braccesi did not overlook the place where he was writing and his local audience. The literary world in Siena was quite different from that of Florence. As Carrai pointed out, if in the first half of the 15th century we encounter the names of eminent Neo-Latin poets such as Panormita, Marrasio, Francesco Patrizi, and Enea Silvio Piccolomini, during the second half there was virtually no relevant Latin poetry, with the exception of the oratory poetry of Agostino Dati and the *Bucolicum carmen* by Fosco Paracleto da Corneto, dedicated to Enea Silvio Piccolomini. The real protagonist in literary Siena half way through the 15th century was the vernacular, starting with Francesco Arzocchi, who, at the beginning of the century, gave way to Tuscan pastoral poetry. The latter became a Sienese speciality that was exported as far as the Veneto and Naples.[46]

Pastoral poetry, however, was not the only focus of Sienese literary circles. Throughout the century a tradition of praising illustrious women took several forms and the three main names in this genre were Bernardo Lapini (better known by his pseudonym Ilicino), Benedetto da Cingoli, and Niccolò Angeli, all of whom taught at the Studio in Siena during the second half of the century. From these works we can construct a genealogy of Sienese women praised during the two decades between the 1460s and the 1470s:[47]

- Onorata Orsini, who lived between 1435 and 1458, was the subject of *Vita di madonna Onorata*, a biography in the form of a *prosimetrum* written by Ilicino between 1469 and 1470.[48]
- Bianca Saracini, Onorata Orsini's daughter, born in 1453 and subject of a *capitolo ternario* written in the 1460s by Benedetto da Cingoli. The same author dedicated to her some *Epigrammata in Blancam*, published in 1503 and 1511.[49]
- Ginevra di Bartolomeo Luti, for whom Bernardo Ilicino wrote a small *canzoniere* and an experimental work in prose called *Somnium*.[50]
- Caterina Orlandi, dedicatee of another *canzoniere* by Benedetto da Cingoli.[51]

---

46   Carrai 2009 (*Enea Silvio Piccolomini*), pp. 32–36; Carrai 2009 (*Benedetto da Cingoli*), pp. 43–44.
47   On this topic see Cracolici 2009 (*Agiografie laiche*).
48   See the dating in Carrai 2009 (*Benedetto da Cingoli*), p. 45; Lapini 1843.
49   Carrai 2009 (*Benedetto da Cingoli*), p. 47; Benedetto da Cingoli 1503; and Bendetto da Cingoli 1511.
50   Cracolici 2009 (*L'etopea di Ginevra*).
51   Carrai 2009 (*Benedetto da Cingoli*), p. 47; Carrai 2009 (*Un commento quattrocentesco*), pp. 54–55.

– Francesca Benassai or *Cervia* because of her *senhal*, a deer, praised by both Bernardo Ilicino and Angeli.[52]

The reason why this sequence of women and poems forms a proper tradition rather than being simply a literary trend of praising illustrious women, lies in the relationship between these women and the works dedicated to them; this is particularly evident in the case of Onorata, Bianca, and Ginevra.

This list has been arranged in chronological order by birth, when, in fact, the first praise written was the *capitolo ternario* for Bianca, dated by Carrai at some point during the 1460s, when Ilicino taught medicine at the Studio in Siena, before he moved to Ferrara. This long *capitolo* for Bianca can be found in its entirety in the 1503 edition printed in Rome by Johann Besicken; part of it is in Florence (ms. Palatino 211 at the National Library of Florence), with an illumination by Francesco di Giorgio Martini.[53] The portrait depicts Bianca Saracini holding a snowball (symbolizing her purity), and hovering above the city of Siena. The events narrated in the *capitolo* are briefly the following. As Bernardo wanders in the outskirts of Siena, lamenting the impossibility of writing a poem for Bianca, a woman too perfect to be fully described by his limited intellect, he suddenly encounters Apollo himself, who explains the reason for such ineffability. Bianca is simply a gift from the gods of Olympus, who, in an act of generosity, decided to give men a gift so perfect that it might rescue them from their misery.

Some years later, Benedetto da Cingoli wrote the biographical *prosimetrum* entitled *Vita di madonna Onorata*, a homage to Onorata Orsini. Onorata, despite her very short life, was a model of absolute virtue for both men and women in Siena, and so she was loved by every citizen. By recounting her life, Benedetto refers to events that happened from 35 to 15 years earlier, as Onorata was the mother of Bianca and wife of Iacomo Saracini.

Finally, Ginevra Luti, like Onorata a "mirror [reflecting the] glory and honour of all living women,"[54] is the main character of a work that seems to combine the *Capitolo* for Bianca and Onorata's biography. It is yet another *prosimetrum*, this time by Ilicino, who describes a dream he had with historical characters and gods arguing for or against Love and Modesty; and of course Ginevra appears in the dream as the only living being capable of reconciling the two.

Stefano Cracolici has correctly defined this sequence of praises for illustrious women as a "secular hagiography,"[55] even though there is another point

---

52 See more details on both in Carrai 2009 (*Benedetto da Cingoli*), p. 45.
53 Bellosi 1993, p. 262.
54 "Spechio, gloria et honore di tutte le donne viventi."
55 Cracolici 2009 (*Agiografie laiche*), p. 106.

deserving attention: the praise of these women exists only in relation to the city of Siena. Both Ilicino and Benedetto da Cingoli emphasize their role in Siena, as these women contributed to the prestige of their city.

It is no coincidence that Braccesi chose to honour a female member of the Saracini family, like Onorata and her daughter Bianca. Tellingly, Braccesi addressed Siena and its citizens quite vehemently in all three poems for Camilla. *Piangete donne belle, et chon voi amore* is directly addressed to Camilla's peers. In *Ben puoi, Sena, dolerti del mal fato*, the city itself is addressed and Camilla's eyes likened to its sun (III.1–3). In the *carmen* it is explicitly stated that Camilla's honour and beauty were the best in all of Siena: "Heu, Saracina, decus splendorque et gloria formae / pulchrius in vestra qua fuit urbe nihil." And again, the personification of Siena mourns the loss of someone even more powerful than Cupid (1.18–20). Camilla's ancestor Bianca, according to the art historian Marilena Caciorgna, symbolizes the virtues and qualities of the city of Siena itself and her descendant Camilla plays an identical role in the personification of Siena.[56]

5 Conclusion

Nearly halfway through the century, in 1441, the polymath Leon Battista Alberti organised a *certame coronario*, i.e., a juried competition among a select group of poets whose submissions on the topic of friendship were to demonstrate the capability of the vernacular to rival Latin with respect to specific parameters. Notwithstanding the uncertain results of the competition, the event was a landmark in the history of the vernacular. By the 1460s, the efforts of a new generation of Florentine literates to revitalize Italian as a language of culture had grown in intensity and sophistication; a product of this environment was the *Raccolta Aragonese*, an anthology of Tuscan poetry delivered by Lorenzo de' Medici to Frederick of Aragon, the King of Naples, around 1477. Latin, however, remained the essential language of intellectual exchange and it was part of humanistic debate along with its grammatical and syntactical rules. This prominence is evident in a number of treatises that discuss the Latin language during the first half of the Quattrocento, the most important written by Lorenzo Valla, who, for instance in his *Elegantiae linguae latinae*—dated 1441 like Alberti's competition on vernacular poetry—endorses classical Latin as the first tool of thinking and writing for every kind of intellectual. Latin poetry

---

56 Caciorgna 2005, pp. 154–57.

had not died in Florence, and Braccesi was only one interlocutor among a complex network of humanists corresponding and exchanging Latin verses.

In 1491, however, with his relocation to Siena, Braccesi's lyric poetry, both vernacular and Latin, was contaminated by a different tradition. Siena and its histories of illustrious women forge the homage to Camilla Saracini. Braccesi was clearly uncomfortable in choosing either the vernacular or Latin, and could not make up his mind, writing in both languages and using overlapping content that pertained to Florence, his hometown, and Siena, the place where he worked. The content of the *carmen* seems tightly linked to a Sienese approach to describing women by idealizing their virtues and making them the icons of a whole city. Neoplatonic hints that belonged to Florence and the revival of Platonic philosophy were transferred into either the vernacular poems, or the paratext, i.e., the letters. Braccesi, therefore, seemed to reach an impasse, due to the cultural and political baggage that the two languages carried with them, unable to give preference to either or to merge successfully the two traditions.

Despite the profound knowledge and curiosity that brought Braccesi to experiment all his life with his translations and renditions between Latin and the vernacular, the small corpus dedicated to Camilla was not enough to grant him the enduring memory among his peers for which he had probably hoped. Its multiple factors, however, paint a vivid picture of what *diglossia* culturally and linguistically entailed at this point in the 15th century.

Abbreviations

Catasto	Florence, Archivio di Stato, Catasto.
L	Florence, Biblioteca Medicea Laurenziana, Plut. 91 sup. 41
SDO	Florence, Archivio di Stato, Signori, Dieci di Balìa, Otto di Pratica, Legazioni e Commissarie Missive e Responsive.

Bibliography

Primary Sources

Benedetto da Cingoli. *Sonecti, barzelle, et capitoli del claro poeta B. Cingulo*. Rome: Johann Besicken, 1503.

Benedetto da Cingoli. *Opere del preclarissimo poeta B. Cingulo novamente stampate. Con molte piu opere che non sono negli altri: cioe Sonetti. Barzellette. Capitoli*. Siena: Simone Nardi and Giovanni Landi, 1511.

Braccesi, Alessandro. *Carmina*, edited by Alessandro Perosa. Florence: Bibliopolis, 1943.

Braccesi, Alessandro. *Soneti e canzone*, edited by Franca Magnani. Parma: Studium Parmense, 1983.

Ficino, Marsilio. *El libro dell'amore*, edited by Sandra Niccoli. Florence: Olschki, 1987.

Landino, Cristoforo. *Carmina omnia*, edited by Alessandro Perosa. Florence: Olschki, 1939.

Lapini, Bernardo. *Vita di Madonna Onorata. Scritta da Bernardo Ilicino, pubblicata per la prima volta sopra un codice del secolo 15 da Giuseppe Vallardi figlio*. Milan: Giuseppe Bernardoni, 1843.

Stabili, Francesco [Cecco d'Ascoli]. *L'acerba: (Acerba etas)*, edited by Marco Albertazzi. Trento: La Finestra, 2002.

Secondary Sources

Agnoletti, Bice. *Alessandro Braccesi. Contributo alla storia dell'umanesimo e della poesia volgare*. Florence: Passeri, 1901.

Barasch, Moshe. *Blindness. The History of a Mental Image in Western Thought*. New York: Routledge, 2001.

Battaglia, Salvatore. *Grande dizionario della lingua italiana*, 24 vols. Turin: UTET, 1961–2009.

Bellosi, Luciano, ed. *Francesco di Giorgio Martino e il Rinascimento a Siena, 1450–1500*. Milan: Electa, 1993.

Bertolini, Lucia. "Latino-volgare e viceversa. Le traduzioni a Firenze fra XV e XVI." In *Le Choix du vulgaire: Espagne, France, Italie (XIIIe–XVIe siècle)*, edited by Nella Bianchi Bensimon, Bernard Darbord, and Marie-Christine Gomez-Géraud. Paris: Classiques Garnier, 2015, pp. 201–19.

Brown, Alison. *Medicean and Savonarolan Florence. The Interplay of Politics, Humanism, and Religion*. Turnhout: Brepols, 2011.

Caciorgna, Marilena. "*Mortalis aemulor arte deos*. Umanisti e arti figurative a Siena tra Pio II e Pio III." In *Pio II e le arti. La riscoperta dell'antico da Federighi a Michelangelo*, edited by Alessandro Angelini. Siena: Monte dei Paschi di Siena-Silvana Editoriale, 2005, pp. 151–79.

Carrai, Stefano. "Enea Silvio Piccolomini e la poesia senese." In *La letteratura a Siena nel Quattrocento*, edited by Stefano Carrai, Stefano Cracolici, and Monica Marchi. Pisa: ETS, 2009, pp. 31–42.

Carrai, Stefano. "Benedetto da Cingoli e la poesia a Siena nella seconda metà del Quattrocento." In *La letteratura a Siena nel Quattrocento*, edited by Stefano Carrai, Stefano Cracolici, and Monica Marchi. Pisa: ETS, 2009, pp. 43–52.

Carrai, Stefano. "Un commento quattrocentesco 'ad usum mulieris': Jacopo de' Buoninsegni sopra un sonetto del Cingoli." In *La letteratura a Siena nel Quattrocento*,

edited by Stefano Carrai, Stefano Cracolici, and Monica Marchi. Pisa: ETS, 2009, pp. 53–72.

Catana, Leo. "Readings of Platonic Virtue Theories from the Middle Ages to the Renaissance: the Case of Marsilio Ficino's *De amore*." *British Journal for the History of Philosophy* 22 (2014), pp. 680–703.

Ciociola Claudio. "Poesia gnomica, d'arte, di corte, allegorica e didattica" in *Storia della letteratura italiana*, edited by Enrico Malato, vol. 2. Rome: Salerno, 1995, pp. 327–454.

Cracolici, Stefano. "Agiografie laiche. Bernardo Ilicino e le donne illustri di Siena." In *La letteratura a Siena nel Quattrocento*, edited by Stefano Carrai, Stefano Cracolici, and Monica Marchi. Pisa: ETS, 2009, pp. 91–108.

Cracolici, Stefano. "L'etopea di Ginevra, o il *Somnium* di Bernardo Ilicino." In *La letteratura a Siena nel Quattrocento*, edited by Stefano Carrai, Stefano Cracolici, and Monica Marchi. Pisa: ETS, 2009, pp. 109–34.

De Marinis, Tammaro and Alessandro Perosa. *Nuovi documenti per la storia del Rinascimento*. Florence: Olschki, 1970.

Isenberg, Nancy. "Censimento delle lettere di Niccolò Michelozzi." *Giornale italiano di filologia* 13 (1982), pp. 271–91.

Kristeller, Paul Oskar. "An Unknown Correspondence of Alessandro Braccesi with Niccolò Michelozzi, Naldo Naldi, Bartolommeo Scala, and other Humanists (1470–72) in Ms. Bodl. Auct. F. 2. 17." In *Classical Medieval and Renaissance Studies in Honor of Berthold Louis Ullman*, edited by Charles Handerson Jr., vol. 2. Rome: Edizioni di storia e letteratura, 1964, pp. 311–59.

Martin Craig. *Renaissance Meteorology: Pomponazzi to Descartes*. Baltimore: Johns Hopkins University Press, 2011.

Orvieto, Paolo. "Un esperto orientalista del '400: Benedetto Dei." *Rinascimento* 9 (1969), 205–75.

Perosa, Alessandro. "Braccesi, Alessandro." In *Dizionario biografico degli italiani*, vol. 13. Rome: Istituto della Enciclopedia italiana, 1971, pp. 602–08.

Perosa, Alessandro. "Storia di un libro di poesie latine dell'umanista fiorentino Alessandro Braccesi." *La bibliofilia* 45 (1943), pp. 138–85.

Signoriello, Federica. *Satire of Philosophy and Philosophers in Fifteenth Century Florence*. London: University College London, 2014, doctoral thesis.

Viti, Paolo. "I volgarizzamenti di Alessandro Braccesi dell'*Historia de duobus amantibus* di Enea Silvio Piccolomini." *Esperienze letterarie* 6 (1982), pp. 49–68.

Viti, Paolo. "Censimento delle lettere di Alessandro Braccesi." *Archivio storico italiano* 142 (1984), pp. 377–420.

CHAPTER 11

The Reception of Petrarch and Petrarchists' Poetry in Marcantonio Flaminio's *Carmina*

Giacomo Comiati

In his *Considerazioni sopra le Rime del Petrarca*, an exegetical work on Petrarch's vernacular poems published in Modena in 1609, the Italian writer Alessandro Tassoni records at the end of a series of annotations devoted to Petrarch's canzone, 'Chiare, fresche et dolci acque' that:

> Marc'Antonio Flaminio con leggiadria grande trasportò questa canzone in un'oda latina, che comincia "O fons Melioli sacer / omni splendidior vitro". E si legge stampata co' versi latini del Flaminio e del Molza.[1]

Tassoni was not the first to mention and praise this text by Flaminio (1498–1550).[2] More than 40 years earlier, in 1560, Bernardino Partenio referred to the same Latin ode in the fourth book of his *Dell'imitatione poetica* and compared a few strophes of Flaminio's *carmen* (1.6.45–64) to the fourth stanza of Petrarch's 'Chiare, fresche et dolci acque' (*RVF* 126.39–51).[3] The proximity of the two texts was later underlined by the Italian poet and co-founder of the Roman Accademia dell'Arcadia, Giovanni Mario Crescimbeni, in his *Dell'istoria della volgar poesia*,[4] as well as by the 19th-century scholar, Ettore Cuccoli, who presented the imitation of 'Chiare, fresche et dolci acque' as one of the most crucial pieces of evidence in support of Flaminio's admiration for Petrarch. Yet,

---

1 Tassoni, *Considerazioni*, p. 192.
2 On Flaminio's life and work, see Cuccoli 1897; Maddison 1965; Pisanti 1976; Pastore 1981; and Pisanti 1982.
3 Partenio, *Dell'imitatione poetica*, pp. 153–54. Partenio explicitly refers to Flaminio's ode as "la bella imitatione di Flaminio sopra questi versi del Petrarca." Ibid. p. 153. Flaminio's Latin poems are quoted from Massimo Scorsone's edition of Flaminio's *Carmina* (see Flaminio's *Carmina* 1993). I refer to Flaminio's poems by book, text number, and line. Petrarch's texts are, instead, quoted from Rosanna Bettarini's edition of the *Canzoniere* (which will be henceforth referred to as RVF, i.e., *Rerum vulgarium fragmenta*). See Petrarch, *Rerum vulgarium fragmenta*. English translations of Petrarch's RVF are quoted from Petrarch, *Lyric Poems*.
4 Crescimbeni, *Dell'istoria della volgar poesia*, p. 306. I consulted the Google-books copy of this edition that can be found at https://books.google.it/books?id=BaT8nGGpYHsC (accessed 2 October 2018).

Cuccoli explicitly, albeit vaguely, also pointed out that Flaminio's links with Petrarch's poetry were not exclusively limited to this literary episode.[5] Echoing this last judgement, another scholar, Carol Maddison, stated that Flaminio's early poems:

> have a carefully balanced structure which owes more to the sonnet than to the classical ode, an easy rhythm, descriptions of nature that reveal the poet's emotional submergence in the vital processes around him, and a colouring of Petrarchan romanticism.[6]

In this observation, Maddison underlined what might appear to be a characteristic trait of Flaminio's poetry. According to her, Flaminio's Petrarchan reception extended beyond the poet's Latin imitation of Petrarch's canzone 126, exactly as Cuccoli pointed out in referring to some other (unspecified) odes by Flaminio in addition to his poem, 'O fons Melioli sacer,' as texts in which he recognized a "non lontana imitazione petrarchesca."[7] It seems, therefore, worth investigating Flaminio's lyrical production through a Petrarchan lens in order to reveal what Cuccoli and Maddison alluded to. I will conduct this analysis by focusing on the first four of the eight books of Flaminio's *Carmina*, namely those books whose poems deal with love, encomiastic, moral, hymnological, and eulogistic themes rather than those related to epistolary subjects (books 5 and 6), or biblical and religious matters (books 7 and 8).[8] Indeed, book 1 is a collection of poems in various lyric metres on love, encomiastic,

---

5 Cuccoli 1897, pp. 209–10: "l'ammirazione del Flaminio per il Petrarca ci è nota. Di lui [...] tradusse una canzone e ne rese meravigliosamente il sentimento nel più eletto latino; e in alcune delle odi erotiche [...] è forse non lontana imitazione petrarchesca."
6 Maddison 1965, p. 18.
7 On Flaminio's ode, 'O fons Melioli sacer' (1.6), and its Petrarchan links, see Scorsone 2004, p. 206.
8 The actual division of Flaminio's lyrical corpus into eight books of poems (which is followed in Scorsone's edition of Flaminio's *Carmina*) was introduced in the 18th century by Francesco Maria Mancurti, editor of both the Padua 1727 and 1743 editions of Flaminio's opera omnia (Flaminio, *Carminum libri VIII* and Flaminio, *Carmina* 1743). Mancurti's organization of Flaminio's books was largely based on the book organisation of the 1552 edition of Flaminio's Latin poems, printed in Florence by Torrentino (Flaminio, *Carmina* 1552). Mancurti only partially changed the placement of some books within the collection. In fact, in the 1552 volume, Flaminio's books of *carmina* were printed according to the following order: books 1, 5, 2 + 3 (as a single book), 4, 6, 7, and 8. In placing book 5 after book 1 and combining books 2 and 3, Torrentino followed the scheme in which Flaminio's books appeared in the 1548 Venice volume of *Carmina quinque illustrium poetarum* (Flaminio, *Carmina* 1548). Torrentino simply added books 6 and 8, absent in the 1548 edition, in the making of which it seems that Flaminio played an important, albeit unofficial, role, by contributing to organize his poetical

hymnological, and moral topics; book 2 is largely composed of poems in hexameters and elegiac couplets, devoted to various subjects; book 3 gathers short *lusus pastorales* (poems in elegiac couplets mainly dealing with love-related themes set in bucolic scenery); and book 4 collects other *lusus pastorales* organized into a free-standing series on the loves of the shepherd Iolla for the beautiful shepherdess Hyella.[9]

By choosing to study the first four books of Flaminio's *Carmina*, I am taking into consideration those poetical works that were written before the years 1539–40,[10] when the poet met the Spanish reformer Juan de Valdes in Naples and, attracted by his ideas on Christian renovation and evangelism, decided to distance his work from Renaissance 'pagan' culture.[11] Prior to this encounter, Flaminio was not only a prolific poet who dealt with a wide range of different topics in his Latin lyrical compositions (assembled in books 1–4), but he also was interested in theology and philosophy. However, after his meeting with Valdes he mainly devoted himself to religious works and scriptural studies. From the mid-1540s until the year of his death (1550), Flaminio decided to abandon non-religious poetry and, apart from a few letters in Phalaecian hendecasyllables (later collected in books 5 and 6), he composed only lyrical works of religious content (a poetical paraphrase of the *Psalms* and a collection of spiritual poems addressed to Margaret of France), gathered in what would have become books 7 and 8 of his *Carmina* respectively.[12]

A close reading of the first four books of Flaminio's Latin poetry reveals a multifaceted series of Petrarchan elements. Each of these elements might be

---

corpus. See Ferroni 2015, p. 318. On the history of the editions of Flaminio's texts, see Cuccoli 1897, pp. 167–70; and Scorsone 1993.

9   On Flaminio's pastoral poetry, see Ferroni 2012, pp. 225–70; Ferroni 2015; and Di Iasio 2018. On Renaissance *lusus pastorales*, see Grant 1957; Cooper 1977; Kennedy 1983; Nichols 1998; Scorsone 1997; Ferroni 2012; and Marsh 2014.

10 Flaminio wrote the poems collected in books 1–4 before 1539–40. See Cuccoli 1897, p. 169; and Ferroni 2015, pp. 309–10.

11 Valdes has been widely studied. See, at least, Nieto 1970; Otto 1989; Firpo 1990; Crews 2008; Firpo 2016; and Valdes, *Alfabeto christiano*. On Valdes's influence on Neapolitan culture, see Lopez 1976; and Firpo 2016, pp. 42–56. On Valdes's links with Flaminio, see Scorsone 1996–1997; Ferroni 2014; Ferroni 2015; and Ferroni 2016.

12 Flaminio's paraphrase of the *Psalms* appeared as a single book in 1546 (Flaminio, *Paraphrasis*), while his collection of religious poems to Marguerite of France was published in 1551 in Paris and in 1552 in Venice (Flaminio, *De rebus divinis carmina*, and Flaminio, *Carminum liber ultimus*), before being collected together with the other poetical works by Flaminio in the 1552 Florence edition of his opera omnia (Flaminio, *Carmina* 1552). On the poet's biblical and religious works, see Scorsone 1996–1997; Ferroni 2014; Ferroni 2015; Ferroni 2016; and Pietrobon 2018.

THE RECEPTION OF PETRARCH AND PETRARCHISTS' POETRY   191

viewed as an interesting but secondary aspect of Flaminio's work, yet once all the references to Petrarch are put together, arranged as a constellation pinpointing similar poetical features, and then analysed as a system, they appear as fragments of a much more significant literary phenomenon and can shed new light on the role of Petrarchan—and, generally, Italian vernacular—poetry in Flaminio's Latin poetical production.

The Petrarchan elements present in Flaminio's Latin poems can be split into two main categories: first, the so-called "textual memories"—in accordance with the terminology that Elisa Curti employed in her study on Dantean reuses in Poliziano's vernacular poems[13]—which refer to all those forms of literary quotations, lexical calques, and syntactic and metrical features derivable from Petrarch's texts that pertain to formal imitation; second, the "thematic memories" that denote any recourse to Petrarchan topoi, themes, or images. Obviously, these two categories do not imply rigid divisions, nor do they exclude possible overlapping reminiscences, which often occur in the material we will analyse. Furthermore, in Flaminio's odes, various Petrarchan memories are perceivable at both a micro[14] and macro level (such as Flaminio's odes 1.6, imitation of Petrarch's canzone 126, and his ode 2.33, 'Iam ver floricomum, Posthume, verticem,' a re-modulation of Petrarch's sonnet 310, 'Zephiro torna, e 'l bel tempo rimena').

We begin this investigation by considering ode 2.33, Flaminio's Latin adaptation of Petrarch's sonnet 'Zephiro torna,' since this work displays one of the first tributes that Flaminio pays to Petrarchan lyrical work. This *carmen*, written in second Asclepiadean meter (composed of three minor Asclepiadeans followed by a Glyconic verse), appeared within the collection of the poet's juvenile Latin compositions, edited by Flaminio himself and printed in Fano in 1515—when the author was just eighteen—together with Michele Marullo's *Neniae* and *Epigrammata*.[15] It is one of the three poems of this first collection dealing with love and the sole work among these love odes that was chosen to be later republished among Flaminio's books of *Carmina*. While the two other texts—an elegy addressed to Flaminio's friend Posthumus to bring him consolation for his star-crossed love and an ode to the poet's beloved Lygda—are mainly written in accordance with Latin elegiac topoi, the *carmen*, 'Iam ver

---

13   Curti 2000.
14   Petrarchan memories at a micro level are, for instance, the textual memory of Petrarch's canzone 53, 'Spirto gentil, che quelle membra reggi,' in Flaminio's ode, 1.42, 'Iam modum figas nimio dolori,' or that of Petrarch's metrical epistle 3.24, 'Salve, cara Deo tellus sanctissima, salve,' in ode 2.7, 'Pausilypi colles, et candida Mergillina.'
15   Flaminio, *Carminum libellus* 1515.

floricomum' (addressed to the same friend Posthumus), follows a vernacular model rather than a classical one and deals with a subject (the arrival of spring) that will continue to be at the centre of Flaminio's poetical oeuvre throughout the following years.[16] In this poem the theme is modulated according to a binary scheme that opposes the seasonal blossoming of the natural world to the poet's sufferings, described as a perennial winter:

> Iam ver floricomum, Posthume, verticem
> Profert puniceo Chloridis ex sinu,
> Iam pellunt Zephyri frigus, et horrida
> Tellus exuitur nives.
>
> Cantantes Hadriae marmora navitae,   5
> Audent velivolis currere puppibus:
> Nec tendens avidis retia piscibus
> Hibernas metuit minas
>
> Sardus: iam virides gramina vestiunt
> Campos, et tumidis palmes agit graves   10
> Gemmas corticibus: iam volucres suis
> Mulcent aera cantibus.
>
> At nos dum gravibus finis eat malis,
> Noctes, atque dies flemus, et intimis
> Urgemus (dominae sic Veneri placet)   15
> Divum numina questibus.
>
> Nil dives posito mensa iuvat mero,
> Nil defessa quies lumina, nil lyrae
> Cantus, nil vario tibia carmine
> Moerorem eluere efficax.   20
>
> Sed curae, heu! miseri sunt animi dapes,
> Sed cordis lacrimae pocula, sed quies
> Confectum rigidae corpus humi iacens,
> Sed carmen mihi flebiles

---

16 See, for instance, Flaminio's ode 3.5, 'Fugit hiems, nitidis vestitur frondibus arbor.'

>   Questus, et dominae nomina: sic mihi   25
>   Numquam veris eunt tempora: sic mihi
>   Soles non aliquo tempore candidi:
>   Sic mi perpetua est hiems.[17]

In contrasting his misery and his love labours with the flourishing of spring, Flaminio recurs to both thematic and textual memories drawn from Petrarch's sonnet 310. Even though the opening of the poem might also allude to the initial lines of Horace's ode 4.12, 'Iam veris comites, quae mare temperant,'[18] the structure of Flaminio's ode, with its opposition between the first three strophes (where the natural blossoming and vital elements are described) and the beginning of the fourth (in which the poet's sorrow emerges), openly echoes Petrarch's text, in which "bel tempo," "i fiori e l'erba," "et primavera candida e vermiglia" (ll. 1–4) all stand in opposition to Zephyr's return, bringing along conflict with the author's grief.[19] The emergence of this Petrarchan pattern in Flaminio's *carmen* can be observed in the opening of the first line of his fourth stanza, "At nos [...] urgemus" ("yet [...] we cry," ll. 13–15), which, in fact, invokes

---

17 Flaminio, *Carmina* 1993, 2.33, "O Posthumus, now spring shows her multi-coloured head from the purplish breast of Chloris, now Zephyrs cast away the cold, and the rough earth gets undressed from the snow. The sailors dare to navigate the roaring waves of the Adriatic Sea with their sailboats: the Sardinian does not fear the winter risks while casting nets towards prurient fish: now green grass covers the meadows, and the vineyard lets the heavy buds with turgid peel come out: now birds soothe the air through their songs. Yet, while the end arrives with great suffering, we cry night and day, and we torment the holy power of gods with deep laments (so mistress Venus likes it). The rich banquets arranged with wine do not help, nor the quietness, once the daylight has fallen, nor the song of the lyre, nor the flute with its various melodies are efficient in cancelling pains. But, alas, food is painful for a suffering soul, the glasses are tears of the heart, but an exhausted body lying on the rigid soil [represents] the quietness, feeble lamentations and the names of my mistress are a song to me: so springtime never comes to me: so the sun is no more bright to me: so a perpetual winter awaits me."

18 Horace, *Odes* 4.12.1–4: "Iam veris comites, quae mare temperant, / impellunt animae lintea Thraciae, / iam nec prata rigent, nec fluvii strepunt / hiberna nive turgidi." ("Now the Thracian breezes, spring's companions that calm the sea, drive forward the sails; now the fields are no longer frozen and the rivers no longer roar, swollen with winter snow"). The translations of Horace's odes are quoted from Horace, *The complete Odes and Epodes*.

19 Petrarch, RVF 310: "Zephiro torna, e 'l bel tempo rimena, / e i fiori et l'erbe, sua dolce famiglia, / et garrir Progne et pianger Philomena, /et primavera candida et vermiglia. // Ridono i prati, e 'l ciel si rasserena; / Giove s'allegra di mirar sua figlia; / l'aria et l'acqua et la terra è d'amor piena; / ogni animal d'amar si riconsiglia. // Ma per me, lasso, tornano i piú gravi / sospiri, che del cor profondo tragge / quella ch'al ciel se ne portò le chiavi; // et cantar augelletti, et fiorir piagge, / e 'n belle donne honeste atti soavi / sono un deserto, et fere aspre et selvagge."

a vivid textual reminiscence of *RVF* 310.9–10, "ma per me, lasso, tornano i più gravi / sospiri." Similarly, the closing lines of Flaminio's text—where the poet affirms through a rhetorical reduplication that "sic mihi / numquam veris eunt tempora: / sic mihi soles non aliquot tempore candidi: / sic mi perpetua est hiems" ("so springtime never comes to me: so the sun is no more bright to me: so a perpetual winter awaits me," ll. 25–28)—rephrase Petrarch's words "e cantar augelletti e fiorir piagge / [...] sono un deserto" (ll. 12–14).

The ode is much longer than the sonnet and all elements of the latter are not strictly followed. For example, Flaminio makes no mention of Procne (the swallow) or Philomena (the nightingale)—as Petrarch did in the third line of his poem—but he simply refers to "volucres" that "suis mulcent aera cantibus" ("birds" that "soothe the air through their songs", ll. 11–12). Neither does he allude to Jupiter's happiness in seeing Venus again when spring returns (see *RVF* 310.6). Yet, Flaminio adds new components to the lyrical picture painted by Petrarch. For instance, he does not simply linger on terrestrial or aerial elements while describing the arrival of spring, as his model did, but also devotes the second strophe to the good effects of the fair season on the aquatic world, which Petrarch simply touched upon with a single word in his text ("l'aria et l'acqua et la terra è d'amor piena," l. 7). Similarly, while contrasting springtime with his sorrow, Flaminio indulges in a reference to the uselessness of any remedy to console his pains (ll. 17–25), whereas Petrarch does not even allude to this detail. Nevertheless, since the two poems share their main traits and are modulated according to the same poetical pattern, it is possible to pair them and consider Flaminio's ode an example of a literary imitation of Petrarch's sonnet.

In the first books of Flaminio's *Carmina*, there are other odes in which some traits of Petrarch's works are clearly present. The Latin poem 1.42, 'Iam modum figas nimio dolori,' for instance, conveys an example of Petrarchan textual memory. In this text, written in Sapphic stanzas, Flaminio tries to console Cardinal Rodolfo Pio for the loss of his brother, Costantino. Both the images to which the poet refers and the formulas he employs in this poem are of Stoic tonality, exactly like those used in the following text of the collection, ode 1.43, 'Ergo (proh superum fidem!),' another *consolatio*, addressed to the author's friend Achille Bocchi. The Stoic moral climate of both these *carmina*, equidistant from pagan and Christian principles, seems to be characteristic of the first texts composed by Flaminio.[20] In ode 1.42, after having invited Cardinal Pio to confront his despair with an awareness of the common mortal doom of every human being, Flaminio turns to the mythological example of Orpheus

---

20   Flaminio, *Carmina* 1993, p. 51.

and refers to his vain efforts to bring his beloved Eurydice back to daylight in order to show the impossibility of modifying humanity's deadly fate. He then recalls the unforeseen duration of one's life, by stating that while some die very young, others are doomed to face a long, fatiguing old age:

> Mors rapit cunis cita vagientem:
> Flore sub primo cadit alter aevi:
> Hic nimis vivax queritur caducae
> Damna senectae.[21]

This strophe is organized in accordance with the pattern and rhetorical features of a passage from Horace's ode 2.16. At the beginning of the eighth strophe of this text (ll. 29–30), one reads: "abstulit clarum cita mors Achillem / longa Tithonum minuit senectus" ("an early death overtook the famous Achilles, a protracted old age wasted Tithonus away"). Both the opposing images and the binary structure of this Horatian passage (whose first element is redoubled by Flaminio through the reference not only to the infant in the cradle but also to the youth) find a parallel in Flaminio's ode, but in the latter another element, absent in the classical subtext, is present. Unlike Horace, Flaminio colours the image of those to whom death allowed to reach elderliness with a note of dejection: he presents some of the aged as people who feel the harm of a harsh decline (ll. 31–32). In these lines, a textual memory drawn from Petrarch's song 53, 'Spirto gentil che quelle membra reggi,' is clearly discernible. Indeed, while referring to elderly people, Petrarch describes them as "vecchi stanchi" (*RVF* 53.58) who "hanno sé in odio e la soverchia vita" (*RVF* 53.59). An echo of these vernacular lines appears in Flaminio's ode, which, through this Petrarchan allusion, is veiled with a melancholic tonality.

Another textual memory drawn from Petrarch is exhibited in Flaminio's ode 2.7, 'Pausilypi colles, et candida Mergillina.'[22] This poem, written in elegiac couplets, describes Flaminio's arrival in Naples "post tantos terraeque marisque labores" ("after so many wearing voyages by land and sea," l. 3). In this text, the poet greets Naples as the safe harbour where one may rest after many troubles and as a place sacred to the Muses where he could "otia digna sequi" ("devote himself to worthy literary otium," l. 50). He probably composed this ode in the late 1530s, when he left Verona and his position as secretary to bishop Gian

---

21 Flaminio, *Carmina* 1993, 1.42.29–32, "Death quickly steals infants from their cradle; others are taken in their early youth; another one, much more long-lived, feels too much the injuries of an unstable old age."
22 On this poem, see Akkerman 1994.

Matteo Giberti because of his irreconcilable differences with him in religious matters—Flaminio was getting closer to evangelism, while Giberti remained faithful to Catholicism—and moved to Campania, where he was hosted by his friends Galeazzo Florimonte and Gian Francesco Alois. Flaminio's detachment from Giberti may be echoed in a line of the poem where Flaminio asserts that he was not held in high esteem by the bishop of Verona (lake Benacus): "mihi Benaci laetissima litora sordent" ("the beautiful costs of lake Garda do not think highly of me," 2.7.105). Whereas the first part of the ode is in praise of a simple and humble life, which, though not the sort of existence chosen by the poet, brings about a modest albeit palpable happiness, the second half of the text pays homage to the beauties of Naples, described as "terra beata" ("blessed land," l. 107) and the sole place where the pleasant life, previously celebrated, can be enjoyed. At the end of this eulogistic passage, Flaminio salutes Naples as the corner of the world where he wishes that his bones could find an eternal rest:

> Me tibi, terra beata, dico; tu meta laborum,
> Iamque senescentis grata quies animi.
> Tu, dum fata sinunt, lucemque, auramque ministras:
> Tu, precor, exstincti corporis ossa tege.[23]

These concluding lines of Flaminio's ode echo a passage from one of Petrarch's metrical epistles, letter 3.24, 'Salve, cara Deo tellus sanctissima, salve,' a touching salute to Italy. This poem was composed in the springtime of 1353, when Petrarch left Avignon and moved towards his native land. On the top of Montgenèvre, the crossing place he went through to pass over the Alps, he glimpsed the peninsula to which he addressed the moving words recorded in his Latin epistle. In lines 11–13 of this metrical letter, Petrarch greets Italy with the following words:

> tu diversoria vite
> grata dabis fesse, tu quantam pallida tandem
> membra tegant prestabis humum.[24]

23　Flaminio, *Carmina* 1993, 2.7.107–10: "I consecrate myself to you, o happy land, o ending of every effort, and relish the rest for a soul already getting old. Until the doom allows it, take care of the light and the air; [then] I beseech you: cover the bones of my dead body."
24　Petrarch, *Epistole metriche* 3.24.11–13, p. 804: "you will give my life a grateful rest and you will finally grant to the bones of my dead body as much land as it is necessary to cover them."

Flaminio probably alluded to this passage at the end of his ode 2.7. The textual memory in this case can also convey a thematic link between the two texts. Petrarch addressed his words to the Italian peninsula, his real native land, presented as the place he had selected where he could find peace and rest from the anxieties of existence and where he also would like to be buried. In contrast, Flaminio in his Latin poem greets a city—Naples—that was not his hometown (he was born in Serravalle, now Vittorio Veneto, in the north east of Italy). Later, forced by life's vicissitudes, he moved around in Italy, and at the time he composed this ode, he could have considered Naples as the safest harbour in the midst of the storm and the likeliest place where he could find refuge. Therefore, he might have used the textual memory drawn from the Petrarchan Latin epistle (and the thematic memory it evoked) in order to highlight the salvific function of his new city and his affection towards it.

Other forms of the reception of vernacular literature are present in Flaminio's *Carmina*. Yet, the author echoes not only Petrarch's works, but also some Italian poems written by Petrarch's 16th-century lyrical followers. The links existing between Petrarchists' texts and Flaminio's odes also merit attention because they further our understanding of the phenomenon of the literary reception of vernacular works into Flaminio's Neo-Latin production. Indeed, an array of significant echoes of features, themes, and colourings drawn from 16th-century vernacular poems is displayed in the series of *lusus pastorales*, composed in 1539–40 in Caserta (and later published in book 4 of Flaminio's *Carmina*). In these works, the author tells the love story of the shepherd Iolla and the shepherdess Hyella. The latter dies because her beloved, against his will, is forced to marry another woman, Nisa. The whole series of *carmina* gives voice to Iolla's suffering over the death of Hyella, whom he cannot forget. His sorrow is so fierce that he finally decides to abandon his wife, Nisa, and mourn his first unforgotten love night and day, until he resolves to kill himself in order to meet his beloved Hyella in the underworld.

The entire collection of Flaminio's *lusus pastorales* establishes close connections with the Italian literary tradition. The first example of this literary reception is offered by the proemial text, 'O quae venusta Sirmionis litora' (4.1). In this *carmen*, the lyrical speaking 'I' asks for the Muses' inspiration in order to sing "Hyellam fistula dulci" ("Hyella with the sweet flute," 4.1.11). A similar opening appears quite unusual in the Latin elegiac context. It is true that Flaminio stands outside the classical elegiac tradition by deciding to organize his *lusus* in accordance with a plot that does not have a clear correspondence with that of any Latin elegiac source. Nevertheless, the choice of employing a rhetorical feature, such as the invocation to the Muses, at the opening of his book could be viewed as an imprudent derogation from the poetical rules of the genre. One can only justify the author's decision by linking this feature with Flaminio's intention to follow a scheme that only gained authority thanks to the example offered by Pietro Bembo's *Canzoniere* a decade before the composition of the *lusus*. Bembo chose to open his book of Italian rhymes with a sonnet, 'Piansi e cantai lo strazio e l'aspra guerra,' in whose second strophe the Muses are invoked to sustain the poet's song: "Dive, per cui s'apre Elicona e serra / use far alla morte illustri inganni / date a lo stil che nacque de' miei danni / viver, quand'io sarò spento e sotterra."[25] Following Bembo's model, Flaminio decided to open his lyrical collection of love poems by addressing a prayer to the muses and composed his poem, 'O quae venusta Sirmionis litora.'

From a wider perspective, other connections can be found between Flaminio's Latin *lusus* and Renaissance Italian poetry. Some of Flaminio's *carmina* deal with themes close to those developed by the vernacular lyrical tradition, such as psychological introspections of love or meditations on the links and contrasts between love and moral duty. Confirmation of the idea that Flaminio developed topics and gave voice to feelings that were perceived as proper to (and recognized as such by) modern sensitivity can be found in the Italian poetical translations of some of his *lusus* written by contemporary poets. For instance, *carmen* 4.9, 'Quisquis es, upiliove bonus, bona vel caprimulga,' a meditation on Hyella's sepulchre addressed to any wanderer who passed by the shepherdess' grave, was rendered by Claudio Tolomei into an Italian sonnet, 'O sia caprar, che la sampogna suoni.'[26] Tolomei also translated many other *lusus* by Flaminio. The majority of these texts were printed among Tolomei's Italian poems, published in the second volume of the anthology of Italian lyrical poetry edited by Dionigi Atanagi in 1565,[27] whereas another of his translations

---

25 Bembo, *Prose e Rime*, sonnet 1.5–8.
26 See *De le rime di diversi nobili poeti toscani*, fol. 28v.
27 Tolomei translated seven *lusus* by Flaminio: Flaminio's *lusus* 3.3, 'Heu quid ago? moritur mi animus, mellita Nigella' in the sonnet, 'Oimé che farò io? ch' io muoio, e muore' (*De le rime di diversi nobili poeti toscani*, fol. 27r, and *Lirici europei del Cinquecento*, pp. 196–97); *lusus* 3.5, 'Fugit hiems, nitidis vestitur frondibus arbor,' in the sonnet, 'Ecco 'l verno si fugge, e già si veste' (*De le rime di diversi nobili poeti toscani*, fol. 28r); *lusus* 3.7, 'Dum sonat argutis late vicinia gryllis,' in the sonnet, 'Mentre s'odon sonar i larghi campi' (*De le rime di diversi nobili poeti toscani*, fol. 29v); *lusus* 3.8, 'Et tonat, et vento ingenti nemus omne remugit,' in the sonnet, 'Tuona e soffiano intorno horridi venti' (*De le rime di diversi nobili poeti toscani*, fol. 28r); *lusus* 3.15, 'Hos tibi purpureos in serta nitentia flores,' in the sonnet, 'Vieni tosto, o cara Hiella, eccoti i fiori' (*De le rime di diversi nobili poeti toscani*, fol. 29r); *lusus* 3.20, 'Irrigui fontes, et fontibus addita vallis,' in the sonnet, 'Gelidi fonti in fresca valle ombrosa' (*De le rime di diversi nobili poeti toscani*, fol. 29r); and *lusus* 3.29, 'Luna decus coeli, astrorum regina bicornis,' in the sonnet, 'Hespero sacra, ed amorosa stella' (*De le rime di diversi nobili poeti toscani*, fol. 28v).

was collected by Tolomei in his volume *Versi et regole della nuova poesia toscana* (1539).[28] As a whole, this series of poetical translations can be taken as a proof of the affinity existing between Flaminio's Latin poems and contemporary vernacular tradition in terms of expressed themes and thoughts.[29]

Another more explicit episode of Flaminio's reception of Italian lyrical poetry into his *lusus* can be observed in the *carmen* 4.21, 'Ingrate Sol, ortum quid approperas tuum?,' written in Iambic trimeters. This Latin poem is a translation of a passage from Jacopo Sannazaro's 12th eclogue, 'Qui cantò Meliseo, qui proprio assisimi,' the last poetical text of Sannazaro's *Arcadia*.[30] Flaminio renders lines 203–13 of this eclogue as an 18-line *lusus*. Even though the *carmen* is slightly longer that the vernacular text, Flaminio closely follows his literary source and neither adds nor changes any aspect of the content of Sannazaro's passage. The few additions that can be observed in the Latin *lusus* are either rhetorical embellishments or lyrical circumlocutions, such as, for example, the translation of Sannazaro's hendecasyllable, "Ovunque miro par che 'l ciel si obtenebre? (l. 211), that Flaminio turned into three iambic trimeters ("Sed fulgeas licebit, et radiantibus / terras, maria, caelumque lustres ignibus, / tamen omnia tenebris inhorrescunt mihi," "even though it is legitimate that you shine and cross lands, seas, and air with your shining beams, yet, to me everything is overshadowed by darkness," ll. 14–16). Notwithstanding these minor divergences, Flaminio's *lusus* is written in complete accordance with the Italian eclogue. Both texts give voice to the love pains of a shepherd, who expresses his sorrow for the death of his beloved and blames the sun for rising, since

---

28   The rhymes that Tolomei collected in this anthology had a single aim: to transfer Latin quantitative metrics into Italian accentual prosody, thereby establishing a direct correspondence between the quantities of the classical verses and the accents of the vernacular metrical system. On this anthology, see *Versi et regole*, pp. 1–78; Mancini 1994; Mancini 1999; Mancini 2004; and Mancini 2006. The text that translates Flaminio's *lusus* 3.21, 'Rivule, frigidulis Nympharum e fontibus orte,' is included in Tolomei's anthology *Versi et regole* as the poem 'Nato da' fonti puri, rivo bel, delle Ninfe gelate,' and is written in Italian "barbaric" elegiac couplets. This text can be read in *Versi et regole*, fol. MIIr, and in *La poesia barbara*, p. 266.

29   Other contemporary Italian poets also rendered in Italian certain other texts by Flaminio. See, for instance, Bernardo Tasso's Italian ode *A l'aurora*, 'Ecco che 'n Oriente' (Tasso, *Rime*, vol. 2, pp. 249–52), which closely follows Flaminio's ode 1.5, 'Ecce ab extremo veniens Eoo.' On Tasso's ode, see Williamson 1951, pp. 67–68; Albonico 1990; p. 42 n. 75 and p. 43; and Ferroni 2009, p. 444.

30   Sannazaro, *Arcadia*, pp. 224–37. The passage that Flaminio translates (ll. 203–13) can be read at pp. 232–33. An English translation of this eclogue can be read in Sannazaro, *Arcadia and Piscatorial Eclogues*, pp. 142–51. The lines that were translated by Flaminio and quoted above are on p. 147. On the link between Sannazaro's 12th eclogue and Flaminio's *lusus* 4.21, see Cuccoli 1897, p. 223.

daylight will be forever painful to him, who cannot see his shepherdess anymore. In Flaminio's case the protagonist is Iolla, whereas in Sannazaro's text it is Melibeo—even though his words are not conveyed through a direct speech but are rather reported by another shepherd, Barcinio, who had previously listened to his friend's moaning. Echoing Melibeo's words, Iolla accuses the sun of ingratitude, because—according to him—it could only rise either to invite him to devote himself to new tasks or to see his grief, since daylight is unable to either brighten his face, or comfort him from his misery.

This literary translation of a passage from Sannazaro's *Arcadia* is significant not only in confirming a tendency that—as we have seen in the case of the poetical reception of 'Zephiro torna e 'l bel tempo rimena'—is not uncommon in Flaminio's *Carmina*;[31] but also offers the possibility to further our understanding of the re-modulation practice employed by the author in his Latin poems. *Lusus* 4.21 could have been composed by Flaminio simply to show his poetical competence and to compete with an illustrious literary model, as Sannazaro would have been considered. However, the author might have chosen to translate that specific fragment of Sannazaro's eclogue and not another one for a specific reason. Moreover, since the *lusus pastorales* form a progressive series of texts that are important not just as single pieces of literary works but also as part of a poetical group, we should further consider that there might be some reason behind Flaminio's decision to place his literary translation precisely a few texts before the end of the fourth book of his *Carmina*, and that there might also be some connections between the subject of *lusus* 4.21 and its place in the progression of the lyrical texts.

It is not implausible to think that Flaminio chose to translate those specific lines of Sannazaro's eclogue and position his *lusus* quite close to the end of book 4 in order to give a vivid intensity and an impulse of universality to Iolla's torments. Indeed, after having expressed his sorrow for Hyella's death in the first half of the series of the *lusus*, in the second half of the collection Iolla makes a fatal resolution: he is determined to die in order to join his beloved. In accordance with this decision, Iolla gradually begins to distance himself from the world: in *lusus* 4.19 he expresses his intention to die; in 4.20 he offers his farewell to the gods of the woods and the forests, where he spent his entire life; in 4.21 he accuses the sun of ingratitude and implicitly takes his leave from the unbearable daylight; and in 4.22 he hangs his lyre, with which he once

---

31 Flaminio was not only familiar with poetical translation from Italian texts, but in his *Carmina* he also rendered in Latin a few Greek poems. He translated a Greek epigram, 'De Ortyade,' in his ode 2.30, while his *carmen* 2.35 is a free lyrical paraphrase of a poem by Empedocles. Flaminio, *Carmina* 1993, pp. 94 and 99.

celebrated his love for Hyella, on a pine tree and prepares to commit suicide. In this particular moment of the *lusus* series, the pathos is high and *carmen* 4.21 can be seen as part of a dramatic escalation that is bringing Iolla to a final resolution. While the young shepherd takes his leave from the accursed sun, he expresses his decision to say farewell not only to his native place, but also to his whole world. Sannazaro's words must have then appeared particularly appropriate to Flaminio as a way to bring to his Latin poem both new colourful tonalities and also those features proper to the dramatic feelings of love that the vernacular tradition had refined. It is indisputable that in translating the chosen passage from Sannazaro's eclogue the author aims to display his poetical mastery, but he also uses his literary vernacular model to convey a higher level of literary expressionism to his text and bring a tone of universal grief to Iolla's torments.

Unexpectedly, in the last lines of poem 4.22, Iolla suddenly changes his mind and abandoning his previous resolution, realizes that although he has lost his beloved, he does not also have to lose himself; rather should devote the rest of his existence to singing of his love for Hyella and thus preserve her memory through poetry for all eternity (4.23). This last poem represents a significant turning point within the series of *lusus*; perhaps Flaminio decided to underline this aspect through a vague Petrarchan textual memory in the final elegiac couplets of the *carmen*—where one might perceive an elusive echo of the narrative movement of the opening line of Petrarch's sonnet 230 ('I' piansi, or canto'). After this text (4.23), there are only two other *carmina* before the conclusion of book 4: *lusus* 4.24, in which Iolla plants a laurel close to Hyella's tomb and consecrates his eternal grief to both the tree and his beloved, and 4.25, where he takes his leave from the bucolic world and closes the collection with a poetical valediction. According to this scheme, *lusus* 4.21, in which Flaminio translates Sannazaro's eclogue, is a salient moment in the series, representing the penultimate step before the point of highest tension in the collection (the distich 4.22–23). The function of this text within the lyrical sequence thus can explain why the author decided to place it close to the end of his book of *lusus pastorales* and not elsewhere in the collection.

After this analysis of Flaminio's literary works, we can state that while incorporating stylistic traits, images, themes, and rhetorical forms drawn from vernacular literature into his *Carmina*, the poet is specifically assimilating certain lyrical elements of the Italian poetical tradition into a non-vernacular framework. In doing so, he enriches Renaissance Latin poetry with new features, different from those derivable from the Roman love poems. Furthermore, through his re-modulation of vernacular works, Flaminio also increases the thematic range of topics that could be considered proper to Neo-Latin poetry.

Through his concrete example, he shows, for instance, that Renaissance authors in their Latin poems could deal with new psychological introspections and inner meditations on both love itself and the poet's status that generally were distinctive subjects of the vernacular lyrical world. As we have seen, the poet dealt with these topics throughout the entire first part of his lyrical production (books 1–4) and articulated them in several passages of his oeuvre. Since Flaminio aimed at voicing in his *Carmina* thoughts and feelings that were typical of modern sensitivity but that had not been widely modulated in Neo-Latin poetry, he found in certain texts of the Italian vernacular tradition (and, particularly, in Petrarch's *Canzoniere*) suitable examples upon which to base his innovative poetical discourse and from which to borrow new literary, thematic, and rhetorical features to adorn his works.

I cannot conclude this analysis without returning to the lyrical episode that opened my investigation: Flaminio's re-modulation of Petrarch's canzone 126, 'Chiare, fresche et dolci acque' into his ode 1.6, 'O fons Melioli sacer.' This poem was probably composed in the summer of 1526[32] and was first published in 1529.[33] It is written in tetrastich strophes, made of three Glyconic verses and a Pherecratean—Flaminio derived this metrical scheme from Catullus, who used it in his hymn to Diana (poem 34, 'Dianae sumus in fide'). In closely rendering a Petrarchan rhyme in a Latin text, Flaminio was not a literary pioneer. On the contrary, he inserted himself within a branch of Renaissance Latin poetry (Latin translations of Petrarch's poems) that thrived during the 16th century, but first flourished two centuries earlier with the Latin translations of *RVF* 132 and 134 by Coluccio Salutati.[34] Throughout the Cinquecento, other authors, in addition to Flaminio, translated some Petrarchan texts into various Latin *carmina*: Monseigneur Henri Louis Fenogliet, bishop of Montpellier, translated *RVF* 208, 'Rapido fiume che d'alpestre vena,' in a short poem in hexameters, 'Gurgite saxoso, rapida qui concitus unda,'[35] while Pietro Amato Spagnuolo wrote a text in Sapphic strophes, 'Virgo quae Solis radians amictu,' in which he rendered Petrarch's *RVF* 366, 'Vergine bella, che di sol vestita.' This text was

---

[32] Maddison 1965, p. 50.

[33] The poem 1.6, 'O fons Melioli sacer,' can now be read in Flaminio, *Carmina* 1993, pp. 14–17, and in *Musae reduces*, vol. 1, pp. 199–205 (with a French translation).

[34] Coluccio Salutati translated Petrarch's sonnets *RVF* 132, 'S'amor non è, che dunque è quel ch'io sento?' and 134, 'Pace non trovo et non ho da far guerra,' into two Latin sonnets by using Latin hexameters instead of the Italian hendecasyllables: 'Si fors non sit amor, igitur quid sentio? Vel si' and 'Nec pacem invenio, nec adest ad bella facultas,' respectively. See Duso 2004, pp. 25–26. On the Latin sonnet in the Italian 14th century, see Duso 2004, pp. XXIX–LXVII and 5–35; Novati 1906–1907; and Biadene 1889, pp. 178–82.

[35] Ménage, *Mescolanze*, p. 28 and Crescimbeni, *Dell'istoria della volgar poesia*, p. 306.

favoured by other early modern poets, who composed other Latin versions of this canzone, such as, for example, the hexametric *carmen* by Filippo Beroaldo, 'Paeanes sive canticum de laudibus Divae Virginis,' or the poem in elegiac couplet by Marco Marullo.[36] This tendency of translating Petrarch in Latin can be considered not simply as a counterproof of the concrete authority that Italian works had acquired in the 16th century but also as a sign of the Renaissance authors' intention to emulate and compete with both classical and vernacular literary models by exhibiting their wide-ranging and manifold poetical ability and metric mastery. Furthermore, by turning Petrarchan poems into Italian, poets elaborated in their Latin compositions themes and modes that were proper to vernacular tradition and, consequently, opened the lyrical field of Renaissance Latin poetical *inventio*, as happened in the case of Flaminio, whose interest in colouring some of his *Carmina* with Petrarchan tints appears less isolated once situated within this broader context.

One of Flaminio's most refined texts that displays these Petrarchan colours is ode 1.6, entitled 'De Delia' after the young lady whom the poet wanted to praise. The poem's first two lines ("O fons Melioli sacer, / Lympha splendide vitrea," "O source sacred to Meliolus, o superbly transparent waters") echo the beginning of Horace's *Odes* 3.13 ("O fons Bandusiae splendidior vitro," "O fountain of Bandusia, shining more brightly than glass").[37] Yet, after this classical opening (to which Petrarch's canzone also alluded, even though less explicitly), Flaminio's *carmen* elegantly and carefully follows the text of 'Chiare, fresche et dolci acque.' As Petrarch in his first stanza had evoked successively all the elements that witnessed his beloved lying down along the spring of the river Sorgue (i.e., the waters, the branch, the grass, and the air),[38] so Flaminio devotes his first four strophes to the same elements, mentioned in unchanged order, and composes his poetical picture by syntactical juxtapositions:

---

36   Crescimbeni, *Dell'istoria della volgar poesia*, p. 306; Malinar 1984–1985, p. 121; and Scorsone 2004. Marullo, who was famous for having translated the first canto of Dante's *Divine Comedy* in Latin hexameters, also translated in elegiac couplets two other Petrarchan poems: RVF 99, 'Poiché voi et io più volte abbiam provato,' and 365, 'I vo' piangendo i miei passati tempi.' On Marullo, see Dionisotti 1952 and Malinar 1984–1985.

37   In its first version, Flaminio's poem 1.6 echoed even more closely Horace's *Odes* 3.13, since its two opening lines were: "O fons Melioli sacer / omni splendidior vitro." See Flaminio, *Carmina* 1529, and Tassoni, *Considerazioni*, p. 192.

38   Petrarch, RVF 126.1–13: "Chiare, fresche et dolci acque / ove le belle membra / pose colei che sola a me par donna / gentil ramo, ove piacque, / (con sospir mi rimembra) / a lei di fare al bel fianco colonna; / erba e fior che la gonna / leggiadra ricoverse con l'angelico seno; / aere sacro sereno / ove Amor co' begli occhi il cor m'aperse: / date udienza insieme / a le dolenti mie parole estreme."

O fons Melioli sacer,
Lympha splendide vitrea,
In quo virgineum mea
Lavit Delia corpus;

Tuque lenibus enitens   5
Arbor florida ramulis,
Qua latus niveum, et caput
Fulsit illa decorum;

Et vos prata recentia,
Quae vestem nitidam, et sinum   10
Fovistis tenerum uvida
Laeti graminis herba;

Vosque aurae liquidi aetheris,
Nostri consciae amoris, ad-
Este, dum queror, atque vos   15
Suprema alloquor hora.[39]

In the following three strophes, Flaminio prays to the evoked natural elements to fulfil his hope to be buried among them when the fates decide that his last hour has arrived, since he believes that death will be less harsh in that corner of the Earth (ll. 17–29). In these lines Flaminio modulates Petrarch's images and conveys the same meaning of the second stanza of RVF 126, but he paraphrases, in slightly shorter sentences, his model's discourse, as is proven by the fact that this time, Petrarch's 13-line strophe is rendered in three Latin quatrains rather than four. Indeed, Flaminio reduces the rhetorical embellishment of some vernacular expressions: Petrarch's hope "ch'Amor quest'occhi lagrimando chiuda" (l. 16) becomes "ut nobis amor impia / morte lumina condat" ("that love close our eyes with cruel death," ll. 19–20), as well as the lines "qualche grazia il meschino / corpo fra voi ricopra, / e torni l'alma al proprio albergo ignuda" (ll. 17–19) are converted in two short verses ("Ut corpus liceat

---

[39] "O source sacred to Meliolus, o superbly transparent waters, in which Delia washes her body, you, o flourishing tree rich in tender branches, on which she leaned her white side and her beautiful head, you, o fresh meadows that sustained her white dress and her tender body with the soft grass of your happy plants, and you, o breezes of the pure air, being aware of my love, come closer, while I lament and suffer my last hour." Flaminio, *Carmina* 1993, 1.6.1–16.

mihi / Vestra ponere terra" ["let me be allowed to abandon my body on your land"], ll. 23–24).

As in Petrarch's first strophe, the third one of the canzone is in complete correspondence with four Latin quatrains of Flaminio's ode (ll. 29–44), in which the poet gives voice to his hope to one day see his beloved return to the place where he glimpsed her along the Sorgue and weep over his tomb. In these lines Flaminio openly displays his poetical mastery by impeccably turning some vernacular settenari into the eight-syllable length of the Glyconic verse, such as, for instance, "O si tempus erit modo" ("o if only time comes", l. 29), which matches Petrarch's "Tempo verrà ancor forse" (l. 26). In the following stanza of the canzone, the lyrical 'I' remembers his beloved, surrounded by the allure of nature, within a paradisiac realm. Flaminio transforms the lyricism of this recollection into iconic verses that condense the delicate description of Petrarch's lines with some classical reminiscences:

> Pulchris undique ramulis 45
> Instar imbris in aureum
> Manabant dominae sinum
> Flores suave rubentes.
>
> Talis Idalia Venus
> Silva, sub viridi iacet 50
> Myrto, puniceo hinc et hinc
> Nimbo tecta rosarum.
>
> Hic flos purpureas super
> Vestes, hic super aureos
> Crines, hic rosei super 55
> Oris labra cadebat.[40]

Whereas the first and third Latin strophes of this passage follow the poetical discourse and the lyrical style of lines 40–42 and 45–46 of the vernacular model respectively,[41] the central quatrain is markedly different from Petrarch's

---

40 "From every lovely branch red flowers tenderly felt as rain on the fair breast of my beloved. Similarly, in the Idalion wood Venus lays down under the green myrtle sprinkled onto a rainfall of red roses. Here a flower is on her purple dress, there another on her golden hair, there another one felt on the lips of her rosy mouth." Flaminio, *Carmina* 1993, 1.6.45–56.
41 Petrarch, *RVF* 126.40–42 ("Da' be' rami scendea, / [dolce ne la memoria] / una pioggia di fior sopra 'l suo grembo") and 45–46 ("qual fior cadea sul lembo, / e qual su le trecce bionde").

text, introducing a simile of classical tints that is absent in the vernacular source. Here, as well as in a few other passages of his ode, Flaminio creates a gap between his lines and those of his model by returning to either words or images of the Roman lyrical tradition in order to translate certain expressions of Petrarch's vernacular text. He renders, for instance, Petrarch's line 55, "costei per fermo nacque in paradiso," with the sentence "aut venit ab aethere / haec alto, vel Oreadum / certe sanguinis una est" ("either she comes from the highest sky, or her blood certainly is that of an Oread nymph," ll. 66–68). In another case, he transforms Petrarch's delicate syntagm to designate Laura, "la fera bella e mansueta" (l. 29), into a much more vivid expression: "ea quae nos ante diem nigros / cogit visere manes" ("she that forces me to see dark Manes before my time," ll. 31–32). In a few other passages Flaminio opts for a Latin phrase of concrete intensity to convert an expression that Petrarch painted with vague tonalities, as emerges, for example, from a comparison of Petrarch's lines "ove le belle membra pose / colei" (ll. 2–3) with Flaminio's verses "in quo [...] / lavit Delia corpus" ("in which Delia washes her body," ll. 3–4). In some other cases, he instead increases the lyrical tone of the vernacular discourse with rhetorical elegances drawn from the classical repertoire, as in the concluding lines of the ode where Petrarch's undetermined temporal expression "da indi in qua" (l. 63) becomes "seu nox tenebris diem / pellit, seu rapidum fugit / solem" ("when either night puts daylight to flight, or [the night] runs away from the swift sun," ll. 85–87), thus decorated with a Virgilian echo.[42]

Notwithstanding these few minor differences existing between the two texts, Flaminio's *carmen* is clearly modulated in close accordance with Petrarch's canzone, and it can be considered a properly refined poetical translation of RVF 126. But why did Flaminio decide to turn this Petrarchan poem into an ode? A proper answer certainly needs to consider that Flaminio might have wanted to compete with the undisputed literary authority of the Italian lyrical tradition in order to exhibit his poetical and metrical skills—and this aspect corroborates our understanding of how vital were the mutual influences and the bilateral exchanges between Neo-Latin literature and its vernacular counterpart during the Italian Renaissance.[43] Yet, a broader answer must contemplate the idea that, in his ode, Flaminio intended to articulate some of the traits and features that were quintessential to modern sensitivity, but which could not be derived from classical elegies and lyrics. Specifically, he wanted

---

42 Virgil, *Georgics* 4.466: "te veniente die, te decedente canebat" ("[Orpheus sang] of you as day neared, of you as day departed").

43 On the dynamic nature of the interplay between Neo-Latin and the vernacular, see Deneire 2014, p. 5, and the Introduction to this volume.

to deal with the tender and effusive aspects of love. Thanks to his imitation of Petrarch, he succeeded in this aim and allowed Renaissance Latin poetry to be enriched with original and innovative traits and features.

Bibliography

Primary Sources

Bembo, Pietro. *Prose e Rime*, edited by Carlo Dionisotti. 2nd ed. Turin: UTET, 1966.

Crescimbeni, Giovan Mario. *Dell'istoria della volgar poesia*. Venice: Basegio, 1731.

De le rime di diversi nobili poeti toscani, raccolte da M. Dionigi Atanagi, libro secondo. Venice: Avanzo, 1565.

Flaminio, Marcantonio. "Carminum libellus." In *Michaelis Tarcaniotae Marulli neniae. Eiusdem epigrammata numquam alias impressa. M. Antonii Flaminii carminum libellus.* Fano: Soncino, 1515.

Flaminio, Marcantonio. "Carmina." In *Actii Synceri Sannazarii Odae. Eiusdem Elegia de malo Punico. Ioannis Cottae Carmina. M. Antonii Flaminii Carmina.* Venice: Nicolini da Sabbio, 1529.

Flaminio, Marcantonio. *Paraphrasis in triginta Psalmos versibus scripta ad Alexandrum Farnesium Cardinalem amplissimum.* Venice: Valgrisi, 1546.

Flaminio, Marcantonio. "Carmina." In *Carmina quinque illustrium poetarum quorum nomina in sequenti charta continentur.* Venice: Valgrisi, 1548.

Flaminio, Marcantonio. *De rebus divinis Carmina ad Margheritam Henrici Gallorum Regis sororem.* Paris: Etienne, 1551.

Flaminio, Marcantonio. *Carminum liber ultimus Eius amicorum cura in lucem nuper editus.* Venice: Giunta, 1552.

Flaminio, Marcantonio. "Carmina." In *Carmina quinque illustrium poetarum quorum nomina in sequenti charta continentur.* Florence: Torrentino, 1552.

Flaminio, Marcantonio. *Carminum libri VIII.* Padua: Comino, 1727.

Flaminio, Marcantonio. "Carmina." In *Marci Antonii, Joannis Antonii et Gabrielis Flaminiorum Forocorneliensium Carmina.* Padua: Comino, 1743.

Flaminio, Marcantonio. *Carmina*, edited by Massimo Scorsone. Turin: RES, 1993.

Horace. *The Complete Odes and Epodes*, edited and translated by David West. Oxford, Eng.: Oxford University Press, 1997.

La poesia barbara nei secoli XV e XVI, edited by Giosuè Carducci. Bologna: Zanichelli, 1881 (reprint edited by Emilio Pasquini. Bologna: Zanichelli, 1985).

Lirici europei del Cinquecento. Ripensando la poesia del Petrarca, edited by Gian Mario Anselmi, Keir Elam, Giorgio Forni, and Davide Monda. Milan: BUR, 2004.

Ménage, Gilles. *Mescolanze*. Rotterdam: Leers, 1692.

Musae reduces. Anthologie de la poésie latine dans l'Europe de la Renaissance, edited by Pierre Laurens and Claudie Balavoine, 2 vols. Leiden: Brill, 1975.

Partenio, Bernardino. *Dell'imitatione poetica*. Venice: Giolito, 1560.
Petrarch. *Epistole metriche*, edited by Enrico Bianchi. In Petrarch. *Rime, Trionfi e poesie latine*, edited by Ferdinando Neri, Guido Martellotti, Enrico Bianchi, and Natalino Sapegno. Milan: Ricciardi, 1951, pp. 706–805.
Petrarch. *Lyric Poems. The* Rime sparse *and Other Lyrics*, edited and translated by Robert M. During. Cambridge, MA: Harvard University Press, 1976.
Petrarch. *Rerum vulgarium fragmenta*, edited by Rosanna Bettarini, 2 vols. Turin: Einaudi, 2005.
Sannazaro, Jacopo. *Arcadia*, edited by Francesco Erspamer. Milan: Mursia, 1990.
Sannazaro, Jacopo. *Arcadia and Piscatorial Eclogues*, translated by Ralph Nash. Detroit, MI: Wayne State University Press, 1966.
Tasso, Bernardo. *Rime*, edited by Domenico Chiodo and Vercingetorige Martignone, 2 vols. Turin: RES, 1995.
Tassoni, Alessandro. *Considerazioni sopra le Rime del Petrarca*. Modena: Cassiani, 1609.
Valdes, Juan de. *Alfabeto cristiano*, edited by Massimo Firpo. Turin: Einaudi, 1994.
Versi et regole de la nuova poesia toscana, edited by Massimiliano Mancini. Manziana: Vecchierelli, 1996.

Secondary Sources

Akkerman, Fokke. "Marcantonio Flaminio's Voyage to Naples: On Carmen 2.7." In *Acta Conventus Neo-Latini Hafniensis. Proceedings of the Eighth International Congress of the Neo-Latin Studies, Copenhagen 12 August to 17 August 1991*, edited by Rhoda Schnur. Binghamton, NY: Center for Medieval & Renaissance Studies, 1994, pp. 285–97.
Albonico, Simone. *Il ruginoso stile. Poeti e poesia in volgare a Milano nella prima metà del Cinquecento*. Milan: Franco Angeli, 1990.
Biadene, Leandro. "Morfologia del sonetto nei secoli XIII e XIV." *Studi di filologia romanza* 4 (1889), pp. 1–234.
Cooper, Helen. *Pastoral. Medieval into Renaissance*. Ipswich: Brewer, 1977.
Crews, Daniel A. *Twilight of the Renaissance. The Life of Juan de Valdes*. Toronto: University of Toronto Press, 2008.
Cuccoli, Ercole. *M. Antonio Flaminio. Studio con documenti inediti*. Bologna: Zanichelli, 1897.
Curti, Elisa. "Dantismi e memoria della *Commedia* nelle *Stanze* del Poliziano." *Lettere italiane* 52.4 (2000), pp. 530–68.
Deneire, Tom, ed. *Dynamics of Neo-Latin and the Vernacular. Language and Poetics, Translation and Transfer*. Leiden: Brill, 2014.
Di Iasio, Valeria. "Prime note sulla struttura del *Liber tertius* di Marcantonio Flaminio." In *Acta Conventus Neo-Latini Vindobonensis. Proceedings of the Sixteenth International*

Congress of Neo-Latin Studies (Vienna 2015), edited by Astrid Steiner-Weber and Franz Römer. Leiden: Brill, 2018, pp. 238–48.

Dionisotti, Carlo. "Marco Marullo traduttore di Dante." In *Miscellanea di scritti di bibliografia ed erudizione in memoria di Luigi Ferrari*, edited by Anna Saitta Revignas. Florence: Olschki, 1952, pp. 232–42.

Duso, Elena Maria. *Il sonetto latino e semilatino in Italia nel Medioevo e nel Rinascimento*. Padua: Antenore, 2004.

Ferroni, Giovanni. "*Vivere al par delle future genti*: Poetica in versi di Bernardo Tasso." In *Gli dei a corte. Letteratura e immagini nella Ferrara estense*, edited by Gianni Venturi and Francesca Cappelletti. Florence: Olschki, 2009, pp. 415–47.

Ferroni, Giovanni. *"Dulces lusus." Lirica pastorale e libri di poesia nel Cinquecento*. Alessandria: Edizioni dell'Orso, 2012.

Ferroni, Giovanni. "*Liber ultimus*. Intorno ai *De rebus divinis carmina* di Marco Antonio Flaminio." In *Roma pagana e Roma cristiana nel Rinascimento. Atti del XXIV convegno internazionale (Chianciano Terme-Pienza, 19–21 luglio 2012)*, edited by Luisa Secchi Tarugi. Florence: Cesati, 2014, pp. 301–10.

Ferroni, Giovanni. "A Farewell to Arcadia. Marcantonio Flamino from Poetry to Faith." In *Allusions and Reflection. Greek and Roman Mythology in Renaissance Europe*, edited by Elisabeth Wåghäll Nivre. Cambridge, Eng.: Cambridge Scholar Publishing, 2015, pp. 309–24.

Ferroni, Giovanni. "*Siculis et Tarentinis*. Teologia, esegesi e poetica nei *De rebus divinis carmina* di Flaminio." *Bollettino della società di studi valdesi* 218 (2016), pp. 33–70.

Firpo, Massimo. *Tra alumbrados e spirituali: studi su Juan de Valdés e il valdesianesimo nella crisi religiosa del Cinquecento*. Florence: Olschki, 1990.

Firpo, Massimo. *Juan de Valdes e la Riforma nell'Italia del Cinquecento*. Bari: Laterza, 2016.

Grant, William Leonard. "The Neo-Latin *Lusus pastoralis* in Italy." *Medievalia et Humanistica* 11 (1957), pp. 94–98.

Kennedy, William J. *Jacopo Sannazaro and the Uses of Pastoral*. Hanover, NH: University Press of New England, 1983.

Lopez, Pasquale. *Il movimento valdesiano a Napoli: Mario Galeota e le sue vicende col Sant'Uffizio*. Naples: Fiorentino, 1976.

Maddison, Carol. *Marcantonio Flaminio. Poet, Humanist and Reformer*. London: Routledge, 1965.

Malinar, Smiljka. "Una parafrasi umanistica del primo canto della *Divina Commedia*." *Studia Romanica et Anglica Zagrabiensia* 29–30 (1984–1985), pp. 119–35.

Mancini, Massimiliano. "L'imitazione metrica di Orazio nella poesia Italiana." In *Orazio e la letteratura italiana. Contributi alla storia della fortuna del poeta latino. Atti del convegno svoltosi a Licenza dal 19 al 23 aprile 1993 nell'ambito delle celebrazioni del bimillenario della morte di Quinto Orazio Flacco*. Rome: Istituto Poligrafico e Zecca dello Stato, 1994, pp. 489–532.

Mancini, Massimiliano. "Un episodio del classicismo romano: I *Versi et regole della nuova poesia toscana.* (Roma, Blado, 1539)." In *Studi in onore di Gennaro Savarese*, edited by Rosanna Alhaique Pettinelli. Rome: Bulzoni, 1999, pp. 239–79.

Mancini, Massimiliano. " La versificazione *neoclassica* fra Italia ed Europa in età rinascimentale." In *Letteratura italiana, letterature europee. Atti del Congresso Nazionale dell'ADI (Associazione degli Italianisti), Padova-Venezia, 18–21 settembre 2002*, edited by Guido Baldassarri and Silvana Tamiozzo. Rome: Bulzoni, 2004, pp. 341–57.

Mancini, Massimiliano. "Sperimenti estremi: i *Versi et regole della nuova poesia toscana* (Roma, Blado, 1539)." In *Il petrarchismo: un modello di poesia per l'Europa*, edited by Loredana Chines, vol. 2. Rome: Bulzoni, 2006, pp. 423–38.

Marsh, David. "Pastoral." In *Brill's Encyclopaedia of the Neo-Latin World*, edited by Philip Ford, Jan Bloemendal, and Charles Fantazzi. Leiden: Brill 2014, pp. 425–36.

Nichols, Fred J. "Navagero's *Lusus* and the Pastoral Tradition." In *Acta Conventus Neo-Latini Bariensis: Proceedings of the Ninth International Congress of the Neo-Latin Studies, Bari, August 29–September 3 1994*, edited by Rhoda Schnur. Tempe, AZ: Medieval & Renaissance Texts and Studies, 1998, pp. 445–52.

Nieto, José C. *Juan de Valdes and the Origins of the Spanish and Italian Reformation*. Geneva: Droz, 1970.

Novati, Francesco. "Sonetti latini e semilatini nel trecento." *Studi Medievali* 2 (1906–1907), pp. 109–12.

Otto, Wolfgang. *Juan de Valdes und die Reformation in Spanien im 16. Jahrhundert*. Frankfurt am Main: Peter Lang, 1989.

Pastore, Alessandro. *Marcantonio Flaminio: fortune e sfortune di un chierico nell'Italia del Cinquecento*. Milan: Franco Angeli, 1981.

Pietrobon, Ester. *La penna interprete della cetra. I Salmi in volgare e la tradizione della poesia spirituale italiana nel Rinascimento*. Rome: Edizioni di storia e letteratura, 2018 (forthcoming).

Pisanti, Tommaso. "L'umanesimo inquieto del Flaminio." In *Interrogativi dell'Umanesimo*, edited by Giovannangiola Tarugi, vol. 1, Florence: Olschki, 1976, pp. 87–98.

Pisanti, Tommaso. "Marcantonio Flaminio tra Umanesimo, Riforma e Controriforma." In *Il Rinascimento. Aspetti e problemi attuali. Atti del X Congresso dell'Associazione internazionale per gli studi di Lingua e Letteratura italiana (Belgrado, 17–21 giugno 1979)*, edited by Vittore Branca et al. Florence: Olschki, 1982, pp. 575–88.

Scorsone, Massimo. "Nota bibliografica." In Flaminio, *Carmina* 1993, pp. 319–22.

Scorsone, Massimo. "Musae severiores: Della lirica sacra di Marcantonio Flaminio." *Atti dell'Istituto veneto di Scienze, Lettere ed Arti* 155 (1996–1997), pp. 83–115.

Scorsone, Massino. "Il *lusus pastoralis*: lineamenti di storia di un genere letterario." *Proteo: Quaderni del Centro Interuniversitario di Teoria e Storia dei Generi Letterari* 3.1 (1997), pp. 23–33.

Scorsone, Massimo. "Petrarchismo e lirica neolatina tra i secoli XVI–XVII: una ricognizione in limine." In *Petrarca in Barocco*, edited by Amedeo Quondam. Rome: Bulzoni, 2004, pp. 199–226.

Williamson, Edward. *Bernardo Tasso*. Rome: Edizioni di storia e letteratura, 1951.

CHAPTER 12

Pietro Angeli da Barga's *Syrias* (1582–91) and Contemporary Debates over Epic Poetry

Alexander Winkler

1   The Codification of Poetry in the Late 16th Century[1]

The *Secondo Cinquecento* in Italy was a period characterized by lively debates on poetics.[2] It witnessed the 'rediscovery' of Aristotle's *Poetics* as well as other important treatises on rhetoric and style, such as Ps.-Longinus's *De sublimitate*, Ps.-Demetrius's *De elocutione*, or Hermogenes's *De ideis*, as well as a series of commentaries on these texts.[3] Moreover, a plethora of treatises, discourses, and other forms of scholarly debate were produced, which had a considerable impact on how people read, wrote, and talked about poetry. In the 16th century Italian context, most debates concerned vernacular literature, first and foremost Dante's *Divine Comedy*, Petrarch's *Canzoniere*, Guarini's *Pastor Fido*, and Tasso's and Ariosto's chivalric and epic poetry, respectively.[4] These discussions dealt with vernacular literature and were held predominantly in vernacular contexts. It is no wonder that the Neo-Latin literature produced in Italy during this period rather stays in the background. However, Neo-Latin literature did not cease to be produced, nor did it remain uninfluenced by the discussions that have just been mentioned.

A case in point is the following statement of Roberto Titi (1551–1609), professor of humanities at the University of Bologna. In one of his introductory lectures to his course on Virgil's *Georgics*, held in 1597, Titi referred to the recent codification of literary discourse as something very useful for the learned:

---

[1]   I would like to extend my gratitude to Alessandra Origgi and Alice Spinelli for their patient and often enlightening discussions with me on this essay.
[2]   Weinberg 1974 is still the most comprehensive and useful introduction to this topic.
[3]   The bibliography on the reception of each of these texts is rather vast. Most useful for a first approach are the following: on Ps.-Longinus, see Weinberg 1971b and Huss 2011; on Ps.-Demetrius, see Weinberg 1971a; and on Hermogenes, despite her focus on the vernacular, see Patterson 1970.
[4]   On these debates, see, respectively, Sberlati 2001; Jossa 2002; and Huss/Mehltretter/Regn 2012.

Aristotle, Horace, and other masters of these things have disclosed to us the precepts of the art of poetry in such a way that what the ancients could achieve relying only on the powers of their genius, we nowadays can accomplish much better as we are imbued with the precepts of discipline and science. Thanks to these precepts Giovanni Pontano, Giacomo Sannazaro, Girolamo Vida and same-named Fracastoro, Scipione Capece, Pietro Angeli, Francesco Benci and quite a few others, whom I am deliberately not going to mention, have, according to me, clearly outstripped several ancient poets, and in the opinion of most people they have at least equalled some of them [...][5]

Titi mentions only the critics of the previous generation, but referencing Aristotle and Horace in that time meant dealing with Castelvetro, Piccolomini, Vettori, and others who had written important commentaries on these classical works on poetics.[6] Thanks to the attempts by literary critics and theorists to define the rules of writing good poetry, contemporary poets are given the chance to catch up with their ancient models. He affirms that Neo-Latin poets are clearly handicapped as they have to use a language that is not their own.[7] With the recent discovery and description of the innermost 'mechanics' of poetry, modern poets are now capable of competing with the otherwise linguistically superior ancient poets. In order to prove his point, he proudly presents his listeners with a list of modern poets who, according to him, have succeeded in their *aemulatio* of the ancients.[8] This canon comprises modern 'classics,' such

---

5 "[V]el quod Aristoteles, & Horatius alijque huiusc. rerum magistri artis Poeticae praecepta ita nobis aperuerunt, ut quod veteres illi viribus ingenii tantummodo freti praestabant, nostri homines disciplinae ac scientiae praeceptis imbuti multò sanè melius efficere potuerint, quorum praeceptorum ope, & auxilio Iouianus Pontanus, Iacobus Sannazarius, Hieronymus Vida, atque alter eiusdem nominis Fracastorius, Scipio Capitius, Petrus Angelius, Franciscus Bencius, alij non sanè pauci, quos consultò praetereo, aliquot veteres Poetas non dubiè meo quidem iudicio superarunt, certè plurimorum sententia nonnullos exaequarunt [...]" Titi, *Praelectiones*, pp. 18–19.

6 The most important of these are Castelvetro's *Poetica d'Aristotele vulgarizzata e sposta* (1570); Maggi's and Lombardi's *In Aristotelis librum de Poetica communes explanationes* (1550); Piccolomini's *Annotazioni nel libro della Poetica d'Aristotele* (1575); Robortello's *In librum Aristotelis de Arte Poetica explicationes* (1548); and Vettori's *Commentarii in primum librum Aristotelis de Arte Poetarum* (1560). On these commentators, see Weinberg 1974 *ad indicem*.

7 In relation to this argument, see Pietro Angeli da Barga's similar comment in the preface to the 1591 edition of his *Syrias*, sig. ★3r, in which he refers to Latin as a language "quae iamdiu ex usu, atque ore hominum quasi exul, & extorris excidisset" ("which has long ago fallen in disuse and is, so to speak, exiled and banished from the mouth of man").

8 While it is not surprising to find the 'modern classics' Pontano, Vida, Sannazaro, and Fracastoro in the list, the other three names require an explanation. Scipione Capece (1480–1551) is

as Sannazaro and Vida, who wrote, of course, before the 'Aristotelian turn.' The poets who more convincingly prove his statement are his contemporaries Pietro Angeli and Francesco Benci, both steeped in Aristotelian theory.

Of course Titi, as a teacher of rhetoric and poetry, is convinced of the benefits that the codification of poetry entails. He can hardly be expected to bite the hand that feeds him. Yet the set of rules established by scholars in the wake of the Aristotelian turn in the *Secondo Cinquecento* could also create difficulties. Torquato Tasso (1544–95), for example, struggled throughout his life with the rigid rules imposed on poetry. His *Gerusalemme liberata* is consequently a compromise between what 'pleases' and what is 'fitting'.[9] To put it more clearly, the *Gerusalemme* marks the end of a long and difficult attempt to reconcile the obscenely popular model of Ariosto's *Orlando furioso* with the requirements of post-Tridentine morals and Aristotelian poetics. There is no need to retell Tasso's notoriously painstaking quest for that compromise.[10]

In this essay on vernacular influences on the Neo-Latin poetic production, a closer look will be taken at a seemingly minor poet who has been called the first epigone of Tasso.[11] This poet, the aforementioned Pietro Angeli da Barga, wrote—just as Tasso did—an epic poem on the First Crusade. As a proponent of late Renaissance humanism, he wrote his poem in Latin; as a professor of humanities, he knew the rules of and the ongoing debates on poetics, and as someone who entertained close relations with the Roman Catholic elite, he tried to produce something in line with the decrees of the Council of Trent.[12]

---

known for his *De principiis rerum*, a didactic poem in Lucretian style, first published in Venice in 1546 and again in Naples 1594. He also wrote an epic poem on the life of John the Baptist (*De vate maximo*). Pietro Angeli da Barga (1517–96) is discussed in greater detail in the remainder of this article. He was a major intellectual figure in the Medicean Duchy of Tuscany. Francesco Benci (1542–94) was a Jesuit in Rome. Once a pupil of Marc Antoine Muret, he is remembered for his *Carmina* (Rome 1590) and above all his epic poem *Quinque martyres* in praise of the Jesuit martyrs who died on their mission to India (Venice 1591). For Benci's epic and its context see Gwynne 2018.

9   This is the famous dilemma in Goethe's *Torquato Tasso* where Tasso's hedonistic maxim "Erlaubt ist, was gefällt" is opposed by the Princess' "Erlaubt ist, was sich ziemt" (Act two, scene two).

10 For a good overview of the vicissitudes of the long period of reviewing and rewriting the *Gerusalemme*, see Bocca 2014; Gigante 1996 and Girardi 2002.

11 See Belloni 1893, pp. 1–28.

12 This conformity is confirmed, for example, by Antonio Possevino, *Bibliotheca Selecta*, p. 289, who recommended Bargeo's *Syrias* as a specimen of a truly Catholic epic poem.

2 Pietro Angeli da Barga and His Epic Poem on the First Crusade[13]

Although he was among the most renowned intellectuals of his time, today Pietro Angeli is only little known.[14] As his nicknames, *Bargeo* (in Latin, *Bargaeus*), or simply *Barga* indicate,[15] he was born in the small Tuscan town of Barga in 1517. He studied law in Bologna but soon fell under the spell of the teachings of the humanist and famous defender of the use of Latin, Romolo Amaseo.[16] When the hot-blooded student ran into serious trouble over an unfortunate love affair, he had to leave Bologna. He went to Venice, where he entered the service of the French ambassador. In the service of the French Crown, he embarked on an eastbound journey during which he travelled in various parts of the Middle East for more than one year. Upon his return, he was appointed professor at the University of Reggio Emilia, from which place Duke Cosimo de' Medici called him to the prestigious chair of the humanities at the University of Pisa in 1549. As the dukedom's chief Latinist, he was asked to draft documents, including public inscriptions and was expected to produce verses in praise of the Medici. In 1572, he was commissioned to teach Cosimo's son Ferdinando, who was destined to pursue an ecclesiastical career and to act as a Medicean outpost in the strategically crucial Roman *curia*. Bargeo seems to have enjoyed the intellectually stimulating milieu of the Roman intelligentsia. During his regular stays in Rome, he entered, albeit indirectly, into contact with Torquato Tasso, for it is in this Roman context that he became acquainted with Scipione Gonzaga, who organized the so-called *Revisione Romana* of Tasso's *Gerusalemme* in 1575–76.[17] Tasso—always worried about the orthodoxy of his epic on the First Crusade—had asked the notoriously learned cardinal for advice on his work. Gonzaga put together a small *équipe* of experts. Bargeo, as a major intellectual figure in Rome, was on this committee and commented on various episodes of the *Gerusalemme*.[18] There is no need to go into the details of his work as a reviser for the purposes of this essay.[19] It is enough to note that Bargeo was certainly conversant with contemporary literary debates

---

13   For the text of the *Syrias*, I refer to the first complete edition printed in Florence in 1591.
14   For the life of Bargeo, the most useful study is still Manacorda 1904. A brief overview is provided by Asor-Rosa 1961.
15   "Il Barga" is the form of the name Tasso regularly uses in his *Lettere Poetiche*.
16   Amaseo is, for example, the author of two speeches *De linguae Latinae usu retinendo*. Amaseo, *Orationes*, pp. 101–46.
17   This process is documented in his so-called *Lettere Poetiche*. See also Bocca 2014.
18   Bargeo also served on a similar committee in the revision of Stella's *Columbeis*; see the 'Letter to the Reader in Stella,' *Columbeidos libri priores duo*, pp. 5–9.
19   For a discussion of Bargeo's work as a reviser of the *Gerusalemme*, see Gigante 2003, pp. 96–101.

and problems. This means that he not only knew the works of Aristotle and Horace's *Ars poetica*, but also the main commentaries of the *Secondo Cinquecento*.[20] Moreover, he was perfectly aware of the problems Tasso had to cope with; in his youthful years, he produced a collection of *Carmina*, which was not entirely void of erotic themes—due to pressure probably exerted by his patron Ferdinando de' Medici, he even had to redact his poems for a revised edition in 1585.[21]

Bargeo must have been aware of the literary discussions in the many academies that were being founded in the second half of the 16th century. In addition to lyric poetry, these academies were peculiarly concerned with epic poetry.[22] They did not, however, usually debate Neo-Latin poetry; they most likely rather talked about Ariosto and Tasso. There generally seems to have been no major debate on a Neo-Latin text,[23] although, as the revision of Sannazaro's *De partu Virginis*, the two editions of Stella's *Columbeis* or Tortoletti's apologetic treatise *Iuditha vindicata*, in the appendix of his epic poem *Iuditha vindex* (Rome 1628) show,[24] Neo-Latin poetry was by no means unaffected by, or *a priori* exempt from, criticism. We have to acknowledge, however, that the most significant discussions in the literary field were clearly instigated by typically vernacular issues. This comes as no surprise, as the discussions were often held in the markedly vernacular contexts of the Italian academies, as demonstrated, for example, by the important role of the *Academia della Crusca* in the debate on Tasso's *Gerusalemme liberata*.

The *Syrias* tells the story of the First Crusade in chronological order, from the divine vision of Peter the Hermit in Jerusalem, to the Council of Clermont, to the siege of Nicaea and Antioch and—at the very end of the 12th and last book—the conquest of Jerusalem. Bargeo published the first two books of his

---

20 We know that Bargeo lectured on Horace's *Ars poetica*, as we have some notes on this text preserved in a codex now at the National Library in Florence (shelf mark: II.IV.192); on this manuscript, see also Weinberg 1974, pp. 156–57. In one place Bargeo refers to Maggi's commentary on the *Ars poetica*, thus confirming the very predictable fact that he both knew and used that commentary.

21 Bargeo's letter to Baccio Valori on 26 April 1585 (BNCF Rinuccini 27, cassetta 1, ins. 6): "per ubbidire sono stato forzato a scancellar tutti gli epigrammi, Elegie, Hendecasyllabi et altre sorti di uersi, che contenessero in se sospetto di lasciuie amorose, non che manifesto argum<en>to."

22 For an exemplary list of topics discussed in one of the Florentine *Accademia degli Alterati*, see Weinberg 1954.

23 Exceptions, such as the brief (ecclesiastical) censure of Sannazaro's *De partu Virginis*, discussed in Deramaix 1991 confirm the rule. See also Deramaix 2008.

24 For a brief comparison between the two editions of Stella's poem, see Hofmann 1994, pp. 468–71, and for Tortoletti's epic poem see Carpané 2006, pp. 9–65.

Syrias in 1582. The second instalment, comprising books three and four, appeared in 1584, followed one year later by the first hexad; all 12 books were printed in 1591. By the time Bargeo decided to publish his poem, he not only had carefully read and commented upon Tasso's *Gerusalemme* but had also witnessed the first reactions to the first pirated editions of that text, which began to be published in 1581. It was especially in the year 1585 that a great number of pamphlets were produced for or against Tasso.[25] Bargeo's poem, appearing in this very period and dealing with the same topic and poetological issues as Tasso's *Gerusalemme*, thus fell on the fertile ground of heated and controversial debates.

3 Engaging with Vernacular Debates in the Paratext of the *Syrias*

The *Syrias* apparently caused a minor literary debate, and we are in the fortunate position of having at least some records of this debate, since Bargeo reacted to the criticism in the preface to the first complete edition that appeared in 1591.[26] As there are no further documents regarding this controversy, it is impossible to know where, how, and among whom the debate took place—whether it occurred via letters, in one of the academies, or elsewhere. Some characteristics of this debate can nonetheless be derived from the little that is known. Bargeo's poem had evidently been exposed to typically Aristotelian criticism, along the lines of the arguments proffered against Ariosto and Tasso. The critics who had sharpened their teeth against the whetstone of vernacular romance or epic poetry also turned to Pietro Angeli's Neo-Latin epic poem.[27]

In the preface to the final edition of 1591, Bargeo says that he "has encountered above all two reproaches *apud criticos*."[28] The first reproach targeted the

---

25   Weinberg 1961, pp. 954–1073.
26   Angeli, *Syrias*, preface to the reader, sig. ★2r–★★★4r.
27   The *Syrias* is written in Latin and it seems that as a consequence the usual questions of style and language do not apply. This does not, of course, mean that the *Syrias* is of immaculate elegance. This is highlighted, for example, by a German—Protestant at that—reader of the *Syrias*. When Roberto Titi states in the introduction to his commentary on the *Syrias* that he would prefer Bargeo even to Virgil, the German reader loses his patience for a moment. His (Caspar von Barth's?) harsh comment reads "Desine asinorum asinissime" ("Stop it, you most asinine of asses!", copy in Zwickau, RSB 25.3.10/9, p. 403). This judgement, however, is not completely unsubstantiated as he also marked and annotated several stylistic flaws in his copy.
28   "[L]ibri illi duo [i.e. the first two books of the *Syrias*, printed 1582 in Paris] [...] in duas potissimum reprehensiones apud criticos inciderunt." Angeli, *Syrias*, preface to the reader, sig. ★★1r).

very definition of poetry as opposed to history. The *argumentum*—i.e., the plot—of the *Syrias* looks like historiography rather than poetry, and that is why it could be maintained that the *Syrias* is not an epic poem but rather a historical account in hexameters. A debate along these lines was already well established in the Middle Ages with regard to Lucanus's *Pharsalia*,[29] and a very similar concern had been voiced against Tasso as well by the Florentine humanist Leonardo Salviati.[30] It was also a commonplace criticism insofar as it had repeatedly been addressed, for example, in the commentaries on Aristotle.[31]

Were his critics right? Was Bargeo no poet, after all? Not quite, Bargeo ripostes, for it all depends on the exact definition of 'poetry.' According to the Stagyrite (*Poetics*, chapter nine), he explains, a poet has to tell "either as things should happen or as they plausibly or necessarily could happen."[32] If a story is implausible, it is impossible to engender joy in the reader. Indeed, who could deny that what has actually happened is much more plausible or probable than what has not? Poetry is not a matter of fiction but of verisimilitude.[33] Angeli admits that a poet who invents his story is to be considered "more skilful and ingenious," but he contents himself with pointing out that his poem is in accordance with the Aristotelian rules and that he himself is consequently a poet. His aim is not to prove that his poem is a particularly good piece of literature; he just wants to show that it has to be considered as poetry.

Bargeo does not take into account the literary taste of his reading public, at least not in the preface to the 1591 edition of the *Syrias*. Popular success, however, had become an increasingly important criterion for the general fortune of a literary work. Ariosto's *Orlando furioso* was an unprecedented best-seller and thus established itself as a literary model.[34] Neo-Latin authors, in particular, from the deceiving heights of their classicist viewpoint, tended to overlook this fact.[35] In Bargeo's view, it was apparently more important for his poem to be in

---

29   On the subject of this debate, see von Moos 1976, p. 94–95.
30   Salviati voices this concern in his *Difesa dell'Orlando Furioso*; see Weinberg 1961, p. 1006.
31   Kappl 2006, pp. 72–169.
32   For a broader discussion of the problem of fiction and truth in the commentaries on Aristotle, see also Kappl 2006, pp. 71–169.
33   A very similar case is made by Tasso in his late *Giudicio* in which he tries to defend the *Gerusalemme* against critics following Speroni's view that poetry has to describe the action of a single person. Tasso resolves the problem by referring to the importance of the "maraviglioso." *Giudicio* II, 177.
34   This literary impact of favourable reception by a wider readership is convincingly demonstrated by Javitch 1991.
35   A famous example of this detrimental miscalculation is Trissino's *Italia Liberata dai Goti* which, according to Tasso's oft-cited judgement, is "mentovato da pochi, letto da pochissimi, prezzato quasi da nissuno." Tasso, *Discorsi dell'arte poetica*, discorso secondo, p. 23.

line with the prerequisites of an orthodox poem than to please a wider public: "As a Christian, I preferred to act in a Christian way dealing with a true story, than to crave for some fame in an un-Christian way by writing on a fictitious and false subject."[36] The argumentative technique by which Bargeo reconsidered his work against the backdrop of the Aristotelian definition of poetry was by no means unusual.[37]

The second critique regards the *dispositio*, more specifically the question whether the *ordo naturalis* is admissible in epic poetry (as opposed to the *ordo artificialis* recommended by Horace in his *Ars poetica*, particularly vv. 147–48). Bargeo's critics point out that Homer's *Iliad* begins *in medias res*, that is, in the tenth year of the Trojan War, whereas Bargeo commences *ab ovo*, even before the actual beginning of the Crusade, and tells the story more or less in chronological order. This could be argued as going against Aristotle's *Poetics*, in which Aristotle praises Homer for not describing the Trojan War in its entirety:

> Homer's inspired superiority over the rest can be seen here too: though the war had beginning and end, he did not try to treat its entirety, for the plot was bound to be too large and incoherent, or else, if kept within moderate scope, too complex in its variety. Instead, he has selected one section, but has used many others as episodes, such as the catalogue of ships and other episodes by which he diversifies the composition.[38]

Bargeo, however, tries to reject this reproach by explaining what he thinks is the correct understanding of Homer's poems and the underlying rules of poetry: Homer could not have told the Trojan War from the beginning because it would either have been too long or simply too boring. In this, Bargeo roughly follows Aristotle's line of argument. However, he adds another thought: Had Homer recounted the entire Trojan War, he would have missed the point, as the actual topic of the *Iliad* is, according to Bargeo, Achilles's wrath or virtue, a subject to which the representation of the first nine years of the war would have had nothing to contribute. For this interpretation, Bargeo refers to the

---

36   "[M]alui enim in aliquo vero argumento christianus christianè agere, quam in re ficta, ac mendaci, nescio quam ingenii gloriam parum christianè aucupari." Angeli, *Syrias*, preface to the reader, sig. ★★2r.

37   See, for example, Lombardelli's defense of Tasso's *Gerusalemme* as outlined by Weinberg 1961, p. 1027.

38   Aristotle, *Poetics*, chap. 23.

authority of (Ps.-)Plutarch[39] as well as that of "many other [...] learned men."[40] The *Iliad* begins with Achilles's wrath (which is hinted at in the first word of the poem, *mênin*, or wrath), and at the end his anger is quenched. The *Iliad* is, in consequence, not the account of (a part of) the Trojan War but rather the story of the wrath of Achilles which unfolds in a linear manner and by no means *in medias res*. Bargeo thus has followed the Homeric model and consequently committed no mistake. The beginning of the plot has to be—according to Bargeo's interpretation of the Philosopher—the "head and the source of the ending of the story."[41] If Bargeo has his story of the Crusade begin with the vision of Peter the Hermit in Jerusalem, he does this because it is right where the Crusade begins. The conquest of Jerusalem, which is told at the very end of the *Syrias*, is the natural conclusion of what had previously been begun with the vision. The *Syrias* thus matches perfectly the Aristotelian definition. A true *ab ovo* beginning, Bargeo goes on to argue in what might appear a *reductio ad absurdum*, would have been if his epic poem on the Crusade had started from the birth of Mohamed. In this way, Bargeo manages to turn the tables on his critics by proving that both Homer and he himself had employed an *ab ovo* beginning.

Bargeo defended his poem against the two reproaches by showing that it adhered to the authority of Aristotle and the Homeric model. The argumentative and discursive methods he employed had been prominently used in the debates on vernacular epic poetry in the Italian *Secondo Cinquecento*.[42] The particular discussion on the *Syrias* that has just been summarized shows, on the one hand, that Latin poems could be subjected to the same kind of criticism as their vernacular counterparts and, on the other hand, that the way criticism is dealt with is similar in both languages. It appears that the vernacular debates on poetics in the Italian academies and the discursive techniques developed in vernacular commentaries, treatises, and discourses could be adapted to Neo-Latin poetry. Nevertheless, it seems that no Neo-Latin epic poem featured in

---

39   Pseudoplutarchea, *De vita et poesia Homeri*, 1.8: "ὁ δὲ ποιητὴς ἀπὸ τοῦ ἐνάτου ἔτους ἤρξατο, ἐπεὶ τὰ πρὸ τῆς Ἀχιλλέως μήνιδος ἦν ἀτονώτερα καὶ πράξεις οὐκ ἔχοντα λαμπρὰς οὐδ' ἐπαλλήλους." ("The poet began from the ninth year because the action was less intense before Achilles' anger, and the heroic deeds were not spectacular or frequent." *Pseudo-Plutarch* 1996.).

40   Angeli, *Syrias*, preface to the reader, sig. ★★★r–★★★v. We know from Tasso that a very similar view was held in particular by Sperone Speroni. Tasso, *Giudicio* II.100: "ma dell'Iliade d'Omero si porta [...] opinione, ch'ella sia azione d'una persona solamente, cioè d'Achille adirato; e questa opinione fu difesa acutamente da lo Sperone mentre egli visse."

41   Aristotle, *Poetics*, chapter seven.

42   This is demonstrated by Weinberg's discussion of the "Quarrel over Ariosto and Tasso." Weinberg 1974, pp. 954–1073.

a major literary debate in late Renaissance Italy. In spite of the considerable production of Neo-Latin epic poetry in the Cinquecento, there seems to have been no extensive 'culture of debate' on these texts and in the Latin language. The reasons for this are rather difficult to pin down. One factor certainly lies in the cultural infrastructure of late 16th century Italy, with its learned societies that put a special (if not exclusive) emphasis on vernacular culture. Another explanation could be provided by the sociocultural status of Latin literature in the early modern period. The debates over vernacular literature often arose from a lack of canonicity and a plurality of potential models. In the field of epic poetry, there is the case of Ariosto's *Orlando furioso*, which prompts discussion by its contrasts with the authoritative models and rules of epic poetry. Neo-Latin epic poetry generally followed indisputable models (above all, Virgil and Homer) and faced consequently no major problems in justifying itself.

With this in mind, one must at least wonder why the *Syrias* aroused the criticism to which Bargeo responded in the preface to the 1591 edition. The *Syrias* is by no means an inherently unorthodox and poetologically adventurous work. Therefore, it was probably not its literary character that caused the debate. Two other hypotheses seem to have a stronger claim to the truth. First, Bargeo was a major poet in the late 16th century who was active in Florence, a vibrant centre of Renaissance literary criticism. His reputation as an erudite writer gave him a great deal of public visibility, which might have facilitated a debate on his work. The second and probably most cogent hypothesis concerns the overt similarity between Tasso's *Gerusalemme* and Bargeo's *Syrias*. As there already existed a more or less heated debate over the former, it was easy for the latter to become involved in a similar dispute. If this is true, the vernacular influence did not limit itself to the contents and arguments of the debate but rather also functioned on a more abstract level: the vernacular debate about Tasso's *Gerusalemme* was a condition of possibility for the debate about Bargeo's *Syrias*.

4   The Influence of the Debates over Poetic Practice: *Admiratio* between Fiction and Historicity

As demonstrated in the first part of this essay, Bargeo was conversant with and—*nolens volens*—also actively participating in the ongoing debates on poetics. In the second part of this essay, the impact of discussions about (predominantly vernacular) poetics on the text of Bargeo's *Syrias* will be explored using the example of the issue of *admiratio* (marvel), which is a major and recurrent theme in Renaissance poetics in general and in Tasso in particular. Poets are required to provoke marvel in the reader. Marvel is aroused by the grand, unexpected, and supernatural. In the universe of chivalric romance, marvel is produced by such figures as sorcerers, griffins, or giants. This, however, was quite difficult to accept for someone like Bargeo, who professedly wanted to write Christian poetry without any trace of non-Christian elements. The poet avowedly pursued a strictly Catholic approach, stating that he wanted to write a poem "in which there is no trace of that impious cult of the ancient Greeks and Romans," a truly Christian poem in which there is "no space left for myths or fiction."[43] This is a clearly post-Tridentine ambition directed both against ancient pagan epic and especially against the modern fancy for monsters, magicians, and witches that was popularized by the (vernacular) *romanzo*. Bargeo, however, professed he had no intention to invent or adapt anything according to the "clamores & admirationes"[44] of the people. He thus explicitly refers to and rejects a popular tendency of vernacular poetry. This was, in view of the eventual success of his work, a bold step, as Tasso, for example, had stated: "Of little delight is indeed the poem that does not have the marvels that move not only the mind of the ignorant but also that of the judicious." Tasso continued to list some of the popular inventions to be found in Ariosto's *Orlando*.[45] Bargeo is confident that the subject matter he has chosen by itself is sufficiently grand and impressive, so he thinks there is no need for him to add anything fictitious or marvellous to the historic account, which he found in the chronicles of the First Crusade, above all in that of William of Tyre. Tasso himself was aware of the problems such fantastic inventions entailed in the post-Tridentine period, but he also understood that he could not do without them if he wanted to find a wider public. He consequently developed the concept of the *maraviglia cristiana* through which he confines (more or less strictly) the supernatural in his poem to direct or meditated divine or infernal intervention.[46] Bargeo adopts this post-Tridentine tendency and categorically shuns magicians, sorcery, incantations, and other stock elements of the tradition of the vernacular *romanzo*, which not even Tasso could eschew completely (see in particular the Saracen sorceress Armida). He thus proudly declares:

---

43 "[C]hristianum poema [...], in quo ne vestigium quidem impii illius veterum Graecorum & Latinorum cultus extaret. Sed omnia ad CHRISTI DEI liberatoris nostri laudem & gloriam referrentur. Videbam igitur in huiusmodi re nullum fermè locum aut fabulae, aut fictioni relinqui [...]." Angeli, *Syrias*, preface to the reader, sig. ★★1v.

44 Angeli, *Syrias*, preface to the reader, sig. ★★2r.

45 "Poco dilettevole è veramente quel poema che non ha seco quelle maraviglie che tanto muovono non solo l'animo de gl'ignoranti, ma de' giudiziosi ancora." Tasso, *Discorsi dell'Arte Poetica* I, p. 6.

46 Kerl 2014, pp. 290–332 and Baldassarri 1977.

> I do not see why I should be blamed and accused for having decided to do away with fictitious digressions and invented stories and tell instead which great and marvellous (*admirabilia*) things happened to the Christians.[47]

It comes as no surprise that the epic account of the *Syrias* is generally based on the solid foundations of the historiography on the First Crusade. Nonetheless, Bargeo seeks to increase the potential of *maraviglia* in the plot and resorts to the following series of techniques that allow him to widen the sometimes rather narrow boundaries of the historical account: He (1) selects and expands particularly suitable episodes from his sources, (2) elaborates hints given therein, or (3) incorporates theologically plausible additions. In rare cases, (4) he even invents secondary episodes from scratch.

(1) Bargeo regarded the mere history of the First Crusade as sufficiently grand and interesting, as noted above. In fact, there are numerous episodes in the chronicles that make for a 'marvellous' epic adaptation, and Bargeo does not fail to include at least some of them. There is, for example, the enthusiastic unanimity with which the Christians who were gathered in Clermont-Ferrand responded to Pope Urban II's exhortation to the Crusade[48] or the accounts of various prophetic visions.[49] Another episode worth mentioning is the discovery of the Holy Lance during the siege of Antioch,[50] in which an angel is sent to a crusader, named Laas in the *Syrias*.[51] He is told to look for the lance with which the Christians could finally bring the conquest of the city to an end. The discovery is a historical fact in the sense that it can be found in the historical sources of the crusade.[52] It is worthy of note, though, that Bargeo stretches the scene to a considerable length (about 180 verses). By providing the Christian soldiers with this powerful weapon, God intervenes (by means of an angel as an intermediary) in a decisive way in the action. It is he who makes the victory possible. This scene is certainly appropriate for arousing *marvel* or *admiratio*, as it involves supernatural elements. In this particular case, Bargeo

---

47 "[N]on video, cur ego reprehendi, & accusari debeam, si reiectis fabulosis digressionibus, & commentitiis fabulamentis, ea, quae christianis magna, & admirabilia acciderunt [...] describenda esse censui." Angeli, *Syrias*, preface to the reader, sig. ★ ★ ★ 2r.

48 See *Syrias*, book one, p. 48, which is dramatically much more intense than the corresponding account in William of Tyre, *Chronicon* 1.16.

49 See, for example, Peter of Amiens' vision in *Syrias* book one, pp. 5–6, corresponding to William of Tyre, *Chronicon* 1.12.

50 *Syrias*, book 12, pp. 354–58.

51 In some sources, he is called Peter Bartholomew; see Runciman 1968, p. 229.

52 William of Tyre, *Chronicon* 6.14.

did not have to alter the historical account, since William of Tyre also describes the discovery of the Holy Lance as the turning point in the siege of Antioch. With the aid of the Holy Lance, God can be shown as something like a *deus ex machina* who comes to the rescue of the crusaders in a difficult, if not desperate, moment of their undertaking. The episode of the Holy Lance is, from a dramatic point of view, very effective and shows that the ideas of poetry that Bargeo had explained in his preface can actually work in particularly suitable circumstances, i.e., when the sources provide a sufficiently 'marvellous' story. In this case, the historic account did not need to be altered in order to transform the sober prose of the chronicle into something that works on a dramatic and narrative level and arouses *admiratio* and *maraviglia* in the reader.

(2) Other episodes can be seen as substantial elaborations of hints provided in the sources. This is the case with the extensive dream vision in book six of the *Syrias*, in which Goffredus's mother, Ida, appears to her son and allows him to see not only the outcome of the Crusade but also into the far future, up to the second half of the 16th century.[53] This vision is a sublime reworking of the model of the *Somnium Scipionis*—perhaps also mediated by Petrarch's *Africa* (books one and two). The metaphysical experience in book six is reminiscent, of course, of the Virgilian *katábasis*. There is no way to reproduce anything like a 'visionary' descent into the underworld in a strictly Christian framework, but the dream vision is a very plausible and expedient substitute. In the case of the *Syrias*, the dream vision derives its historic plausibility from a very brief allusion in William of Tyre's chronicle, in which William claims that Ida had predicted the future of her sons when they were still children, and thus was already endowed with prophetic gifts during her lifetime.[54] It was evidently important for Angeli to underscore the probability of the dream vision by attributing it to someone who had been described in the historical account as graced with the gift of prophecy.

(3) Episodes capable of arousing marvel can derive their plausibility not only from historical sources but also from theology. Bargeo combines a clear-cut celestial and demoniacal hierarchy from God to Lucifer via archangels, angels, and guardian angels on one side and respective 'choirs' of demons on the other.[55] In book one, the epic action is initiated by God, who dispatches an angel to talk to Petrus the Hermit (book one, pp. 4–5). God's counterpart, the *Regnator Erebi* (an epithet used in book four, p. 110), is impressively introduced

---

53 *Syrias*, book six, pp. 162–89.
54 William of Tyre, *Chronicon* 9.6.
55 The most elaborate representation of both the celestial and infernal machinery is found in book four.

in book four. Furthermore, there is a constant interaction between the human and the supernatural spheres with angels and demons acting as intermediaries. At the beginning of book four, for example, two angels meet in heaven before God. These two angels are explicitly described as guardian angels, one in charge of the Christian crusaders, the other protecting the Muslims.[56] While the former eloquently argues in favour of the crusade in order to free the Christians suffering from Muslim suppression in Jerusalem, the latter is against a war that might cause the death of many Muslims and their eternal damnation, as they will not have converted to Christianity in time. This celestial encounter is an overtly fictitious addition to the historical plot, as there is no trace of it in the chronicles of the First Crusade. At the same time, it is in line with the rules Bargeo had previously established insofar as it is theologically plausible. It is a theological truth that there is a guardian angel on both sides and it is likely, if not necessary, for them to intercede before God in view of the events on earth. This is a particularly expedient episode even from a merely literary viewpoint, as it recalls similar scenes in ancient models in which gods try to intercede in favour or against the protagonists of the epic action.[57] The celestial encounter thus serves a twofold aim: it lends a classicising flavour to the epic and manages to enhance the epic cosmos with theologically plausible actors capable of evoking a sense of (orthodox) marvel in the reader.

(4) Although Bargeo had pronounced against fictions and fairy tales in Christian epic poetry and, as has just been shown, generally strove not to deviate from the precept of historicity, the *Syrias* is not entirely free from fictitious insertions. An episode in the *Syrias* that has no historical source at all is one featuring Tomyris, a brave female warrior who sets out to free Nicaea from the siege against the city by the crusaders (book eight, pp. 232–347). This episode is an obvious imitation of the Virgilian Camilla (*Aeneid* 11.532–867) and has no historical foundations whatsoever. It may also be due to the success of Tasso's Clorinda that Bargeo could not resist the temptation of introducing a female warrior. This supposition corresponds to Tasso's opinion that "nothing seems more marvellous than female prowess and fortitude."[58] Tomyris cannot, of course, bear the comparison with Camilla or Clorinda, her mesmerizing

---

56 The theological background for the divine protection of non-Christians is discussed, for example, by Thomas Aquinas, *Summa Theologiae*, I[a] q. 113.

57 The most prominent examples are probably Juno's visit to Aeolus in *Aeneid*, book one, and Venus's plea to Jupiter in the same book to put an end to the Trojans' plight, caused by Juno's intervention.

58 Tasso, *Giudicio* II.125: "dovendo il poeta cercar la maraviglia, niuna cosa ci pare piú maravigliosa de l'ardire o de la fortezza feminile; laonde Virgilio occupò questa parte del maraviglioso de la quale Omero s'era dimenticato."

forerunners. But she is still the heroine of a remarkable and, to a certain extent, creative episode. Tomyris volunteers to lead a group of female warriors against the crusaders who are besieging Nicaea, Tomyris's home town. Although the Amazon-like warriors give proof of their courage, Tomyris is killed in combat, whereupon her comrades commit suicide *en masse*.[59] This episode is hardly compatible with the unconditioned historicism to which Bargeo repeatedly professes to aspire. However, it is legitimated by the Virgilian model to which Tasso's Clorinda must also be reduced. Considering the early success of the Tassian heroine, however, it is by no means far-fetched to assume that Bargeo's Tomyris is influenced by her famous vernacular counterpart. Structural intertextuality corroborates this assumption; in the particularly successful Canto XII (octavas 1–17 and 42–48) of Tasso's *Gerusalemme liberata*, Clorinda volunteers for a nocturnal mission, during which she seeks to set the Christian siege tower on fire. In the *Syrias*, Tomyris likewise undertakes a nightly expedition to kill some of the Christian besiegers. The *nyktomachia* is, of course, a typically epic motif. Nevertheless, it is a telling fact that Bargeo blends the episode in which the heroic deed of the female warrior is related with the theme of the nocturnal expedition. Tasso's *Gerusalemme* might have acted as the intermediary here that induced Bargeo to create with Tomyris his own version of Camilla/Clorinda.

As this short discussion of *admiratio* in the context of the *Syrias* has shown, Bargeo holds up the ideal of poetic truth, which can be either historical or theological truth. With regard to the latter, Bargeo develops Tasso's concept of *meraviglia cristiana*, introducing the new personage of the guardian angel.[60] In this way, he confers a more orthodox structure onto the celestial hierarchy. A more obvious case of vernacular—and especially Tassian—influence occurs in Bargeo's Tomyris episode which has arguably been inspired by Tasso's famous heroine Clorinda.

5   Conclusion

A question one might ask in light of the argument presented in this essay is the following: would the *Syrias* have been written or discussed in a fundamentally different way had there been no vernacular debates about poetics? How decisive was the vernacular influence? With respect to the debates outlined in the

---

59   Angeli, *Syrias*, book eight, pp. 246–47.
60   This innovation seems to be immediately adopted by Stella in the second edition of his *Columbeis* published in 1589; see Hofmann 1994, p. 468.

first part of this essay, the answer is affirmative. Thanks to the lengthy discussions on Ariosto and Tasso among the northern Italian intellectuals, there was a culture of literary debate that was particularly alert to some stock issues of (vernacular) poetry, such as the question of the definition of poetry (i.e., history versus poetry) or the permissible structure of epic poetry (i.e., *dispositio*). It is thus very unlikely that the criticism against Bargeo's *Syrias* would have been voiced had there been no well-established literary discourse in the vernacular.

As to Bargeo's poetic practice, arguably the most obvious vernacular influence on the *Syrias* is evidenced in the subject matter shared with Tasso's *Gerusalemme*. Bargeo knew Tasso's work when he published the *Syrias*. He was also aware that he was entering into a very challenging competition with a vernacular text that had already become immensely popular. Bargeo was in a difficult situation. As Titi notes in the passage quoted at the beginning of this essay, Latin was decreasing in popularity, at least in Italy, and was in danger of becoming a language accessible only to the learned few. Bargeo himself hints to this fact in the preface to his *Syrias* when he points out the difficulties of writing in a language that "has fallen in disuse for a long time and is now almost exiled and banished."[61] A Latin poem could not expect to find as large a readership in late-16th century Italy as the vernacular *romanzi* and *poemi eroici*; moreover, readers' taste had become used to the stories of magic, marvels, and pleasures in the vernacular. In this context, the Latin *Syrias* could not and explicitly would not compete with its vernacular counterpart. In the case of the *Syrias*, the poet's willingness to conform to the values of the Counter-Reformation was quite high. Nonetheless, Bargeo tries, as has been shown in the second part of this essay, to widen to some extent the post-Tridentine rigorist maxims of poetic historicism. He banishes overtly fictitious elements from the chivalric tradition but at the same time tries to exploit the historical sources in order to produce *admiratio*. In doing so, he adopts the idea of *meraviglia cristiana* as used, theorized, and disseminated by Tasso. In the particular case of his heroine Tomyris, Bargeo even appears to have entered in a direct intertextual dialogue with Tasso.

Bargeo's epic poem can be regarded as an attempt to compete with the successful contemporary vernacular literature of the Italian Cinquecento. In hindsight, we know that this competition was difficult to win. On the one hand, vernacular culture in Italy had already gained considerable momentum, producing highly successful works that were almost instantly canonized (as in the case of Ariosto). Latin literature, on the other hand, faced formidable

---

61 "[E]a lingua in pangendo carmine vti deberem, quae iamdiu ex vsu, atque ore hominum quasi exul, & extorris excidisset." Angeli, *Syrias*, preface to the reader, sig. ★3v.

difficulties. The Latinate reading public in the late 16th century was declining in comparison to that of the vernacular. The 'democratization' of literary taste made it more difficult for an elaborate, classicising, and in this sense 'elitist' text to appeal to a wider public. However, it would be inappropriate to view the *Syrias* as a reactionary product. Rather it tries to implement the ideas of an orthodox post-Tridentine literary criticism and in this sense is perfectly in line with the culture of the time. There are also attempts to hold up Bargeo's specifically post-Tridentine virtues against his less strict vernacular counterpart. Roberto Titi, who added a short commentary to the 1591 edition of the *Syrias*,[62] tried to valorise Bargeo in comparison to Tasso on the grounds of the former's major historical faithfulness.[63] He concludes, without mentioning Tasso's name: "For many reasons I think that this poem of Angeli's is to be preferred to the other one [*sc.* Tasso's]."[64]

Even though Titi incessantly showcases Bargeo's orthodoxy and historicity, Bargeo's work never achieved lasting success. Its language was losing ground to the increasingly successful vernacular, and, as a result of its very orthodoxy, it had to lack most of what was popular in those years, for example, chivalric stories of love and magic. The *Syrias* was a poem almost perfectly in line with the Aristotelian post-Tridentine ideas about poetics, but it disregarded the "gusto degli uomini volgari"[65] to which Tasso managed perfectly to cater. The *Syrias* was 'fitting', but it failed to please.

Bibliography

Primary Sources

Amaseo, Romolo. *Orationum volumen.* Bologna: Rubrio, 1564.
Angeli, Pietro. *Syriados liber primus et secundus.* Paris: Patisson, 1582.
Angeli, Pietro. *Syriados liber tertius et quartus.* Paris: Patisson, 1584.
Angeli, Pietro. *Syriados libri sex priores.* Rome: Zannetti, 1585.
Angeli, Pietro. *Syrias.* Florence: Giunti, 1591.

---

62 This commentary is part of the 1591 edition of Bargeo's *Syrias* and printed on pp. 403–96.
63 Titi notes on the lemma "Tancredus" that those "who for other people's sake have attributed to Rinaldo the praise [*sc.* of having first entered Jerusalem], have departed very far from the truth." This innuendo is evidently directed at Tasso, although he is not explicitly mentioned by Titi. Ibid. p. 495.
64 "[H]oc Angelii poema multis de causis ei esse anteponendum censeo." Ibid. p. 495.
65 Tasso, *Discorsi dell'Arte Poetica* I, p. 6.

Aristotle. *Poetics*, edited and translated by Stephen Halliwell. In *Aristotle, Poetics / Longinus, On the Sublime / Demetrius, On Style*. Cambridge, MA: Harvard University Press, 1995, pp. 27–141.

Castelvetro, Lodovico. *Poetica d'Aristotele vulgarizzata e sposta*, edited by Werther Romani, 2 vols. Bari: Laterza, 1978–1979.

Possevino, Antonio. *Bibliotheca Selecta. Qua agitur de ratione studiorum in historia, in disciplinis, in salute omnium procuranda*. Rome: Typographia Apostolica Vaticana, 1593.

Pseudo-Plutarch. *Essay on the Life and Poetry of Homer*, edited by J. J. Keaney and Robert Lamberton. Atlanta, GA: Scholars Press, 1996.

Robortelli, Francesco. *In librum Aristotelis de arte poetica explicationes*. Florence: Torrentini, 1548.

Stella, Julio César. *La Columbeida*, edited by Jávier Sánchez Quirós. Alcañiz: Instituto de Estudios Humanisticos/Madrid: Consejo Superior de Investigaciones Cientificas, 2010.

Tasso, Torquato. *Giudicio sovra la* Gerusalemme *riformata*, edited by Claudio Gigante. Rome: Salerno, 2000.

Tasso, Torquato. *Discorsi dell'arte poetica e del poema eroico*, edited by Luigi Poma. Bari: Laterza, 1964.

Titi, Roberto. *Ad Georgica Virgilii praelectiones quatuor*. Bologna: Rossi, 1597.

Vettori, Pietro. *Comentarii in primum librum Aristotelis De Arte Poetarum*. Florence: Giunti, 1573.

William of Tyre. *Chronicon*, edited by R. B. C. Huygens, 2 vols. Turnholt: Brepols, 1986 (Corpus Christianorum Continuatio Medievalis 38 & 38a).

Secondary Sources

Asor Rosa, Alberto. "Àngeli, Pietro degli (nome umanistico Pier Angelio Bargeo)." *Dizionario Biografico degli Italiani*, vol. 3. Rome: Istituto dell'Enciclopedia Italiana, 1961, pp. 201–04.

Baldassarri, Guido. *Inferno e cielo: Tipologia e funzione del Meraviglioso nella Liberata*. Rome: Bulzoni, 1977.

Belloni, Antonio. *Gli epigoni della Gerusalemme liberata con un'appendice bibliografica*. Padua: Draghi, 1893.

Bocca, Lorenzo. *Le Lettere poetiche e la revisione romana della Gerusalemme liberata*. Alessandria: Edizioni dell'Orso, 2014.

Carpané, Lorenzo. *Da Giuditta a Giuditta. L'epopea dell'eroina sacra nel Barocco*. Alessandria: Edizione dell'Orso, 2006.

Deramaix, Marc. "*Inepta et indecora comparatio: sacris prophana miscere*. Une censure ecclésiastique post-tridentine et inédite du *De partu Virginis* de Jacopo Sannazaro pour Nadine Robert." *Bulletin de l'Association Guillaum Budé* 2 (1991), pp. 172–93.

Deramaix, Marc. "*Non mea uoluntas sed tua*. La révision académique du *De Partu Virginis* de Sannazar et l'expression littéraire latine du sentiment religieux." In Marc Deramaix, Perrine Galand-Hallyn, Ginette Vagenheim, and Jean Vignes, eds. *Les Académies dans l'Europe Humaniste. Idéaux et pratiques*. Geneva: Droz, 2008, pp. 211–48.

Gigante, Claudio. *Vincer pariemi piú sé stessa antica: La Gerusalemme Conquistata nel mondo poetico di Torquato Tasso*. Naples: Bibliopolis, 1996.

Gigante, Claudio. "Poetica del Bargeo." In Idem, *Esperienze di filologia cinquecentesca. Salviati, Mazzoni, Trissino, Costo, Il Bargeo, Tasso*. Rome: Salerno, 2003, pp. 96–117.

Girardi, Mariateresa. *Tasso e la nuova 'Gerusalemme.' Studio sulla 'Conquistata' e sul 'Giudicio.'* Naples: Edizioni Scientifiche Italiane, 2002.

Gwynne, Paul. *Francesco Benci and the Origins of Jesuit Epic. An Edition with Translation and Commentary of the 'Quinque Martyres'.* Leiden: Brill, 2018.

Hofmann, Heinz. "*Adveniat tandem Typhis qui detegat orbes!* Columbus in Neo-Latin Epic Poetry (16th–18th Centuries)." In Wolfgang Haase and Meyer Reinhold, eds. *The Classical Tradition and the Americas*, vol. 1,1. Berlin: de Gruyter, 1994, pp. 420–656.

Huss, Bernhard. "Anmerkungen zur Rezeption von Longins ‚Erhabenem' im Cinquecento." *Romanistisches Jahrbuch* 62 (2011), pp. 165–87.

Huss, Bernhard, Florian Mehltretter, and Gerhard Regn. *Lyriktheorie(n) der italienischen Renaissance*, Berlin: de Gruyter, 2012.

Jossa, Stefano. *La fondazione di un genere: il poema eroico tra Ariosto e Tasso*. Rome: Carocci, 2002.

Kappl, Brigitte. *Die Poetik des Aristoteles in der Dichtungstheorie des Cinquecento*. Berlin: de Gruyter, 2006.

Kerl, Katharina. *Die doppelte Pragmatik der Fiktionalität. Studie zur Poetik der Gerusalemme Liberata (Torquato Tasso, 1581)*. Stuttgart: Steiner, 2014.

Manacorda, Guido. "Petrus Angelius Bargaeus (Piero Angeli da Barga)." *Annali della R. Scuola Normale Superiore di Pisa. Filosofia e Filologia* 18 (1905), pp. 1–131.

Patterson, Annabel M. *Hermogenes and the Renaissance*. Princeton NJ: Princeton University Press, 1970.

Runciman, Steven. *Geschichte der Kreuzzüge*. Munich: Beck, 1968.

Sberlati, Francesco. *Il genere e la disputa: la poetica tra Ariosto e Tasso*. Rome: Bulzoni, 2001.

von Moos, Peter. "*Poeta* und *historicus* im Mittelalter. Zum Mimesis-Problem am Beispiel einiger Urteile über Lucan," *Beiträge zur Geschichte der deutschen Sprache und Literatur* 98 (1976), pp. 93–130.

Weinberg, Bernard. "Argomenti di discussione letteraria nell'Accademia degli Alterati (1570–1600)." *Giornale storico della letteratura italiana* 131 (1954), pp. 175–94.

Weinberg, Bernard. "Demetrius Phalereus." In: Paul Oskar Kristeller and F. E. Cranz, eds., *Catalogus Translationum et Commentariorum: Medieval and Renaissance Latin*

Translations and Commentaries, vol. 2. Washington DC: The Catholic University of America Press, 1971a, pp. 27–42.

Weinberg, Bernard. "ps. Longinus, Dionysius Cassius." In: Paul Oskar Kristeller and F. E. Cranz, eds., *Catalogus Translationum et Commentariorum: Medieval and Renaissance Latin Translations and Commentaries*, vol. 2. Washington DC: The Catholic University of America Press, 1971b, pp. 193–98.

Weinberg, Bernard. *A History of Literary Criticism in the Italian Renaissance*, 2 vols. Chicago: University of Chicago Press, 1974.

CHAPTER 13

Didactic Poetry as Elitist Poetry: Christopher Stay's *De poesi didascalica dialogus* in the Context of Classical and Neo-Latin Didactic Discourse

Claudia Schindler

Didactic poetry is among the most popular and long-lasting genres of Neo-Latin literature. In the wake of the recovery at the start of the Renaissance of the two most important didactic poems in the Latin language, Virgil's *Georgics* and Lucretius's *De rerum natura*, didactic poetry enjoyed immense popularity and became firmly established in the Neo-Latin genre. Today, around 400 Neo-Latin didactic poems of varying provenance, covering a wide array of different subject matter, are known. These poems adhere to the ancient models in the classical manner and deal, in hexameters, with every topic imaginable, including sericulture and chess, the art of war, horticulture, seafaring, and even electricity. Their authors were to be found not just in nearly all European countries but overseas as well.[1] The complexity of the topics and the need to present them adequately in classical Latin and in close connection with its generic traditions constituted a particular challenge for the authors. As a consequence, Neo-Latin didactic poetry is a very specific literary form that is substantially different from vernacular didactic poetry. The choice of Latin as the language of didactic poetry offers special opportunities that ensure longevity. Therefore, there are differing regional variations of didactic poetry, which can also be identified in other Neo-Latin genres. In the choice of topic and the arrangement of the poems, for example, there are discernible differences among the Neo-Latin didactic poems that originated in Italy, France, or Germany. Occasionally, one can discern an explicit aspiration for a regional identity, as in the micro-culture of Neo-Latin didactic poetry in Naples, which, despite the universality of its topics, did not tire of emphasising regional references.[2] At the same time, the authors of Neo-Latin didactic poetry always belonged

---

[1] For a survey of Neo-Latin didactic poetry in the 15th and 16th centuries, see Roellenbleck 1975; Hofmann 1988; Ludwig 1989; Haskell 1999; Hofmann 2001, esp. pp. 173–74; Haskell 2003; Monreal 2010, esp. pp. 10–12 (overview of earlier research); Haskell 2014. On (vernacular) didactic poetry in Italy in the 18th and 19th centuries, see Necchi 2013. On didactic poetry in the German-speaking area, see Kühlmann 2016.
[2] Schindler 2016.

to international networks—for example, as members of the Jesuit order—of which they deftly made use to disseminate their works. In this case, the writing of these works in Latin not only had the advantage of being readily understood in Europe and its overseas colonies; it also added value to the works by marking them as part of the scholarly discourse. Neo-Latin didactic poetry, in particular, drew its success from the fact that it can be placed in a kind of 'twilight zone' between regional and international and that, with regards to content as well as language, it also met the expectations of the educated European elites. The decision to write in Latin, therefore, represents a conscious choice and a mark of distinction.

In stark contrast to the prominence and popularity enjoyed by Latin didactic poetry in the poetic practice of the early modern period (especially in Italy and France), little attention was granted to it in theoretical treatises about poetry. Until the second half of the 18th century, with few exceptions, didactic poetry was not perceived or defined as a separate literary genre, neither in Latin nor in vernacular poetics.[3] Poetological reflections on didactic poetry, if they originated from the poets themselves or early modern or later poetics, were always geared towards individual representatives of the genre, mostly from Greco-Roman antiquity.[4] As their first point of reference, therefore, they predominantly turned to the didactic poems of Empedocles, Lucretius, and Virgil. Most statements on didactic poetry from this period are incidental and not very complex;[5] they are ensnared in the objectives of the respective poetics and are, as a rule, limited to brief remarks. They do not indicate a cohesive, internally consistent estimation of didactic poetry but instead present a multitude of varying viewpoints disparate in their approaches and, at times, even contradictory.[6] To summarise: the vitality of Neo-Latin didactic poetry in practice during the late 17th and early 18th century is reflected only to a very limited extent in contemporary poetic theory.

One exception to this common practice of dealing either very briefly with didactic poetry in the course of more general poetological discussions (or even ignoring it completely), is the *De poesi didascalica dialogus* by the Croatian Christopher Stay (Stojković, Staj). Little is known about Stay himself or his literary works. The *Dialogue on the Didactic Poem* was printed as a paratext for the third and last volume of the thoroughly comprehensive

---

3   Akkermann 1988, p. 410.
4   Akkermann 1988, p. 410 and Ludwig 1989, p. 100.
5   Pantin 1999, p. 22: "I assume that poets are concerned with theoretical problems; but, at first sight, these problems did not lead them to very complex reflections."
6   For an overview, see Hathaway 1962; Fabian 1968.

philosophical-scientific didactic poem, *Philosophiae recentioris libri decem*[7] by Christopher Stay's Jesuit-educated brother, Benedetto Stay ('Beno' Stojković),[8] in Rome in 1792. In the second edition of his earlier didactic poem, the *Philosophiae versibus traditae libri sex*, which appeared in print in Rome in 1747, Christopher Stay had already recorded several thoughts that he included in his later treatise, an *Epistula dedicatoria* to his brother.[9] Encompassing 30 pages of print, Stay's *Dialogus* is practically the only Neo-Latin treatise ever written that specifically examines the theory of the didactic poem; moreover, it also represents what was until that point the most extensive, cohesive examination of this literary genre,[10] even if the relationship between poetry and science was definitely taken into consideration only in the 18th century.[11] The framework and scenery of the dialogue are conventional. It is most likely in the tradition of Cicero's rhetorical dialogues, Tacitus's *Dialogus de oratoribus*, as well as one of the most famous Renaissance treatises on poetry, Fracastoro's *Naugerius sive de poetica dialogus*.[12] Stay styles his treatise on the didactic poem as a discourse among three people, two fictitious speakers: the older, highly educated and highly intelligent Antonius,[13] the younger, brilliant Balbus,[14] and himself. According to the fiction of the dialogue, these three men meet in Antonius's house, where they find him reading Hesiod's *Theogony*.[15]

---

7   The didactic poem was published in instalments: The first volume appeared in 1755, the second in 1760, and the third in 1792. In its initial publication, this difficult and complex poem was already accompanied by a commentary by the Croatian mathematician Roger Joseph Boscovich. The *Philosophiae recentioris libri decem* earned Benedict Stay the name 'Croatian Lucretius'. Zubrinic 1995, s.v. Benedikt Stay-Stojkovic.

8   On his biography, career, and didactic poetry, see Haskell 2003, pp. 179–80.

9   *Philosophiae a Benedicto Stay Ragusino versibus traditae libri sex*, editio secunda. Rome: Pallas 1747, pp. xi–xx.

10 Before Stay, to the best of my knowledge, only Joseph Trapp deals with the didactic poem in particular in his chapter "praelectio quindecima: de poemate didactico seu praeceptivo" of his *Praelectiones poeticae*, vol. 2, pp. 90–104.

11 Roberti, *Lettera sopra l'uso della fisica nella poesia*; Haskell 2003, pp. 183–86; Spaggiari 2015, p. 35.

12 Whether this is really a remake of the *Naugerius*, as Haskell maintains, is debateable, given the long tradition of poetics in the form of dialogues. Haskell 2003, p. 186.

13 Stay, *Dialogus*, pp. ii–iii. There is no evidence to support the idea that contemporaries of Stay might be hidden behind 'classical' names. Possibly, the name 'Antonius' is a reference to Pontano's poetological treatise, *Antonius*. In Cicero's *De natura deorum*, 'Balbus' plays the role of the sceptic in the dialogue.

14 "Balbum eximiae indolis juvenem, quique ad excellens ingenium parem diligentiam, ac discendi cupiditatem adjunxerat." Stay, *Dialogus*, pp. ii–iii.

15 "Hesiodi Theogoniam paulo attentius perlegebam; siquidem vetustissimum ac in primis nobilem poetam considero tanquam praeclarum quoddam religionis ac doctrinae illorum Graeciae temporum nobis reliquum monumentum." Stay, *Dialogus*, p. iii.

Based on this 'prototype of a mythical didactic poem', as all participants in the dialogue agree, a conversation ensues that is held partly in the manner of an Aristotelian lecture, partly as brief exchanges among the participants. The dialogue seems to remain open-ended. The participants agree on a temporary consensus, as friends are expected to arrive and, although they do not wish to exclude them from the discussion, they also do not want to draw them awkwardly into their long-winded debate.[16]

Stay's dialogue on the didactic poem is interesting not simply because his is the first in-depth didactic poetics of the early modern period and the only such poetry that was penned in Latin. With this *Dialogus*, the author participates in a discourse on the didactic poem whose roots extended back to antiquity; one that had been continued up to his time in endless variations and with different approaches. This discourse was not so much about the 'practical' aspects of didactic poetry as it was about the general position of didactic poetry in the poetic system. Stay's estimation and positioning of didactic poetry differs significantly from that of his predecessors. While the authors of earlier poetics consider didactic poetry, as a poetic genre in general, either with a dismissive or, at best, benevolently neutral attitude, and content themselves with allowing didactic poetry to be considered poetry at all, Stay's *Dialogus* is a unique plea in favour of didactic poetry as the best of all poetic forms. For Stay, didactic poetry is the very poetry that satisfies the highest of intellectual needs and that addresses an exclusive circle of recipients, who alone are able to appreciate its difficulty and complexity. Although Stay developed his analysis on the basis of representations in the relevant poetics on didactic poetry that preceded him, he does add new inflections that constitute a logical continuation of his predecessors' approaches, eventually going on to achieve his own concept. In this essay, three examples will be used to illustrate Stay's line of argument. These examples also represent central points in the early modern discourse on didactic poetry, thereby leading directly into early modern poetological discussions on the didactic poem. One of the questions most frequently and most intensely debated in early modern poetics in connection with didactic poems was whether didactic poetry could actually be considered proper poetry at all. The early modern discussion of this question was a reaction to Aristotle's verdict that provided the starting point for what Fabian has called the "Problemgeschichte des Lehrgedichts"[17]—a verdict that, however,

---

16 "Nam et familiares nostros brevi huc adfuturos opinor, qui, si nos in eadem disceptatione deprehendent, aut ad redintegrandam controversiam adigent, aut exclusos se aegre ferent. Quare quae reliqua sunt, si ita videtur, in aliud tempus differamus." Stay, *Dialogus*, p. xxx.
17 Fabian 1968, p. 68.

originally did not refer to didactic poetry *in toto* but rather to one of its particular forms. In his *Poetics*, Aristotle had very decisively drawn the line between Empedocles's nature poems and Homeric verses. For Aristotle, Empedocles's philosophical observations on nature did not meet the criterion of μίμησις, the imitation of human activity, which, according to Aristotle's approach in *Poetics*, is an essential feature of poetry. Empedocles and Homer, in his famous statement, have nothing in common besides metre. For this reason, Empedocles is to be regarded more as a naturalist than a poet.[18] Aristotle made this verdict only about the presentation of natural science research in hexametric verses as practised by Empedocles and concluded that his work was "amimetic."[19] Nevertheless, after the Aristotelian *Poetics* became well-known in Western Europe in the 16th century,[20] his judgement was then applied to all didactic poetry in a generalised manner and led to many controversial discussions.[21] While some participants in this discourse sought to declare didactic poetry *in its entirety* an unpoetic genre and exclude it from poetry,[22] others attempted to modify the Aristotelian statement in order to turn didactic poetry into a genre of poetry after all. For example, in the above-mentioned *Naugerius sive de poetica dialogus*, first printed in 1549, Girolamo Fracastoro has his dialogue participant Bardulo represent the view that the principle of μίμησις does not need to be limited to imitating people and their actions; after all, μίμησις, that is *imitatio*, lies in every utterance made by the poet.[23] He thus held a very firm ("durum") opinion that somebody who imitated people was a poet but that Empedocles, who did not do this, was not, for otherwise this would mean that Virgil was writing as a poet in the *Aeneid* but not in the *Georgics*.[24] Besides,

---

18 "οὐδὲν δὲ κοινόν ἐστιν Ὁμήρῳ καὶ Ἐμπεδοκλεῖ πλὴν τὸ μέτρον, διὸ τὸν μὲν ποιητὴν δίκαιον καλεῖν, τὸν δὲ φυσιολόγον μᾶλλον ἢ ποιητήν" (Aristotle, *Poetics* 1447b).

19 Fabian 1968, 69–70.

20 The first Latin translation of Aristotle's *Poetics* (by Giorgio Valla) was published in 1498; the *editio princeps* of the Greek original was printed by Aldus Manutius in 1508. See Buck 1952, p. 146; Weinberg 1961, pp. 361–71 (for further editions and commentaries, pp. 371–563); Plett 1994, p. 10. For the further reception of the *Poetics*, see Buck 1952, pp. 143–90; Weinberg 1961, pp. 564–634; Kappl 2006.

21 Hathaway 1962, pp. 66–67; Fabian 1968, pp. 74–89. For the German-speaking region, see Siegrist 1974, pp. 20–30.

22 See esp. Speroni, *Dialogo sopra Virgilio*; see also Hathaway 1962, pp. 69–70 for Benedetto Varchi, Piero Vettori, Bernardino Partenio, and Antonio Sebastiano Minturno.

23 "Ponamus igitur imitationem esse, quodcunque Poeta scribat: et non solum cum personas inducit." Fracastoro, *Naugerius*, p. 156 D. For the earliest expansion of the term *imitatio* (without references to didactic poetry) in the commentary on the *Poetics* by Francesco Robertello (Florence 1548, p. 2), see Fabian 1968, pp. 76–77.

24 "Quod si dicas, quanquam poeta non est simul, ac quis personas est imitatus, poeta tamen non est vocandus ille, qui hanc non assumpsit materia, ut Empedocles, profecto et hoc

a distinctive characteristic of poetry, he continues, is also the *modus dicendi*, not the *materia*. Horace, he argues, had already recognised this when he determined that any material can become poetic material if it is treated using *poetico more*.[25] The human mind, he asserts, has two parts, *voluntas* and *intellectus*, and the goal of *voluntas* is *prudentia*, while that of the *intellectus* is *cognitio* and *intellectio*. Accordingly, a poet who not only imitates people but also all things concerning nature, complies with this specification particularly well, since in imitating people he achieves *prudentia*, and by imitating things in the natural world, he achieves *cognitio*.[26] For Fracastoro, therefore, "dichterische Erkenntnis und dichterische Lehre" are "die vollkommenste Form der Lehre."[27] This extension allows him to reclaim didactic poetry as poetry and thus save his own poetic production, the Latin didactic poem *Syphilis sive de morbo Gallico*, published in 1530, from the accusation that it was 'unpoetic.'

The question whether didactic poetry is 'mimetic' and therefore constitutes a 'poetic' genre is also taken up by Stay in his *Dialogus*:

> As there are many non-living beings among the entirety of things and there are those that are not equipped with any internal sensation but nevertheless are of maximum power [...]: that is why it will be sufficiently obvious that if poets express the image of these things, a large number of options is similarly available to them in order to inspire desire, sorrow, admiration and other sensations in us. These very poets ought to be considered the true imitators, because they have achieved the imitation of nature in its entirety.[28]

In an opinion similar to Fracastoro and various other early modern poetry theorists,[29] Stay also maintains—as is made clear by the context of the

---

valde durum videtur. Primum quod Vergilium circa Aeneida poetam esse, circa Georgica vero non esse valde mirum est [...]." Fracastoro, *Naugerius*, p. 157 A. Donati, *De arte poetica*, book 1, pp. 38–41; Akkermann 1988, p. 414.

25 "Horatius videtur, cum publicam omnem, et communem materiam dixit propriam poetae fieri, si poetico more tractetur." Fracastoro, *Naugerius*, p. 157 A–B.

26 Fracastoro, *Naugerius*, p. 157 B/C; Fabian 1968, pp. 82–83.

27 Fabian 1968, p. 83.

28 "Nam cum in hac rerum universitate permulta sint inanima quidem, nulloque sensu praedita, in quibus tamen plurima vis inest [...], satis erit manifestum in earundem rerum imagine exprimenda magnam aeque poetis relictam esse copiam ad voluptatem, tristitiam, admirationem, aliosque sensus in nobis excitandos. Iidemque tum tandem germani imitatores erunt putandi, cum hanc universae naturae imitationem fuerint assecuti." Stay, *Dialogus*, pp. xi–xii.

29 For Bernardino Tomitano and Speroni, see Hathaway 1962, pp. 67–69.

above quotation—that Aristotle's concept of μίμησις cannot be limited to the imitation of human actions in drama, especially since this would mean that all of the non-dramatic parts of Homer's epic poems, in particular his descriptions of gods and nature, would have to be excluded from poetry. In addition, he declares—attributing the words to the character of Balbus—that it is completely unfathomable not to consider Vergil's *Georgics* and Lucretius's *De rerum natura* to be the works of great poets due to a lack of μίμησις.[30] The term *imitatio*, he therefore asserts, must inevitably be more broadly defined and also expanded to include inanimate things, such as descriptions of the sky.

However, Stay bases this modified concept of μίμησις on a new foundation. Even before discussing μίμησις, he justifies the ontological state of philosophical-scientific didactic poetry. The starting point for his argument is formed by a general consensus among the dialogue's participants that myths such as those found in Hesiod's *Theogony* obscure facts, produce ambiguities, and extend an invitation to read more into the myths than what the poets had intended. For difficult thought processes in particular, Stay maintains, myths are in conflict with poetry's aspiration to truth:

> How can myths be interpreters of the truth if they, which themselves intended as clarification, need to be clarified?[31]

He concludes that to be at all comprehensible in presenting difficult and complex issues, one must do away with myths completely and rely on explicit representation.[32] Examples from philosophy, such as the cosmogony found in the Platonic *Timaeus*, as well as cosmogonies from non-didactic poetry, such as the song of Silenus in Virgil's sixth *Eclogue* and Pythagoras's speech in the 15th book of Ovid's *Metamorphoses*, provide factual arguments and also, as it were, 'evidence' for the accuracy of the statement. Stay's finding that a 'mythless' poetry can by all means be justified with regard to substance and facts forms the premise of his successive statements. Before introducing the reader of his *Dialogus* to the arguments in favour of an expansion of the Aristotelian

---

30 "aegre enim adduci poteram, ut Virgilii Georgica ob eam imitationis inopiam non divini poetae opus existimarem, aut ipsum Lucretium tametsi sedulo, ac naviter philosophantem, ob sublimem ac singularem illam dicendi rationem, non item homericum, ac summum poetam crederem." Stay, *Dialogus*, pp. xii–xiii.

31 "Quo enim pacto fabulae veritatis interpretes esse possunt, si ipsae interpretes alio interprete indigebunt?" Stay, *Dialogus*, p. vi.

32 "Sed huiusmodi festivitates a gravioribus doctrinis omnino removendas censeo, et tanquam inutiles ornatus in palaestra adhiberi solitos, in veris certaminibus, quia oneri sunt, motusque corporis impediunt, abjiciendas." Stay, *Dialogus*, p. viii.

conception of *mimesis*, he is made familiar with another idea of the author's, namely his opinion that philosophical-scientific content, in its specific clarity, has primacy over mythical narrations, which are only preliminary stages on the way to as lucid a depiction as possible of complex philosophical-scientific subject matters. For Stay, 'myths' and allegorical speech (as an example, he names the parable of Menenius Agrippa of the belly and the members[33]) constitute a form of presentation employed before anything like a 'scientific' mode of expression was known, and was later dismissed as primitive. Accordingly, he concludes:

> And I think that for this single reason myths were gradually displaced from the poems of early philosophers, and thus finally the principle to present their philosophy in verse without myths was introduced by Empedocles and Parmenides and other [southern] Italian philosophers.[34]

The denunciation of mythical narrative as 'primitive' and 'not appropriate for facts that fulfil complex and scientific standards' is an essential part of Stay's reasoning. Implicitly, without expressing it directly, Stay in fact makes it clear at this early point in his dialogue that the *imitatio* and representation of inanimate objects has a higher intellectual standing than the *imitatio* of human actions. The *imitatio* of a didactic poet who chooses scientific topics ranks above the *imitatio* of an epic poet who devotes himself to mythology.

A further point that Stay repeatedly raises in discussing the poeticity of didactic poetry and whether it ought to be considered poetry at all (a point related to μίμησις) is the definition of 'poetry' as 'narration' or the 'imitation of action.' According to this fundamentally Aristotelian view,[35] only works on mythological subjects with a narrative structure and a temporal succession

---

33   "Nota est illa Menenii Agrippae ad plebem, quae in montem Sacrum secesserat, fabella [Liv. 2.32.9–12], qua rudi populo, qui justitiae, et civitatis constituendae neque vim neque nomen teneret, illa corporis humani membrorum inter se dissidentium imagine utilitatem legum ac magistratuum in animos intulit. In ipsis philosophiae incunabulis eadem fabulandi industria sapientes usos scimus ad morum doctrinam imperitorum mentibus communicandam." Stay, *Dialogus*, p. xviii.

34   "Atque hanc unam ob causam opinor fuisse fabulas a veterum sapientium carminibus paulatim rejectas, atque ab Empedocle, Parmenide, atque aliis Italicae disciplinae philosophis idcirco hunc apertis versibus philosophandi usum fuisse demum introductum." Stay, *Dialogus*, pp. vi–vii.

35   "ἔστιν δὲ τῆς μὲν πράξεως ὁ μῦθος ἡ μίμησις, λέγω γὰρ μῦθον τοῦτον τὴν σύνθεσιν τῶν πραγμάτων; [...] δῆλον οὖν ἐκ τούτων ὅτι τὸν ποιητὴν μᾶλλον τῶν μύθων εἶναι δεῖ ποιητὴν ἢ τῶν μέτρων, ὅσῳ ποιητής κατὰ τὴν μίμησίν ἐστιν, μιμεῖται δὲ τὰς πράξεις." Aristotle, *Poetics* 1450a; 1451b.

should be considered as poetry. However, didactic poetry—especially if it dispenses with the addition of mythical stories—lacks this basic structure of narrative; this also is an argument found in various Renaissance treatises that favour excluding it from poetry. Joseph Trapp, who holds Lucretius's didactic poetry in high regard, nevertheless criticises the lack of poetic fiction in *De rerum natura* in his *Praelectiones poeticae* (1715).[36] For Trapp, narrative digressions (*digressiones fabulosae* and *figmenta poetica*) belong to didactic poetry as a matter of course. With a similar argument, Giovanni Pietro Capriano had already completely excluded Empedocles and Lucretius from poetry in his treatise *Della vera poetica* (1555): these are not poets, he argues, since no poetic fictions are present in their works.[37] Stay, who also examines this problem, represents an entirely different point of view. To this end, he starts by associating mythical narrations (*fabulae*) with rhetoric (*dicendi comptus*):

> What happened during the invention of individual elements of writing [was] that faithful images of things that were initially used for the reproduction of these things were gradually abstracted and turned into characters, the very same seems to have happened with the speech of people: just like letters, mythical stories—so to speak as images of thought— initially used to understand raw facts, were then concentrated into this

---

[36] "Illud quoque Lucretio objiciendum est, quod in digressiones fabulosas, et figmenta poetica, nunquam excurrat. Sunt quidem illi suae digressiones; eae vero non fabulosae, sed philosophicae potius quam poeticae; quae idcirco argumentum non satis varium reddunt, et diversum, neque lectorem recreant satis, et oblectant. Etiam excursus sunt philosophici, sed et impii; nimirum contra providentiam, religionem, et immortalitatem animae, compositi: Unum si excipias, de Peste Atheniensi; qui descriptionem quidem poeticam continet, non fabulam." Trapp, *De poemate didactico*, p. 95.

[37] "e pero giustissimamente Aristotele giudico Empedocle che senza fittione alcuna scrisse in versi cose physice et naturali, si come anchora appresso di noi Lucretio, non essere meritamente da esser' detto poeta in altro che forsi in qualche parte della eloquution' delle parole." Capriano, *Della vera poetica*, p. B ii; see Hathaway 1962, p. 71. On digressions in the didactic poem in poetics in German, see Siegrist 1974, pp. 73–74. A sort of middle course is steered by the most comprehensive poetics of the 17th century, the *Palaestra Eloquentiae ligatae* by the Jesuit Jacob Masen. Although the didactic poem is mentioned as an epic sub-genre within the explanations of heroic epic ('*Poesis heroica*') ("est vero Epicum carmen universe illud, quod rem quamcumque hexametro versu ac gravi oratione imitatur. Hoc vel Physicum est, de natura rerum creatarum, artiumque ac scientiarum, ut Manilius et Lucretius, tum in Georgicis Virgilius, scripsere; vel ethicum de vita hominum, ut ceteri plerique Poetarum dedere," p. 125), it is subsequently not taken into further consideration—also due to the fact that Masen is concerned with epics characterised by noteworthy poetic fictions and with a high stylistic level ("nota aliqua ac laude singulari, cum fictionis, tum elocutionis," p. 126) and because he deems hexametric poetry without *fictio poetica* to be incomplete.

shorter ornament of speech. Both general speech and the speech of the poet became more elegant because of it.[38]

Rhetoric (*dicendi comptus*), according to the core idea in the above-quoted excerpt, is derived from mythical narrations (*fabulae*), just as letters originated from images; similes and comparisons are thus related to narrations. Ultimately, therefore, according to this core idea, rhetoric is an abstraction and sublimation of mythical narratives in which the poet realises his poetic intuition. Based on this thought, Stay can then go beyond his predecessors to establish the supremacy of the didactic over the narrative epic. He claims that a poetic form such as didactic poetry, which makes use of 'abstracted' and 'sublimated' myths to a great extent, accommodates the intuition of a poet in a special way; this inevitably makes it 'more poetic' than poetry, which uses the conventional mythical fictions in its long forms. Ultimately, on the basis of this line of argument, he then goes yet *another* step further: the structure of the narrative plot is to the epic and tragedy, as establishing a conclusive argument is to the didactic poet.[39] As Stay's Antonius claims in the dialogue, epics/tragedies and didactic poems differ most notably in their choice of topics: on the one hand, epic and tragedy deal with events in the human realm, while didactic poetry, on the other hand, takes its subject matter from the cosmic, that is, the divine realm. Based on this attribution, the subject matter drawn from natural science always has priority—an opinion that was reason enough for Francesco Patrizi to prefer Empedocles to Homer in his work *Della poetica*.[40] With an obviously contemptuous reference to what Aristotle characterised as the exemplary drama, *Oedipus Tyrannus*, Stay asks:

---

38 "Unde quod in scripturae inveniendis elementis accidit, ut ipsae rerum picturae, quae initio ad res designandas adhibebantur, paulatim contractae in litterarum notas transierint, illud idem etiam in hominum sermone videtur contigisse: nimirum ut fabulae quasi cogitationum imagines ad rudiorum intelligentiam primo adhibitae, deinde contraherentur in hos breviores dicendi comptus, quasi figuras, quibus et communis sermo, et poetarum oratio praesertim esset elegantior." Stay, *Dialogus*, p. xviii.

39 "Nam si ex ipsa rerum conjunctione potest isthaec carminis colligatio proficisci, qua ex re aptius eadem, quam ex his Didascalicorum argumentis orietur? Quod unquam facinus, quae hominum actiones possunt tam multas, ac tam varias res tam apte colligare atque connectere [...]." Stay, *Dialogus*, p. xxviii.

40 "Ora vengasi al paragone, delle favole di Empedocle, e di Omero. Quelle di Omero sono d'huomini, e di Dei. E quelle di Empedocle, sono altresi di Dei per l'una parte. E d'altra, più alto, che d'huomini, di cose, e d'opere di Natura favolleggiate. E in questa parte quanto Natura è ad huom superiore, tanto sono le favole d'Empedocle alle Omeriche superiori." Patrizi, *Della Poetica*, book 7, p. 143.

> What changes, what unexpected events that arise from the fact that someone learns something about his parents against his expectation, can be so sweet that they are equal to this convenience of knowledge; if we, as far as we can achieve it with the mind, can recognise this very long chain of causalities and the effects they have among themselves, and learn together with those effects that produce them, so to say neighbourhoods and relationships?[41]

Based on these observations, Stay suggests an obvious conclusion to his audience: since, on the one hand, subject matter from the divine realm must be given precedence over human topics, but, on the other hand, poetry possesses the greatest possibilities for a sublime representation of these topics, the depiction of subject matter in epics and tragedies must inevitably yield precedence to didactic poetry with its depiction of cosmic phenomena.

A third aspect of the discourse on didactic poetry that Stay incorporates in his *Dialogus* is already hinted at in the previous quotation. There he observes that the revelations of familial relationships in tragedies (as already mentioned, he alludes to the revelation of incest in the case of Oedipus) would hardly be so "pleasant" ("suaves") that they could equal the "pleasing quality" ("jucunditas") that knowledge of nature provides.

The question of whether poetry should 'instruct' or 'delight,' and how poetic pleasure and instruction relate to each other, had been controversially discussed since Horace's programmatic phrase, presumably based on that of Neoptolemus of Parion[42] "aut prodesse volunt aut delectare poetae / aut simul et iucunda et idonea dicere vitae" (*Ars poetica* 333–34).[43] Namely, according to the *communis opinio*, poetry may and must have a certain intent to teach, but, in any case, delight, or *delectare*, should be at the forefront. This attitude, in turn, placed didactic poetry specifically in the spotlight of the criticism that accused it of being far too obtrusive in its intention of 'teaching' and too little concerned with 'delighting.' In some instances such a critique simply categorised it as purely instructive[44]—a view that is reflected even in Goethe's essay

---

41 "Quae mutationes, qui repentini eventus ex ignotis antea cujuspiam parentibus praeter opinionem compertis derivati tam suaves esse possunt, ut pares sint huic cognoscendi jucunditati; cum quoad animo consequi possumus, longissimam illam causarum aliarum ex aliis succedentium seriem intelligimus, earumque inter se, et cum iis, quos gignunt, effectibus, tanquam propinquitates et cognationes ediscimus?" Stay, *Dialogus*, p. xxx.
42 Fabian 1968, pp. 73–74 (with further literary references).
43 For an overview, see Till 2005.
44 Ps.-Acro, *Scholia in Horatium vetustiora, ad artem poeticam*, v. 333: "Delectant bucolica, prosunt Georgica."

on the didactic poem.[45] In his line of argument, Stay takes the Horatian *delectare* and *prodesse* as the primary characteristics of poetry:

> Therefore poets have earned a unique opportunity to delight and entertain because of the limitations, due to which they are restrained and held in place out of obedience towards the spirit and respect for the body.[46]

The essence of poetry is to evoke joy through a pleasant and admirable mode of expression; to have an emotional effect on the reader.[47] Stay, however, adds an important detail here, giving *delectare* another orientation. Only by being filled with content, he declares, does poetry achieve its true grandeur; certainly, instrumental flute playing, for example, also elicits emotions, but it is surely much more effective to combine tones and rhythms with words.[48] The ultimate poetic harmony, Stay claims, only comes about as a result of the interplay between form and content:

> Whose (i.e., of a poem appropriate in content and form) characteristic will be real harmony which coalesces from this harmony of rhythm with things and verbal statements.[49]

According to Stay, the poet must make use of precisely this special potential of his expression in order to depict unusual and difficult things—that is to say, subjects that evince a certain erudition. With this, he determinedly

---

45 "Alle Poesie soll belehrend sein, aber unmerklich: sie soll den Menschen aufmerksam machen, wovon sich zu belehren werth wäre; er muß die Lehre selbst daraus ziehen wie aus dem Leben." Goethe, *Über das Lehrgedicht*, p. 225.

46 "Ita ex ipsis angustiis, quibus animi obsequio et indulgentia corporis adstricti coercentur, poetae egregiam et delectandi, et juvandi opportunitatem quaesiverunt." Stay, *Dialogus*, p. xvi.

47 In the *Philosophiae libri sex*, a quotation from Cicero's *Tusculanae* in which delighting the reader was declared to be the foundation of every literary work, was the motto of Benedict Stay's poem ("Sed mandare quemquam litteris cogitationes suas, qui eas nec disponere, nec illustrare possit, nec delectatione aliqua allicere lectorem, hominis est intemperanter abutentis et otio et litteris," Cic. Tusc. 1.6). See also Christopher Stay, *Epistola dedicatoria*, p. xiii: "Nam Veteres humanissimam artem non ad delectandum tantummodo (ut nunc ea abutimur) adhibuerunt: sed idcirco praeclare invenerunt, quae maxime jucunditate traheret, eadem esset ad juvandum aptissima."

48 Tomitano, *Quattro libri della lingua thoscana*, fol. 86v: "si come l'harmonia del poeta è più conosciuta dall'intelletto, che da i sensi: il contrario è del musico, usato di dilettar à l'orecchie, più che à la mente."

49 "Cujus illa demum erit germana concinnitas, quae ex hac numerorum cum rebus ac sententiis consensione coalescet." Stay, *Dialogus*, p. xx.

opposes Ludovico Castelvetro's hedonistic interpretation in his commentary on the Aristotelian *Poetics*, in which he had defined the art of delighting as the only objective of poetry, thereby excluding all scientific matters as topics of poetic portrayal. Castelvetro claimed that "diletto" was the duty of poets, and "giovare" that of scientists and philosophers; poetry should appeal to the masses ("rozza multitudine") and common folk ("commune popolo"), while the discovery of the secrets of nature should be left to philosophers and artists.[50] Stay, in contrast, takes the view that one can elicit joy in the listener especially with philosophical-scientific subjects. He makes his point by referring to the heroic epic: both the song of the sirens in the *Odyssey* as well as the song of Iopas in the *Aeneid* dealt with scientific subject matter and yet had, as their primary goal, the *delectatio* of their audience. Similarly, Joseph Trapp, in his *Lectures on Poetry*, had argued for the happy union of poetry and philosophy in the didactic poem, using the song of Iopas as an example.[51]

The dichotomy between *docere* and *delectare*, which Castelvetro and the authors of previous poetics had built upon, is dissolved by Stay in favour of a correlation between the two poles, which he had appropriated for his own

---

50 "Percio che se speculando havessono trovata la verita di quella scienza, o di quella arte, havrebbono trovato quello, che era, et sara in perpetuo nella natura delle cose, intorno alle quali s' è compresa quella scienza, et s' è constituita quella arte, et usato ufficio di buono philosopho et di buono artista, ma non gia di buono poeta, che è di speculando rassomigliare la verita degli accidenti fortunosi degli huomini, et di porgere per rassomiglianza diletto a gli ascoltatori lasciando il trovamento della verita nascosta delle cose naturali, o accidentali al philosopho, et all'artista con la loro propria via di dilettare, molto lontana da quella del poeta, o del giovare. Ma oltre a questo la materia delle scienze, et delle arti per un'altra ragione piu manifesta al senso non puo essere soggetto della poesia, conciosia cosa che la poesia sia stata trovata solamente per dilettare, et per ricreare, io dico per dilettare et per ricreare gli animi della rozza moltitudine, et del commune popolo, il quale non intende le ragioni, ne le divisioni, ne gli argomenti sottili, et lontani dall'uso degi idioti, quali adoperano i philosophi in investigare la verita delle cose, et gli artisti in ordinare le arti, et non gli' intendendo conviene quando altri ne favella, che egli ne senta noia, et dispiacere, perciochè c'incresce fuori di modo naturalmente, quando altri parla in guisa che non lo possiamo intendere. Laonde, se concedessimo, che la materia delle scienze, et dell'arti potesse essere soggetto della poesia, concederemmo anchora che la poesia o non fosse stata trovata per dilettare, o non fosse stata trovata per le genti grosse ma per insegnare, et per le persone assottigliate nelle lettere, et nelle dispute. Il che anchora si conoscera essere falso per quello che si provera procedendo oltre. Hora perche la poesia è stata trovata, come dico, per dilettare, et ricreare il popolo commune, dee havere per soggetto quelle cose, che possono essere intese dal popolo commune, et intese il possono rendere lieto, le quali sono quelle, che tutto di avengono, et delle quali tra il popolo si favella, quali sono quelle, che sono simili alle novelle del mondo." Castelvetro, *Poetica d'Aristotele vulgarizzata et sposta*, fols. 16v–17; Buck 1952, p. 149.

51 Trapp, *De poemate didactico*, p. 93.

reasoning. The essence of poetry, the *delectatio*, as he has Antonius state, can be enhanced by the choice of topic: the more demanding and difficult the subject matter, the greater the associated *delectatio*:

> How we are delighted by our ingenuity, how we think of ourselves quite educated, and are pleased with ourselves! How divine then and gifted with superhuman strength we will consider the poets who bring unusual and strange topics to us and make us happier and more erudite than usual![52]

In this line of argument, *delectare* is redefined as a purely intellectual pleasure. The fact that only a small, highly-educated readership could appreciate this type of poetry is happily accepted by the author of the *Dialogus*. Unlike Castelvetro, Stay purposely does not assume that delighting the *populus communis* must be the aim of poetry. Pindar's work, he argues, also contains great intricacies, and yet he is treasured as a poet; moreover, if somebody writes something that meets with the approval of the best, the opinion of the masses is no longer at all necessary: "Si quae quis scriberet, probare optimis posset, quid jam plurimorum sententias quaereret?" (Stay, Dialogus, p. xxvi).

This survey of Stay's *Dialogus* has already shown that discussions on the didactic poem, which had been ongoing in poetics since the beginning of the Renaissance, were for the author only the foundation and starting point for an elitist concept of poetry[53] in which didactic poetry, specifically didactic poetry in Latin, was promoted to the highest-rank as the best of all poetic genres. This evaluation represents a novelty in the history of poetological discourse on the (Neo-Latin) didactic poem and goes considerably beyond the attempts of other poetics to integrate the didactic poem into poetry. It seems all the more astonishing, therefore, that Stay articulated his upgrading of didactic poetry at what was really an end point of the early modern, Neo-Latin production of didactic poetry. The third volume of the *Philosophiae recentioris libri decem* by his brother, Benedict, is arguably the last extensive Neo-Latin didactic poem with universalistic ambitions. Although science and poetry did enter into the most varying of unions in the 19th century,[54] the production of classic didactic

---

52 "Quam ingenio nostro delectati satis docti nobis videbimur, nobisque placebimus! Quam vero divinos, ac humana majore vi praeditos hujusmodi poetas arbitrabimur, qui cum inusitata omnia ac peregrina nobis afferant, tum nos ipsos solito beatiores, ac doctiores pene faciant!" Stay, *Dialogus*, pp. xx–xxi.
53 Haskell 2003, p. 188: "candidly elitist vision."
54 In his instructive contribution on Darwin and Goethe, Olav Krämer describes literary forms that—despite their similar topics—have little in common with the Neo-Latin didactic poems that were based on classical models. Hufnagel/Krämer 2015, pp. 37–67.

poems written in Latin came almost entirely to an end. The few Latin didactic poems of the 19th century, such as Didacus Vitrioli's didactic poem on the swordfish (*Xiphias*) in 1845 or Alexander Zappata's didactic poem on eel fishing in the bay of Comacchio, printed in 1897, would hardly have satisfied Stay's elitist demands.

What, then, are the reasons for this curious lack of a sense of finite time in Stay's theory? I think that, paradoxically, *precisely* this abandoning of hexametric didactic poetry in Latin in the 19th century and Stay's *Dialogus* must be brought into close relation—and this is where vernacular languages come into play. This decline, and the *Dialogus*, ought to be seen in conjunction with the very reasons that accelerated the marginalisation of classical-style Latin didactic poetry in the late 18th and early 19th century. By the middle of the 18th century, a new understanding of poetry had emerged, especially in vernacular treatises on poetry, that emphasised subjectivity and emotion, placed enthusiasm at the centre of poetry, and left no room for the more 'rational' didactic poetry. In the vernacular languages, these changes led to a subjectification and an emotionalisation that the translator of the songs of Ossian, Melchiore Cesarotti, tried to capture in his *Saggio sulla filosofia del gusto* as *orrore augusto*.[55] Accordingly, the understanding of what should be deemed 'sublime' also shifted from the classic ideal of order and regularity to the 'hideously' or the 'terribly beautiful.'[56] These changes, which had a significant effect on the poetic perception of nature, also influenced didactic poetry, as Christoph Siegrist sums up for the German-speaking countries.[57] It was not just the scholarly language of Latin, which drew from a limited corpus of canonical texts and was strictly standardised with regard to both its grammatical

---

55 "Un cuore profondamente sensibile, e penetrato da quella melanconia sublime che sembra il distintivo del genio, una fantasia in cui s'improntano, anzi si scolpiscono tutti gli oggetti, un'anima che trabocca e riversasi sopra tutto ciò che la circonda, sono i caratter<i> principali che lo rendono singolare anzi unico nella sua specie. Alternative perpetue d' affetti grandi e patetici, quadri i più toccanti di tenerezza domestica, narrazione animata che ti trasporta imperiosamente in mezzo all' azione, scene silvestri spiranti un orrore augusto, fenomeni della natura rappresentati ora con imponente maestà, ora col più dolce vaneggiamento, espressione pregna della cosa, brevità comprensiva, energia d' evidenza, tratti or di foco or di lampo, vibratezza e rapidità inarrivabile, formano un cumulo di pregi che riuniti e portati ad un grado così eminente si cercherebbero indarno in tutto il regno poetico." Cesarotti 1800, pp. 315–16.

56 Föcking 2000, pp. 177–79. The fact that Stay so explicitly maintains that didactic poetry is related to the *sublime* ("Verum quot genera hujusmodi sublimium rerum pertractari a Didascalicis possunt, quae ipsis Epicorum argumentis nec admirationis minus habeant, nec nostra minus intersint?", Stay, *Dialogus*, pp. xxi–xxii) is perhaps to be read as a reaction to the contemporary discussions.

57 Siegrist 1974, pp. 248–49.

set of rules and the literary genera, that lost ever more ground in the face of these new concepts; the new understanding of poetry also left no room in particular for the more artificially rational Neo-Latin didactic poetry, and disparaged it as a prototype of pedantry and outdated scholarliness. In the vernacular languages, therefore, didactic poetry, especially technical didactic poems in the ancient style, had already been abandoned to the greatest extent possible since the middle of the 18th century,[58] even though, particularly in the German-speaking area, there were in fact theoretical reflections on what the (vernacular) didactic poem of the future could look like.[59] In connection with the developments originating from the vernacular languages, Stay's *Dialogus* comes across in a slightly different light; not so much as the long-overdue poetics of the Latin didactic poem, which as the sum of earlier approaches and considerations finally establishes this long-standing genre in the system of poetry, but instead as an *apologia* against an altered understanding of poetry, against which Christopher Stay attempted to justify and establish, in the larger literary historical context, the somewhat outdated didactic poem by his brother. Stay was a proponent of Latin didactic poems at a time when poets were turning away not only from the Latin language but also from didactic poetry in the classic sense as a mode of expression. The dialogue, *De poesi didascalica*, with its plea for the primacy of the didactic poem is thus a highly interesting testimony for the intellectual resistance of certain church-based circles against a new paradigm that led to a radical re-evaluation of what should be deemed an essential feature of poetry. Of course, Stay's *Dialogus* was unable to stop this paradigm shift and prevent the extinction of the Latin didactic poem: the *Dialogus* met with no response. After 1792, it was not even printed a second time and fell almost completely into oblivion. But its existence serves to point out once more that, to a much greater degree than Aristotle's verdict, it was ultimately the altered concept of poetry and the Latin language's loss of prestige from the second half of the 18th century that banished didactic poetry from the literary corpus. This understanding of poetry initiated and shaped a perspective on the genre that, with its negative evaluation,[60] influenced even scholarly approaches to ancient and Neo-Latin didactic poems until well into the 20th century.

---

58 Albertsen 1967, p. 339; Siegrist 1974, pp. 248–49.
59 Albertsen 1967, pp. 349–69.
60 As, for example, in Kroll 1925, esp. col. 1848 on Aratus: "ein von vornherein veraltetes, schwer verständliches und selbst dem Verstehenden geringe Reize bietendes Werk"; col. 1855 on Vergil's *Georgics*: "Gegen das Ganze lassen sich erhebliche Bedenken äußern […]."

Bibliography

Primary Sources

Capriano, Giovanni. *Della vera poetica*. Venice: Bolognino Zaltieri, 1555.

Castelvetro, Ludovico. *Poetica d'Aristotele vulgarizzata et sposta*. Vienna: Gaspar Stainhofer, 1570.

Donati, Alessandro. *De arte poetica*. Rome: Facciotti, 1631.

Fracastoro, Girolamo. *Naugerius sive de poetica dialogus*. In *Opera omnia*, Venice: Juntas, 1555; modern edition edited by Ruth Kelso and Murray Wright Bundy. Urbana, ILL: The University of Illinois, 1928.

Goethe, Johann Wolfgang von. "Über das Lehrgedicht." In *Sophien-Ausgabe*, vol. 41.2, Weimar: H. Böhlau 1903, pp. 225–27.

Masen, Jacob. *Palaestra Eloquentiae ligatae*. Cologne: Busaeus, 1661.

Patrizi, Francesco. *Della Poetica. La Deca disputata*. Ferrara: Vittorio Baldini, 1586.

Roberti, Giambattista. "Lettera sopra l'uso della fisica nella poesia (1763)." In *Scelta di lettere erudite del padre Giambatista Roberti*, Venice: Alvisopoli 1825; modern edition edited by Stefania Baragetti. Milan: LED, 2014.

Speroni, Sperone. *Dialogo sopra Virgilio*. Venice: Maietti, 1596.

Stay, Christopher. *Philosophiae a Benedicto Stay Ragusino versibus traditae libri sex*, editio secunda. Rome: Pallas, 1747.

Stay, Christopher. *De poesia didascalica dialogus*. In *Philosophiae recentioris versibus traditae a Benedicto Stay libri decem*, third ed. Rome: Palearinianus, 1792, pp. i–xxx.

Tomitano, Bernardino. *Quattro libri della lingua thoscana*. Padua: Marcantonio Olmo, 1570.

Trapp, Joseph. *De poemate didactico seu praeceptivo*. In *Praelectiones poeticae in schola naturalis philosophiae Oxonii habitae*, vol. 2, Oxford: Clements, 1715, pp. 90–104.

Vitrioli, Didaco. *Xiphias*. Amsterdam: Johannes Müller, 1845.

Zappata, Alexander. *De anguillarum Comaclensium piscatione*. Amsterdam: Johannes Müller, 1897.

Secondary Sources

Akkermann, Fokke. "Auf der Suche nach dem Lehrgedicht in einigen neulateinischen Poetiken." In Hofmann 1988, pp. 409–17.

Albertsen, Ludwig. *Das Lehrgedicht*. Aarhus: Akademisk Boghandel, 1967.

Buck, August. *Italienische Dichtungslehren. Vom Mittelalter bis zum Ausgang der Renaissance*. Tübingen: Niemeyer, 1952.

Cesarotti, Melchiorre. *Saggi sulla filosofia delle lingue e del gusto*. Pisa: Tipografia della Societa Letteraria, 1800.

Fabian, Bernard. "Das Lehrgedicht als Problem der antiken und modernen Poetik." In *Die nicht mehr schönen Künste*, edited by Hans Robert Jauss. Munich: Fink, 1968, pp. 67–89.

Föcking, Marc. "Sublime. Funktionen des Erhabenen im Diskurssystem des italienischen Settecento." In *Beiträge zur Begriffsgeschichte der italienischen Aufklärung im europäischen Kontext*, edited by Helmut C. Jacobs and Gisela Schlüter. Frankfurt am Main/Berlin: Peter Lang, 2000, pp. 167–85.

Haskell, Yasmin Annabel and Philip Hardie, eds. *Poets and Teachers. Latin Didactic Poetry and the Didactic Authority of the Latin Poet from the Renaissance to the Present.* Bari: Levante, 1999.

Haskell, Yasmin Annabel. *Loyola's Bees. Ideology and Industry in Jesuit Latin Didactic Poetry*, Oxford, Eng.: Oxford University Press, 2003.

Haskell, Yasmin Annabel. "The Classification of Neo-Latin Didactic Poetry from the Fifteenth to Nineteenth Centuries." In: *Brill's Encyclopaedia of the Neo-Latin World*, edited by Philip Ford, Jan Bloemendal, and Charles Fantazzi. Leiden: Brill, 2014, pp. 437–48.

Hathaway, Baxter. *The Age of Criticism. The Late Renaissance in Italy.* Ithaca, NY: Cornell University Press, 1962.

Hofmann, Heinz. "Seminar: Das neulateinische Lehrgedicht (contributions by Bernd Effe, Fokke Akkerman, Georg Roellenbleck, Mario A. Di Cesare)." In *Acta Conventus Neo-Latini Guelpherbytani. Proceedings of the Sixth International Congress of Neo-Latin Studies, Wolfenbüttel 12 August to 16 August 1985*, edited by Stella P. Revard, Fidel Rädle, and Mario A. Di Cesare. Binghamton, NY: Center for Medieval and Early Renaissance Studies, 1988, pp. 401–36.

Hofmann, Heinz. "Von Africa über Bethlehem nach America. Das Epos in der neulateinischen Literatur." In *Von Göttern und Menschen erzählen. Formkonstanten und Funktionswandel vormoderner Epik*, edited by Jörg Rüpke. Stuttgart: Steiner, 2001, pp. 130–82.

Hufnagel, Henning and Olav Krämer, eds. *Das Wissen der Poesie. Lyrik, Versepik und die Wissenschaften im 19. Jahrhundert.* Berlin: de Gruyter, 2015.

Kappl, Brigitte. *Die Poetik des Aristoteles in der Dichtungstheorie des Cinquecento.* Berlin: de Gruyter, 2006.

Krämer, Olav. "Transformationen des Wissenschaftlichen Lehrgedichts um 1800. Erasmus Darwins *The Temple of Nature* und Johann Wolfgang Goethes *Metamorphose der Tiere*." In Hufnagel/Krämer, pp. 37–67.

Kroll, Wilhelm. "Lehrgedicht." In *Pauly's Realencyclopädie der classischen Altertumswissenschaft*, vol. 12.2 (1925), cols. 1842–57.

Kühlmann, Wilhelm. *Wissen als Poesie. Ein Grundriss zu Formen und Funktionen der frühneuzeitlichen Lehrdichtung im deutschen Kulturraum des 16. und 17. Jahrhunderts.* Berlin: de Gruyter, 2016.

Ludwig, Walther. "Neulateinische Lehrgedichte und Vergils Georgica." In *Walther Ludwig. Litterae Neolatinae. Schriften zur neulateinischen Literatur*, edited by Ludwig Braun. Munich: Fink, 1989, pp. 100–27.

Monreal, Ruth. *Flora neolatina. Die Hortorum libri IV von René Rapin S.J. und die Plantarum libri VI von Abraham Cowley. Zwei lateinische Dichtungen des 17. Jahrhunderts*. Berlin: de Gruyter, 2010.

Necchi, Rosa. *Scienziati e pastori. Poesia didascalica fra Sette e Ottocento*. Milan: LED, 2013.

Pantin, Isabella. "*Res contenta doceri?* Renaissance Cosmological Poetry, Classical Models and the Poetics of Didascalica." In Haskell/Hardie 1999, pp. 21–34.

Plett, Heinrich F. "Renaissance-Poetik. Zwischen Imitation und Innovation." In *Renaissance-Poetik / Renaissance Poetics*, edited by Heinrich F. Plett, et al. Berlin: de Gruyter, 1994, pp. 1–20.

Roellenbleck, Georg. *Das epische Lehrgedicht Italiens im fünfzehnten und sechzehnten Jahrhundert. Ein Beitrag zur Literaturgeschichte des Humanismus und der Renaissance*. Munich: Fink, 1975.

Schindler, Claudia. "La cultura letteraria dei Gesuiti a Napoli (1680–1730): Tradizioni locali come propaganda per una rete mondiale." In *Per la valorizzazione del patrimonio culturale della Campania. Il contributo degli studi medio- e neo-Latini*, edited by Giuseppe Germano. Naples: Paolo Loffredo, 2016, pp. 117–21.

Siegrist, Christoph. *Das Lehrgedicht der Aufklärung*. Stuttgart: Metzler, 1974.

Spaggiari, William. *Geografie letterarie: Da Dante a Tabucchi*. Milan: LED, 2015.

Till, Dietmar. "Prodesse-delectare-Doktrin." In *Historisches Wörterbuch der Rhetorik*, vol. 7 (2005), cols. 130–39.

Weinberg, Bernard. *A History of Literary Criticism in the Italian Renaissance*, vol. 1. Chicago, ILL: University of Chicago Press, 1961.

Zubrinic, Darko. "Croatian Humanists, Ecumenists, Latinists, and Encyclopaedists." In http://www.croatianhistory.net/etf/lat.html-stay (Zagreb 1995, accessed July 26, 2016).

Index

Aelius Spartianus (Historia Augusta)   26
Alaric   16n
Alberti, Leon Battista   11–14, 15n, 24, 184
Albertus Magnus   178n
Alfonso of Aragon   16n, 22, 27
Alois, Gian Francesco   196
Amaseo, Romolo   215
Amato Spagnuolo, Pietro   202
Ammianus Marcellinus   26
Anacharsis   53, 54
Angeli, Niccolò   182
Angeli, Pietro (da Barga)   9, 125, 213–28
Angelo Beolco see Ruzzante (Angelo Beolco)
Anguillara, Giovanni Andrea dell'   120
Anjou, René of see René of Anjou
Anselm, Thomas   56n
Appian   170
Aquinas, Thomas   178n, 225n
Aragon, Alfonso of see Alfonso of Aragon
Aragon, Frederick of see Frederick of Aragon, Frederick IV (King of Naples)
Arco, Nicolò d'   114n
Ariosto, Ludovico   8, 113–24, 117, 137, 212, 214, 216–18, 221–22, 227
Aristotle   40, 103, 107–8, 120, 178, 212, 213, 216, 218–20, 235–36, 238, 241, 247
Arzocchi, Francesco   182
Ascoli, Cecco d'   178n
Atanagi, Dionigi   198
Augustus (Roman emperor)   26, 140, 142
Aurispa, Giovanni   15n
Aventinus, Johannes (Johann Georg Turmair)   56

Baggesen, Jens   74
Barbaro, Daniele   38
Barbaro, Francesco   19, 20, 24n
Barbolani, Torquato   125
Barclay, John   154
Barth, Caspar von   217n
Beauvillier, Paul de (duc de Saint-Aignan)   148
Beccadelli, Antonio (Panormita)   182
Becchi, Ricciardo   168

Bembo, Pietro   37, 39–41, 43–45, 107, 198
Benassai, Francesca   183
Benci, Francesco   213–14
Beroaldo, Filippo   203
Bertalo, Antonio   153n
Bertolini, Lucia   12
Besicken, Johann   183
Biondo, Flavio   11–27, 29, 37, 42n, 98–99
Biondo, Girolamo   19–20, 22
Boccaccio, Giovanni   14, 39–40
Bocchi, Achille   114n, 194
Bocchi Bianchi, Maria Clorinda de Franceschi   171n
Bonamico, Lazzaro   7, 36–37, 39–41, 43–49
Bonsi, Domenico   168
Boscovich, Roger Joseph   234n
Bovelles, Charles de   107
Braccesi, Alessandro   9, 166–67, 169–72, 175–78, 180–82, 184–85
Braccesi, Rinaldo   167
Braccio da Montone (condottiere)   26
Bracciolini, Poggio   13, 15n, 98
Bruni, Francesco   44
Bruni, Leonardo   12–13, 16, 24, 37, 96, 98–110
Budé, Guillaume   107
Burchiello (Domenico di Giovanni)   169
Burke, Peter   2, 3

Caesar, Gaius Iulius   20, 107, 154
Caligula (Gaius Caesar Augustus Germanicus, Roman emperor)   26
Campani, Giovanni Antonio   54
Capece, Scipione   213, 215
Capriano, Giovanni Pietro   240
Casanova, Giacomo Girolamo   82
Castelvetro, Lodovico   213, 244–45
Catullus, Gaius Valerius   6, 202
Caux de Cappeval, N. de   163
Celtis, Conrad   54n, 56–57
Cesarotti, Melchiore   246
Ceva, Cristoforo   125
Ceva, Tommaso   125
Charlemagne   64, 120n, 148
Charles V   46, 136–37

Chrestien, Florent 114
Chrysoloras, Manuel 13, 16, 100
Cicero (Pseudo-) 97
Cicero, Gaius Tullius 16, 19, 42, 91, 96, 98, 102–3, 105, 107–8, 234
Cingoli, Benedetto da 182–84
Claudian 151
Clement VII, Pope 42
Colonna, Francesco 37
Colonna, Prospero 14
Compagni, Dino 16
Contarini, Gasparo 46
Conversini, Giovanni 13, 16
Cornazzano, Antonio 23
Cornelius Nepos 154
Corte-Real, Jerónimo 25, 132, 133, 135–37, 139, 144–45
Covarrubias y Orozco, Sebastián de 131
Crescimbeni, Giovanni Mario 188
Crivelli, Lodrisio 23
Croce (Della Croce), Giulio Cesare 121
Croce, Benedetto 11
Cruceo, Annibale 114n
Cuccoli, Ettore 188–89
Cueva, Martín de la 138
Curtius Rufus (Quintus Curtius Rufus) 154

Dante, Alighieri 1, 5, 14, 21, 40, 98, 101–2, 117, 154n, 178
Dati, Agostino 182
Dati, Leonardo 15n
Decembrio, Pier Candido 23, 170
Dei, Benedetto 167
Demetrius of Phalerum (Pseudo-) 212
Desfontaines, Pierre François Guyot 77
Destouches, Joseph Claude 154, 156–58, 161, 163
Didymus Chalcenterus 58n
Dionisi, Antonio 121–24
Dionisi, Iacopo 121
Dionisi, Ottavio 121
Dobson, William (fl. 1750) 163
Dolce, Ludovico 120
Dolet, Étienne 96, 106–10
Donato, Bernardino 47
Doria, Andrea 46, 141, 143
Du Bellay, Guillaume 107
Du Bellay, Joachim 109, 149–50
Dubois, Jacques 107

Einhard 64n
Empedocles 200n, 233, 236, 239–41
Erasmus, Desiderius 56, 59n, 133, 139, 144
Escrivano, Alonso 130n
Eugene IV, Pope 13–15, 28
Ezzelino III da Romano 26

Fenogliet, Henri Louis 202
Ferguson, Charles 3–4, 96n
Ferretti, Angelo 118
Ficino, Marsilio 1, 167, 170, 178–81
Filelfo, Francesco 21–23
Filippino, Bernardo 124
Fiocchi, Andrea 13, 15n
Firenzuola, Agnolo 169
Flaminio, Marcantonio 9, 188–206
Florimonte, Galeazzo 196
Florus (author of the Epitome of Roman History) 53, 154
Foiano, Andrea da 168
Ford, Philip 5
Fornari, Simone 118
Fracastoro, Girolamo 213, 234, 236–37
Frederick of Aragon, Frederick IV (King of Naples) 184
Fénelon, François (François de Salignac de La Mothe-Fénelon) 8, 109n, 147–51, 157–58, 161, 163
Fénelon, Gabriel-Jacques 147n

Gaddi, Francesco 171–72, 176
Giberti, Gian Matteo 195–96
Giolito, Giovanni 120
Giovanni, Count of Carpgena 170
Giovanni da Ravenna see Conversini, Giovanni
Godwin, Francis 82
Goethe, Johann Wolfgang von 214n, 242
Goro da Colcellalto 121
Gottlob, Joachim 163
Gottsched, Johann Christoph 156
Grosseteste, Robert 103
Guarini, Giovanni Battista 212
Guarino da Verona 62, 63
Gómez de Ciudad Real, Alvar 140, 144–45

Hadrian (Roman emperor) 26
Hermogenes 212
Herodian 53
Herodotus 131

INDEX

Herrera, Fernando de   8, 130–32, 138, 144
Hesiod   234, 238
Holberg, Ludvig   72, 78–79, 81–82, 84–85, 86n, 92
Homer   107, 125, 137, 140, 147, 151–52, 163, 219, 221, 236, 238, 241
Horatius (Quintus Horatius Flaccus)   6, 97, 139, 193, 195, 213, 216, 219, 237, 242

Ilicino see Lapini, Bernardo
Irenicus, Franciscus (Franz Fritz Friedlieb)   7, 53–55, 57, 59, 61–68

Jerome (Saint)   97
Joanaqui, Athanasios   153n
John, of Austria (Don Juan de Austria)   138, 140–43
Jouvancy, Joseph de   155–56
Justin (Marcus Iunianus Iustinus)   120

Klopstock, Friedrich Gottlieb   163
Kunić, Rajmundo   163

Lactantius, Lucius Caecilius Firmianus   133, 139, 144
Landino, Cristoforo   25, 167, 169n, 181
Lapini, Bernardo (Ilicino)   182–84
Lascaris, Janus   39–40
Le Tellier, Michel (Jesuit)   153
Livy (Titus Livius)   26, 91, 154
Lombardelli, Orazio   219n
Lombardi, Bartolomeo   213n
Longinus (Pseudo-)   212
Loschi, Antonio   13, 15n, 98
Louis V (Count Palatine of the Rhine)   55
Louis XI of France   27
Louis XIV (the Great, King of France)   148
Louis XV (the Beloved, King of France)   150
Louis de France, Duc de Bourgogne   148–49, 157
Lucan (Marcus Annaeus Lucanus)   137, 144, 151
Lucretius (Titus Lucretius Carus)   232–33, 238, 240
Luna y Roja, Joaquín Hernandez de   154
Luna y Roja, José de   154
Luther, Martin   59n
Luti, Ginevra   182–83
López, Alonso (El Pinciano)   131n

Machiavelli, Niccolò   37, 168
Macrobius (Macrobius Ambrosius Theodosius)   176–78
Maggi, Vincenzo   213n, 216n
Magno, Celio   47
Mal Lara, Juan de   130
Mancurti, Francesco Maria   189n
Manetti, Gianozzo   105n
Manuzio, Aldo   44, 236n
Manuzio, Paolo   46
Margaret of France (Duchess of Berry)   190
Maria of Austria (Holy Roman Empress)   132, 134
Marino, Giambattista   122
Marinis, Tammaro de   171n
Marrasio, Giovanni   182
Marsuppini, Carlo   15n
Martini, Francesco di Giorgio   183
Marullo, Marco   203
Marullo, Michele   191
Masen, Jacob   240n
Maurizi, Visito   113, 118–21, 124
Mauvillon, Jakob Eléazar de   81
Maximilian III Joseph (elector of Bavaria)   157
Medici, Cosimo de' (Grand Duke of Tuscany)   215
Medici, Ferdinando de'   215–16
Medici, Lorenzo de'   25, 167–68, 171–72, 176, 181
Melanchthon, Philip   55–56, 59n
Mena, Juan de   137
Metello, Antonio   22
Mey, Joan   131
Michelozzi, Niccolò   167, 171–73
Milton, John   163
Minturno, Antonio Sebastiano   236n
Minuti, Antonio   23
Molza, Francesco Maria   188
Montefeltro, Guidobaldo I da (Duke of Urbino)   169–70
Montesquieu, Charles-Louis de Secondat, Baron de La Brède de   78n
Mosquera de Figueroa, Cristóbal   130–31, 138, 144
Muret, Marc Antoine   214n
Musuro, Marco   44
Mutian, Konrad   56

Naldi, Naldo   167
Nardini, Stefano (Archbishop of Milan)   21, 27
Nebrija, Antonio de   140n
Neoptolemos of Parion   242
Nepos see Cornelius Nepos
Nerva (Roman emperor)   26
Neukirch, Benjamin   156
Neuman, Ludwig Bertrand   163
Niccoli, Niccolò   100
Nicholas v, Pope   16

Opitz, Martin   5
Orlandi, Caterina   182
Orsini, Onorata   182
Ovid (Publius Ovidius Naso)   62–63, 120, 161, 238

Pachel, Leonhard   170
Palmieri, Matteo   12
Paracleto da Corneto, Fuscus (?)   182
Parmenides   239
Partenio, Bernardino   188, 236n
Patrizi, Francesco   182, 241
Paul the Deacon (Paulus Diaconus)   62–63
Pedrosa, Francisco de   8, 130–32, 135–41, 144–45
Petrarch (Francisco Petrarca)   1, 9, 13, 16, 23n, 39–40, 62–63, 107, 117, 125, 137, 169, 188–89, 191, 193–97, 199, 201–7, 212, 224
Petronius (Gaius Petronius Arbiter)   83–84, 91
Philip I (Margrave of Baden)   58n
Philipp II (King of Spain)   132, 134, 137–39, 143–44
Pibrac, Guy Du Faur de   114–15
Picardo, Alonso   130n
Piccolomini, Alessandro   16n, 19, 54, 170, 182, 213
Piccolomini, Enea Silvio   182
Pinciano, Alonso López see López, Alonso (El Pinciano)
Pindar   245
Pio di Carpi, Rodolfo   194
Piovan, Francesco   45
Pirckheimer, Willibald   56, 59n
Pius II, Pope   16, 18, 19, 170
Pius V, Pope   136, 141

Plato   100–1, 107, 179, 238
Plessen, Volrad von   114–21, 124
Pliny the Elder (Gaius Plinius Secundus)   62–63
Plutarch (Lucius Mestrius Plutarchus)   26, 53, 101
Plutarch (Pseudo-)   220
Pole, Reginald   46
Poliziano, Angelo   25, 167
Pomponazzi, Pietro   39, 44, 45
Pontano, Giovanni   213
Pope, Alexander   163
Possevino, Antonio   214n
Prandini, Aurelio   122
Preuss, Jacob   79–81
Prior, Matthew   163
Priscianese, Francesco   47
Prudentius (Aurelius Prudentius Clemens)   6
Prévost, Augustin   114

Quintilian (Marcus Fabius Quintilianus)   103n

Rab, Christoph   115
Ramsay, André Michel   151–52
Rapin, René   154–55
René of Anjou   27
Requesens, Berenguer de   143n
Reuchlin, Johann   59n
Rhenanus, Beatus   56, 59n
Richard de Dijon, Jean   114
Robertello, Francesco   213n, 236n
Rufo, Juan   132–33, 135–37, 144–45
Ruscelli, Girolamo   120
Rustici, Cencio de'   13, 15n, 98
Ruzzante (Angelo Beolco)   40

Sadoleto, Iacopo   46
Sallust (Gaius Sallustius Crispus)   26, 107, 131, 154
Salutati, Coluccio   101, 202
Salverte, Eusèbe   158–59
Salviati, Leonardo   218
Sannazaro, Jacopo   107, 199–201, 213–16
Saracini, Bianca   182–83
Saracini, Camilla   166, 170–73, 176–77, 179–80, 185
Sassetti, Francesco   169

INDEX

Savonarola, Girolamo   168, 169
Scala, Bartolomeo   167, 171–72
Scanello, Cristoforo   121
Scinzeler, Uldericus   170
Selim II, Sultan of the Ottoman Empire   135–36
Sforza, Attendolo   23
Sforza, Francesco (Duke of Milan)   11, 12, 15, 20–23, 25–27
Sigbert von Geamblou   64n
Silius Italicus   151
Simonetta, Cicco   24
Soderini, Giovan Vittorio   169
Speroni, Sperone   1, 7, 36–39, 40n, 41, 42n, 43n, 44–49, 218n, 220n, 236n, 237n
Statius (Publius Papinius Statius)   151
Stay, Benedetto   9, 234
Stay, Christopher   9, 232–35, 237–43, 245–46, 247
Stella, Giulio Cesare   215n, 216, 226n
Suetonius (Gaius Suetonius Tranquillus)   26
Swift, Jonathan   73–74, 77, 82n, 88, 92–93

Tacitus (Publius Cornelius Tacitus)   26, 64, 131, 154, 234
Tasso, Bernardo   199n
Tasso, Torquato   120, 122, 125, 143, 163, 212, 214–18, 221–22, 225–27
Tassoni, Alessandro   188
Terence (Pubius Terentius Afer)   98
Terracina, Laura   117, 121–22
Themon Judaeus   178n
Thomasius, Christian   5
Thucydides   107, 131
Titi, Roberto   212–14, 217n, 227–28
Tolomei, Claudio   198–99
Tomitano, Bernardino   44, 237n
Torrentino, Lorenzo (Laurens van den Bleeck)   189n
Tortoletti, Bartolomeo   216
Toscanella, Giovanni   22
Toscanella, Orazio   118
Trajan (Roman emperor)   26
Tranchedini, Nicodemus   22
Trapp, Joseph   234n, 240, 244
Trautwein, Georg   154–56
Trebeta, mythological founder of the city of Trier   65

Trevisan, Zaccaria   20n
Trissino, Gian Giorgio   218n
Trithemius, Johannes   59
Tuisco, mythological father of the Germans   66
Turisano, Bernardo   46
Tyre, William of see William of Tyre

Urban II, Pope   223

Valdes, Juan de   190
Valgrisi, Vincenzo   120
Valla, Giorgio   236n
Valla, Lorenzo   18, 42n, 102, 184
Valori, Baccio   216n
Valverde, García de   137
Varchi, Benedetto   236n
Vasoli, Cesare   41
Vegio, Maffeo   15n
Vehus, Hieronymus   58n
Velleius Paterculus   154
Venningen, Florentius de   56
Verino, Ugolino   167
Veronese, Guarino see Guarino da Verona
Vettori, Pietro   213, 236n
Vianello, Valerio   38
Vida, Marco Girolamo   140, 144–45, 213–14
Viel, Etienne Bernard Alexandre   154, 158–59, 161, 163
Villani, Giovanni   16
Virgil (Publius Vergilius Maro)   82, 91, 107, 120, 125, 137, 144–45, 151, 155, 158–59, 212, 221, 225, 232–33, 236, 238
Visconti, Bianca Maria   26
Visconti, Filippo Maria   23n, 27
Vitrioli, Didacus   246
Voltaire (François-Marie Arouet)   163

Walkowitz, Rebecca   74–76, 79, 81, 83, 86, 88–91
Waquet, Françoise   3, 76n
William of Tyre   222, 224
Wimpfeling, Jacob   64n

Zacharias, Lilius   64n
Zanni, Domenico   163
Zapata, Luis   131, 137
Zappata, Alexander   246